LONDON

www.marco-polo.com

Sightseeing Highlights

The British Museum, Buckingham Palace, Big Ben – everyone knows these and other highlights of London. But some other sights, not quite so well known, are equally worth seeing.

Do You Feel Like ...

... enjoying a fantastic view of the city from above, drinking a pint in a historic pub, seeing London from the water, exploring interesting cemeteries and graves, or doing something really traditional?

VIEWS FROM ABOVE

DOCKS AND SHIPS

A HISTORIC PUB

GRAVES

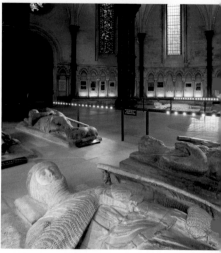

BRITISH TRADITION

BACKGROUND

ENJOY LONDON

TOURS

PRICE CLASSES
Restaurants
(main course)
££££ = over £25
£££ = £20–£25
££ = £10–£20
£ = up to £10
Hotels
(double room)
££££ = over £300
£££ = £200–£300
££ = £120–£200
£ = £70–£120

New architecture: the »Gherkin«

SIGHTS FROM A TO Z

The opening ceremony of the London Olympics 2012

PRACTICAL INFORMATION

BACKGROUND

London is an exciting place: a centre of global finance, multicultural with imperial heritage. Read on for background information on one of the world's leading cities.

Facts

Population · Politics · Economy

London is a colourful melting pot for all the peoples of the world and a centre of global finance. The powerhouse that generates employment is the City. And anyone who is dissatisfied or wants to change the world only has to go to Speakers' Corner in Hyde Park.

As early as the 17th century, when the city had a population of 500,000, London's importance as a place of manufacturing and trade attracted immigrants from all over the world. Huguenots in the 17th century were followed by the Irish in the 18th century. In the early 19th century African and Chinese immigrants settled in the dock areas, and after 1880 the main newcomers to the East End were Jews from eastern Europe. After the Second World War immigrants came from the West Indies, Africa, Cyprus, India and Pakistan. In the last 30 years, the mix has become even more diverse, including people from the expanding European Union and every continent. Many parts of London are dominated by a particular ethnic group: Jamaicans in Brixton, Trinidadians in Notting Hill, Bangladeshis in the East End, Indians in Southall, Chinese in one part of the West End and wealthy Arabs in Kensington. The resulting **mixture of peoples** produces a unique cultural diversity expressed in restaurants, shops, festivals and traditions (▶MARCO POLO Insight p. 286).

Ethnic diversity

The number of residents in the City decreased steadily from the mid-19th century (1851: 130,000, today about 13,000), whereas the population of Greater London rose from 2.2 million in 1841 to 8.3 million today. Based on the high birth rate and levels of migration, a population of 10 million is forecast for 2030. This growth and London's diversity cause conflicts over issues of local autonomy, educational and cultural institutions, equal career opportunities – ethnic minorities are clearly under-represented in top political and business positions – and religion. On top of this there are social problems arising from cuts in the welfare state following the global financial crisis. In summer 2011 riots erupted, accompanied by arson and looting. The rate of unemployment in London is above the national average, and young people are especially affected.

Poverty in the most expensive city in Europe

INNER AND OUTER LONDON

Twelve of the 33 London boroughs are grouped together to form Inner London. The others are known as Outer London. After the dis-

Democracy in action: everyone can express an opinion at Speakers' Corner

Facts and Figures

Location:
South-east England
near the estuary of the Thames

Area:
1579 sq km/610 sq mi
(Greater London)
2.6 sq km/1 sq mi
(City of London)

Population:
8.3 million
(Greater London)
3.2 million (Inner London)
13,000 (City of London)

In comparison:
Berlin 3.5 million
Paris 2.2 million
New York 8.2 million

Time:
GMT

2° 21' 07"
longitude east

London

722km/448mi   Hamburg

933km/579mi   Ber

343km/213mi

48° 51' 24"
latitude north

Paris ■

▶ Coat of arms ...

... of the City,
with its motto
»Guide us, Lord «

▶ Transport

Principal airport:
Heathrow, third-largest in the world
with 70 million passengers in 2012
Main system of transport:
underground railway (the Tube),
3 million passengers per day

▶ Addresses

London's postal districts are designated
by an alphanumeric code. The first
part of the postcode gives a broad
indication of where the address is
located: the letters show the compass
direction, and the number stands
for a district, e.g. SW 3 is Chelsea.

▶ Government

33 Boroughs
Head of government: Mayor of London

E: east	**SE:** south east
EC: east central	**SW:** south west
N: north	**W:** west
NW: north west	**WC:** west central

▶ Economy

Leading stock exchange in the world measured by number of stocks quoted

World's largest insurance market

World's largest banking centre (daily turnover £300 billion)

Centre of the **British press**

No. 1 European destination for city breaks

No. of overnight stays per year (million)

35.8 Paris
48.7 **mil.**
20.8
London Berlin

▶ Climate

Average temperatures

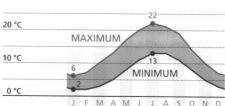

30 °C

22
20 °C MAXIMUM
6 13
10 °C MINIMUM
2
0 °C
J F M A M J J A S O N D

Precipitation and sunshine

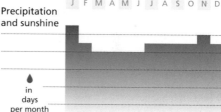

in days per month | 11 9 8 8 8 9 9 9 9 9 10 9

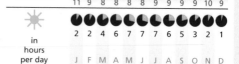

in hours per day | 2 2 4 6 7 7 7 6 5 3 2 1
J F M A M J J A S O N D

▶ The »Tube« in figures

London's underground railway is the oldest and, with a length of 405km/250mi, the second-longest in the world.

Network

Total length:
405km/250mi

Proportion of network underground:
 45 %

Annual distance covered per train:
184,000km/ 114,000mi

Escalators

Total number:
426

Station with the most escalators: Waterloo
23

Longest escalator: Angel Station

80m/267ft
27.5m/90ft

Passengers

Total number per year
1107 million

Employees:
19,000

Busiest station: Waterloo
57,000 👤
57,000 per day at peak time (3 hrs)

82,000,000 👤
per year

London • Boroughs

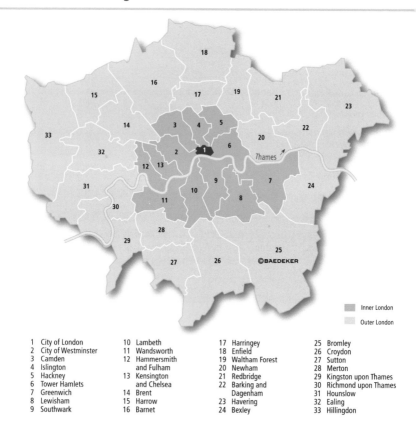

Inner London

Outer London

1 City of London	10 Lambeth	17 Harringey	25 Bromley
2 City of Westminster	11 Wandsworth	18 Enfield	26 Croydon
3 Camden	12 Hammersmith	19 Waltham Forest	27 Sutton
4 Islington	and Fulham	20 Newham	28 Merton
5 Hackney	13 Kensington	21 Redbridge	29 Kingston upon Thames
6 Tower Hamlets	and Chelsea	22 Barking and	30 Richmond upon Thames
7 Greenwich	14 Brent	Dagenham	31 Hounslow
8 Lewisham	15 Harrow	23 Havering	32 Ealing
9 Southwark	16 Barnet	24 Bexley	33 Hillingdon

solution of the Greater London Council (GLC) in 1986 by the Conservative government – the city council was too left-wing for Margaret Thatcher – the city administration was an unworkable mix of responsibilities exercised by local authorities and government bodies. In May 2000 under the Blair government, the citizens of London elected a mayor for the whole city for the first time. They chose a left-wing critic of Blair, Ken Livingstone, re-elected him in 2004, but opted for the Conservative Boris Johnson in 2008 and again in 2012. The Greater London Authority, democratically controlled by the 25-strong London Assembly, replaced the boroughs as the highest administrative entity. The government of the City of London (►MARCO POLO Insight p. 206), by contrast, goes back to the Middle Ages.

THE FINANCIAL HEART OF THE WORLD

There are two pre-eminent dates in London's recent business history: The first was the **Big Bang** on 27 October 1986, when the London Stock Exchange abolished a host of restrictions and became an open market for transactions in stocks and financial instruments that were yet to be invented – a market that was scarcely regulated. In the years that followed the City became the world's leading financial centre and remains the place with the largest number of bank transactions, which peaked at a value of over £450 billion daily (►MARCO POLO Insight p. 186). A larger number of stocks are traded on the London Stock Exchange today than on any other exchange. The London Metal Exchange is one of the leading markets for raw materials and precious metals, Lloyd's of London is the world's largest and oldest insurance exchange, and the Baltic Exchange is one of the principal global markets for container shipping – over half of the world volume is transacted here. More American banks have a branch in London than in New York. 360,000 people were employed in the »square mile« alone before the crash of 2008, from top earners trading in derivatives down to the reception staff in the bank towers, but the second important date, 25 September 2008 marked a break. On that day the New York investment bank Lehmann Brothers collapsed, sparking a financial crisis that hit the city of London harder than most business centres. London had concentrated on pure finance, inventing new investment products and neglecting the real economy. Tens of thousands of bankers lost their jobs, and many suppliers of services who had once prospered now shared the pain: wine dealers, tailors, jewellers, nannies, chauffeurs, hairdressers, estate agents and others. The auction houses Sotheby's and Christie's, too, felt the consequences, even though London's status as a **global centre for the art business** has not been endangered.

... in need of a pacemaker

In spite of the crisis, 220 of the 500 largest British companies, including Shell, BP and BAT, have their headquarters in London. As the importance of trade and services has increased to a level which can hardly rise further (97% of total employment, including low-paid jobs), so manufacturing production has fallen. New factories in high-tech industries have mainly been established in the south-east region, to profit from the London market and the infrastructure of the capital, which includes Heathrow Airport, the third-largest in the world, and the Port of London, which remains one of the world's leading

Powerhouse of the British economy

Welcome to Everyday Life

Some tips for experiences off the tourist track and meeting some »completely normal« Londoners:

PROTECT URBAN NATURE

TCV (The Conservation Volunteers) is an organisation that carries out practical projects to protect the natural world – and that includes London. TCV is open to all age groups.
www.tcv.org.uk
www.btcv.org.uk/volunteer/ index2.html

JOIN A COURSE

The London boroughs run all kinds of adult education courses. Details are on the websites of the individual councils, e.g.
www.camden.gov.uk,
http://rbkc.gov.uk
(Kensington and Chelsea),

BED & BREAKFAST

Some B & Bs are anonymous, but in others you can get to know your hosts and see how they live. If this is your aim, it is best to enquire personally by phone rather than book online and to opt for an address in the suburbs well away from the main tourist sights.

www.londonbb.com
www.visitlondon.com
www.airbnb.com

FIND LIKE-MINDED PEOPLE

City Socialising is a network that connects people who have interests in common, whether cultural, gastronomic or sports, or who simply live in the same neighbourhood. Anyone who is staying in London for a longer period of time can join:

http://london.citysocialising.com/home.html

WALK OR CYCLE IN A GROUP

The London Strollers organise group walks in the city and its surroundings without aiming to do challenging hikes. Their website also has links to similar groups: Click on »Contact us«. The London Cycling Campaign tries to improve the conditions for cycling in the city and holds bike tours as part of its work:

www.londonstrollers.org.uk
http://lcc.org.uk/events

Rush hour on London Bridge: Every working day tens of thousands of commuters cross from London Bridge Station to their offices in the City

ports. Here, however, the centre of activity has shifted. Whereas ocean-going vessels unloaded at the 19th-century docks in the east of London until the 1960s, the container port is now about 25km/16mi east of Tower Bridge in Tilbury. The oil terminals Shellhaven, Thameshaven, Canvey Island and Coryton are even further downstream. Tourism is a further important pillar of the economy: The annual number of visitors will soon reach 15 million, making London Europe's top city as a tourist destination.

Transport | It goes without saying that London is the traffic hub of Britain. Travellers heading to London from other parts of the country by car or bus often end up on the 188km/120mi-long **M25 motorway** (»London Orbital«), which is chronically congested, not only at peak times. When driving into the city centre, motorists have to pay the congestion charge, which is intended to reduce the volume of traffic.

The region has **five airports**. Most international scheduled flights are handled by Heathrow, the world's third-largest airport. Gatwick is among the biggest European airports for charter flights, while Stansted and to a lesser extent Luton are destinations for budget airlines. The small City Airport is used by business travellers.

London has a large number of **rail terminals**, of which St Pancras is the most important for international traffic: It is the destination of the Eurostar trains that come from the Channel Tunnel.

Public transport within Greater London is handled by the London Underground (Tube) with its twelve lines and a network amounting to 405km/250mi (►MARCO POLO Insight p. 15), and by countless buses running on more than 700 routes – but the old-time Routemaster double-deckers are only in operation on two routes used by many tourists: no. 9 (Kensington – Aldwych) and no. 11 (Trafalgar Square – Tower). In 2011 a completely new model, inspired by the old Routemaster, was presented. A design specially conceived for London has three doors, making this bus larger than all its predecessors, but greener thanks to its lightweight construction. The new model is being progressively introduced.

City History

Tradition of the Empire

From the »fortress on a pool« – this is thought to be the meaning of the Celtic name for London – to the capital of an empire: The history of London is also the history of Britain and the British Empire. The empire no longer exists, but its traditions live on.

ROMAN LONDINIUM

AD 43	Start of Roman rule in Britannia
61	Rebellion of Celtic tribes led by Boudicca
449	End of Roman rule

In AD 43 the army of Emperor Claudius conquered Britannia, a land occupied by Celts. The Romans established a »colonia« and built a trading-place, Londinium, on the north bank of the Thames. The resistance of the Celts was unsuccessful: In AD 61 the tribal queen **Boudicca** burned the Roman settlement to the ground, but it was quickly rebuilt. The buildings of Roman London included a forum, a temple to Mithras and the first bridge across the Thames, made of wood. Londinium became a prosperous Roman city, even though Eboracum (York) and Verulamium (St Albans) were more important. From the year 200 the city was enclosed by a wall, the course of which still approximately marks the boundary of the City. Emperor Diocletian made Londinium the capital of one of the four late Roman provinces of Britannia. However, from 410 the Britannic legions were transferred to Germany, and Roman rule in Britannia came to a final end in 449. Londinium fell into decay.

SAXON LUNDENWIC

796	Lundenwic becomes capital of the kingdom of Essex.
From 1016	Capital of England

Before long the island of Britain was occupied by Jutes, Angles and Saxons. It was the Saxons who established the port of **Lundenwic** outside the Roman walls. In 796 this settlement became capital of the Anglo-Saxon kingdom of Essex. In 851 Lundenwic was destroyed by the Danes, and old Londinium was not resettled until 35 years later, under Alfred the Great. It then grew to be the largest and wealthiest

An inglorious end: the execution of Charles I on the scaffold in front of Banqueting House on Whitehall

town in England by the 10th century. This period was followed after 1016 by a Danish interlude that had far-reaching consequences for the city: London replaced Winchester as capital city of the kingdom under Canute I, and Canute's Anglo-Saxon successor Edward the Confessor moved his residence from what is now the City to the new monastery of St Peter in Westminster – thus establishing the second of the two centres from which modern London developed.

NORMAN PERIOD

1066	Battle of Hastings
1176	First stone bridge across the Thames
1189	First election of a Lord Mayor
1215	Magna Carta: right to elect the Lord Mayor
1381	Wat Tyler's rebellion

In 1066 the Normans invaded England and defeated King Harold at the Battle of Hastings. Duke **William of Normandy** (William the Conqueror) was crowned in Westminster Abbey as King William I and confirmed the traditional rights of the city of London. The first demonstration of his power was the erection of the White Tower. The following centuries were a period of economic growth, manifested both in buildings – in 1176 Peter de Colechurch built the first stone bridge across the Thames – and in the pride of the London merchants, who established their own governmental institutions: As early as 1189 the guilds elected Henry Fitzailwyn as the first Lord Mayor of London. The Crown was repeatedly forced to recognise the citizens' rights: In the reign of Henry I, when London became the capital of England once and for all, it retained its independence as a self-governing city responsible only to the King; Richard the Lionheart signed a charter guaranteeing London citizens' rights on the river Thames. The independence of the city was sealed in 1215 by the signing of Magna Carta, in which King John recognised the right of the guilds to elect the Lord Mayor each year. Regular meetings of the Common Council, an assembly of the Lord Mayor and aldermen that had existed informally since the 13th century, began in 1376. It became an official institution in the late 14th century. Peasants and the poor had

The shrine of Edward the Confessor in Westminster Abbey

no rights; their discontent was expressed in protests such as Wat Ty-ler's rebellion against poll tax in 1381 and Jack Cade's rebellion of 1450.

TUDORS AND STUARTS

1485	Start of Tudor rule
1509–1547	Reign of Henry VIII
1565	Foundation of the Exchange
1605	Gunpowder Plot
1649	Execution of Charles I
1665	Plague in London
1666	Great Fire

The rule of the house of Tudor began in 1485 with the accession of **Henry VII** and is traditionally taken to mark the end of the Middle Ages in England. The 16th century was a period of accelerated economic growth for London, thanks to the foundation of trade companies and the establishment of the Exchange by Thomas Gresham in 1565. By the end of the century London was the leading trading centre in the western world with a population of 200,000. The political events of this period include the establishment of the Anglican church by **Henry VIII**, who initiated a major building programme – most of it outside the city, for example in Greenwich and at Hampton Court – and brought well-known artists such as Hans Holbein to London.   **Tudor period**

The 17th century was one of the most turbulent periods in the history of London. The ill-fated attempt of **Guy Fawkes** and a group of Catholic conspirators to blow up Parliament in 1605, the Gunpowder Plot, was a prelude to the struggle for power between the Puritan parliament and the Catholicising tendencies of the Stuarts, who held the throne from 1603. London was a focal point of the conflict, which led to civil war in 1642 and culminated in the victory of **Oliver Cromwell** and his party and the execution of **Charles I** at the Banqueting House in 1649. Eleven years of republican rule (the Commonwealth) were followed in 1660 by the restoration of the Stuart dynasty under Charles II. Hardly had the situation settled down when an outbreak of the plague in 1665 claimed the lives of almost 100,000 Londoners.   **Stuart period**

A second catastrophe occurred just a year later: On the morning of 2 September 1666 the Great Fire broke out and raged for four days and nights, reducing four fifths of the City to ashes and destroying 13,200 houses and 84 churches. 100,000 people were made homeless. The   **Great Fire**

The Great Fire: an Eye-Witness Account

The most vivid account of the Great Fire was written by Samuel Pepys (1633–1703), First Secretary to the Admiralty, who described the catastrophe in his diary, one of the most interesting sources on 17th-century London:

2 September 1666

... Jane comes and tells me that she hears that above 300 houses have been burned down tonight by the fire we saw, and that it was now burning down all Fishstreet by London Bridge. So I made myself ready presently, and walked to the Tower and there got up upon one of the high places ... and there I did see the houses at that end of the bridge all on fire, and an infinite great fire on this and the other side the end of the bridge ... So down, with my heart full of trouble, to the Lieutenant of the Tower, who tells me that it begun this morning in the King's bakers house in Pudding lane, and that it hath burned down St. Magnes Church and most part of Fishstreete already. So I down to the waterside and there got a boat and through the bridge, and there saw a lamentable fire ... Everybody endeavouring to remove their goods, and flinging into the River or bringing them into lighters that lay off. Poor people staying in their houses as long as till the very fire touched them, and then running into boats or clambering from one pair of stair by the waterside to another. Having stayed, and in an hour's time seen the fire rage every way, and nobody to my sight endeavouring to quench it, but to remove their goods and leave all to the fire ... and the wind mighty high, and driving it into the city, and everything, after so long a drought, proving combustible, even the very stones of churches ... We ... stayed till it was dark almost and saw the fire grow ... and in Corners and upon steeples and between churches and houses, as far as we could see up the hill of the City, in a most horrid malicious bloody flame, not like the flame of an ordinary fire ... We stayed till, it be-

The City in flames, seen from the south bank of the Thames, with London Bridge on the right

MARCO POLO TIP

! *Hear Samuel Pepys* ^{Insider} Tip

To hear Samuel Pepys, go to the Museum of London, where an audio-visual show presents extracts from the diary about the Great Fire.

ing darkish, we saw the fire as only one entire arch of fire from this to the other side of the bridge, and in a bow up the hill, for an arch of above a mile long. It made me weep to see it.

4 September 1666

This night Mrs. Turner and her husband supped with my wife and I at night in the office, upon a shoulder of mutton from the cook's, without any napkin or anything in a sad manner but were merry. Only, now and then walking into the garden and saw how horridly the sky looks, all on a fire in the night, was enough to put us out of our wits; and endeed it was extremely dreadfull – for it looks just as if it were at us, and the whole heaven on fire. I after supper walked in the dark down to Tower street, and there saw it all on fire … and the fire with extraordinary vehemence. Now begins the practice of blowing up of houses in Tower street, those next to the Tower, which at first did frighten people more than anything; but it stopped the fire where it was done … And [St] Pauls is burned and all Cheapside.

7 September 1666

Up by 5 a-clock and, blessed be God, find all well, and by water to Paul's wharfe. Walked thence and saw all the town burned, and a miserable sight of Pauls church, with all the roofs fallen and the body of the Quire fallen into St Fayths – Paul's school also – Ludgate – Fleet street – my father's house, and the church, and a good part of the Temple the like …

A hopeless struggle

First Secretary to the Admiralty, **Samuel Pepys**, recorded the events in his diary (▶p. 28). **Sir Christopher Wren** was the principal architect entrusted with the task of rebuilding the city. In addition to his greatest work, St Paul's Cathedral, he had built a further 52 churches by the time of his death in 1711. In spite of all disasters, London consolidated its position as a centre of world trade and had a population of 500,000 by the end of the 17th century.

IMPERIAL CAPITAL

1750	Westminster Bridge is opened, the second Thames bridge in central London
1829	Foundation of the Metropolitan Police

In the 18th century Britain began to conquer an empire that spanned the globe and established its position as the leading maritime power. London benefited greatly from this. Magnificent buildings, wide paved streets and a flowering of the theatre reflected its wealth. The Industrial Revolution brought more and more people to the city. The first official census in 1801 recorded a total population of 860,035, which made London the world's largest city. Social problems grew in step with the population; the foundation of the London Metropolitan Police in 1829 can be seen as an indicator of the growing conflicts. In 1845 Friedrich Engels (1820–95) described the contradictions of this period in The Condition of the Working Class in England: *I know nothing more imposing than the view which the Thames offers during the ascent from the sea to London Bridge. The masses of buildings, the wharves on both sides, especially from Woolwich upwards, the countless ships along both shores, crowding ever closer and closer together, until, at last, only a narrow passage remains in the middle of the river, a passage through which hundreds of steamers shoot by one another; all this is so vast, so impressive, that a man cannot collect himself, but is lost in the marvel of England's greatness before he sets foot upon English soil. But the sacrifices which all this has cost become apparent later. … The most extensive working-people's district lies east of the Tower in Whitechapel and Bethnal Green, where the greatest masses of London working-people live. Let us hear Mr G. Alston, preacher of St. Philip's, Bethnal Green, on the condition of his parish. He says: »It contains 1,400 houses, inhabited by 2,795 families, comprising a population of 12,000. The space within which this large amount of population are living is less than 400 yards square (1,200 feet), and it is no uncommon thing for a man and his wife, with four or five children, and sometimes the grandfather and grandmother, to be found living in a room from ten to twelve feet square, and which serves them for eating and working in.«*

Construction of a tunnel for the first underground line

VICTORIAN LONDON

1837–1901	Reign of Queen Victoria
1851	Great Exhibition
1863	The first underground railway goes into operation

London developed by leaps and bounds in the reign of Queen Victoria, which began in 1837. The first train ran from London Bridge to Greenwich in 1836. In 1863 the underground railway started operation on the Metropolitan Line between Paddington and Farringdon. A broad belt of suburbs arose around the city. Steam power enabled the docks and factories to grow rapidly, and the demand for workers drew people from the surrounding regions, and increasingly also from the European continent, to London. The Crystal Palace, which was built for the **Great Exhibition** of 1851 can be regarded as a symbol of the period. It no longer exists, but other buildings and streets bear witness to the wave of change that swept over the city: the Houses of Parliament, Trafalgar Square, Victoria Embankment and Regent Street. When Victoria died in 1901, London had a population of 4.5 million and was undisputedly the world's leading city.

Life in the Underground: the Tube tunnels protected Londoners from the Blitz, entertainment was provided, too

THE 20TH AND 21ST CENTURIES

1940–1945	German air raids
1948	Olympic Games
1952	Coronation of Queen Elizabeth in Westminster Abbey
1986	Big Bang
1997	Funeral of Princess Diana
2000	Greater London has a mayor again
2005	On 7 July, a day after London was chosen as the venue for the 2012 Olympic Games, a terrorist attack on the underground railway claims 56 lives
2008	The financial crisis shakes the foundations of the banking world
2012	London is the venue of the 30th Olympic Games, 60th jubilee of Elizabeth II

In London, as elsewhere, the two world wars were the dominant events of the first half of the 20th century. In the First World War – the first attack by a Zeppelin airship was in 1915 – the number of casualties of German air raids, approximately 700 killed and 2000 injured, was relatively small. In the Second World War, however, the German bomber raids of 1940–41 (»The Blitz«) and attacks by the V1 and V2 flying bombs in 1944–45 killed more than 30,000 people. In the City hardly any buildings remained undamaged.

Swinging London, Big Bang and banking crisis Nevertheless, the 1948 Olympic Games were held in London. The mood of optimism lasted: In the 1960s the world of music and fashion revolved around »Swinging London« (►MARCO POLO Insight p. 80). However, the end of the British Empire meant a decline in the political and economic importance of London. The demise of the London docks and the associated wave of strikes in 1968 were perhaps the most dramatic illustration of this. The creation of the Greater London Council in 1965 to direct the government of the city was an attempt to solve London's growing problems, but this Labour-dominated body was dissolved in 1986 by Margaret Thatcher. In one other respect, too, 1986 marked a break with the past: The deregulation and reform of the stock exchange, the so-called Big Bang, helped London to become a major global financial centre. A city of docks and manufacturing became a centre for the service sector – a development visible from 1982 in the transformation of the Docklands to an office district and an up-market residential area.

In May 2000 the Labour government gave Greater London not only a new representative assembly and its first mayor – Tony Blair's old enemy **Ken Livingstone** (»Red Ken«) – but also spectacular new buildings for the new millennium (▶p. 40). Livingstone's congestion charge for the inner city resulted in a noticeable reduction of road traffic. In 2005 London was chosen to hold the 2012 Olympic Games. The celebrations were short-lived, as four Muslim suicide bombers caused explosions on three underground trains and a bus, killing 52 people, on the following day. 2006 was the end of the road for a much-loved sight on the streets of the capital: The last Routemaster double-decker buses with their open platform at the back were withdrawn from service. In consolation they continued to run as a tourist attraction on two routes. 2008 saw the opening of a fifth terminal at Heathrow Airport and a disappointment for Ken Livingstone: On 1 May he lost the mayoral elections to the equally flamboyant and controversial Conservative candidate, Boris Johnson, who is also known for a green-minded transport innovation: »Boris bikes«, which can be hired at many places all around the city, and ambitious plans for new cycle paths.

New Labour

Boris Johnson's first term was overshadowed by the world financial crisis and its severe effects on the City banking sector, but by the time of his re-election in 2012, things were looking up thanks to two major, happy events in that year: the Olympic Games (▶MARCO POLO Insight p. 226) and the 60th jubilee of Elizabeth II, celebrated with street parties and a procession of boats on the Thames. The **tallest building in western Europe** was completed on the south bank near London Bridge: The Shard (▶p. 297), 310m/1017ft high. As the years of recession ended in 2013–14, London's economy and population were growing faster than in the rest of England, and property prices were booming again. The adequate provision of housing, education and social services for all residents, and transport issues such as whether to expand Heathrow Airport or build a new one, are among the big challenges for the future.

Arts and Culture

Art and Architecture

What remains of Roman London? Where is the finest Norman and Gothic architecture in London? What did Sir Christopher Wren build after the Great Fire? Which monuments to their periods in government were left by Margaret Thatcher and Tony Blair?

REMAINS OF THE ROMAN PERIOD

Following the establishment of Roman rule under Emperor Claudius in the years after AD 43, Londinium became a centre of trade. The construction of a wooden bridge near today's London Bridge, where many coins from the Roman period have been found, encouraged the prosperity of the city, which had become the largest in Roman Britannia by the last quarter of the first century AD. Where Leadenhall Market now stands, an imposing **basilica** was erected with a huge **forum** next to it. The city had a drainage system and many bath-houses. The harbour, warehouses and the governor's palace were on the banks of the Thames. In 1954 a **Temple of Mithras** was excavated. The **city wall** built in the late 2nd century was 6m/20ft high and up to 2.5m/8ft thick. It enclosed an area between the Tower and Ludgate Hill, where the Fleet River flows into the Thames. Many exhibits in the Museum of London, behind which a stretch of the city wall has been preserved, demonstrate the quality of life in Londinium.

NORMAN LONDON

The Normans were responsible for an enormous increase in building activity from the 11th century. The characteristics of Norman architecture are round arches, doorways with archivolts, rectangular and, in the later period, round or clustered piers, arcades and plain wooden roofs, which later evolved into barrel vaults or groin vaults. Decorative elements consisted of simple geometric forms and capitals with human or animal figures. From 1078 to 1097 William the Conqueror had the massive **White Tower** built within the Roman city wall using limestone from Caen. It marked the beginning of Norman building in the city. **St John's Chapel**, the apse of which can be seen in the south-east corner of the Tower, is one of the most significant works

This portrait of Charles I by the court painter Anthony van Dyck is unfortunately no longer in London – it can be admired in the Louvre

of early Norman architecture in London. It consists of a nave and two aisles, which continue around the choir. A passage in the form of a gallery runs all around the upper storey, an architectural feature typical of the south of France. A further impressive example of Norman architecture is the choir of St Bartholomew-the-Great. The massive masonry, the narrowness of the bays, the sturdy piers and the moulded blind arcades of the upper storey from the Norman period contrast with the late Gothic windows in the Perpendicular style. The first stone bridge across the Thames was the 20-arched London Bridge, built from 1176 by **Peter de Colechurch**. Immediately after its completion houses, shops and a chapel were built on the bridge on both sides of the roadway (model in St Magnus-the-Martyr, ▶ p. 244).

THE HIGH MIDDLE AGES: THE GOTHIC PERIOD

Architecture Many elements of Norman architecture are evident in the early Gothic period in England. However, there was a trend for walls to be pierced more, columns to become more slender and windows to take on the form of lancets. This first phase of **English Gothic style**, Early English, can be seen in exemplary form in **Westminster Abbey**. The proportions of the church, with its nave and two aisles, choir,

Gothic architecture of the highest order: Westminster Abbey

sanctuary and radiating chapels are those of a French cathedral. The clear and simple tracery shows the influence of Amiens and Reims, while the round-arched trefoils in the arcades above the sedilia are characteristic of the very early Gothic period.

In the **Decorated style** which follows, the walls are broken open even more, and lively forms of tracery and arch adorn windows and openings. Doorways are decorated with strongly pierced gables, capitals are freer in style and more ornamental, and rib vaulting evolves. An excellent example of this style is the late 13th-century Chapel of **St Etheldreda** near Smithfield Market.

The **Perpendicular style** was the dominant style in English architecture until the 16th century. The characteristics of this specifically English version of late Gothic are greater complexity of detail in walls and vaulting, a reduction of flexibility and spontaneity of form, stylised ornamentation and more clearly structured design. Arches and windows, which become even larger, gain a stronger horizontal accentuation. In addition to lierne and stellar vaults, the fan vault, a form unique to England, came into favour. Here the ribs radiate in the shape of a fan from a single point. The Chapel of Henry VII with its remarkable fan vault adorned with cone-like pendants is an exceptionally fine example of the Perpendicular style.

The outstanding **secular building** among the few that have survived from the Gothic period is **Westminster Hall**, now part of the Houses of Parliament, with its hammer-beam roof and window tracery. The crypt, assembly hall and main doorway of **Guildhall** date back to the period 1411 to 1439.

Developments in the art of sculpture can be seen by studying funerary monuments. Recumbent figures on stone tombs such as the effigies in the **Temple Church** are characteristic of the 13th century. In **Westminster Abbey** the tomb of Edmund Crouchback († 1296) represents a new departure. Its lavish architectural framework is derived from the shrines of saints. The sinuous pose of the mourning figure on the tomb of John of Eltham displays the tendency to create flowing forms that is apparent by 1250 and was to be a defining characteristic of English sculpture.

Sculpture

In the 12th century the art of book illustration flowered in England as at no other time. The native tradition of linearity combined with influences from the European continent in a lively interchange that is most conspicuous in motifs of the Angevin dynasty. **Matthew Paris**, the most important English painter of miniatures, decorated the manuscript of *Historia Anglorum* with illustrations in a manner that appears somewhat archaic and influenced by the classical style, but is nevertheless of its time in its naturalism and the emphasis on emotions. The panels of an altarpiece in Westminster Abbey that has

Painting

been dated to the last quarter of the 13th century depict elegant, elongated figures with light, soft drapery standing close together, one behind the other. An impression of the secular painting of the period is given by the panels commissioned by Henry III in the mid-1230s in the Painted Chamber of Westminster Palace. Only two of these works, likely by the court painter **Walter of Durham**, survived the fire which destroyed the palace in 1834. They had been already removed in 1816 and are now in the British Museum in room 40.

RENAISSANCE LONDON

Architecture   The Perpendicular style retained its importance throughout the Renaissance period. The **Tudor style** (approx. 1485–1558) marks a time of upheaval and transition. Tudor buildings in London include the gatehouse, audience chamber and chapel of **St James's Palace**, and Staple Inn in Chancery Lane. At **Hampton Court Palace** (1514–40) Italian decoration in the shape of terracotta medallions showing the heads of Roman emperors adorns a Gothic building that is typical of the Tudor period in its brickwork and especially in the slender chimneys with their geometrical decoration. The **Elizabethan style** (approx. 1558–1603) is the expression of a magnificent courtly culture that has, however, left few architectural traces in London. New theatres, in particular Shakespeare's Globe Theatre, are the principal evidence of the flowering of culture in this period. In the **Jacobean period** (1603–25) Gothic elements are increasingly replaced by classical forms: Classical columns, classical entablatures and symmetry take centre stage, and decoration becomes considerably more lavish. In the period after 1625 the **Palladian style** gained influence. Its leading exponent was **Inigo Jones** (1573–1652), whose buildings for royal and aristocratic patrons charted a course that was to be followed in later centuries. Sparing, refined decoration and solidity are characteristics of his work, as the severely Palladian **Queen's House** in Greenwich (1616–35) superbly exemplifies. Jones's principal work, however, is the **Banqueting House** (1619–22), the only part of Whitehall Palace that still stands today.

Painting and sculpture   The Hornebolte family, invited to England from the Netherlands in about 1530 by Henry VIII, provided a stimulus to miniature painting. **Nicholas Hilliard** (1537/38?–1618) specialised in portraits limited to the head and shoulders. **Hans Holbein** (1497–1543) played a pioneering role in the development of painting. At first he worked mainly for the merchants of the Steelyard, the London premises of the Hanseatic League, and later became court painter to Henry VIII. Rational observation and the precise rendering of physiognomy are the basis of his portraiture.

Renaissance sculpture in London begins with the commission award-ed to **Pietro Torrigiano** (1472–1528) from Florence to create the tomb of Henry VII and Elizabeth of York in Westminster Abbey (1512–18). It shows the couple in the traditional manner as separate recumbent figures, richly robed with hands folded. The individual physiognomy and the representation of the bodies, which can be dis-cerned even under the drapery, was much imitated in London.

SIR CHRISTOPHER WREN'S CENTURY

The 17th century was a golden age for English architecture. Initially Inigo Jones's style led the way, but the enormously productive figure of the second half of the century was Sir Christopher Wren (1632–1723), particularly through his rebuilding work after the Great Fire of 1666. His church building, including St Paul's Cathedral and a fur-ther 52 city churches, demonstrates a diverse range of adapted styles. In many instances, however, he continued local tradition. To begin with he continued the work begun by Inigo Jones in Greenwich, ex-tending the Royal Naval Hospital, Queen's House and Observatory. Wren's masterpiece is **St Paul's Cathedral** (1675–1711): The façade with its twin towers and the dome broke new ground. For the two colonnades he was indebted to the Parisian architecture of Perrault, while the upper storeys of the towers are influenced by Borromini's Roman Baroque and reappear in similar form on other towers by Wren. The interior represents a compromise between the basilica plan with a spacious choir, as the Anglican church demanded, and the architect's favoured design of a central plan with dome. As a »tri-al run« for St Paul's Wren built **St Stephen Walbrook**, where in the choir a large area with a square ground plan was crowned with a dome as an experiment in central-plan architecture. Wren designed fewer secular buildings; one of them is the somewhat monotonous cuboid east wing of Hampton Court Palace (1689–92). Along with Sir John Vanbrugh and Nicholas Hawksmoor, Wren evolved a strangely heterogeneous style of English late Baroque around the year 1700.

17th century – a period of architectural achievement

18TH CENTURY

Richard Boyle, Earl of Burlington, the main proponent of the classi-cal and Palladian ideology, regarded Baroque as an unenlightened Roman Catholic style and brought together a small group of archi-tects who chiefly took their inspiration from Italy. **William Cham-bers** (1723–96), for example, drew on French and Roman influences for his classical design of Somerset House. At Kenwood House **Rob-**

Architecture

ert **Adam** (1728–92) emphasised the façade with aediculae and a classical portico, but attached more importance to elegant and refined neo-Roman interior decoration. In 1630 with Covent Garden Plaza, Inigo Jones had been the first to implement the idea of a uniform row of buildings on the model of the Place des Vosges in Paris. However, rebuilding work after the Great Fire was not initially carried out in a uniform manner. Not until the construction of the east side of Grosvenor Square was the concept of a standardised façade elevated to the status of an aesthetic principle, expressed in the design of residential buildings on several storeys as a harmonious ensemble in the form of a square, crescent or circus. Grey and yellow brick, light-coloured stucco and, as rhythmic elements, columns, pediments and doorways are the typical features of this restrained style. One of its leading practitioners was **John Nash** (1752–1835), whose major legacy is Regent Street and Regent's Park. At the time of construction from 1811 onwards, this was Europe's largest town planning project.

Painting Until the early 18th century painters from continental Europe were at the forefront in England. The German artist Sir **Godfrey Kneller** (1646–1723), for example, produced elegant portraits, while Italians established the genre of historical painting. The only outstanding English painter was Sir **James Thornhill** (1675–1734) with decora-

A moral portrait of London:
William Hogarth's Beer Street (left) and Gin Lane (right)

tive work such as the dome of St Paul's and ceilings at Hampton Court Palace. The generation that followed re-established the international reputation of English painting: **William Hogarth** (1697–1764) used popular narrative paintings to treat moral issues. He is also famous for his prolific production of copperplate engravings, in which his satirical scenes are based on close observation. Sir **Joshua Reynolds** (1723–92), taking up the tradition of van Dyck and Rembrandt's manner of chiaroscuro colouring, was a major influence on the development of portraiture. He depicted his subjects, who were taken from polite society, in the poses of well-known antique statues or recreated famous compositions of the Renaissance period. The election of Reynolds as the first president of the Royal Academy in 1768 reinforced his pre-eminent position in the artistic life of London. **Thomas Gainsborough** (1727–88) provided fresh impulses in the field of landscape painting and established an English Arcadian tradition with carefully composed scenes in which harmonious light colouring is prevalent.

THE 19TH CENTURY

The most significant architectural commission of the 19th century was the rebuilding of the Houses of Parliament, for which the Gothic or Elizabethan style was specified. In 1836 a design proposed by Sir **Charles Barry** (1795–1860) was chosen. It was not until 1860 that the Gothic Revival style achieved complete dominance for secular as well as religious architecture, as at the Royal Courts of Justice. **Sir John Soane** (1753–1837) was appointed as architect of the Bank of England in 1788. Industrialisation created a demand for housing, docks, markets and railway stations. Robert Stephenson and Philip Hardwick built Euston Station between 1835 and 1839 with a monumental entrance in the form of a Doric portico (demolished in 1963); Lewis Cubitt's design for King's Cross Station (1851–52) had platforms with 24m/80ft-wide barrel vaults and a glass façade. Towards the end of the great age of railway building the engineer William Henry Barlow constructed the widest train shed of all at St Pancras (1867–77), and George Gilbert Scott added the magnificent Gothic hotel in front of it. The greatest achievement of iron-and-glass architecture was the **Crystal Palace** for the Great Exhibition of 1851. In 1860 work began on the first underground railway. Not long after its

Architecture

> ! *Traces*   Insider Tip
>
> MARCO ⊕ POLO TIP
>
> Nothing remains of the magnificent Crystal Palace built for the Great Exhibition of 1851, but a model can be seen in the Museum of London, and something remains of one of the main attractions of the exhibition: life-size plaster models of prehistoric animals in Crystal Palace Park.

opening advertising space could be rented in underground stations and colourful posters soon added to the charm of the new transport system. Market halls and arcades such as Covent Garden, Burlington Arcade, Smithfield Market and Leadenhall Market bear witness to the prosperity of a city which gained a new landmark of the Victorian Gothic style with the construction of **Tower Bridge** from 1886 to 1894.

Painting   In landscape painting **John Constable** (1776–1837) developed his own way of handling colour and light: He captured nuances of light and air, aiming to put atmospheric moods on canvas by painting with free, concise brush-strokes that lent his works the character of sketches in oil rather than of paintings. **J. M. W. Turner** (1775–1851) was a self-taught painter who later attended Reynolds's master classes and was influenced by his studies of Poussin and Lorrain. He became famous for impressionistic landscapes flooded with light, for scenes of hazy atmosphere and scintillating reflections which he painted without tangible contours, thus creating visionary images that sometimes have symbolic character. The fantastical and mystic art of **William Blake** (1757–1827) has caused him to be seen as a precursor of the **Pre-Raphaelites**. They took a romantic view of the past, concentrating on the period before Raphael, to which they were attracted by its expression of emotions and moods.

THE 20TH AND 21ST CENTURIES

Architecture   The dominant mode of architecture until just after the end of the First World War was a tradition of monumentalism derived from the 18th century. The Piccadilly Hotel and Reginald Blomfield's Regent Street Quadrant are examples of this. A task that became increasingly urgent was the building of suburbs; the Tecton group designed the residential blocks Highpoint One and Highpoint Two with incomparable elegance and artistry.

After the Second World War the **Festival Hall** represented a new style: Concrete, horizontal lines and an impression of built landscape with platforms and bridges are the trademarks of this complex designed by Robert Mathew and Leslie Martin. The 1980s saw the emergence of post-modern architecture: **James Stirling** was the architect of the Tate Gallery extension, and in 1986 **Richard Rogers** was responsible for the spectacular new Lloyd's Building. The Docklands became a laboratory for modern architecture, bringing forth interesting work such as Cesar Pelli's office tower One Canada Square and Piers Gough's residential building The Cascades.

At the start of the new millennium the face of London once again changed significantly. The erection of the world's largest observation

The tilt is intentional: the new City Hall

wheel, the 135m/443ft-high **Coca-Cola London Eye** on the bank of
the Thames opposite Parliament, is more interesting in technical than
architectural terms. In a further contribution to the world of superla-
tives, **Richard Rogers** built the Millennium Dome in Greenwich, a
tent 320m/350yd in diameter and 50m/165ft in height enclosing the
world's biggest venue for events. The other British star architect, Sir
Norman Foster, did not remain idle. His was the intricate design of
the **Millennium Bridge**, a pedestrian link between St Paul's Cathedral and the new Tate Modern in the former Bankside Power Station.
He also remodelled the Great Court of the British Museum, covering
it with a glass dome. Two of the newest London landmarks are also
Foster's work: City Hall close to Tower Bridge and the 180m/590ft-
high Swiss Re Tower, which has been nicknamed the »gherkin«. For
the 2012 Olympic Games, an Olympic Park has been built in the eastern district of Stratford. The principal new structures there are the
Olympic Stadium, designed by the Populous architectural practice,
and the Aquatics Centre, which unmistakably bears the signature of
Zaha Hadid.
In the same year the tallest building in western Europe was completed in the new London Bridge Quarter: **The Shard**, designed by

Renzo Piano (▶p. 294). Since then the high-rise trend in the City has continued with the construction of 20 Fenchurch Street (named the »walkie-talkie«, due to its shape), the Leadenhall Building (225m/737ft known as the »Cheesegrater« due to its wedge shape) and The Pinnacle on Bishopsgate, which is planned to reach 288m/945ft.

Painting and sculpture
There were three main currents in modern art before the Second World War: The presence of a number of artists from continental Europe such as Hans Arp, Lázló Moholy-Nagy and Piet Mondrian reinforced the trend to Constructivism, harmonies of pure geometric forms and the rejection of representational art. The most popular avant-garde school was Surrealism, which met with a response in England through, among other influences, Roland Penrose's manifesto. These two currents came together in »Unit One«. The third trend drew on the Impressionist origins of Modernism and took as its subject matter the First World War, but also sexuality, as the sculpture of Jacob Epstein shows.

Post-war art was characterised by a revival of figurative work and the addition of new media: Richard Hamilton and Eduardo Paolozzi employed the imagery of the consumer and media society in computer collages. Pop Art became the art form of the Sixties. In the early 1950s **Henry Moore** stood for moderately figurative sculpture, which Anthony Caro developed towards abstraction. In the 1960s the principles of Constructivism were widened to permit a greater degree

Eye-catching, for most people at least: the works of Gilbert & George

of expression and emotion. Artists who went their own way were **Francis Bacon**, who took cruelty, violence and suffering as the themes of large-scale works; Frank Auerbach, who practised a wild and seemingly spontaneous style of painting; and **Lucian Freud**, who unashamedly captured the voluptuousness of his models on canvas. The preferred medium of **Gilbert & George** and Bruce McLean was initially performance art. Later they expressed their ideas as »permanent solutions«. In the early 1990s artists such as Rachel Whiteread and **Damien Hirst**, who are now established figures, made waves in the art world. The provocative works of these YBAs (Young British Artists) are inseparably associated with the name of Charles Saatchi, patron of the movement.

The prestigious **Turner Prize** is the highest honour for young artists who are out to shock. One winner of the prize, Chris Ofili (1998), caused outrage by his use of elephant dung and pornographic collages in images of the Virgin Mary. The prize-winner in 2003, the »transvestite potter« Grayson Perry, combines traditional ceramics with subversive motifs. In 2007 Mark Wallinger carried off the prize with an installation that criticised the Iraq war, although his official entry was a film of him wandering around an empty museum dressed as a bear. In 2010 Glasgow-born Susan Philipsz was the first to win the Turner Prize with a sound installation, in which she sang an old Scottish lament under three bridges of her home city.

Famous People

WILLIAM BOOTH (1829 – 1912)

The soldiers of the Salvation Army command respect in their tireless work to spread the word of God and provide much-needed help in red-light districts and shelters for the homeless. The founder and first general of the organisation was William Booth, born on 10 April 1829 in Nottinghamshire. He served an apprenticeship as a pawnbroker, became a Methodist, arrived in London in 1849 and preached on the streets.

Founder of the Salvation Army

As his popularity increased over a number of years, his meetings attracted large crowds. In 1865 he and his wife Catherine founded the Christian Revival Society in the East End. Later it was renamed Christian Mission, and in 1878 became the Salvation Army, which Booth structured along the lines of the British army. Despite the hostility and derision which they attracted, General Booth and his soldiers succeeded in establishing their organisation all over the world and gaining widespread recognition by the end of the 19th century. Booth died on 20 August 1912.

CHARLIE CHAPLIN (1889 – 1977)

Oversized shoes, moustache, bowler hat and walking stick: Charlie Chaplin's »**tramp**« is one of the immortal figures in film history. Chaplin was born in Lambeth on 16 April 1889 as the son of a music-hall artist and performed on stage as a child. In 1915 he played the tramp for the first time in the film of the same name. He kept faith with this role, which made him world-famous as early as the 1920s, in such films as The Kid and The Gold Rush in the United Artists film company, which he founded in 1919 in collaboration with Mary Pickford, Douglas Fairbanks and D. W. Griffith. Chaplin's career continued after the advent of sound films with Modern Times and, above all, The Great Dictator, a satire on Nazi Germany that, for all its comic side, was a profoundly moving appeal to resist barbarity.

Actor

After the Second World War his political activity earned him a summons to the Committee for Un-American Activities, and the US government took the opportunity of a trip that Chaplin made to Britain to deny him re-entry to the country. Chaplin then settled in Switzerland. He took on a different type of role in later films such as Monsieur Verdoux, in which he played a confidence trickster who married and murdered widows. He died on Christmas Day 1977 in Vevey on Lake Geneva. Although he came to fame in the USA, he always retained his British citizenship.

Henry VIII, notorious for his succession of wives

DIANA, PRINCESS OF WALES (1961 – 97)

There is no adequate rational explanation for what happened on 6 September 1997 between Kensington Palace and Westminster Abbey. Over 1.5 million people lined the route of the funeral procession of Diana, Princess of Wales, and London drowned in a sea of flowers. Diana Spencer became a legend in her own lifetime and the most public personality of the 1990s. When she married the future monarch of the United Kingdom on 29 July 1981 in St Paul's Cathedral, she perhaps did not realise what she had taken on. Her husband knew all too well what was at stake: »**Love, whatever that means.**« The nation needed an heir to the throne. It was not long before the heir was born, and he soon had a brother, but by then the marriage

Diana, Queen of Hearts

had already broken down. The images and headlines are familiar: personal coldness shown in public, bulimia, Charles and Camilla Parker Bowles, Diana and her riding-teacher. Separation followed in December 1992, divorce in 1996. But the pursuit of Diana by the paparazzi had only just begun, and it ended on a concrete pillar in Paris on 30 August 1997. The public gave Diana what family life failed to provide: warmth and affection. Diana had clearly succeeded in bridging the gulf between herself and the »common people«. Her own personal fate lent credibility to her sympathy for Aids sufferers, the victims of mine accidents and sick children. Even the royal family now showed signs of human emotions: Against all court protocol Elizabeth II ordered that the Union Jack should fly at half-mast over Buckingham Palace, and on the evening before the funeral she even made a TV broadcast to her people. Diana's grave in Althorp (125km/80mi north of London) has become a place of pilgrimage. The Princess of Wales Memorial Fountain in Hyde Park commemorates her.

CHARLES DICKENS (1812 – 70)

Author The works of Charles Dickens, who was born on 7 February 1812, provide an outstanding and sympathetic portrait of the life of the poor in London. Dickens had, after all, experienced this life of poverty in his early years in the dockland districts when his father was in prison. Despite this, Dickens worked his way up to become a law clerk, parliamentary stenographer, journalist and, in the end, the **most successful author of his time** and publisher of the *Daily News*. He made his name in 1837 with The Pickwick Papers; in such novels as *Oliver Twist, Nicholas Nickleby* and *David Copperfield* he created characters with a place in world literature. London was often the scene of his stories, which deal with the plight of the poor and the injustice done to them. Dickens's social campaigning never took place at the expense of his humour, and he was also capable of writing touching pieces such as his Christmas stories. Charles Dickens died on 9 June 1870.

HENRY VIII (1491–1547)

Henry VIII of the house of Tudor ruled England from 1509 to 1547. He is remembered as the founder of the Anglican church, for his immoderate life and because he had six wives. Henry was born on 28 June 1491 in Greenwich. He had a humanist and theological education, was a model of courtesy, a good dancer and huntsman and a physically imposing figure. Thanks to his chancellor, Thomas Wolsey, the first years of his reign seemed to confirm the high expectations placed in him. In recognition of a polemic that he wrote against Luther (in fact its main arguments came from Thomas More), Pope Leo X even awarded him the title »Defender of the Faith«. When his marriage to Catherine of Aragon failed to produce the desired male heir, Henry resolved to divorce his queen, but the pope refused. The resulting conflict ended in 1533 with the separation of the English church from Rome and the establishment of the Anglican church. Henry then married Anne Boleyn, who bore him a girl, the later Elizabeth I. However, he executed Anne in 1536 and married Jane Seymour, who died in 1537; then Anne of Cleves, whom he quickly divorced; Catherine Howard, whom he executed in 1542; and finally Catherine Parr, who survived him. In the last years of his life – he died on 28 January 1547 – after he had sent his chancellors Sir Thomas More and Thomas Cromwell to the scaffold, Henry VIII was a mistrustful tyrant.

King of England

ALFRED HITCHCOCK (1899 – 1980)

»Suspense« was the key concept in the work of Alfred Hitchcock, who was born in London on 13 August 1899. By this he meant not the usual excitement of wondering »who dunnit?«, but a state of tension in the film-goer arising from the fact that the heroes seen on the screen, who are usually perfectly normal people, are caught up in completely irrational situations which either leave the viewer wholly in the dark (e.g. in North by Northwest and Rear Window) or on the contrary let the viewer know more than the film characters (e.g. in Psycho). Hitchcock, who was educated at a Jesuit college, is regarded as one of the greatest film directors. He worked with the leading Hollywood stars and appeared in his own films in fleeting roles. He died on 29 April 1980 in Los Angeles.

Film director

WILLIAM HOGARTH (1697–1764)

Painter   William Hogarth, the son of a schoolteacher, was born in London on 10 November 1697. He trained as an engraver, and his early employment was to produce copper engravings of book illustrations, but in his spare time he studied painting, and was to become equally distinguished as a painter and engraver. Hogarth was a talented portraitist, as his *Shrimp Girl* in the National Gallery shows, but his forthright nature and unwillingness to flatter were obstacles to success in this field. He is best known for his depiction of the high and low society of the time in narrative series such as *The Rake's Progress* and *The Harlot's Progress*, which he painted with a moral and satirical intent. Two works that highlighted social problems in 18th-century London were *Gin Lane* and *Beer Street*, contrasting the happy residents of Beer Street, where mode-ration and hard work ruled, with the drunken and impoverished inhabitants of Gin Lane. Hogarth regarded beer as a healthy, truly British beverage and cultivated a patriotism that verged on xenophobia, as in *The Gate of Calais*, showing the arrival of English roast beef in France, and *Taste in High Life*, a defence of English tradition against the perceived foppery of the French and Italians. Indeed Hogarth had a liberating effect on English art, which had previously been dominated by Italian influences. The moralising narrative series of paintings were conceived as the basis for engravings, which were widely sold. Hogarth died on 26 October 1764 and was buried in the churchyard of St Nicholas in Chiswick in the west of London.

JACK THE RIPPER

Murderer   The most notorious murderer in the criminal history of London was »Jack the Ripper«. To this day the identity of the man behind the name remains a mystery. He (or she) bestially murdered five prostitutes in Whitechapel in the dark East End of London between August and November 1888: He cut the throats of all victims, and from most he removed organs and arranged them around the body. The murderer taunted the police in several letters signed »Jack the Ripper« and announced further murders, but the killing of the 25-year-old Mary Kelly on 9 November 1888 was the last. Panic gripped the East End and the police made enormous, but unsuccessful, efforts – they even photographed the eyes of one victim in

> **❗ MARCO ⊕ POLO TIP**
>
> *The Ripper: Read All About It*
>
> ... at www.casebook.org: the victims, the suspects, the theories, the witnesses, the newspaper reports. Even Jack the Ripper's letters are reproduced in facsimile.   *Insider Tip*

the hope that the face of the killer had been captured on the retina. Today the identity of Jack the Ripper is still the subject of wild speculation; the suspects have included the grandson of Queen Victoria and heir to the throne, the Duke of Clarence, the artist Walter Sickert, a Russian secret agent and a cousin of the writer Virginia Woolf.

Who was Jack the Ripper?

SAMUEL JOHNSON (1707–84)

Samuel Johnson, generally known as Dr Johnson, was born in Lichfield on 18 September 1709, the son of a bookseller. His first visit to London was at the age of three, when he suffered from scrofula, then known as »the king's evil«, and was brought by his parents to be touched by Queen Anne as a cure. After studies at Oxford and an unsuccessful venture as a schoolmaster, a task in which his scarred face, nervous tics and melancholia were a handicap, Johnson came to London in 1737. His early years in the city were marked by poverty. He worked hard as a journalist and parliamentary reporter, and in 1746 began to produce the first dictionary of the English language, for which he wrote definitions of over 40,000 words and illustrated them with about 114,000 quotations drawn from all fields of knowledge. He also wrote *The Lives of the English Poets* and edited the works of Shakespeare. His fame as the pre-eminent man of letters of the 18th century rests not only on his prolific literary output but also on the brilliance of his conversation, as recorded in the biography written by his Scottish friend James Boswell. He expressed trenchant and much-quoted opinions about Scotland, foreigners, women and many other subjects, but could also be humorous at his own expense, as in his famous definition of a lexicographer: »A maker of dictionaries, a harmless drudge«. He went abroad only once: London, particularly the area around Fleet Street, and its inns and coffee-houses, was his world. He died on 13 December 1784 at his home in Bolt Court. His legacy of quotable remarks includes one of the greatest tributes that could be paid to the city he loved: »A man who is tired of London is tired of life.«

KARL MARX (1818 – 83)

Philosopher

After the failure of the revolution of 1848 in Germany, Karl Marx, born on 5 May 1818 in Trier on the Moselle and publisher of the newspaper Neue Rheinische Zeitung in Cologne, was expelled from the state of Prussia. Via Brussels he came to London, where after a period living in Dean Street in Soho he settled at 41 Maitland Park Road with his wife Jenny. He struggled to support his family with journalism, often helped by his wealthy friend and collaborator Friedrich Engels. In London – mainly in the Reading Room of the British Library – he wrote his major work, Das Kapital. Karl Marx died in London on 14 March 1883; his much-visited grave is in Highgate Cemetery in north London.

SIR THOMAS MORE (1477 – 1535)

Philosopher
and Lord
Chancellor

Sir Thomas More, born on 7 February 1477 as the son of a lawyer, attended the best school in London, St Anthony's, and the University of Oxford, and studied law at Lincoln's Inn. In December 1516 he published Utopia, the first-ever work of fiction about an ideal society. It describes a state ruled – in complete contrast to contemporary England or France – by reason and equality where there was no place for exploitation and envy. More had a career at court as adviser to Henry VIII. In 1523 he was elected speaker of the House of Commons and succeeded Wolsey as Lord Chancellor in 1529. His disagreement with Henry came when the king divorced Catherine of Aragon. After the break from the Catholic church, More declined to have any part in Henry's wedding to Anne Boleyn. He finally refused to recognise the King as head of the Anglican church and was thrown into the Tower in April 1534. A sentence of death was passed in July 1535, but More was given five days' time to reconsider. He still refused to take the oath and was beheaded on 6 July 1535. His head was placed on a spike at the south end of London Bridge as a warning. Pope Pius XI canonised him in 1935.

FLORENCE NIGHTINGALE (1820 – 1910)

Nurse

Even as a young woman Florence Nightingale, who was born on 12 May 1820 in Florence, had the reputation of being an expert on health. After managing a hospital during the Crimean War, she devoted herself to organising medical care for the British army and became inspector general of nursing in military hospitals. In 1860 she founded the Nightingale School for Nurses in London, the world's first nursing college. Until her death on 13 August 1910 Florence

Nightingale mainly lived in London and pursued her cause with great energy, but not without ruthlessness towards others. From 1857 she was an invalid, although no illness was ever diagnosed, and in addition she was blind from 1901.

VIRGINIA WOOLF (1882 – 1941)

Virginia Woolf's house in the Bloomsbury district of London was the meeting place of the »Bloomsbury Group«, an association of friends which included E. M. Forster, Vita Sackville-West and John Maynard Keynes. Woolf, born on 25 January 1882 and married to the publisher Leonard Woolf, founded the Hogarth Press with her husband and wrote literary criticism for *The Times*. Through her work as an essayist, diarist and novelist she became the most celebrated female author in England in the 1920s. She suffered from severe depression and committed suicide on 28 March 1941.

Writer

SIR CHRISTOPHER WREN (1632 – 1723)

Sir Christopher Wren, born on 20 October 1632, became Professor of Astronomy at Gresham College in London in 1657 and in Oxford in 1661. At Oxford he began to study architecture and eventually found his vocation in this field after the Great Fire of 1666. He was appointed Surveyor General and directed the rebuilding of London. He designed a total of 53 London churches, the Greenwich Hospital and the Chelsea Royal Hospital. His great work, however, was the new building of St Paul's Cathedral, in which he was buried after his death on 25 February 1723 beneath the following inscription: »Lector, si monumentum requiris, circumspice« – »Reader, if you seek a monument, look around you.«

The man who built London

ENJOY LONDON

Shopping in the West End or the East End? A pint in a traditional pub or a cocktail in a hip bar? And what kind of evening meal would you prefer – Chinese? Indian? African? Lebanese? Or even English?

Accommodation

Variety in the Capital City

All the diversity of London is reflected in its places to stay overnight. Every wish can be met.

HOTELS

The low end of the scale is represented by hostels of character that compete on the basis of free extras, by classic youth hostels and by campsites from which the city centre can be reached in an astonishingly short time. The mid-range is covered by chain hotels that may be anonymous but often provide good value for money, by bed & breakfasts both old-fashioned and comfortable, and by hotels that can either be unwelcoming and staffed by people who hardly speak English or full of atmosphere and friendly. Higher up on the price scale are historic townhouses with a great deal of charm, boutique hotels that seem to have come from the pages of a glossy style magazine, and great hotels that are part of the history of the international hospitality business. Examples of this are the reopening in recent years of two legendary addresses, the Savoy Hotel and St Pancras Hotel.

Prices The bad news is that London's hotels are still among the most expensive in the world, so most people will spend a large part of their travel budget on accommodation. For a double room in a lower mid-range hotel, expect to pay £120 per night, for a bed & breakfast £100. Those travelling alone usually have to pay a substantial »single supplement«. The good news is that fierce competition and the internet age have led to innovation and diversification. In the budget category there is now a wider choice, including hotel-hostel hybrids and hotels with tiny rooms that do without the usual amenities such as room service, hair dryer and kettle. At weekends prices are often lower, or the hotels have package offers with extras: a bottle of champagne, use of a spa or tickets for a musical. When comparing hotel prices, check whether 20% VAT is included – what looks like an offer of £99 per night can actually cost almost £120.

Facilities Lifts and air-conditioning are only available in the larger modern hotels; if you have difficulty climbing stairs, ask for a ground-floor room in older places; fans are often available on request. WiFi is usually included in the price, but where this is not the case, the costs tend

The Milestone is one of the finest hotels in London

Brought back to life: the Savoy

to be exorbitant. Hotels increasingly offer bikes for hire.

In choosing accommodation it is worth considering (apart from the costs) how much time you will actually spend there, and how important it is to be able to reach the city centre quickly. It is cheaper to stay outside the London Transport zones 1 and 2, but the higher transport fares and time spent travelling to and fro (standing up during the rush hour) are the disadvantage.

OTHER ACCOMMODATION

Bed & breakfast is well worth considering as an alternative to a hotel. A room in a private house and a classic English breakfast is one way to see a bit of real London life, as long as the room is not in one of those inhospitable low-grade guesthouses in districts like Victoria which go under the name B & B. Whereas B & Bs once had a reputation for being chintzy and old-fashioned with worn-out mattresses and instant coffee, today there are modern design B & Bs and private homes full of antiques and tasteful furnishings where the owners actually have time to talk to their guests. Some B&Bs have a lounge for guests. If not, then the unwritten rule is that guests will not hang around the house during the day.

Hostels For the young and young at heart, London's fast-moving hostel scene is an attractive option. Most hostels have double rooms and decent service (ticket and information desks, dorms for women, free city tours) that are worlds away from the traditional idea of what a youth hostel is like. There are also hostels for travellers who are no longer quite so young and are not looking for party atmosphere round the clock but still happy to make contacts in sociable surroundings. The kitchen facilities for self-catering also save a lot of money. And even those who turn up their nose at the idea of staying in a tent in London might be pleasantly surprised by campsites with such innovations as comfortable double »cocoons« with proper beds and service.

Recommended hotels

PRICES

The prices given below are average prices for a double room and vary considerably (in the luxury category they can be much higher). As a rule only continental breakfast is included; a supplement is charged for English breakfast. The prices quoted do not normally include the 20% VAT which will be added. It is worth asking about special group and weekend rates.

£ £ £ £ above £300
£ £ £ £200 – 300
£ £ £100 – 200
£ £70 – 100

❶ see plan p. 102–103
Addresses without a number are outside the area shown.

RESERVATIONS

www.visitlondon.com/
accommodation

⓱ The Connaught **£ £ £ £**

Carlos Place, W 1
Tel. 020 7499 7070
www.the-connaught.co.uk
Tube: Bond Street
90 rooms. Old-style British hotel tradition with an interior carved in oak in 1897: Discretion is the guiding principle, and guests' wishes are treated like holy writ. The best chance of making a reservation is to write a courteous letter, but the hotel does not take everyone, and regular guests take precedence.

⓲ The Dorchester **£ £ £ £**

53 Park Lane, W 1
Tel. 020 7629 8888
www.dorchesterhotel.com
Tube: Hyde Park Corner
244 rooms. Marble was one of the principal materials used when the hotel was built in 1900. Wonderful view across Hyde Park. Guests can use Brompton folding bicycles for a ride in the park or to take on the Tube.

⓴ The Milestone Hotel **£ £ £ £**

1 Kensington Court, W 8
Tel. 020 7917 1000
www.milestonehotel.com
Tube: High Street Kensington
45 rooms, 12 suites. The Milestone is one of the world's finest hotels and the recipient of many awards. Behind the red-brick façade of two Victorian houses are individually and tastefully furnished rooms that reflect the traditional style of the house but are fitted with all modern technology. Friendly and helpful staff attend to every wish with old-fashioned courtesy. The location directly opposite Kensington Palace is unbeatable.

❶ Renaissance St. Pancras **£ £ £ £**   Insider Tip

Euston Road, NW1
Tel. 020 7841 3540
www.marriott.co.uk
Tube: King's Cross/St Pancras
283 rooms. A few steps away from the platform for those who arrive in London on Eurostar. George Gilbert Scott's monument,

turreted fantasy architecture for what was then called the Great Midland Hotel, was a highlight of the Victorian railway age and has an enchanting atmosphere once again, having reopened in 2011 after thorough renovation with all modern facilities.

⑲ The Ritz £ £ £ £
Piccadilly, W 1
Tel. 020 7493 8181
www.theritzlondon.com
Tube: Green Park
129 rooms. A flagship of the London hotel trade, situated right next to Green Park. All rooms are furnished in the Louis XVI style. Teatime in the Palm Court is an institution.

⑯ Savoy £ £ £ £
Strand, WC 2
Tel. 020 7836 4343
www.fairmont.de/savoy-london
Tube: Charing Cross
200 rooms. A legendary Victorian hotel with an Art Deco foyer where afternoon tea is served. Reopened after a thorough renovation in 2010. Rooms with a view of the Thames are more expensive. It was the first hotel with electric lighting in every room, and has bathrooms in a wonderfully old-fashioned style – though they are not old!

Insider Tip

⑬ W Hotel £ £ £ £
10 Wardour Street, W1
Tel. 020 7758 1000
www.wlondon.co.uk
Tube: Leicester Square
192 rooms. Glitz, glamour and a theatrical atmosphere are the watchwords of this branch of the

Starwood chain, which opened in 2011 in the heart of the entertainment quarter. The rooms have VIP styling from top to toe, the restaurant is South-East Asian, the cocktail bar is ultra-cool and the nightclub has what must be the biggest glittering disco globe in London.

㉑ Aster House £ £ £
3 Sumner Place, SW 7
Tel. 020 7581 5888
www.asterhouse.com
Tube: South Kensington
12 rooms. An elegant bed and buffet-breakfast house in high-class Kensington, perfect for museum fans, as the Science, Natural History and V & A Museums are just round the corner. Air-conditioned rooms, attentive service, for non-smokers only.

⑪ Grazing Goat £ £ £
6 New Quebec Street, W 1
Tel. 020 7724 7243
www.thegrazinggoat.co.uk
Tube: Marble Arch
8 rooms. Opened in 2010, a skilful combination of the traditional British pub with a comfortable country-house-style hotel. Its location is ideal for shopping, but also for cultural activities and a trip to Notting Hill.

㉕ Rafayel £ £ £
34 Lombard Road, SW 11
Tel. 020 7801 3610
www.hotelrafayel.com
Tube: Clapham Junction
65 rooms, 15 apartments. For ecologically-minded guests who want comfort but do not need to be in the city centre, this hotel

Insider Tip

west of Battersea Park is a good choice. High-tech energy efficiency, rainwater collection, no plastic, electronic newspapers, bikes for getting into town – which can be left at the Tube station, where they are picked up. Hotel guests pay half price in the in-house Asian restaurant.

⑭ Hazlitt's £ £ £
6 Frith Street, W 1
Tel. 020 7341 1771
www.hazlittshotel.com
Tube: Tottenham Court Road
23 rooms. In the middle of Soho, and the very antithesis of a sleazy establishment. This was once the house of the Prussian consul and the essayist William Hazlitt, who is said to have died from drinking too much tea, now furnished in traditional English style.

⑳ The Levin £ £ £
28 Basil Street, SW 3
Tel. 020 75 89 62 86
www.thelevinhotel.co.uk
Tube: Knightsbridge
12 rooms. Boutique hotel in cottage style round the corner from Harrods. Very cosy, with continental breakfast but a brasserie that serves a British grazing menu of delicious titbits, washed down with Sauvignon Blanc from the proprietor's own vineyard on the Loire.

❷ Rough Luxe £ £ £
1 Birkenhead Street, WC 1
Tel. 020 7730 7000
www.roughluxe.co.uk
Tube: King's Cross/St Pancras
9 rooms. A bed & breakfast in a listed heritage house with the very London idea of being half luxury, half rough. Copper bathtubs, furnishings from style magazines and some artistic shabbiness. Breakfast in the courtyard.

❹ The Zetter £ £ £
St John's Square
86–88 Clerkenwell Road, EC 1
Tel. 020 7324 4444
www.thezetter.com
Tube: Farringdom
59 rooms. Modern and well-designed with a green touch, and good value for money compared to the West End. Clerkenwell is a historically interesting and newly fashionable district, great for gourmets and near both the traditional and the East End attractions. Folding bikes for hire without charge. The new bistro serves Asian-influenced dishes with a touch of the Maghreb.

㉓ Belgravia B & B £ £
64-66 Ebury Street, SW 1
Tel. 020 7759 8570
www.bb-belgravia.com
Tube: Victoria
17 rooms, 9 apartments. A Georgian townhouse refurbished in contemporary style in one of the poshest parts of town, but only 10 minutes' walk from Victoria Station. Black-and-white decor, private garden, guest lounge. The studios, a few houses further along, share a sunny terrace.

⑮ Fielding £ £
4 Broad Court, Bow Street, WC 2
Tel. 020 7836 8305
www.the-fielding-hotel.co.uk
Tube: Covent Garden

26 rooms. Don't expect luxury here, as the rooms are small (mini showers!), but the positives are English breakfast and the central location in Covent Garden, handy for cultural attractions and shopping. Hotel guests have use of a spa around the corner.

❺ The Hoxton Hotel £ £
81 Great Eastern Street, EC 2
Tel. 020 7550 1000
www.hoxtonhotels.com
Tube: Old Street
205 rooms. The Hoxton advertises its mixture of »urban hip« and »country lodge living«. The rooms are not large but modern, with internet and breakfast in the fridge. Clubbers' destinations are just round the corner.

⓬ The Main House £ £
6 Colville Road, W 11
Tel. 020 7221 9691
www.themainhouse.co.uk
Tube: Notting Hill Gate
Elegant and individual B & B, with a friendly welcome. Minimalist style in the large rooms. The French Suite is ideal for families who need two rooms.

❻ Shoreditch Rooms £ £
Ebor Street, E 13
Tel. 020 7739 5040
www.shoreditchrooms.com
Overground: Shoreditch High Street
26 rooms. Shoreditch embodies the creative renaissance of the old East End. Here trendy travellers find bright and airy rooms with a vintage look on the five floors of a former warehouse.

❿ The Sumner £ £
54 Upper Berkeley Street, W 1
Tel. 020 7723 2244
www.thesumner.com
Tube: Marble Arch
20 rooms. A charming, award-winning boutique hotel in a Georgian terraced house near Marble Arch but quietly situated. Good breakfast, WiFi and helpful staff.

㉔ Windermere £ £
142–144 Warwick Way, SW 1
Tel. 020 7834 5163
www.windermere-hotel.co.uk
Tube: Victoria
19 rooms. The hotel, which has a pleasant breakfast room and clean guest rooms, is much prettier than the street.

❸ Clink 261 £ £ £
Gray's Inn Road, WC 3
Tel. 020 7833 9400
www.clinkhostels.com
Tube: King's Cross/St Pancras
177 beds. An extremely comfortable boutique hostel between King's Cross and Bloomsbury with dorms (separate for women), double rooms and a common room where people of all ages from all over the world meet.

❾ Lincoln House Hotel £
33 Gloucester Place, W 1
Tel. 020 7486 7630
www.lincoln-house-hotel.co.uk
Tube: Marble Arch
22 rooms. Friendly Georgian hotel near Oxford Street and Hyde Park. Small rooms (two for smokers), but English breakfast.

❽ Parkwood Hotel £
4 Stanhope Place, W 2

Tel. 020 7402 2241
www.parkwoodhotel.com
Tube: Marble Arch
16 rooms. Large rooms in a
award-winning B&B in a quietly
located historic building, only a
few minutes from Hyde Park and
Oxford Street. No lift, fan in summer instead of air-conditioning.

❼ Tune Hotel £
13-15 Folgate Street, E 1
www.tunehotels.com
Tube: Liverpool Street
183 rooms. You can save a lot of
money if you are content to book
a very small room. Those with a
window and any extras such as a
hair dryer, TV, towels, internet
cost more.

YHA HOSTELS
Central reservations
www.yhalondon.org.uk
Tel. *0800 0191 7008

St. Paul's
36–38 Carter Lane, EC 4
Tel. *0845 317 9012

Oxford Street
14 Noel Street, W 1
Tel. *0845 317 90 33

Holland Park
Holland Walk, W 8
Tel. *0845 317 9022

OTHER HOSTELS
**The London Hostels
Association**
54 Eccleston Square, SW 1

www.london-hostels.co.uk
Ten hostels with basic facilities
and a total of 1100 beds.

CAMPING
Information
www.campingandcaravanning
club.co.uk

Abbey Wood
Federation Road, Greenwich,
SE 2, tel. 020 8310 2233
www.caravanclub.co.uk
Historic Greenwich with its Unesco attractions and the boat pier
on the Thames are not far away.

Crystal Palace Caravan Club
Crystal Palace Parade, SE 19
Tel. 020 8778 7155
In south London via the A 205
near the National Sports Centre,
with a regular bus connection to
Oxford Circus. Close to pretty
Dulwich Village.

**Lee Valley Campsite
& Caravan Park**
Sewardstone Road,
Chingford, E 4
Tel. 020 8529 5689
Cosy cocoons with electric light
and camp beds or wooden family
cabins. A great way to take the
family to London. With a big
park, boating, nature-watching,
rafting, mountainbiking. By bus
and Tube less than an hour from
inner London.

Children in London

Never Get Bored!

London provides so much entertainment and so many suitable sights for young visitors that children need never be bored in the city – if they are, it must be the parents' fault.

London caters for families: On buses and the Tube children under five travel free, and up to the age of 15 they pay half fare on the Tube and travel free on buses. Museums and other attractions have reduced admission prices for children and family tickets; the big museums, in particular, make great efforts to please children. Many restaurants have a children's menu, and most hotels can help to find babysitters. There is a wide range of information at www.timeout.com/london/kids and www.visitlondon.com.

In London with children

The Changing of the Guard at Buckingham Palace and Horse Guards is a delight for kids. A sightseeing tour on a double-decker bus (upstairs of course, and ideally at the front) is a must – if anything is better than this, then perhaps a trip on the London Eye. A boat trip on the Thames is also not to be missed, and parents who want a quieter activity on the water can hire a rowing boat on the Serpentine in Hyde Park. There is no shortage of other parks for running about and working off energy: Regent's Park, Hampstead Heath (flying kites!), Primrose Hill, Greenwich Park, Battersea Park (with its zoo) and many more. In the brass-rubbing centres at ▶St Martin-in-the-Fields, where anyone can make copies of the brass figures on medieval tombs (knights, dragons, etc.), small children are the most active participants.

Activities with children

Bethnal Green ▶V & A Museum of Childhood has a superb collection of toys and organises imaginative activities for children. In many other museums, especially the major institutions, they can do hands-on experiments for themselves, for example in the ▶Natural History Museum (above all the dinosaur department, the Darwin Centre and the Earth Galleries) and in the ▶Science Museum. Programmes for children are also run by the London Transport Museum, the ▶National Maritime Museum (where a simulator allows you to steer a container ship into port) and the Museum in Docklands. Other attractions that go down well with kids are the Cutty Sark in ▶Greenwich, the Golden Hinde, the ▶Tower, ▶Madame Tussaud's and London Zoo. There are even farmyards and petting zoos in the city, for example Mudchute Park & Farm in the Docklands, Hackney City Farm in east London and Vauxhall City Farm south of the river. Whatever parents may think about this, it cannot be denied that Lon-

Museums and other sights

The Beefeaters in the Tower can always help

don's military sights such as HMS Belfast and the Imperial War Museum are often popular with children – not to mention grisly and bloody visitor experiences such as the London Dungeon.

Attractions for children

Internet
www.visitlondon.com/ things-to-do/activities/ family-activities
Up-to-date news of events for families, child-friendly attractions etc.

Platform 9¾ Insider Tip

As every Harry Potter fan knows, the Hogwarts Express leaves from platform 9¾ at King's Cross Station. Not everyone knows that this platform sign exists – between platforms 9 and 10, of course. A great photo opportunity!
If this is not enough, go to Watford north of London to see the »Making of ...« the Harry Potter films in Warner Brothers Studios. Information and tickets: www.wbstudiotour.co.uk.

MARCO POLO TIP

www.timeout.com/london/ kids
The children's pages of London's leading city magazine

CHILDREN'S FARMS
Mudchute Park & Farm
▶ p. 186

Hackney City Farm
1a Goldsmiths Row, E 2
Tue–Sun 10am–4.30pm
Free admission
Tel. 020 7729 6381
www.hackneycityfarm.co.uk
Tube: Hoxton, Berthnal Green

Vauxhall City Farm
Spring Gardens, SE 11
Wed–Sun 10.30am–4pm
Free admission
Tel. 020 7582 4204
www.vauxhallcityfarm.org
Tube: Vauxhall

PLAYGROUNDS
Coram's Fields
Guilford Street WC 1
Tube: Russell Square
A quieter playground close to the British Museum: sandpits, a pond, petting zoo. Adults must be accompanied by a child.

Princess Diana Playground
Kensington Gardens, W 12
Tube: Lancaster Gate
Indian wigwams, a beach and Captain Hook's ship.

Somerford Grove Adventure Playground
Somerford Grove Park, N 17
Overground: Northumberland Park
Tue–Fri 3.30–6.30pm, Sat 1–6pm
Climbing activities and an indoor area for rainy days, but a long way north of the city centre.

THEATRE FOR CHILDREN
Little Angel Marionette Theatre
14 Dagmar Passage, N 1
Tel. 020 7226 1787
Tube: Angel

Welcome to Hamley's, the world's biggest toy shop

Polka Theatre for Children
240 The Broadway, SW 19
Tel. 020 8543 4888
www.polkatheatre.com
Tube: South Wimbledon
Two theatres for children, clowns,
playground and toy shop all in
one.

Puppet Theatre Barge
Little Venice, W 9
Tel. 020 7249 6876
Tube: Warwick Avenue

Puppet theatre on an old barge in
Little Venice.

Unicorn Arts Theatre
6 Great Newport Street, WC 2
Tel. 020 7836 3334
Tube: Leicester Square

TOYS
Hamley's
200 Regent Street, W 1
The world's largest toy shop on
six floors.

Entertainment

Where to Go?

If the phrase »spoilt for choice« applies anywhere, then in London. So why not think about it first over a drink?

The start to an evening in London is often the after-work pint. In summer drinkers crowd the pavements outside **pubs**, and even when it is cooler, smokers can be found huddling around the outdoor heaters. **Smoking** is prohibited in all pubs, bars and restaurants – with the exception of cigar-humidor bars and smoking rooms in a handful of hotels.

Of course the taste of cool Londoners does not just run to beer. **Wine and cocktail bars** with an individual character are everywhere, and plenty of champagne is drunk at prices similar to cocktails: about £10 per glass in hotel bars. The classic gin & tonic is back in fashion, and trendy bars often opt for Victorian theming, style themselves like a speakeasy of the Prohibition, or find some new way of standing out from the others.

First get your bearings. The expensive nightclubs and hotel bars are above all in the **West End**; the City is dead at weekends, and the **East End** is not easily summarised, as it changes so rapidly. Unless you are an insider, the latest district where it's all happening might appear shabby or even threatening. To steer a middle course, not only in geographical terms, between the established nightlife and self-referential chic, it is worth trying out **Clerkenwell**, a historic district that also attracts gourmets, or **Islington** (Tube: Angel), where there are interesting bars and restaurants. Orientation

London is the **world's capital for musicals**, and the range of offerings seems to get wider all the time. London has world-class drama and opera, while remaining less elitist than the theatres in some other major cities: The audience can wear jeans, and there are various ways of getting hold of cheap tickets. Theatre

Theatre tickets are best purchased directly from the theatre, at the official ticket shops or from Visit London. Avoid the unofficial outlets that are often to be found near the big tourist sights, and definitely give a wide berth to the ticket touts who do business outside the theatres – there is no guarantee that their tickets are not fakes. As an alternative to »proper« theatres, consider an evening in a small venue or the back room of a pub for **stand-up comedy**, where the duels between performers and hecklers can be very entertaining, or a play

Spoilt for choice ...

or opera – modest surroundings and a high level of artistry are not a contradiction.

Clubs If you want to go clubbing, it is wise to be well-informed and plan the evening. The articles and listings in Time Out are a valuable guide. For those on business trips: Groups of men will often find it hard to gain admission, so it is better to go in one at a time. If you prefer not to stand around in the rain, consider getting on the **guest list** – there are even services that will organise this for you.

Pubs and bars

❶ See map on p. 74-75

SOME OF THE BEST PUBS
(gastropubs: see p. 99)
⓳ **Black Friar**
174 Queen Victoria Street, EC 4
Tube: Blackfriars
Wonderful Arts & Crafts pub built
in 1905. The poet laureate Sir
John Betjeman campaigned to
save its interior. The »sip before
you sup« policy lets you taste the
beer before ordering a pint.

⓾ **Cittie of Yorke**
22 High Holborn, WC 1
Tube: Holborn
A 17th-century pub with one of
the longest bars in London.

❾ **The Fox and Anchor**
115 Charterhouse Street, EC 1

**The great detective never came here personally, but Arthur Conan
Doyle often took a refreshment in The Sherlock Holmes**

Tube: Farringdon
This was once the local pub for the butchers from Smithfield Market, now with a new owner who has changed the menu from hearty breakfasts for market traders to classic English food without spoiling this lovely Victorian pub.

㉞ The George Inn
77 Borough High Street, SE 1
Tube: London Bridge
London's last coaching inn with a galleried courtyard; the public bar with smooth-polished wooden tables is extremely cosy.

㉛ King's Arms
25 Roupell Street, SE 1
Tube: Waterloo, Southwark A typical corner pub, but it also serves good coffee.

⑱ The Old Bank of England *Insider Tip*
194 Fleet Street, EC4
Tube: Temple
Only opens on weekdays, but the high ceilings and fine interior of this former bank make it a good place for an after-work drink, inside or outside.

㉝ The Old King's Head
King's Head Yard, 45–49 Borough High Street, SE 1
Tube: London Bridge Cosy one-room pub not far from the George Inn.

⑬ Princess Louise *Insider Tip*
208–209 High Holborn, WC 1
Tube: Holborn One of the original gin palaces, complete with a historic lacquered ceiling, and not

too expensive. Order gin and tonic!

㉗ Prospect of Whitby
57 Wapping Wall, E 1
Tube: Wapping
The oldest pub on the Thames, established in 1502, was once a smugglers' nest and popular as it offered grandstand seats for the nearby gallows.

㉔ Salisbury
90 St Martin's Lane, WC 2
Tube: Leicester Square
A superb Victorian interior with mirrors, and a football-free zone.

㉖ Samuel Pepys
Brook's Wharf, Upper Thames Street, EC 4
Tube: Blackfriars
Attractive pub with a view of the Thames. Modern European food and a happy hour from 5pm to 7pm.

㉚ Sherlock Holmes
10 Northumberland Street, WC 2
Tube: Charing Cross
This is where Conan Doyle wrote A Study in Scarlet. The pub is full of mementoes to the great detective.

㊲ Trafalgar Tavern
Park Row, SE 10
DLR: Cutty Sark
A magnificent Victorian pub right on the Thames in Greenwich, one of Charles Dickens's favourites. The traditional dish here is whitebait.

㉟ The White Horse
1–3 Parsons Green, SW 6

Tube: Parsons Green
Called the »Sloany Pony«,
because of the clientele. 60 kinds
of beer, 30 of them on draught,
and a nice beer garden.

 ㉑ Windsor Castle
114 Campden Hill Road, W 8
Tube: Notting Hill Gate,
Kensington High St
This pub in Notting Hill has hardly
changed since the 19th century.

⑰ Ye Olde Cheshire Cheese
145 Fleet Street,EC4
Tube: St Paul's
A little touristy at times, but full of
atmosphere, especially the cellar.
Built in the 17th century, a haunt
of Samuel Johnson and other literary figures.

SOME OF THE BEST BARS
Londoners love their bars – for the
cocktails, the champagne or for
people-watching. Try these addresses for a change from traditional pubs.

❸ Camino
3 Varnisher's Yard,
The Regent Quarter,
King's Cross, N 1
Tube: King's Cross
Spanish bar with tapas and music
in the evening, Camino restaurant
opposite.

❺ 69 Colebrooke Row
69 Colebrook Row, N1
Tube: Angel
At the Islington Green end of
Essex Road, a cocktail bar with
»musical Sundays« and master-
classes in mixing.

㉙ Gordon's Wine Bar
Villiers Street, WC 2
Tube: Embankment
A catacomb-like venue, not far
from Parliament and so a good
place for a confidential talk.

⑫ Paramount *Insider Tip*
101–103 New Oxford
Street, WC 1
Tel. 020 7420 2900
Tube: Tottenham Court Road
On the 30th floor of the Centre
Point tower, a bar with a stunning
panoramic view. Pre-booking is
essential. Will probably close in
2015!

㉜ Skylon
Royal Festival Hall, SE 1
Tube: Embankment, Waterloo
One of the best views in central
London: 180° view of the Thames.
Don't eat straight away, but order
a Bellini and drink at the bar till
sunset.

㊱ Sipsmith
27 Nasmyth Street, W6
Tube: Ravenscourt Park
A micro-distillery for gin and
vodka with a bar.

㉕ Terroirs
5 William IV Street, WC 2
Cross 14–16 Ganton Street, W 1
Tube: Charing
Likeable, French-style wine bar
with a touch of class. The wine list
is wonderfully detailed. Delicious
cheese board and charcuterie.

CLUBS
㉒ Bar Rumba
36 Shaftesbury Avenue, W 1
Tel. 020 7287 6933

www.barrumbadisco.co.uk
Tube: Piccadilly Circus
A Covent Garden institution for jazz, Latin, funk, house. Comedy on Tue, Fri, Sat.

❽ Fabric
77a Charterhouse Street, EC 1
Tel. 020 7336 8898
www.fabriclondon.com
Tube: Farringdon
Enormous club in an old brick-built cold-store. Book in advance if you want to get in on Fri or Sat, don't turn up in a business suit.

㉘ Heaven
Under the Arches, Craven Street, WC 2
Tel. 020 7930 2020
www.heavennightclub-london.com/
Tube: Charing Cross
Long-established spot for gays below Charing Cross Station that also welcomes straight people. A recommendation for Mondays when nothing else is happening elsewhere.

⑳ Notting Hill Arts Club
Insider Tip
21 Notting Hill Gate, W 11
Tel. 020 7598 5226
www.nottinghillartsclub.com
Tube: Notting Hill Gate
Not too large and not too expensive, younger age-group. Wed is rock, indie, punk, Thu is urban music with dubstep, garage. Photo ID is required.

❷ Proud Camden
Stables Market, Horse Hospital, Chalk Farm Road, NW1

Tel. 020 7482 3867
www.proudcamden.com
Tube: Chalk Farm
A blend of bar, gallery and night club, one of Camden's coolest.

❹ Scala
275 Pentonville Road, N 1
Tel. 020 7833 2022
www.scala-london.co.uk
Tube: King's Cross
Dance club, cinema, live concerts, bars in a Victorian theatre in a district that is getting hipper. Four floors, two dance floors and a courtyard for smokers.

JAZZ
⑯ 100 Club
100 Oxford Street, W 1
Tel. 020 7636 0933
www.the100club.co.uk
Tube: Tottenham Court Road
Intimate club with everything from trad jazz to swing, punk and rock, including well-known names.

❻ Café Oto
18–22 Ashwin Street, E8
www.cafeoto.co.uk
Overground: Dalston Junction
New and unusual sounds in run-down but trendy Dalston. A location for fans of avant-garde music.

⑪ Ronnie Scott's
47 Frith Street, W 1
Tel. 020 7439 0747
www.ronniescotts.co.uk
Tube: Leicester Square
Legendary jazz club, still the best in town.

❼ The Vortex Jazz Club

11 Gillett Square, N 16 (Stoke Newington)

Jazz of the highest standard can be heard in London's clubs

Tel. 020 7254 4097
www.vortexjazzclub.co.uk
Tube: Highbury & Islington, then bus 30 or rail to Dalston Kingsland Station
Worth the trip if you are a fan of modern jazz.

COMEDY

㉓ Comedy Store
1 a Oxendon Street, WC 2
Tel. 0844 871 7699
www.thecomedystore.co.uk
Tube: Leicester Square

❶ Jongleurs
11 East Yard, Camden Lock, NW 1
Tel. 08700 111 960
www.jongleurs.com
Tube: Camden Town

NIGHT CLUBS, CABARET

⓯ Madame Jo Jo's
8–10 Brewer Street, W 1
Tel. 020 7734 2473
www.madamejojos.com
Tube: Piccadilly Circus
Kitsch cabaret, Kitten Club, burlesque – lots of glitter, camp and irony, a favourite place for a hen party.

⓮ Volupté *Insider Tip*
9 Norwich Street, EC 4
Tel. 020 7831 1162
www.volupte-lounge.com
Tube: Chancery Lane
Cocktails and cabaret, hula girls, burlesque strip, conjuring shows – Volupté is about enjoying decadence. Afternoon tea with cocktails in the teapot as an option.

Theatre and musicals

TICKETS
tkts
Leicester Square, WC 2
Mon–Sat 10am–7pm, Sun 11am–4.30pm
Normal advance sales and half-price tickets for all kinds of performances on the same day. A screen shows what is on offer. Only two tickets per person.

CLASSICAL AND MODERN
National Theatre
South Bank, SE 1
Tel. 020 7452 3000
www.nationaltheatre.org.uk
Tube: Waterloo
Three theatres, and high-quality productions. Unsold tickets at cheap rates on the day of performance: 9.30am, 12 noon on Sundays, but get there early for popular plays.

Old Vic
Waterloo Road, SE 1
Tel. 0844 871 7628
www.oldvictheatre.com
Tube: Waterloo
Political, timeless and high-calibre.

Royal Shakespeare Company
Barbican Centre, EC 2
Tel. 0870 609 1110
Tube: Barbican/Moorgate

Shakespeare's Globe
New Globe Walk, Bankside, SE 1
Tel. 020 7401 9919
www.shakespearesglobe.com/
Tube: St Paul's, Mansion House, walk across the Millennium Bridge
The season is May–Sept. Plays by Shakespeare and his contempo-raries in the authentically built octagonal theatre. If you don't want to risk getting wet, book tickets in the covered circle.

Theatre Royal Haymarket
Haymarket, SW 1
Tel. 020 7930 8800
www.trh.co.uk
Tube: Piccadilly Circus
Possibly London's most beautiful theatre, and its oldest, now has its own productions once again.

VARIOUS
Lyric
Shaftesbury Ave., W 1
Tel. 0844 412 4661
www.lyrictheatrelondon.org.uk
Tube: Piccadilly Circus

St. Martin's
West Street, WC 2
Tel. 08444 99 1515
www.the-mousetrap.co.uk
Tube: Leicester Square
A non-stop hit since 1962: Agatha Christie's »The Mousetrap«.

COMEDY, FARCE, THRILLERS
Apollo
Shaftesbury Ave., W 1
Tel. 020 7494 5070
Tube: Piccadilly Circus

Comedy
Panton Street, SW 1
Tel. 020 7369 1731
Tube: Piccadilly Circus

EXPERIMENTAL, FRINGE
Donmar Theatre
41 Earlham St., Seven Dials, WC2

Entertainment

Pubs, Bars & Clubs

1. Jongleurs
2. Proud Camden
3. Camino
4. Scala
5. 69 Colebrooke Row
6. Café Oto
7. The Vortex Jazz Club
8. Fabric
9. The Fox and Ancjor
10. Cittie of Yorke
11. Ronnie Scott's
12. Paramount
13. Princess Louise
14. Volupté
15. Madame Jo Jo's
16. 100 Club
17. Ye Olde Cheshire Cheese
18. The Old Bank of England
19. Black Friar
20. Notting Hill Arts Club
21. Windsor Castle
22. Bar Rumba
23. Comedy Store
24. Salisbury
25. Terroirs
26. Samuel Pepys
27. Prospect of Whitby
28. Heaven
29. Gordon's Wine Bar
30. Sherlock Holmes Pub
31. King's Arms
32. Skylon
33. Old King's Head
34. The George Inn
35. The White Horse
36. Sipsmith
37. Trafalgar Tavern

Tel. 0844 871 7624
www.donmarwarehouse.com/
Tube: Covent Garden
One of the foremost producing
theatres in the UK – classics and
contemporary drama.

Lyric Hammersmith
King Street, W 6
Tel. 020 8741 6850
www.lyric.co.uk
Tube: Hammersmith
An interesting mix of contempo-
rary works, plus music, comedy,
children's theatre.

Royal Court
Sloane Square, SW 1
Tel. 020 7565 5000
www.royalcourttheatre.com/
Tube: Sloane Square
The home of the English Stage
Company became famous with its
production of John Osborne's
Look Back in Anger. Today the
tradition of polemical theatre
continues with modern pieces.
Tickets are not expensive, espe-
cially on Mondays.

Young Vic
66 The Cut, SE 1
Tel. 020 7922 2922
www.youngvic.org
Tube: Waterloo
Highly regarded young drama,
cosmopolitan and cutting-edge.
The bar is a fixture on the hip
culture circuit.

THEATRE IN PUBS
Etcetera Theatre
265 Camden High Street, NW1
Tel. 020 7482 4857
Tube: Camden Town
Typical pub theatre above the

Oxford Arms on Regent's Park.
The young team often presents a
choice of two lively shows; Tue–
Sat 7.30 and 9.30pm,
Sun 6.30 and 8.30pm.

Gate at Notting Hill *Insider Tip*
Prince Albert Pub, Pembridge
Road, W 11
Tel. 020 7229 0706
www.thegate.co.uk
Tube: Notting Hill Gate
The only pub theatre in London
that puts on exclusively interna-
tional productions has an excellent
reputation.

King's Head *Insider Tip*
115 Upper Street, N 1
Tel. 020 7478 0160
www.kingsheadtheatre.org
Tube: Angel
A classic pub theatre that has
received the award for the best
Off-West-End Theatre. Now also
stages opera.

POPULAR MUSICALS
Programmes
www.londontheatre.co.uk
visitlondon.com

Stomp
Ambassadors Theatre
West Street, WC 2
Tel. 0844 811 2334
www.theambassadorstheatre.
co.uk
Tube: Leicester Square

The Lion King
Lyceum Theatre
Wellington Street, WC 2
Tel. 0870 243 9000
Tube: Covent Garden

London is Europe's capital for musicals

Mamma Mia
Aldwych Theatre
Aldwych, WC 2
Tel. 0844 482 5115
Tube: Covent Garden

Phantom of the Opera
Her Majesty's Theatre
Haymarket, SW 1
Tel. 0844 412 2707
www.thephantomoftheopera.com
Tube: Piccadilly Circus

Thriller
Lyric Theatre
Shaftesbury Ave., W 1
Tel. 020 7099 0930
Tube: Piccadilly Circus

Wicked
Apollo Victoria
17 Wilton Road, SW 1
Tel. 0870 400 0751
www.wickedthemusical.co.uk
Tube: Victoria

Swinging London

The sound of Britain took the world by storm in the 1960s had such a lasting influence on rock music that two guitars, a bass, percussion, long hair and outlandish clothing almost became the definition of a rock band. The success of the Beatles kick-started this movement, which was centred on London.

When **Alexis Korner** opened his **Rhythm & Blues Club** on Ealing Broadway in 1962, traditional jazz was the dominant force on the music scene, and Lonnie Donegan's skiffle and the instrumental music of the Shadows were all the rage. Korner's club was where Mick Jagger, Keith Richards and Brian Jones first performed. It was the place that inspired Eric Clapton, John Mayall and Ray Davies to start up such legendary bands as the Yardbirds, the Bluesbreakers and the Kinks. The Decca label, which had turned down the Beatles in 1962 as »not commercial enough«, took care not to miss out on the Rolling Stones, whose record sales soon reached unimaginable levels. It was not long before the entertainment industry was signing up practically every group on the scene, provided they had long hair and electric guitars.

Sacred Sites

The leading R&B clubs in London were the cradle of European rock music. The most important venue for the Beatles, after the Cavern Club in Liverpool and the Star Club in Hamburg, was the **Marquee** at 90 Wardour Street in the heart of Soho. This was where the Rolling Stones were first paid to perform and **The Who** destroyed their equipment to the sound of »My Generation«. Until well into the 1970s every band with a reputation had to do a gig at the Marquee at least once a year as a matter of prestige. The queues to get in were long, but alternatives were not far away in Wardour Street: In the **Roundhouse** on the corner of Brewer Street fans could listen to Manfred Mann or newcomers calling themselves the Hoochie Goochies, whose singer, Rod Stewart by name, shared the mike with Long John Baldry; and the **Flamingo Club** at number 33 staged groups whose style was more influenced by the likes of Ray Charles or James Brown. The bands who played there regularly included the Graham Bond Organisation with Jack Bruce, Ginger Baker and John McLaughlin, and Rod Stewart's Steam Packet with Brian Auger and Julie Driscoll. It was only a short walk from Wardour Street to the **100 Club** in Oxford Street, the main base for the Pretty Things, to **Studio 51** in Great Newport Street or to **The Scene** in Ham Yard, where Eric Burdon and the Animals made their London debut. Some way out of the city centre, in West End Lane in West Hampstead, was **Klooks Kleek**, the home of John Mayall's Bluesbreakers. The **Crawdaddy Club**, which had two establishments, one in Richmond and another in Croydon, was almost as famous as the Marquee. The owner, Giorgio Gomelsky, presented his new finds here – the Yardbirds, for example, who took over from the Stones as resident band playing one night every week.

Pop Aristocracy

By 1965 Swinging London was the mecca of the self-styled pop aristocracy. The award of the MBE (Member of the British Empire) to the Beatles, who had long since moved to London, put the seal on social acceptance of the aristocrats of the pop world, even though the Queen was not at all amused to hear, years later, that John, Paul, George and Ringo had passed a joint around in the Buckingham Palace toilets. By now **the mods** were the trendsetters. They reacted against the established bands, wearing suits and ties on principle and listening to the Small Faces and The Who instead of the Beatles and Rolling Stones. The more eccentric their efforts to be different, the more they were copied. Boutiques previously known only to insiders, such as those of **Mary Quant** in Carnaby Street and John Stephen in King's Road, had so many imitators that Pete Townshend's jacket made from the Union Jack, which prompted outrage in conservative circles when The Who appeared on the TV show »Ready, Steady, Go!«, was soon available on every street corner. Op Art, Pop Art and crazy fashion became an integral part of pop culture, and models such as

Twiggy, who wore unprecedentedly short mini-dresses from Mary Quant's store Bazaar, elevated the anorexic look to an aesthetic ideal.

Waterloo Sunset

As the record companies had their headquarters in London, up-and-coming **talent from the provinces** headed for the capital city. They were eager to make a name for themselves, and clubs pulled in the fans with new sensations such as the Hollies from Manchester, The Move and Spencer Davis Group from Birmingham, the Troggs from Andover and Van Morrison's Them from Belfast. London bands reacted to this by putting **local colour** in their songs. Ray Davies, the frontman of the Kinks, was particularly

Thin is in: Twiggy set a trend that not everyone could follow

adept at this. He not only dedicated songs to Berkeley Mews, Denmark Street and Willesden Green, but recorded a lasting memorial to evening on the Thames with »Waterloo Sunset« and commemorated his home area by declaring **»I'm a Muswell Hillbilly Boy«**. Although the Kinks, especially Ray's brother Dave, were notorious London swingers, they made fun of themselves and fashion-mania with **»Dedicated Follower of Fashion«**. In »Play with Fire« Mick Jagger relished the social demise of a nou-

veau-riche lady, now forced to find her lovers in Stepney instead of Knightsbridge, while John Lennon, in »A Day in the Life«, speculated about how many holes it takes to fill the Albert Hall. It was the Small Faces, four born-and-bred Cockneys, who did the most appealing demolition-job on Londoners' pride when, describing the small pleasures of East Enders in »Lazy Sunday«, they used so much local slang that people in Kensington had difficulties understanding the song.

Revolution: Mary Quant (right) invented the mini-skirt

Tea and Acid

From 1967 the scene slowly started to change, even though new blues bands such as Fleetwood Mac, Savoy Brown and Ten Years After still notched up great successes in the old clubs. Flower power and frilly shirts pushed out Op Art and Courège. Tea and acid – marijuana and LSD, that is – replaced whisky-and-coke and Guinness as the way to get high. The best-known places to go to achieve a new state of consciousness were **UFO** in Tottenham Court Road, **Speakeasy** in Margaret Street, **Middle Earth** in Covent Garden and the new **Roundhouse** in Chalk Farm Road. While the Beatles were still proclaiming that »All You Need is Love«, Pink Floyd were already taking their fans into galactic space with »Interstellar Overdrive«. Cream, The Nice, Soft Machine and many other groups were turning with growing success to long, improvised instrumental passages, at which they were all outshone by the new star in the London club heavens: Jimmy Hendrix, who was brought to London in 1967 by Chas Chandler, the former bass player of the Animals, was now the benchmark.

Young and Wild

By 1968 British youth was preoccupied with contemplating its own navel. Tolkien fans made their pilgrimages to Stonehenge and grew magic mushrooms, while the jet-set jumped on the Beatles bandwagon to find fulfilment with swamis, yogis and gurus. It was a little embarrassing when Mick Jagger, who by now only moved in well-to-do circles, sang »In sleepy London town there's just no place for a street-fighting man«, but he was not far from the truth.

At the end of the decade, when sound systems became more elaborate and loud-speakers towered higher and higher, the intimate atmosphere of the smaller clubs no longer suited the latest trend: **hard rock**. New bands like Yes and Genesis were more effective in concert halls or converted theatres. Exorbitant rents and high payments to the bands closed down many inner-city clubs, and new talents like Dr Feelgood, Elvis Costello and Graham Parker played in pubs. In musical terms this pub rock had little in common with punk rock, but it paved the way for bands such as The Clash and the Sex Pistols, who brought about a brief renaissance of the club scene from 1976 and challenged the established bands.

The Legacy

London remains one of the world's top cities for music. Those who are not put off by sky-high prices and big venues are spoilt for choice by a remarkable number of superstar events. However, it is far more exciting to visit the countless pubs and clubs outside the city centre, where undiscovered talent of every description tirelessly performs, dreaming of the big breakthrough. After all, most of the heroes of British rock now commemorated at Madame Tussaud's started out in just the same way more than 40 years ago.

Opera, dance, music

OPERA
English National Opera
London Coliseum, St Martin's
Lane, WC 2
Tel. 020 7845 9300
ww.eno.org
Tube: Leicester Square
A highly regarded ensemble sing-
ing in English in a historic theatre
close to Trafalgar Square.

Royal Opera
Royal Opera House, Covent
Garden/Bow Street, WC 2
Tel. 020 7304 4000
www.roh.org.uk/
Tube: Covent Garden
World-famous stage for opera
and ballet. 60 »rear amphitheatre« seats are sold daily from
10am for up to £10 for performances on the same evening
(only one ticket per person). The
Royal Ballet also performs here.

DANCE AND BALLET
English National Ballet
Venues: various, e.g. Barbican
Theatre. www.ballet.org.uk

Royal Ballet
Covent Garden Royal Opera
House, see above.

Sadler's Wells Theatre
Rosebury Avenue, EC 1
Tel. 0844 412 4300
www.sadlerswells.com
Tube: Angel
High-quality performances by
classical, modern and ethnic
groups from Britain and around
the world: ballet, tango, hip-hop,
contemporary dance…

CONCERTS
Barbican Hall
Barbican Centre, EC 2
Tel. 020 7638 8891
www.barbican.org.uk
Tube: Barbican, Moorgate
London Symphony Orchestra and
English Chamber Orchestra.

Royal Albert Hall
Kensington Gore, SW 7
Tel. 0845 401 50 45
www.royalalberthall.com
Tube: South Kensington
A famous concert hall for famous
orchestras and Proms concerts

St. Martin-in-the-Fields
Trafalgar Square, WC 2
Tel. 020 7766 1100
www.stmartin-in-the-fields.org/
music/concerts
Tube: Charing Cross
Home of a chamber music festival
and frequent concerts. Mon, Tue
and Fri free lunchtime concerts.

South Bank Centre
SE 1, Tel. 020 7 960 4242
www.southbankcentre.co.uk
Tube: Waterloo
Three concert halls – Purcell
Room, Queen Elizabeth Hall and
Royal Festival Hall – for top-class
music.

Wigmore Hall
36 Wigmore Street, W 1
Tel. 020 7935 2141
www.wigmore-hall.org.uk
Tube: Bond Street
Well known for concerts of chamber music, solo concerts and for its
popular Sunday morning concerts.

Cinema

ARTHOUSE AND REPERTORY

BFI London Imax
1 Charlie Chaplin Walk, SE 1
Tel. 0870 787 2525
Tube: Waterloo
Run by the British Film Institute, with Britain's biggest 3D screen.

Renoir@Brunswick Centre
Bloomsbury, WC 1
Tel. 0330 500 1331
www.curzoncinemas.com/cinemas/renoir/
Tube: Russell Square
In the Brunswick Centre in the heart of Bloomsbury, one of the best arthouse cinemas (and a good address for shopping).

Electric Cinema   *Insider Tip*
191 Portobello Road, W 11
Tel. 020 7908 9696
www.electriccinema.co.uk
Tube: Notting Hill Gate
Worth a visit not just for the films: This is the oldest operating cinema in London with an Art Deco foyer.

ICA Cinema
Nash House, The Mall, SW 1
Tel. 020 7930 0493
www.ica.org.uk
The programme is definitely not mainstream.

Pomp and Circumstance

With a proud sense of 2000 years of history, a talent for show-manship and a love of celebrating diverse identity, the people of London excel at putting on celebrations and festivals.

A walk along the Thames Path on the south bank of the river near London Bridge impressively demonstrates the adaptability of Londoners: Tile paintings show how they coped with a severe weather that froze the Thames in 1608. A frost fair with horse-racing and puppet theatre on the ice was organised. In 1683 the chronicler John Evelyn described such a fair on the frozen river as a »Bacchanalian triumph« and a »carnival on the water«.

Today the city calendar is filled with centuries-old royal ceremonies, military commemorations, large and small festivals connected with sports, music, literature and food, archaic rituals of the City guilds, exclusive occasions for members of high society to see and be seen, Cockney traditions and newer ethnic festivals (►MARCO POLO Insight, p. 90). Eccentricity is celebrated whenever possible: On Christmas Day swimmers plunge into the icy waters of the Serpentine, and the Chap Olympiad honours »athletic ineptitude and immaculate trouser creases« with events such as ironing-board surfing and umbrella jousting. Anything and everything gets its own festival: comedy, gay cinema, world street food and real ale, to name a few examples that are fairly mainstream in this city. Many of these events bolster the image of the royal family and the establishment, others celebrate Englishness and fair play, or simply the inexhaustible diversity of the city.

Sports fans have occasions throughout the year to enjoy a spectacle: football matches at Wembley or the grounds of Premier League teams (Arsenal, Chelsea and Tottenham Hotspur above all, but also West Ham United, Fulham, Crystal Palace and others), cricket at Lord's and The Oval, tennis at Wimbledon, rugby at Twickenham, horse-racing outside the city for high-society events at Ascot and Epsom, or greyhound racing for the other end of the social scale.

Events for everybody

Despite all the wigs and uniforms, subtle class barriers and dress codes, ordinary Londoners or visitors find plenty of opportunities to get in on the act. The Proms are a good example. Lovers of classical music can pay a high price for the best seats in advance, or queue up to get tickets in the standing area for the world's best orchestras for just a few pounds. The famous Last Night of the Proms is broadcast on a big screen in Hyde Park, giving everyone a chance to wave the

The Notting Hill Carnival is a loud and colourful occasion

Union Jack and bellow along to »Land of Hope and Glory«. At the summer exhibition of the Royal Academy, everyone can enter works for the show. The Open Garden Squares Weekend in June admits the public to well-tended parks in the city's highest-class areas that are otherwise only open to rich residents who possess a key.

To be a spectator at the Ceremony of the Keys in the Tower of London (▶p. 308), it is necessary to book a place long in advance. For other events, such as street festivals and summer cultural happenings, simply turn up on the day. A lot of fun can be had at charity events, such as the annual Great Gorilla Run, a 4.5-mile race for contestants dressed in gorilla costumes held in September to save the species in question. At the Olympic Games in 2012, the city proved its ability to stage a huge event for the eyes of the world. Royal occasions such as the boat procession for the diamond jubilee of Elizabeth II in the same year demonstrate the continued drawing power of pageantry. And a host of smaller annual events show that London has much more than the big stage and the upholding of traditions.

Events and listings

The city magazine *Time Out* (www.timeout.com) is still the best source for events listings. www.visitlondon.com is also well organised and highly informative.

Trooping the Colour: all the pomp of a royal and military spectacle

PUBLIC HOLIDAYS
1 January: New Year's Day
Good Friday
Easter Monday
First Monday in May: early May bank holiday
Last Monday in May: spring bank holiday
Last Monday in August: summer bank holiday
25 December: Christmas Day
26 December: Boxing Day

EVENTS IN JANUARY
London New Year's Day Parade
One of the world's biggest parades to see in the New Year.
www.londonparade.co.uk

Charles I Commemoration
A wreath is laid at the statue of Charles I on Trafalgar Square and a service of remembrance is held for the »royal martyr« in front of Whitehall Palace (last Sunday in January).

Chinese New Year
In Chinatown (end of January or early February).

IN FEBRUARY
London Fashion Week
Mid-February (and also September), in many locations.

Tossing the Pancake
On Shrove Tuesday in Westminster School (see p. 334).

Great Spitalfields Pancake Day Race
This is no ordinary obstacle race: Costumed contestants carry a pan with a pancake (Shrove Tuesday).

Stationer's Company Service
www.stationers.org
Members of a City guild, the Worshipful Company of Stationers, attend a service in the crypt of St Paul's Cathedral in historic dress (Ash Wednesday).

IN MARCH
Oranges and Lemons Service
Distribution of oranges and lemons in ▶St Clement Danes Church according to ancient tradition.

Chelsea Antiques Fair
www.penman-fairs.co.uk
In Chelsea Old Town Hall (second half of March, **also in September**).

Head of the River Race
Insider Tip
www.horr.co.uk
About 400 teams of over 3000 rowers take part in a race on the Thames from Mortlake to Putney.

Oxford and Cambridge Boat Race
http://theboatrace.org
The same course but only two teams: the world's most famous boat race (end of March or early April).l

EASTER
Royal Maundy Ceremony
On Maundy Thursday, the day before Good Friday, in accordance with an ancient tradition, specially coined »Maundy money« in white leather purses is handed to deserving persons by the monarch, either in Westminster Abbey or in a different city (see www.royal.gov.uk for the location).

IN APRIL

London Marathon
www.virginmoneylondon
marathon.com
One of the world's largest marathons (early April).

Queen's Birthday
Gun salute for the Queen's birthday (21 April).

Anglo-Welsh Cup
Rugby cup final (end of April).

Tyburn Walk
Procession led by the Roman Catholic bishop from Newgate Prison to the old place of execution at Tyburn (dates vary).

IN MAY

FA Cup Final
www.thefa.com
National football cup final.

Royal Windsor Horse Show
www.rwhs.co.uk
Dressage, show jumping, carriage driving and more – with royal presence, of course (second week in May).

Chelsea Flower Show
www.rhs.org.uk
Major event organised by the Royal Horticultural Society (end-May).

IN JUNE

Coronation Day
Gun salute to celebrate the coronation of the Queen (2 June).

Beating the Retreat
www.trooping-the-colour.co.uk/
retreat
Colourful parade of the Household Cavalry on Horse Guards Parade.

Epsom Derby
www.epsomderby.co.uk
One of the most famous horse races (early June).

Royal Academy Summer Exhibition

www.royalacademy.org.uk
High-calibre art exhibition.

Trooping the Colour
www.trooping-the-colour.co.uk
Official birthday parade for the queen on Horse Guards Parade. The royal family drives down the Mall from Buckingham Palace to the parade ground (mid-June).

Royal Ascot Race Meeting
www.ascot.co.uk
Horse races (mid-June), a big society event and the occasion for ladies to wear extravagant hats.

Open Garden Squares
Mid-June, a rare chance to stroll around private gardens in the poshest parts of London.

Election of Sheriffs
Public election of the sheriffs of the City of London in an impressive ceremony in Guildhall (24 June).

The Garter Ceremony
www.royal.gov.uk/
RoyalEventsandCeremonies
The Knights of the Order of the Garter attend a service in St George's Chapel in Windsor. Parade of the Household Cavalry and Yeomen of the Guard.

City of London Festival
www.colf.org
Music and drama, start of street theatre festival in Covent Garden (until July).

IN JULY
All England Lawn Tennis Championships
www.wimbledon.org
The world's most famous tennis tournament in Wimbledon (first half of July).

Test Cricket Matches
www.lords.org
The English cricket team plays test matches at Lord's Cricket Ground and the Oval (dates vary).

Road Sweeping by the Vintners' Company
Procession of the Worshipful Company of Vintners from Vintners' Hall to St James-Garlickhythe Church. They are preceded by the »wine porter« in white jacket and black top hat, who sweeps the route with a birch broom (mid-July).

Doggett's Coat and Badge Race
The world's oldest boat race, upstream from London Bridge to Chelsea Bridge, a tradition established in 1715 by the Irish comedian Thomas Doggett when he could find no-one to take him home after a night on the town. Eventually he found a young man willing to row him upstream against the tidal current.

Swan Upping
www.royalswan.co.uk
By custom the swans on the Thames belong to the Crown, the Company of Dyers and the Company of Vintners. In this colourful boat procession representatives of the three groups row upstream, count the swans and mark the cygnets.

Henry Wood Promenade Concerts
www.bbc.co.uk/proms
In the Royal Albert Hall (mid-July to mid-September).

IN AUGUST
CAMRA Great British Beer Festival
www.camra.org.uk
In mid-August the Campaign for Real Ale brings beer fans to Olympia to try out hundreds of different brews.

Notting Hill Carnival
www.thenottinghillcarnival.com
The carnival of the London Caribbean community is the world's largest event of this kind after the Rio de Janeiro carnival (bank holiday weekend at end of August).

IN SEPTEMBER
Battle of Britain Day
Fly-past of military aircraft to commemorate the air battle over England in the Second World War (15 September, 11am–noon).

London Open House Annual Weekend
www.londonopenhouse.org
Several hundred historic or architecturally significant buildings are open to the public (mid-September).

The Whole World Celebrates Here

In recent years London's festivals have become more diverse, bringing colour from around the globe to grey English skies. Showcasing food, music, dance and beliefs, they help give cohesion a variety of communities and – as it costs nothing to watch – draw big crowds.

Mayor Boris Johnson has espoused the multicultural nature of the capital, and many an establishment event has gained an ethnic counterpart. In addition to the Oxford and Cambridge Boat Race and other traditional rowing races, in summer the **Hong Kong Dragonboat Regatta** pit dozens of brightly decorated boats against each other amidst the sound of pounding drums (www.lclionsclub.co.uk). On the riverbank, with the Docklands skyline as a backdrop, the races are accompanied by kung fu demonstrations, a Chinese wishing tree, food stalls and calligraphy stands.

At the Heart of the City

Some of the best examples for the fresh wind blowing through London's world of festivals can be seen on **Trafalgar Square**. Surrounded by statues of colonial military heroes, the National Gallery and the parish church of Buckingham Palace, St Martin-in-the-Fields, traditions are celebrated by cultures from across the world that have been at home in London for generations. In January or February the **Chinese NewYear's Parade** starts here in a blaze of red and gold, with figures of dragons and tigers, a lion dance, acrobats, fireworks and dim sum stalls. Autumn is the time for **Diwali**, when the Hindu, Sikh and Jain communities

(www.diwaliinlondon.com) celebrate the triumph of light over darkness, of good over evil, with floating lanterns, dancing, Indian music, lucky Rangoli folk designs made from coloured rice and flower petals, and story-tellers. For **Hanukkah**, the Jewish festival of light before Christmas, the candles on the world's largest menorah are lit and salt-beef bagels, a traditional speciality of the East End, are eaten next to the huge Christmas tree from Norway each evening at sunset.

Culinary specialities are one way to arouse curiosity about different cultures. Music is another way. Since 2006 **Eid-al-Fitr**, the official end of the Muslim fasting month Ramadan, has taken its place on the historic square. As well as the singing of religious Nasheed music, this might well feature hip-hop music or another modern style performed by an Islamic singer or band.

Carnival of Cultures

Notting Hill Carnival in west London has evolved from its beginnings in 1959 as a protest against »nigger hunts« to what is probably Europe's biggest street carnival, with a million visitors. Although high earners have now largely displaced the Caribbean community in Notting Hill, once a year calypso

Diwali, the Hindu festival of light, on Trafalgar Square

sounds and hypnotic steele bands make the walls of the expensive residences there vibrate, extravagant feathered costumes produce a colourful spectacle and the aromas of jerk chicken and fried plantains fill the air (www.thenotting hillcarnival.com). This celebration inspired the Latin American community to start its own **Carnival del Pueblo** in 1999 in south London – with the traditions of a dozen different countries. The lively **Brick Lane Curry Festival** (www.curryfes tival.co.uk) is a good opportunity to sample authentic cooking from northern India and Bangladesh and to dance at a Mela street party.

Disharmony

Of course not all is multicultural harmony, despite the best efforts of the marketing people to create that impression. Dislike of immigration, whether from the European Union or more exotic parts of the world, remains one of the hot issues in British politics. Despite his praise for the multicultural nature of the city, Mayor Boris Johnson cut the funding for Rise in east London, Europe's festival of anti-racism, which had attracted 100,000 visitors. Musicians had used it to mobilise opposition to the policies of far right-wing organisations such as the British National Party and the English Defence League. The Metropolitan Police struggles to gain acceptance by young blacks following years of outcry about inadequate investigation of the murder of the teenager Stephen Lawrence and the riots of 2011 in north London, which were sparked by the shooting of the black Mark Duggan by a police officer. The happier events that celebrate London's melting-pot qualities with music, dance and food are thus all the more important as a means of maintaining racial harmony and tolerance.

Great River Race
www.greatriverrace.co.uk
Regatta on the Thames from Ham House in Surrey to the Docklands with a wide variety of vessels.

Last Night of the Proms
www.bbc.co.uk/proms
Final concert in the series of Henry Wood Promenade Concerts in the Royal Albert Hall (end of September).

Costermonger's Harvest Festival
Service of »pearly kings and queens« in the church of ▶St Martin-in-the-Fields at 3.30pm (last Sunday in the month).

IN OCTOBER
Trafalgar Day
Naval parade at Nelson's column in memory of the Battle of Trafalgar (21 October).

Quit Rent Ceremony
in the Law Courts, a public ceremony for the payment of rent for two properties, The Moors in Shropshire and a forge near St Clement Danes Church. For The Moors the Corporation of London pays a bill-hook and an axe, for the forge six horseshoes and 61 nails. The rent is received by an officer known as the Queen's Remembrancer (end of October).

IN NOVEMBER
State Opening of the Parliament
www.parliament.co.uk
The Queen drives from Buckingham Palace to Parliament in the Irish State Coach to open the session of Parliament in the House of Lords. Gun salutes are fired in Hyde Park and the Tower (early November).

London to Brighton Veteran Car Run
www.veterancarrun.com
Veteran car rally starting at Hyde Park Corner (first Sunday in November).

Guy Fawkes Day
Fireworks to mark the Gunpowder Plot of 5 November 1605, an attempt by Guy Fawkes and his supporters to blow up Parliament.

Lord Mayor's Show
www.lordmayorsshow.org
On the second Saturday in November the new Lord Mayor drives from Guildhall to the Law Courts in the State Coach to take the oaths of office from the Lord Chief Justice.

Remembrance Day

Red paper poppies are worn to commemorate the fallen of the two world wars (second Sunday).

Sport

CRICKET
www.lords.org
www.kiaoval.com

DOG RACES
www.wsgreyhound.co.uk

FOOTBALL
www.arsenal.com
www.chelseafc.uk
www.tottenhamhotspur.com

IN DECEMBER
New Year's Eve
Celebrations in Trafalgar Square.

www.whufc.com
(West Ham United)
www.cafc.co.uk
(Charlton Athletic)
www.fulhamfc.com

RUGBY
www.quins.co.uk
www.wasps.co.uk
www.london-irish.com

Cosmopolitan Cooking

For visitors to London from other parts of Britain, the food needs no introduction. For visitors from overseas, some basic guidelines may be helpful.

The poor international reputation of English cooking is no cause for concern, for two reasons: Firstly, the striking characteristic of the London restaurant scene is its cosmopolitan nature. It would be possible to eat food from a different country every night for months without ever tasting an English dish. The variety goes far beyond the familiar choice between Chinese, Indian, Italian or French to include the cuisine of the Caribbean, South America, Africa, eastern Europe, Australia and almost everywhere else. In parts of central London it is difficult to find a traditional English fish and chip shop.

Better than expected

Secondly, the quality of English cooking has improved, though it is still uneven. In the Michelin guide for 2014 there were **53 restaurants in the city with one star**, nine with two stars, and two three-starred restaurants (Gordon Ramsay's Chelsea establishment and Alain Ducasse at the Dorchester Hotel). London is a good place to find out whether the celebrity chefs so often seen on British TV screens can really produce the quality they promote. The famous molecular cuisine of Heston Blumenthal, for example, can be sampled at the Mandarin Oriental Hyde Park Hotel. There are many opportunities to taste the modern style of British cooking,

> **?** *Did you know*
>
> ... that the French philosopher Voltaire is partly to blame for the bad reputation of British food? »In Britain there are 60 different religions, but only one sauce«, was his damning verdict.

MARCO POLO INSIGHT

which is influenced by the Mediterranean, France and Asia, or to stay with time-honoured favourites such as roast beef with Yorkshire pudding or steak and kidney pie, which some old-established restaurants have been serving in high quality for decades, regardless of the latest culinary fashions.

Fans of afternoon tea have abundant opportunities to indulge themselves. The stylish and expensive way is to take tea in one of the grand hotels, where customers are seemingly prepared to pay over £40 per person without batting an eyelid. Here it is necessary to book a table and arrive well-dressed: Men should wear a jacket and tie but not

Afternoon tea

A statement that's hard to contradict

jeans; women are expected to maintain a similar standard. For those unfamiliar with British habits, it is useful to know the difference between afternoon tea, which mainly involves drinking tea and eating cakes, especially scones with jam and cream, and the more substantial but less usual high tea, which also includes a variety of sandwiches and savouries and amounts to a main meal. As for the sandwich, it was thought up by John Montague, fourth Earl of Sandwich, a keen gambler who wanted a bite that would not force him to leave his game of cards – a British invention that went round the world. Following this tradition, Londoners love quick snacking. There are great numbers of sandwich bars where customers can eat inside or carry out their food, and the old-fashioned British sandwich has been joined by the baguette and ciabatta, as well as the varied offerings of French- and Belgian-style patisseries and cafés. Vegetarians, too, are well catered-for in London. Little snack bars serve up the more exotic flavours of Indian, Arab, Chinese and other dishes, and the huge range of street food served from vans and market stalls has been one of the trendy developments of recent years.

Pubs   Pub food varies enormously in quality, from the fashionable dishes of so-called gastropubs to fish and chips and other basics. Visitors from overseas who are not acquainted with pub etiquette should know the following: If food is served, this sometimes takes place in a dining room separate from the bar, where there are properly laid tables and waiter service; but more commonly in the pub lounge itself, where there is no waiter service. Instead, orders are placed at the bar and paid for immediately, and the meal is eaten at a normal pub table with other drinkers. Drinks, too, are bought at the bar, and when several people go out together, each person in turn buys a round for the whole group.

Typical of London   If there is a dish that is truly typical of London, rather than typically English, then it is eel or pie and mash – a minority taste that is no longer widely found. Jellied eel, and the combination of a meat pie with mashed potato eaten with a parsley sauce known as liquor, are East End classics for poor people. Two surviving authentic restaurants that serve these endangered culinary species are Manze's, the oldest one still in business, and F. Cooke's on Broadway Market, where the surroundings are more hip.

Beer   In many countries the British have an undeserved reputation for drinking warm beer. In fact pubs serve many different kinds of beer at varying temperatures. The biggest-selling brands, mostly known as lager, are served cold. These are based on European beers, or are English versions of beers from other countries brewed under licence. Traditional English ale, by contrast, often of a kind known as bitter,

creates hand made, natural ... , av..
the obscure chemicals, additives
and preservatives common
to so much of the
'prepared' and 'fast'
food on the market today.

DS ★   ★ **SANDWICHES** ★

The Earl of Sandwich's innovative idea for snacking while he played cards seems to have caught on

should be served slightly cool, at cellar temperature. Those kinds described as »real ale« or »cask-conditioned« have undergone a second fermentation in the cask and are drawn by hand-pump, rather than under gas pressure. They often have a highly individual flavour, which would suffer if they were served ice cold. Two old-established London breweries, Youngs and Fullers, and a host of small breweries make traditional ales of this kind.

Recommended restaurants

❶ see plan p. 102–103
Addresses without a number are outside the area shown.

PRICES
The average prices given here are for a main course. Bear in mind that eating out in London is expensive, and that in many restaurants it is essential to book a table in advance!

£ £ £ £ over £25
£ £ £ £20 – 25
£ £ £10 – 20
£ up to £10

ENGLISH
㉝ Roast £ £ £ £
The Floral Hall, Borough Market,
Stoney Street SE 1
Tel. 0845 034 7300
www.roast-restaurant.com
Tube: London Bridge
Traditional English cooking in the
gourmet market: fish and chips,
beef, pork belly, Yorkshire long-
horn steak in a high-class but
laid-back ambience. Popular for
family brunch at the weekend.

㉑ Rules £ £ £ £
35 Maiden Lane, WC 2
Tel. 020 7836 5314
www.rules.co.uk
Tube: Charing Cross / Covent
Garden
Rules has been upholding the values of British cooking since 1798
– here this means game shot on
the restaurant's own estate and
Scottish salmon. Ale and Guinness are served in silver tankards,
and those who prefer a cocktail
can order a Kate Middleton –
with pink vodka and crystallised
violets and rose petals.

⑫ St. John £ £ £
26 St John Street, EC 1
Tel. 020 7251 0848
www.stjohnrestaurant.com
Tube: Farringdon
Classic dishes with a modern
touch in a former smokehouse,
e.g. pig's head in aspic, also seafood and an excellent choice of
desserts.

**㉜ Simpson's-in-the-Strand
£ £ £ £**
100 Strand, WC 2
Tel. 020 7836 9112

Tube: Charing Cross /
Covent Garden
Since 1828 a distinguished and
unassailable bastion of English
roast beef, which is wheeled to
the tables on trolleys and served
by master carvers. A less expensive way to see this institution is
to come for a full English breakfast, which can be added to for a
filling menu called the Ten Deadly
Sins. Dark wooden panelling and
heavy chandeliers are a fitting accompaniment to the food.

❺ Fryer's Delight £
19 Theobald's Road, WC 1
Tel. 020 7405 4114
Tube: Holborn
Mon–Sat 12 noon–11pm
A good place to get your strength
back with fish and chips after
exploring Bloomsbury or the historic but trendy designer quarter
of Clerkenwell.

㉞ Manze's £   Insider Tip
87 Tower Bridge Road, SE 1
Tel. 020 7277 6181
www.manze.co.uk
Tube: London Bridge
London's authentic contribution
to international haute cuisine, but
only for strong stomachs: a traditional shop for eel (jellied or
stewed), pies & mash, in business
since 1902, mainly for lunch between 11am and 2pm. Closed on
Sundays.

❽ Pellici's £   Insider Tip
332 Bethnal Green Road, E 2
Tel. 020 7739 4873
Tube: Bethnal Green
Mon – Sat. 7am – 4pm
»Full English« Bethnal Green

tradition in 1940s style. An authentic bit of the East End with an interior listed by English Heritage: formica tables and wooden panelling with Art Deco inlay work and leaded windows.

⑬ Poppies £
6–8 Hanbury Street, E 1
Tel. 020 7247 0892
www.poppiesfishandchips.co.uk
Tube: Aldgate East
Daily 11am–11pm
Best independent UK fish and chip shop in the Seafood UK awards for 2014. Has done a thriving trade since 1945. 1950s interior with jukebox, sustainably sourced fish from Billingsgate Market, hand-cut chips, free-range chicken and home-made sauces.

GASTROPUBS
Pubs that aim to serve a high standard of food have become a fixture on the London gastronomic scene.

A distinguished bastion of roast beef: Simpsons-in-the-Strand

Insider Tip

6 The Duke of Cambridge £ £
30 St Peter's Street, Islington N 1
Tel. 020 7359 3066
www.dukeorganic.co.uk
Tube: Angel
England's first pub where everything is organic, from the beer to
the fish. Generous portions of
seasonal food in a cosy and
straightforward place.

10 The Eagle £ £ / £ £ £
159 Farringdom Road, EC 1
Tel. 020 7837 1353
Tube: Farringdon
The original gastropub, still one of
the best and often full. Mediterranean and world food.

2 The Holly Bush £ £ / £ £ £
22 Holly Mount, NW 3

Tel. 020 7435 2892
www.hollybushhampstead.co.uk
Tube: Hampstead
Open fireplace, original gas lamps
and snugs – a pub with a fantastic
atmosphere and a bright, stylish
dining room on the first floor. Try
the hot apple and rum in winter.

7 Princess £ £
76–78 Paul Street, EC2
Tel. 020 7729 9270
www.theprincessofshoreditch.
com
Tube: Old Street
Award-winning food with excellent ingredients in an elegant dining room upstairs, cheaper British
pub food in the cosy area down-
stairs. This historic pub in trendy
Shoreditch has not been spoiled
by its tasteful recent makeover.

More than just another pub: the Duke of Cambridge

❸ The Wells Tavern
£ £ / £ £ £
30 Well Walk, NW 3
Tel. 020 7794 2785
www.thewellshampstead.co.uk
Tube: Hampstead
Modern and efficient. Rendezvous for well-groomed Hampstead clientele after a walk across the heath. Wonderful in summer, if you can get a seat outside.

MIX
❸❶ Asia de Cuba _Insider Tip_
£ £ £
in St Martin's Lane Hotel, 45 St Martin's Lane, WC 2
Tel. 020 7300 5588
Tube: Leicester Square
Yes, Asian dishes cooked Cuban-style. The restaurant is half library, half Martini bar. Order a la carte is rather expensive, so if you want to make a full evening of it, the tasting menu is a good option, and the pre-theatre menu offers two courses for £22.

❾ Orrery £ £ £
55 Marylebone High St, W 1
Tel. 020 7616 8000
www.orrery-restaurant.co.uk
Tube: Baker Street
Interior by the design guru Terence Conran. Excellent Sunday lunch for less than £30. British-Mediterranean food.

❶❺ Nopi £ £ £
21–22 Warwick Street, W 1
Tel. 020 7288 1454
www.nopi-restaurant.com
Tube: Piccadilly Circus
Come to this restaurant-brasserie in Soho for breakfast, lunch or dinner with Middle Eastern and Asian flavours. Canteen tables with a view of the kitchen on the lower floor, posher upstairs. Good for vegetarians and theatre-goers, part of Yotam Ottolenghi's small culinary empire – other branches in Islington, Notting Hill and Belgravia (www.ottolenghi.co.uk).

AFRICAN
❸❾ Adulis £ £
44–46 Brixton Road, SW 9
Tel. 020 7587 0055
www.adulis.co.uk
Tube: Oval
This Eritrean restaurant serves delicious spicy tsebhi stew of marinated lamb and potato, eaten with light injera bread, and has a good range of vegetarian dishes. If you over-indulge in the Eritrean mead, the coffee ceremony – with popcorn! – is a good pick-me-up.

❷❹ Momo £ £
25 Heddon Street, W 1
Tel. 020 7434 4040
www.momoresto.com
Tube: Piccadilly Circus
Authentic North African cooking with an atmosphere to match. Couscous, fish, lamb, chicken or vegetable tagine. Mo Café next door does breakfast, afternoon tea and mezze, and is noted for its mint tea.

❺ Moro £ £ _Insider Tip_
34–36 Exmouth Market, EC 1
Tel. 020 7833 8336
www.moro.co.uk
Tube: Farringdon
A fusion of fine Spanish and North African cuisine, with all-day tapas, cooked by a couple, Sam and Sam Clark, whose cookbooks

Hotels and Restaurants

Restaurants/Tea Time

1. Mango Room
2. The Holly Bush
3. The Wells Tavern
4. Great Nepalese
5. Moro
6. The Duke of Cambridge
7. Princess
8. Pellici's
9. Orrery
10. The Eagle
11. Fryer's Delight
12. St. John
13. Poppies
14. Aladin
15. Nopi
16. Melati
17. Little Lamb
18. Patisserie Valerie
19. Tokyo Diner
20. Baozi Inn
21. Rules
22. Kolapata
23. Lahore Kebab House
24. Momo
25. Nobu
26. Hakkasan
27. Brown's Hotel
28. Kulu Kulu
29. Fortnum and Mason
30. Mr. Kong
31. Asia de Cuba
32. Simpson's-in-the-Strand
33. Roast
34. Manze's
35. Blue Elephant
36. The Fifth Floor at Harvey Nichols
37. The Capital
38. Chutney Mary
39. Adulis

Accommodation

1. Renaissance St. Pancras
2. Rough Luxe
3. Clink 261
4. The Zetter
5. The Hoxton
6. Shoreditch Rooms
7. Tune Hotel
8. Parkwood
9. Lincoln House
10. The Sumner
11. Grazing Goat
12. The Main House
13. W Hotel
14. Hazlitt's
15. Fielding
16. Savoy
17. The Connaught
18. The Dorchester
19. The Ritz
20. The Levin
21. Aster House
22. The Milestone
23. Belgravia B & B
24. Windermere
25. Rafayel

are found in many London homes. Moro is one of the longer-established restaurants on trendy but charming Exmouth Market.

CARIBBEAN
❶ Mango Room £ £
10 Kentish Town Road, NW 1
Tel. 020 7482 5065
www.mangoroom.co.uk
Tube: Camden Town
Fantastic cocktails and superb, imaginative Caribbean cooking.

CHINESE
⓴ Baozi Inn £ £ / £ £ £
45 Newport Court, WC 2
Tel. 020 7287 6877
www.baoziinnlondon.com
Tube: Leicester Square
The dishes cooked on the food

stalls of Beijing and Szechuan, beautifully cooked for a reasonable price. Try the noodles. Small and busy, so you may have to wait, but that is worthwhile.

㉖ Hakkasan £ £ £
17 Bruton Street, W 1
Tel. 020 7907 1888
http://hakkasan.com
Tube: Oxford Circus
Contemporary Cantonese food, including dim sum. A restaurant with a dedicated following of VIPs, which accounts for the ban on photos and the XXX-size cocktails.

⓱ Little Lamb £ £ Insider Tip
2 Shaftesbury Avenue,
Tel. 020 7287 8078

If you want a Chinese meal, the choice in Chinatown is almost bewildering

Tube: Piccadilly Circus
For sociable diners: The speciality is Mongolian hotpot, eaten communally.

㉚ Mr. Kong £ / £ £
21 Lisle Street, WC 2
Tel. 020 7437 7341
www.mrkongrestaurant.com
Tube: Leicester Square
An old-established and small restaurant on two floors in Chinatown with a wide-ranging menu. Try the Mongolian lamb.

INDIAN / PAKISTANI / NEPALI / BANGLADESHI

⑭ Aladin £
132 Brick Lane, EC 1
Tel. 020 7247 8210
www.aladinbricklane.co.uk
Tube: Aldgate East
Dependable Indian food in »Curry Lane« that was even praised by Prince Charles.

㊳ Chutney Mary £ £
535 Kings Road, SW 10
Tel. 020 7351 3113
www.chutneymary.com
Tube: Fulham Broadway
One of the first restaurants in London to give a modern touch and ambience to Indian, still going strong after almost 25 years.

❹ Great Nepalese £
48 Eversholt Road, NW 1
Tel. 020 7388 6737
www.great-nepalese.co.uk
Tube: Euston
See how Nepalese food differs from Indian cooking – both are on the menu here.

㉒ Kolapata £ Insider Tip
222 Whitechapel Road, E 1
Tel. 020 7377 1200
http://kolapata.com
Tube: Whitechapel
The inevitable chicken tikka masala is a favourite, but this is also an excellent Bangladeshi restaurant serving more than the tourist dishes so often found around Brick Lane.

㉓ Lahore Kebab House £ / £ £
4 Umberston Street, E 1
Tel. 020 7481 9738
www.lahore-kebabhouse.com
Tube: Whitechapel
An excellent balti house: Pakistani and northern Indian dishes prepared in a cast-iron, wok-like balti.

JAPANESE

㉘ Kulu Kulu £
76 Brewer Street, W 1
Tel. 020 7734 7316
Tube: Piccadilly Circus
Sushi heaven: rolled-up goodies from the conveyor belt and first-class noodles.

㉕ Nobu £ £ £ £
19 Old Park Lane, W 1 (in the Metropolitan Hotel)
Tel. 020 7447 4747
Tube: Hyde Park Corner
One of the most authentic Japanese restaurants, and expensive.

⑲ Tokyo Diner £ £
2 Newport Place, WC 10
Tel. 020 7287 8777
www.tokyodiner.com
Tube: Leicester Square
An opportunity to have an

authentic Japanese meal without breaking the bank.

MALAYSIAN
16 Melati £ / £ £
21 Great Windmill Street, W 1
Tel. 020 7437 2745
Tube: Piccadilly Circus
Consistently popular Malaysian, Singaporean and Indonesian food in the heart of Soho.

THAI
35 Blue Elephant £ £ £
4 – 6 Fulham Broadway, SW 6
Tel. 020 7385 6595
www.blueelephant.com
Tube: Fulham Broadway
This is admittedly the most expensive Thai restaurant in London,

but the food and the Far Eastern atmosphere ist incomparable.

TEATIME
36 The Fifth Floor at Harvey Nichols
Knightsbridge, SW 1
Tel. 020 7235 5000
Tube: Knightsbridge
The café and tea room on the fifth floor of Harvey Nichols department store are a London institution serving everything needed for a proper afternoon tea (daily 3–5pm) at a fairly reasonable price.

29 Claridge's
Brook Street, W 1
Tel. 020 7629 8860

www.claridges.co.uk
Tube: Bond Street
Claridge's is a venerable institution where tea is served in the exquisite Art Deco foyer, allowing guests to admire the opulent decoration at leisure from the comfort of a settee. Fixed times: 3, 3.30, 5 and 5.30pm, £50. Reservations can only be made up to 90 days in advance.

18 Pâtisserie Valerie
44 Old Compton Street, W 1
www.patisserie-valerie.co.uk
Tube: Leicester Square
One of London's best-known pâtisseries, much loved since 1926. There are 18 more branches in addition to this one in Soho, e.g. 162 Piccadilly, Duke of York Square (Chelsea), 105 Marylebone High Street, 25 Kensington Church Street.

27 Brown's Hotel
33/34 Albemarle Street, W 1
Tel. 020 7493 6020
www.roccofortehotels.com
Tube: Green Park
The oldest hotel in London, established in 1837, is one of the classic places to take afternoon tea (daily noon–6.30pm), but for a full treat from the range of available options, expect to pay £40 or more.

MARCO POLO TIP | *Patara* | **Insider Tip**

Good service, swish interior, innovative and aromatic dishes at affordable prices are the reasons for going to Patara Thai restaurant in Soho: 15 Greek Street, W 1, tel. 020 7437 1071, Tube: Tottenham Court Road; also at 9 Beauchamp Place in Knightsbridge, tel. 020 7581 8820; 181 Fulham Road in South Kensington, tel. 020 7351 5692; and 7 Maddox Street near Oxford Circus, tel. 020 7499 6008.

---

37 The Capital
22 Basil Street, SW 3
Tel. 020 7589 5171
www.capitalhotel.co.uk
Tube: Knightsbridge
The charming tea room in this small hotel is the right place to take a break after shopping in Harrods. Afternoon tea is served from 2pm to 5.30pm, £29.50.

Museums and Exhibitions

World-class

Hardly any city in the world has such a large number of world-class museums as London. Some of them have made a major contribution to the history of science and scholarship. When the medium-sized and smaller museums are added, the result is an inexhaustible range of activities for the keen visitor to exhibitions.

In many museums, especially the big and famous ones, admission is free, but visitors are asked to pay a voluntary contribution. Other attractions such as the Tower of London can be very expensive. It is worth considering whether the London Pass, which is not cheap but provides free admission to more than 60 attractions and a range of other discounts, is worth buying (▶Practicalities, Prices and Discounts) – obviously this depends on exactly what you want to see.

Admission fees

Apart from Monday there is no day of the week without at least one museum in London that stays open until 8pm or even 10pm. These after-hour visits are extremely popular, as special guided tours or lectures are usually included; in the British Museum even snacks and drinks are on offer on Friday evenings.

A night at the museum

London Museums

HISTORY / ARTS
Abbey Museum
▶Westminster Abbey

Apsley House
▶Hyde Park, Hyde Park Corner

Bank of England Museum
▶Bank of England

Benjamin Franklin House
▶The Strand

British Museum
▶p. 159

Burgh House
▶Hampstead Heath

Churchill War Rooms
▶Whitehall

Clink Prison Museum
▶Southwark

Cutty Sark
▶Greenwich

Eton College Museum
▶Windsor Castle

The National Portrait Gallery honours great Britons in oil or watercolour, miniature or large format

Florence Nightingale Museum
▶Imperial War Museum • Lambeth

Guildhall Library & Clockmakers' Museum
▶Guildhall

Jewel Tower
▶Houses of Parliament

Jewish Museum
129–131 Albert Street, NW 1
www.jewishmuseum.org.uk
Tube: Camden Town
Sun–Thu 10am–5pm, Fri 10am–2pm, admission £7.50
Following a thorough rebuilding and extension in 2007, the museum uses modern technology to present Jewish culture in England. The highlight is a Jewish ritual bath that was excavated in the City in 2001.

London Bridge Experience
▶Southwark

London Canal Museum
▶Regent's Canal

London Dungeon
▶South Bank

Museum of London Docklands
▶Docklands

Museum of London
▶p. 244

Museum of the Order of St. John
▶Smithfield Market

National Archives Museum
▶Kew Gardens, Kew

National Maritime Museum
▶Greenwich

Prince Henry's Room
▶Fleet Street

Ragged School Museum
Copperfield Road, E 3
www.raggedschoolmuseum.org.uk
Tube: Mile End
Wed, Thu 10am–5pm, 1st Sun in the month 2pm–5pm
Free admission
The museum in and about an original Victorian school for needy children in the East End.

Royal London Hospital Museum
St Augustine and St Philip's Church, Newark Street, E 1
Tube: Whitechapel
Mon–Fri 10am–4.30pm
Free admission
History of the hospital, founded in 1740, with original items from Jack the Ripper's murders.

Sikorski Museum
20 Princes Gate, SW 7
www.pism.co.uk
Tube: South Kensington
Mon–Fri 2pm–4pm, first Sat in the month 10.30am–4pm
Free admission
About the Polish government-in-exile in London 1939–45.

Tower of London
▶p. 307

Wellington Museum
▶Hyde Park, Hyde Park Corner

Wesley's Chapel and House
49 City Road, EC 1

www.wesleyschapel.org.uk
Tube: Old Street
Mon–Sat 10am–4pm, Sun 12.30–
1.45pm
Free admission
House of the Methodist John
Wesley (1703–91) and museum of
Methodism.)

Winston Churchill's Britain
at War
▶Southwark

ART, DESIGN AND
ARCHAEOLOGY
Barbican Art Gallery
Silk Street, EC 2
Tube: Barbican
www.barbican.org.uk
Fri–Mon 11am–8pm, Thu until
10pm, Tue and Wed until 6pm
Admission: £12
Changing exhibitions on a wide
variety of themes.

Courtauld Institute Gallery
▶p. 174

Design Museum
▶Docklands

Dulwich Picture Gallery
▶Dulwich

Estorick Collection of
Modern Italian Art
39 a Canonbury Square, N 1
www.estoriccollection.com
Tube: Highbury & Islington
Wed–Sat 11am–6pm, Sun noon–
5pm; admission: £5
Excellent collection of Italian
Futurist works.

Fashion and Textile Museum
83 Bermondsey Street, SE 1

www.ftmlondon.org
Wed–Sun 11am–6pm
Tube: London Bridge
Changing exhibitions about
contemporary London fashion.

Geffrye Museum
Kingsland Road, E 2
www.geffrye-museum.org.uk
Tube: Liverpool Street, then bus
149, 242
Tue–Sat 10am–5pm, Sun noon–
5pm
Free admission
English furniture and interiors
from the 16th to the 20th century
in the former almshouse of the
Ironmonger's Company.

Guildhall Art Gallery &
Roman Amphitheatre
▶Guildhall

Hayward Gallery
▶South Bank

Hogarth's House
Hogarth Lane, Great West Road, W 4
Tube: Turnham Green
Tue–Sun 2pm–5pm
Free admission
Country house of the artist
William Hogarth.

Institute of Contemporary Art
▶The Mall

Leighton House
12 Holland Park Road, W 14
www.rbkc.gov.uk
Tube: High Street Kensington
Wed–Mon 1am–5.30pm
Home of Frederic Leighton
(1830–96), president of the
Royal Academy, decorated in
the Moorish style.

Linley Sambourne House
18 Stafford Terrace, W 8
Tube: High Street Kensington
www.museumoflondon.org.uk
Tours Sat and Sun 10am,
11.15am, 1pm, 2.15pm, 3.30pm
Admission: £6
House of the artist and Punch
caricaturist Edward Linley Sambourne (1844–1910), with a large
collection of Chinese porcelain.

National Gallery
►p. 245

National Portrait Gallery
►p. 252

Petrie Museum of Egyptian
Archaeology
University College London,
Malet Place, WC 1
Tube: Euston Square
www.ucl.ac.uk
Tue–Sat 1pm–5pm
Free admission
Collection of the Egyptologist Sir
Flinders Petrie (1853–1942), one
of the largest of its kind in the
world, with some wonderful and
rare exhibits.

Queen's Gallery
►Buckingham Palace

Royal Academy of Arts
►Piccadilly Circus

Saatchi Gallery
►Chelsea

Serpentine Gallery
►Hyde Park • Kensington Gardens

Sir John Soane's Museum
►Lincoln's Inn

Tate Gallery
►p. 303

Wallace Collection
►p. 324

Whitechapel
Art Gallery

Insider
Tip

77–82 Whitechapel High Street,
E 1
Tube: Aldgate East
www.whitechapelgallery.org
Tue–Sun 10am–6pm, Thu to 9pm
Free admission
One of the leading British galleries
for contemporary art.

Victoria & Albert Museum
►p. 318

LITERATURE, THEATRE
AND MUSIC
British Library
►p. 158

British Music Experience
►Greenwich

Carlyle's House
►Chelsea

Dr. Johnson's House
►Fleet Street

Dickens House Museum
48 Doughty Street, WC 1
Tube: Russell Square
www.dickensmuseum.com
Mon–Sat 10am–5pm, Sun from
11am
Admission: £3
Charles Dickens lived here from
1837 to 1839 while working on
The Pickwick Papers and **Oliver
Twist**. Letters, furniture and first
editions are on display.

Museums and Exhibitions • ENJOY LONDON

Handel House Museum
23–25 Brook Street, Lancashire Court, W 1
Tue–Fri 10am–6pm,
Tube: Bond Street, Oxford Circ.
www.handelhouse.org
Tue–Sat 10am–6pm, Thu until 8pm, Sun from noon
Admission: £6
George Frideric Handel lived here from 1723 to 1759 (and later Jimi Hendrix lived next door).

Keats House
▶Hampstead Heath

London Film Museum
▶South Bank, County Hall

Muscial Museum
▶Kew Garden, Kew Village

Royal Academy of Music Museum
Marylebone Road, NW 1

Tube: Baker Street, Regent's Park
www.ram.ac.uk
Mon–Fri 11.30am–5.30pm, Sat and Sun noon–4pm
Free admission
Instruments and documents of famous composers, soloists and conductors.

Shakespeare's Globe Theatre
▶Southwark

Sherlock Holmes Museum
▶Regent's Park

MILITARY
Museum of the Chelsea Royal Hospital
▶Chelsea

Fusiliers' Museum
▶Tower

Guards Museum
▶Buckingham Palace

A Victorian constable guards the entrance to the Sherlock Holmes Museum

HMS Belfast
►Southwark

Household Cavalry Museum
►Whitehall

Imperial War Museum
►p. 230

National Army Museum
►Chelsea

Royal Air Force Museum
►p. 268

Royal Armouries
►Tower

Royal Artillery Museum
►Docklands, Thames Barrier

NATURE, TRANSPORT AND
TECHNOLOGY
BBC Tours
Broadcasting House, Portland
Place, W 1
Tube: Oxford Circus
www.bbc.co.uk/showsandtours/
tours
Tours (£13.50) Mon–Sat, booking
essential: online or tel. 0370 901
1227.

London Transport Museum
►Covent Garden

Museum of Garden History
►Imperial War Museum •
Lambeth

Natural History Museum
►p. 253

Old Operating Theatre
►Southwark

Chelsea Physic Garden
►Chelsea

Guildhall Clockmakers'
Museum
►Guildhall

Horniman Museum and
Gardens
100 London Road, Forest Hill,
SE 23
Overground: Forest Hill
www.horniman.ac.uk
Daily 10.30am–5.30pm
Free admission
Musical instruments, ethnology
and stuffed animals from the
collection of the much-travelled tea
merchant Frederick John Horniman
(1835–1906); a wonderful assembly of items, presented with modern museum technology.

Hunterian Museum
►Lincoln's Inn

Kew Bridge Steam Museum
►Kew Gardens, Kew Bridge Steam
Museum

London Canal Museum
►Regent's Canal

Old Royal Observatory
►Greenwich

Peter Harrison Planetarium
►Greenwich

Pumphouse Museum
►Docklands

Royal Mews
►Buckingham Palace

It's not all about modern high-tech at the Science Museum

Science Museum
▶p. 281

Sea Life Aquarium
▶South Bank, County Hall

Tower Bridge Exhibition
▶Tower Bridge

Thames Barrier
▶Docklands

Wetland Centre
Queen Elizabeth Walk, Barnes, SW 13
Tube: Hammersmith, then bus 23
www.wwt.org.uk
Daily 9.30am–6pm
Admission: £11
Plants and animals which live in or on the Thames.

PALACES AND STATELY HOMES
Chiswick House **Insider Tip**
Chiswick, W 4
www.chgt.org.uk

Tube: Turnham Green
April–Oct Sun–Wed 10am–6pm
Admission: £6.10
18th-century mansion, the first and one of the most beautiful Palladian houses in England.

Eltham Palace
Court Yard, Eltham, SE 9
www.english-heritage.org.uk
Rail: Eltham from Victoria, Charing Cross or Cannon Street
April–Oct Sun–Wed 10am–5pm, Nov–March Sun: 10am– 4pm
Admission: £9.60
Remains of a Tudor palace in which Henry VIII spent his childhood next to the wonderful Art Deco country house of the Courtauld family.

Fenton House
▶Hampstead Heath

Ham House
▶Richmond

Kensington Palace
▶Hyde Park • Kensington Gardens

Kenwood House
▶Hampstead Heath

Kew Palace
▶Kew Gardens

Marble Hill House
Richmond Road, Twickenham, TW1
www.english-heritage.org.uk
Tours April–Nov Sat 10.30am and noon, Sun additionally 2.15 and 3.30pm
Rail: St Margaret's from Waterloo
Admission: £5.50
Georgian stately home with collection of chinoiserie.

Osterley Park House
Jersey Road, Osterley, Middlesex, W 7
Tube: Osterley
March–Oct Wed–Sun noon–4.30pm, Dec Sat and Sun 12.30–3.30pm
Admission: £8.70
House and park of Sir Thomas Gresham, founder of the Royal Exchange; remodelled by Robert Adam in the 18th century.

Queen's House
▶Greenwich

Spencer House
▶St. James's Palace

Southside House
▶Wimbledon

Syon House
▶Kew Gardens • Syon House

TOYS
Pollock's Toy Museum
41 Whitfield Street, W 1
www.pollockstoymuseum.com
Tube: Goodge Street
Mon–Sat 10am–5pm
Admission: £6

V & A Museum of Childhood
▶p. 323

SPORT
Arsenal Football Club Museum
Emirates Stadium, Drayton Park, N 5
www.arsenal.com
Tube: Arsenal
Mon–Sat 10am–6pm, Sun until 5pm
Admission: £7.50 (museum only); £18 (with stadium tour)

Chelsea Football Club Museum
Stamford Bridge Stadium, SW 6
www.chelseafc.com
Tube: Fulham Broadway
Daily 9.30am–5.30pm
Admission: £11 (museum only); £20 (with stadium tour)

Lord's Cricket Museum
▶Regent's Park

World Rugby Museum
Twickenham Stadium, Rugby Road, Richmond, TW 1
www.rfu.com/museum
Rail: Twickenham from Waterloo
Tue–Sat 10am–5pm, Sun 11am–5pm
Admission: £16 (museum and stadium tour)
The world's largest rugby museum.

Wembley Stadium
►p. 325

Wimbledon Lawn Tennis Museum
►Wimbledon

OTHERS
Baden Powell House
65–67 Queen's Gate, SW 1
Daily 7am–10pm
Tube: South Kensington
Free admission
Small museum about the founder of the Boy Scouts.

Crystal Palace Museum
►Dulwich

Fan Museum
►Greenwich

Freud-Museum
►Hampstead Heath

Fuller's Griffin Brewery
Chiswick Lane South, W 4
www.fullers.co.uk
Tube: Turnham Green
Tours (£10) Mon–Fri 11am, 12noon, 1pm, 2pm and 3pm,
pre-booking required online or Tel. 020 8996 2063
Tour of London's oldest brewery, including samples, of course.

Madame Tussauds
►p. 241

National Library of Women
Old Castle Street, E 1
www.londonmet.ac.uk
Tube: Aldgate
Mon–Fri 9.30am–5.30pm, Thu until 8pm, Sat 10am–4pm
Free admission
Europe's largest library of women's literature; with special exhibitions.

Ranger's House
►Greenwich

Twinings Tea Museum
►The Strand

Vinopolis
►Southwark

Willow Road No. 2
►Hampstead Heath

Shopping

Exciting and Tempting

London is – next to Paris – the most exciting and tempting shopping destination in Europe. It has an unbeatable combination of brand fashion stores, suppliers to the royal court with a distinguished tradition, a booming vintage sector, charity shops for bargain hunters, enclaves of ethnic products, colourful street markets, Europe's biggest shopping mall and rickety market stalls where trends that will later conquer the world are born.

Antiques and classic English clothing – tweed, cashmere, shirts, shoes, hats – are the city's trump cards, and there are vast numbers of shops ranging from the classic to the outlandish. The widest choice for shoppers is to be found in the West End between Oxford Street, Regent Street and Bond Street, as well as around Piccadilly and Jermyn Street (even Carnaby Street has made a comeback!), around Covent Garden and (for second-hand goods) in Soho. Despite the density of international brand outlets and big department stores such as Selfridges, Debenhams, House of Fraser and John Lewis, Europe's busiest shopping drag, **Oxford Street**, is not always a happy experience as you push through heaving masses of shoppers, dodging their carrier bags and the people distributing leaflets. Watch out for pickpockets here – as everywhere in London's crowds. It is worth looking at some smaller-scale islands of good taste with more original offerings – St Christopher's Place, for example, or Seven Dials. Marylebone High Street has a certain small-town character, with non-standard shops and a touch of France. The other main shopping area is Knightsbridge, South Kensington and Kensington around Brompton Road and High Street Kensington. King's Road and Chelsea are less rewarding by comparison, but it is still worth taking a look here, especially at the designer outlets along Sloane Street. Those in search of something out of the ordinary should not miss Camden Town. Finally the **East End**, especially the area around Brick Lane, Old Street and Redchurch Street, has become a destination for creative design.

Shopping districts

The recession years to 2012 and competition from internet shopping have forced the retail sector to come up with new ideas, whether in the form of special offers or by making shopping into a more interesting experience. Pop-up shops appear for a few days all over the city,

New methods

An exclusive shop in Savile Row, the street of bespoke tailors: Huntsman

and »sample sales« charge admission but in return offer brands at knock-down prices without the crowds that come to the regular end-of-season sales.

Souvenirs Visitors from abroad have every opportunity to take back something typically British: tea and marmalade (from Fortnum & Mason or Harrods, for example), tobacco or sweets, and in the higher price bracket perhaps a pipe, scarf, woollens or a Burberry trenchcoat. The museum shops in the British Museum, Victoria and Albert Museum, National Gallery and Natural History Museum have a lot of attractive items. There is any amount of kitsch and tourist tat; a plastic police-man's helmet goes down well with kids. Teenagers will find plenty of streetwear to suit them.

Value added tax Most goods and services (including hotels and restaurants) are sub-ject to 20% value added tax (VAT). When leaving the country citizens of non-EU countries can reclaim VAT on goods bought at shops dis-playing the »Tax Free« sign by taking the relevant form from the store.

Opening hours The usual minimum opening hours for shops are Mon–Sat 9am–5.30pm, though small, owner-run establishments may have restricted hours. Larger stores on the main shopping streets are open for long-er – department stores often until 10pm. Thursday is late-opening day in the West End. Many shops open for a few hours on Sundays, often from 12 noon until 6pm, and in the pre-Christmas season hours are extended. Where markets are held at weekends, the local shops frequently open too.

Addresses

DEPARTMENT STORES
Fortnum & Mason
181 Piccadilly, W 1
www.fortnumandmason.com
Tea, marmalade and jam are typi-cal purchases here. The tea in-cludes single-estate produce from Cornwall. The window decoration is elaborate.

Harrods
87–135 Brompton Road, SW 1
www.harrods.com
A tourist magnet, but for good reasons. ▶p. 213

Harvey Nichols
109 Knightsbridge, SW 1
www.harveynichols.com
An exclusive address for fashion, cosmetics and furniture, with fine dining on the fifth floor.

Liberty
Great Marlborough Street, W 1
www.liberty.co.uk
Fine fabrics and many distinctive products. ▶p. 237

Marks & Spencer
458 Oxford Street, W 1

Fortnum & Mason is known for its beguiling displays of wares

www.marksandspencers.com
Clothing, woollens, underwear.
This retail chain for Middle England is solid rather than chic, of
course, and the main store on Oxford Street has the whole range.

One New Change
1 New Change, EC4
www.onenewchange.com
Opened in 2010 in sustainable architecture designed by Jean Nouvel, on Cheapside opposite St
Paul's Cathedral, this is the only
shopping centre in the City. 60
stores from H&M to upscale outlets such as Hotel Chocolat, an Oliver Bonas gift shop, a Gordon

Ramsay restaurant, and as a special treat the outdoor dining on
the roof, open from 10am.

Selfridges
400 Oxford Street, W 1
www.selfridges.com
A gigantic store, with the largest
shoe, jewellery and cosmetic departments in Europe, and an innovative approach to store design.
Has more than a touch of the
class that most of Oxford Street
lacks.

Westfield Shopping Centre
Ariel Way, W 12 (west of Kensington Park, Tube: White City)

http://uk.westfield.com/london/
Europe's largest inner-city shopping mall, opened in the recession years, with over 265 shops and 50 restaurants. Everything from A for Accessorise and All Saints urban fashion to Z for Zorba sweets and French cashmere from Zadig & Voltaire. All the designers a fashionista's heart could desire. Plus an excellent Waitrose supermarket and a multiplex cinema. Even newer is the Westfield Centre in Stratford City, close to the 2012 Olympics site (Tube, DLR and Overground to Stratford).

MARCO ❂ POLO TIP

Spices galore! **Insider Tip**

In the wonderful shop opposite Books for Cooks you will find more than 1800 different spices – everything you need for the ethnic recipes that make London's culinary scene such fun!

BOOKS

Books for Cooks
4 Blenheim Crescent, W 11
www.booksforcooks.com
Legendary cookbook shop; recipes are tested in the café.

Foyles
113–119 Charing Cross Road
WC 2
www.foyles.co.uk
A leading independent bookseller with a big assortment, a survivor on what used to be London's pre-eminent bookshop street. Has a popular jazz café with excellent Monmouth coffee.

Daunt Books
83 Marylebone High Street, W 1
www.dauntbooks.co.uk
A legendary Edwardian-style bookshop, a leading address for fiction, superbly stocked with classics and new releases.

CDS AND VINYL
Fopp
1 Earlham Street, W 3
www.foppreturns.com
Small but top-quality selection of CDs and records.

His Master's Voice (HMV)
363 Oxford Street, W 1
Under pressure from internet sales, but still Europe's biggest store of its kind.

Honest John
278 Portobello Road, W 8
www.honestjohn.com
Incredible range of jazz, reggae, soul.

Revival
30 Berwick Street, W 1
Oldies, second hand.

Rough Trade Records
Dray Walk, Old Truman Brewery
91 Brick Lane, E1
www.roughtrade.com
The tiny original shop is in Notting Hill at 130 Talbot Road, W 11; Rough Trade East is a mega-outlet with 5500 square feet with a huge selection of CDs and vinyl, and a cool café.

DESIGN, GIFTS
The Button Queen
76 Marylbone Lane, W 1
www.thebuttonqueen.co.uk

Buttons, buttons and more buttons.

Cool Britannia
Piccadilly Circus, SW1
www.coolbritannia.com
A huge souvenir shop ranging from tasteful to kitschy: tea mugs, toys, fridge magnets, football shirts and merchandise for all the latest events.

Davenports Magic Shop
7 Charing Cross Underground Arcade, The Strand, WC 2
www.davenportsmagic.co.uk
For magicians.

The General Trading Company
91 Pelham Street, SW 7
www.generaltradingcompany.co.uk
Exclusive and out-of-the-ordinary kitchen equipment, Far Eastern goods, also a »supplier of fancy goods« to the royal family. One of London's most interesting shops. It pays attention to sustainability and fair-trade issues.

Gill Wing
194–195 Upper Street, N 1
www.gillwing.co.uk
Gifts, joke items, clocks, teapots, toys – a wonderfully eclectic mix.

James Smith
53 New Oxford Street, W 1
www.james-smith.co.uk
Hand-made umbrellas and walking-sticks behind one of London's finest historic shop façades.

Paperchase
213 Tottenham Court Road, W 1
www.paperchase.co.uk
Beautiful writing instruments, cards and unusual gifts.

Waterford Wedgwood
158 Regent Street, W 1
www.waterfordwedgwood.com
Famous ceramics by Wedgwood and Royal Doulton, plus Waterford glass.

MARCO●POLO TIP

Up north **Insider Tip**

Upper Street in Islington is a pleasant shopping street despite heavy traffic. For a break and a bite, Ottolenghi (no. 287) and Afghan Kitchen (35 Islington Green) are recommended.

FASHION FOR WOMEN
Coco de Mer
23 Monmouth Street, WC 2
www.coco-de-mer.com
»Something for the weekend« – London's boutique for erotic decadence, in a street full of fantastic shoe shops.

Laura Ashley
9 Harriet Street, SW 1
www.lauraashley.com
Classically English fashion for girls and ladies, and pretty interior decoration items.

Myla
77 Lonsdale Road
www.myla.com
Delicate lingerie and sexy pyjamas. Branches in Harrods, Selfridges and Old Bond Street. Celebrate the purchasers in the Lonsdale cocktail bar in the same street.

There is no more stylish place to buy an umbrella

Vivienne Westwood
44 Conduit Street, W 1
www.viviennewestwood.co.uk
London's fashion queen, now
Dame Vivienne, made her mark
on the punk scene and still
sparkles with unconventional
ideas for asymmetrical design.
Her first outlet, at 430 King's
Road, SW 3, is still in business.

FASHION FOR MEN
Hackett
137–138 Sloane Street, SW 1
www.hackett.com
Traditional English men's clothing,
reasonable prices.

Lock & Co.
6 St James's Street, W 1
www.lockhatters.co.uk
The inventor of the bowler hats
and court supplier – commoners
can at least look at the window
display.

Ozwald Boateng
9 Vigo Street, W 1
www.ozwaldboateng.co.uk
The most innovative gentlemen's
tailor, expensive.

Turnbull & Asser
71–72 Jermyn Street, SW 1
www.turnbullandasser.com
Fine shirts, ties, scarves and
accessories since 1885. Branches
at 125 Old Broad Street and in
Harrods.

FASHION FOR MEN & WOMEN

Aquascutum

100 Regent Street, W 1
www.aquascutum.com
Tweed and raincoats with tradition going back to 1851 – their waterproof materials were valued in the First World War, hence the name »trenchcoat«, since 2012 under Chinese ownership.

Brora

186 Upper Street, N 1
www.brora.co.uk
Luxury knitted goods, tweeds and cashmere from Scotland.

Browns

23–27 Moulton Street, W 1
www.brownsfashion.com
Leading address for British haute couture; Brown's Focus across the street has the latest trends.

Burberry's

165 Regent Street, W 1
www.burberry.com
Classic trenchcoats, scarves, wallets with the famous Cairo pattern. The model Emma Watson (from the Harry Potter films) has helped to boost the brand. At outlet in Hackney sell's last year's fashion at low prices.

Reiss

114–116 King's Road, W 1
www.reissonline.com
The latest trends off the rack, not too expensive; accessories at 30–31 Islington Green N1.

Stella McCartney

30 Bruton Street, W 1
Beatle Paul's daughter doesn't need her dad's help to shine in the fashion world. Whether daytime and evening wear, her creations are easy to wear, and harm no animals: No leather or fur is used.

Urban Outfitters

200–201 Oxford Street, W 1
For the young and trendy.

FASHION SECONDHAND

Lucy in Disguise   *Insider Tip*

48 Lexington Street, W 1
Pop singer Lily Allen and her half-sister have gathered vintage treasures in Soho. Not cheap, but very, very London.

Red Cross   *Insider Tip*

61–67 Church Street, SW 3
www.redcross.org.uk
One of the city's best charity shops sells wares by classic designers in pleasant surroundings. Get kitted out at a reasonable price in a good cause.

Rokit

255 High Street, Camden, NW 1
42 Shelton Street, Covent Garden, WC2
www.rokit.co.uk
Authentic vintage fashion from the 1940s to 1990s grunge. Lots of accessories and a huge range of men's hats.

FINE FOOD

Cadenhead's

26 Chiltern Street, W 1
www.whiskytastingroom.com
Over 200 sorts of Scotch whisky and Irish whiskey. With a tasting room.

Charbonnel et Walker
1 Royal Arcade,
28 Old Bond Street, W 1
www.charbonnel.co.uk
Hand-made chocolates. English
Rose and Violet Creams are a speciality.

Hope & Greenwood
1 Russell Street, WC 2
www.hopeandgreenwood.co.uk
Shop in Covent Garden in old-
world style that sells sweet childhood dreams – humbugs, lemon
sherbet, candy lipstick and its
own creations. Why not buy their
recipe book and make the sweets
at home?

Neal's Yard Dairy
17 Shorts Gardens, WC 2 and
►Borough Market
www.nealsyarddairy.co.uk
British and Irish artisan cheese.

Partridge's
2–5 Duke of York Square, SW 3
www.partridges.co.uk
Supplier to the royal family of all
sorts of goodies. With a wine bar
and café, not far from Sloane
Square.

Paxton & Whitfield
93 Jermyn Street, SW 1
www.paxtonandwhitfield.co.uk
Supplier of cheese to the royal
family.

JEWELLERY
@work
156 Brick Lane, E 1
www.atworkgallery.co.uk
Three designers make fashionable
jewellery here.

Dinny Hall
Insider Tip

292 Upper Street, N 1 and at
Liberty's (►p. 237)
www.dinnyhall.com
Designer jewellery inspired by
organic forms – bamboo, lotus
flowers, waves.

Mikimoto
179 New Bond Street, W 1
www.mikimoto.com
A sea of pearls – the famous
Akoya cultured pearls.

PERFUME
Jo Malone
150 Sloane Street, SW 1
www.jomalone.com
Beautifully presented scented
candles, fragrances and bath
essences.

Penhaligon's
16–17 Burlington Arcade, WC 2,
125 Regent Street, W 1,
132 King's Road, SW 3 and
elsewhere
www.penhaligons.com
The fragrances sold by the court
perfumer include classics such as
Hamam Bouquet, Blenheim Bouquet, Bluebell and Jubilee.

PIPES AND TOBACCO
Davidoff of London
35 St James's Street, SW 1
www.davidoff.com
This might be the largest selection
of fine cigars in Europe, each one
kept in its own beautiful box.

SHOES
Church's
201 Regent Street, W 1
www.church-footwear.com

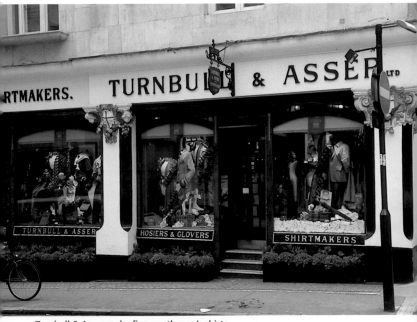

Turnbull & Asser make fine gentlemen's shirts

Tasteful gentlemen's shoes from the first manufacturer to make separate ones for the left and right foot.

Office

210 Camden Hight Street, NW 1
190 Oxford Street, W 1
61–63 Monmouth Street, W 2
A huge range of out-of-the- ordinary shoes. The Monmouth Street branch has the latest designs.

Russell & Bromley

151 Kensington High Street, W 8
Once rather conventional, now a good balance between comfortable and fashionable. Branches in Regent Street and elsewhere.

SPORTS

Lillywhite's

24–36 Lower Regent Street, SW 1
www.lillywhites.com
Whatever your sport is, you will find the right kit here.

TEA

The Tea House

15a Neal Street, WC 2
www.theteahouse.co.uk
Lots or rarities and organic teas, and samplers with four kinds to help you decide.

Twinings

216 Strand, WC 2
www.twinings.co.ukTea has been sold in this long, passage-like

shop for almost 300 years. At the back there is a small museum of company history, and customers can brew their own cup.

TOYS
Hamley's
200 Regent Street, W 1
www.hamleys.com
Claims to be the world's largest toy shop, with lots of treats for young and old, including things to try out – staff are on hand to show you how to do it.

MARKETS
Borough Market
Borough High Street, SE 1; Tube: London Bridge
Mon–Wed 10am–3pm »open for lunch«, Thu 11am–5pm, Fri noon–6pm, Sat 9am–4pm
www.boroughmarket.org.uk
London's oldest produce market, now a foodies' heaven: organic and gourmet produce, designer snacking (►p. 296).

Brick Lane Market
E 1/E 2; Tube: Aldgate East
Sun 9am–5pm
www.visitbricklane.org
All kinds of secondhand goods between the curry houses, cool bars, trendy shops, graffiti and street art.

Brixton Market
SW 9; Tube: Brixton
Mon–Sat 8.30am–5.30pm, Wed to 3pm
www.brixtonmarket.net
Afro-Caribbean, but also African, Asian and Latin American stalls selling household goods, clothes, food, music.

Broadway Market Insider Tip
E 1 near London Fields; bus to London Fields, Overground to Haggerston
Sat 9am–5pm
www.broadwaymarket.co.uk
Farmer's market with lots of organic produce, home-made foodstuffs, an old-established eel and pie shop, pubs and deli cafés, vintage fashion and designers' stalls.

Camden Markets
► Camden

Columbia Road
E 2
Tube: Old Street
Sun 8am–3pm
www.columbiaroad.info
What started out as a flower market has become a big Sunday event, the street is full of independent shops – delis, antiques, design, clothes – with a good choice of pubs and cafés.

Leadenhall Market
EC 3
Tube: Bank, Monument
Mon–Fri 7am–4pm
Meat, poultry, fish in Victorian market hall, ►p. 235

Leather Lane Market
Leather Lane, EC 1
Tube: Chancery Lane
Mon–Fri 10.30am–2pm
Clothes, electrical goods, records and CDs.

Old Spitalfields Market
65 Brushfield Street, E 1
Tube: Liverpool Street
Tue–Fri and Sun 11am–4pm

www.oldspitalfieldsmarket.com
A large market for a hip scene,
selling jewellery, design items,
fashion, crafts. Good array of
ethnic food stalls.

Portobello Road Market
W 11
Tube: Ladbroke Grove,
Notting Hill Gate
Mon–Fri 9am–5pm, Thu to 1pm

A top-ranking event and
tourist attraction. Only fruit
and vegetables on weekdays,
antiques and second-hand goods
on Saturdays, when it is unbeliev-
ably crowded.

Smithfield Market
▶ p. 282

AUCTION HOUSES, GALLERIES, ANTIQUES

The headquarters of the leading international auction houses **So-theby's** and **Christie's** are in London. Phillips and Bonham's are the less well-known players in this business. Smaller auction houses outside the city centre have a less formal atmosphere. The auctions are announced in the press.

Auction houses

There is a concentration of expensive and fabulously expensive dealers selling exclusive items **in Mayfair** around Old and New Bond Street and the side-streets: furniture and crafts in the Bond Street Antiques Centre (124 New Bond Street, W 1), Victoriana at Christopher Wood's (141 New Bond Street, W 1), silver at SJ Philips (139 New Bond Street, W 1), old masters at Richard Green (33 and 147 New Bond Street, 39 Dover Street, W 1), Victorian sculpture and painting at Tryon and Morland (23 Cork Street, W 1). **St James's** is in a similar class, for example Spink & Son (5 King Street, SW 1). Less expensive – though by no means cheap – dealers are based in **Pimlico Road**: Westenholz (68 Pimlico Road, SW 1), for example, sells furniture and interiors items. Outlets in **Kensington** such as those on Kensington Church Street and Christie's salesroom (85 Old Brompton Road, SW 7) also have a good reputation. Last but not least there is **Chelsea**, where bargains can sometimes be found on King's Road, New King's Road and Fulham Road, for example in Lot's Road Galleries (73 Lot's Road, SW 10).

Some antique dealers

Most of the old-established London galleries have addresses in Mayfair in the streets around Old and New Bond Street, where Cork Street is the place to find dealers in contemporary art, in South Kensington and in St James's, where Duke Street is the best location. These galleries sell top-class art with prices to match. Many young gallery owners have set up in the East End and Notting Hill, e.g. in Vyner Street.

Galleries

AUCTION HOUSES
Bonham's
Montpelier Street, SW 7
Tel. 020 7584 9161
wwww.bonham.com

Christie's
8 King Street, SW 1
Tel. 020 7839 9060
www.christies.com

Phillips
101 New Bond Street, W 1
Tel. 020 76 29 66 02
www.phillips-auctions.com

Sotheby's
34 – 35 New Bond Street, W 1
Tel. 020 7493 5000
www.sothebys.com

ANTIQUE AND FLEA MARKETS
Alfie's Antique Market
13–25 Church Street, NW 8
Tube: Edgware Road

Tue–Sat 10am–6pm
www.alfiesantiques.com
London's biggest antiques market
with 370 dealers under one roof.

Battersea Car Boot Sale
Battersea Park School, SW 3
Overground: Battersea Park
Sun 12 noon–5pm
www.batterseaboot.com
Admission 50 p to £3
Highly organised event that
attracts some good-quality wares
as well as some very cheap ones.

Bermondsey Market
Tower Bridge Road, SE 1
Tube: Borough, London Bridge
Fri 5am–2pm
Attracts crowds of dealers and
buyers every Friday. For the
bargains, get up early.

Gray's Antique Market
58 Davies Street, W 1
Tube: Bond Street

The Saturday market on Portobello Road

www.graysantiques.com
Mon–Fri 10am–6pm
200 stalls with quality articles –
jewellery, watches, all sorts of
collectables and curiosities, on
the site of the underground
Tyburn stream. Quaint old-
fashioned bistro.

Kensington Church Street Art & Antique Dealers Association
Church Street, W 8
Tube: Kensington High Street
www.antiques-london.com
60 high-class dealers on a
charming shopping street.

Portobello Road Market
W 11, Tube: Ladbroke Grove,
Notting Hill Gate
Sat 7am–5.30pm
www.portobelloroad.co.uk
Antiques and second-hand market
on Saturdays, on weekdays only
fruit and vegetables. ▶p. 129

Silver Vaults
53 Chancery Lane, WC 2
Tube: Chancery Lane
Mon–Fri 9am–5.30pm, Sat 9am–
12.30pm
www.thesilvervaults.com
A huge range of old and new
silver in subterranean passages.

Tours and Guides

Bus or Not?

A hop-on/hop-off tour on an open-top bus is a good way of getting an overview of London, especially on a first trip. For visitors who already know London a little better, there are many walking tours of the city given by professional guides on a range of themes, some of them creative and unusual.

Original London Sightseeing Tours and Big Bus Company are just two of a number of operators who run hop-on/hop-off tours from fixed stopping-places such as Baker Street, Marble Arch and Piccadilly Circus. Tickets are sold by the driver, commentaries are given over headphones, and there are even disposable plastic rain capes in case of rain. A 24-hour ticket gives you the option of spreading the tour over two days and combining it with a visit to some of the attractions en route. The famous old Routemaster double-decker buses are still alive and well on two routes that are used by many tourists: no. 9 (Kensington – Aldwych) and no. 15 (Trafalgar Square – Tower)

Hop-on/ hop-off tours

! *For experienced travellers*   **Insider Tip**

MARCO ⊕ POLO TIP

Have you done all the guided tours on every conceivable theme? And seen everything? Perhaps there are still discoveries to be made, for example on www. london-footprints.co.uk, where more than 100 walks through well-known and less-known parts of London are described.

Guided walks given by experts on the city are entertaining and interesting. They usually have a theme, such as Roman London, medieval London, Victorian London, »in the footsteps of Jack the Ripper«, Sherlock Holmes's London, etc. The latest programmes are available from the organisers. Original London Walks has a wide range of subjects (▶ MARCO POLO Insight, p. 135, for more ideas).

Guided walks

A trip on the river Thames reveals London from a different angle. A number of different operators run regular boats from Westminster Pier, Charing Cross Pier and Tower Pier downriver via Greenwich to the Thames Barrier and upriver to Hampton Court. Exact departure times are shown and tickets on sale at the piers.
An excursion on the Regent's Canal is gentler than on the Thames. Old barges glide along from Little Venice past Regent's Park to Camden Lock.

River trips

A bus tour is a compact introduction to the highlights of the city

BUS TOURS
The Big Bus Company
48 Buckingham Palace Road,
SW 1
Tel. 020 7233 9533
www.bigbustours.com

Black Cab Heritage Tours
Tel. 0170 769 6034
www.blackcabheritagetours.co.uk
Personal tours in classic London
taxis.

Original London Sightseeing
17 – 19 Cockspur Street, Trafalgar
Square, SW 1
Tel. 020 8877 8120
www.theoriginaltour.com

THEMED GUIDED WALKS
London Walks
Tel. 020 7624 3978
www.walks.com
A big, big range of walks at a
standard price of £9.

London Discovery Tours
Tel. 020 8530 8443
www.discovery-walks.com
Pub walks, Sherlock Holmes
walks, and much more.

ON THE THAMES
River Tours
Piers at Westminster, London Eye,
Tower, St Katharine's, Greenwich,
Richmond, Hampton Court
www.tfl.gov.uk, click on River
Westminster to Greenwich and
Westminster to Hampton Court,
with different stop-offs.

Thames River Services
Tel. 020 7930 4097
http://thamesriverservices.co.uk
Westminster to Greenwich and
Thames Barrier, round trips.

ON THE REGENT'S CANAL
Jason's Wharf
60 Blomfield Rd.,Little Venice, W9
Tel. 020 7286 3428
www.jasons.co.uk

London Waterbus Company
58 Camden Lock Place, NW 1
Tel. 020 7482 2550
www.londonwaterbus.com

Walkers Quay
250 Camden High St., NW1
Tel. 020 7485 4433
www.walkersquay.com

Discovering London from the Thames

A Different View of London

There are now more opportunities than ever to explore London in an unusual and active way with expert guidance. Here are some suggestions.

London on a Bike

One of the best sightseeing tours is done on two wheels. **Spoke'n Motion** (www.guidedbiketour-london.com) give you a completely new perspective, for example on a Sunday morning tour between the high-rise banks and churches of the City or on the Sights By Night Tour, which leads through streets lit by gas lamps behind Westminster Abbey, offers views into the kitchen windows of some of the poshest residences in London and finishes with on benches rather than saddles in what must be London's only Korean barbecue pub.

Follow Your Nose

The **Seven Noses of Soho** (www.peterberthoud.co.uk) is a tour by Peter Berthoud, one of more than a few experts on London who take guests on quirky walks spiced up with surprising stories. The noses were made by a sculptor, Rick Buckley – he made casts of his own nose and placed them on walls in inconspicuous places. If this sounds too special, try a tour of the hidden side of The Strand or Hidden Mayfair.

Discover the Thames

There are alternatives to the standard sightseeing cruise on the river. To set your pulse racing, book a trip on the bright orange **RIB speedboat** (www.londonrib voyages.com). It starts at the London Eye; when the captain has passed Tower Bridge and is able to rev up the engine, then hold tight!

For a quieter, calmer water tour, squeeze into a kayak (www.londonkayaktours.co.uk) and paddle past Hampton Court or upstream in Windsor or along the Regent's Canal.

Green London

London's parks (www.royalparks.org.uk) are perfect for botanical, mushroom or bat walks. For a modern alternative to doing everything on foot, book a **Segway tour around Alexandra Park** (www.intotheblue.co.uk) in the north of the city, where you have panoramic views in the 80-hectare park around the impressive Alexandra Palace.

If you are hungry, how about foraging? The search for edible wild plants is fun and a good way of finding something healthy to eat that costs nothing. Astonishingly, it works very well in Europe's most populous city, e.g. on a day's seminar with www.foragingcourses.com or an event organised by www.urbanharvest.org.uk, an informal network that holds regular meetings and excursions with varied themes.

TOURS

A tour in a sightseeing bus takes in the highlights of London, of course, but the real way to explore the city is on foot. Here are some routes for an entertaining walk.

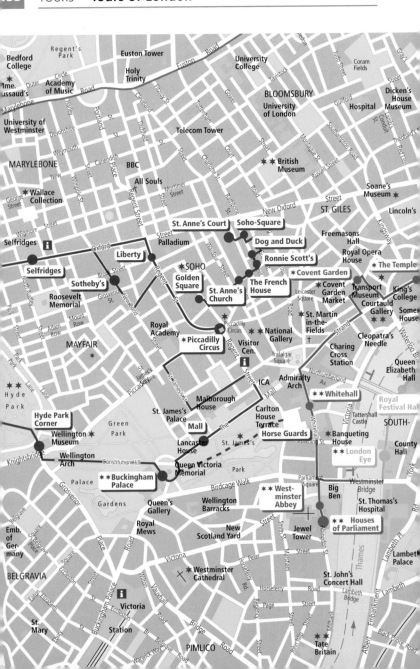

Bedford College
Regent's Park
Euston Tower
Holy Trinity
University College
Coram Fields
Ime. ussaud's
Academy of Music
BLOOMSBURY
University of London
Dicken's House Museum
University of Westminster
Telecom Tower
Hospital
Soane's Museum
MARYLEBONE
BBC
All Souls
British Museum
ST. GILES
Lincoln's
Wallace Collection
St. Anne's Court
Soho-Square
Freemasons Hall
Royal Opera House
The Temple
Selfridges
Liberty
Palladium
Dog and Duck
Covent Garden
Selfridges
Sotheby's
SOHO
Golden Square
Ronnie Scott's
The French House
Covent Garden Market
Transport Museum
King's College
Courtauld Gallery
Somer House
Roosevelt Memorial
St. Anne's Church
St. Martin in-the-Fields
Royal Academy
Piccadilly Circus
National Gallery
Charing Cross Station
Cleopatra's Needle
MAYFAIR
Visitor Cen.
Queen Elizabeth Hall
Hyde Park
ICA
Admiralty Arch
Whitehall
Royal Festival Hall
Hyde Park Corner
Malborough House
SOUTH-
Wellington Museum
St. James's Palace
Mall
Carlton House Terrace
Horse Guards
Banqueting House
County Hall
Wellington Arch
Lancaster House
London Eye
Buckingham Palace
Queen Victoria Memorial
Westminster Abbey
Big Ben
Westminster Bridge
St. Thomas's Hospital
Emb. of Germany
Queen's Gallery
Royal Mews
New Scotland Yard
Wellington Barracks
Jewel Tower
Houses of Parliament
Lambeth Palace
BELGRAVIA
Westminster Cathedral
St. John's Concert Hall
St. Mary
Victoria Station
PIMLICO
Tate Britain

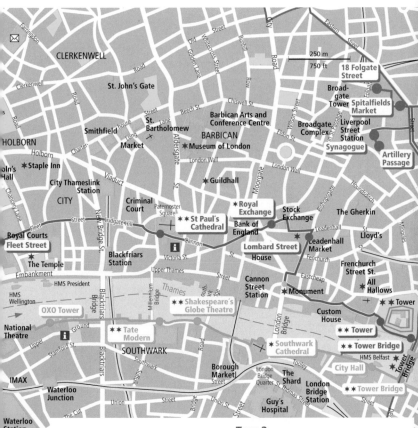

Tours of London

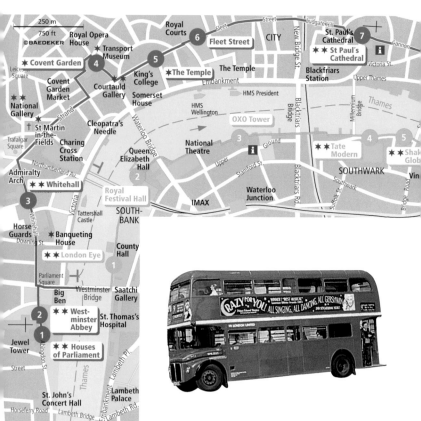

The old-time Routemaster double-deckers are only in operation on two routes used by many tourists

Getting Around in London

Fast trains and cheap flights mean that a day trip to London is possible from most parts of Great Britain and indeed Europe. But to see the main sights, visit a museum or two and do some shopping, three days is a minimum. For people who like to walk it is not difficult to get around in the City and Westminster. However, it quickly becomes tiring to do everything on foot, as London covers an area that makes it one of the largest cities in the world. Fortunately almost every corner of this area can be reached by bus or the underground railway (Tube). The Tube is an indispensable means of transport, even

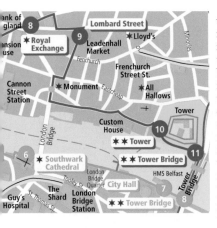

though Londoners are critical of the network, which is in need of modernisation. It is certainly advisable to avoid travelling during the rush hour. As far as transport is concerned, any district not too far from the centre is a suitable choice for accommodation; to stay in pleasant surroundings with good places to go out in the evening, the best option is a hotel in the West End, Knightsbridge or Kensington.

One more point on transport: When travelling to London, it is advisable to leave the car at home. In 2002 London's mayor introduced the congestion charge, a toll of £10 per day for each vehicle that enters the city centre between 7am and 6pm from Monday to Friday. The number plates of vehicles entering the zone system are registered electronically. If this is not a sufficient deterrent, then bear in mind the shortage of parking spaces and the hefty fines for illegal parking.

Westminster and the City – Essential London

Tour 1

Start and finish: Westminster Bridge – Tower Bridge (north bank of the Thames)
Duration: min. 4 hours

This walk takes in many highlights and is an introduction to the city for first-time visitors. To see the Changing of the Guard, plan to be at Horse Guards at 11am (Sunday 10am). To get your bearings take a ride in the London Eye, a 135m/443ft-high observation wheel not far from the starting point.

Start at Westminster tube station. London's famous landmark Big Ben, the clock tower of the ❶ ****Houses of Parliament**, is in view as you emerge from the underground. The best place to enjoy the magnificent architecture of the Houses of Parliament is from Westminster Bridge. From there cross Parliament Square to take a look at

Start at Big Ben

Not to miss: Horse Guards

②**Westminster Abbey**. Set aside another day to make a thorough visit to the abbey and walk up ③**Whitehall** to Horse Guards, which draws crowds of tourists. A little further on is London's finest square, **Trafalgar Square**, which commemorates the British naval hero Lord Nelson. The **National Gallery** occupies the north side of the square. Don't feed the pigeons here, but turn round to look back down Whitehall to Big Ben. Then continue along the *Strand to the City, passing Waterloo Bridge and Somerset House, home of the **Courtauld Institute Gallery**. The pubs and cafés of ④*Covent Garden to the north are the best place to take a break – try the café in the Royal Opera House.

Into the heart of the City | Return to the Strand and the Temple Bar Memorial, where a narrow archway on the right leads to ⑤*The Temple. Beyond Temple Bar is ⑥Fleet Street, once the centre of the newspaper business. It leads into Ludgate Hill and a view of ⑦**St. Paul's Cathedral**. From the cathedral take Cannon Street and Queen Victoria Street to Bank tube station. Here, in the heart of London's financial world, are the **Bank of England** and the ⑧*Royal Exchange. The last part of this route starts at Bank station. Go down Threadneedle Street or ⑨Lombard Street to the Victorian market halls of Leadenhall Market, then along Gracechurch Street to the *Monument and on via Lower Thames Street to the ⑩**Tower and ⑪**Tower Bridge**.

South Bank of the Thames   Tour 2

Start and finish: Westminster Bridge – Tower Bridge
Duration: min. 2 hours

This walk takes you to a part of London that has become more and more attractive and offers wonderful views of Westminster and the City.

Start at Westminster Bridge to get the best view of the ****Houses of Parliament**. Steps lead down to the path along the south bank of the Thames near the 135m/443ft-high observation wheel, the ❶****London Eye**, which gives a completely different angle on Parliament and the whole city. From here the walk follows the river to Tower Bridge, with views north to the opposite bank and plenty of opportunities for shopping or taking a break in a pub or restaurant.

Start at London Eye

At the Hungerford Railway Bridge and further along from the bridge, there is a marvellous view of the City with ****St. Paul's**, the »Gherkin« and other bank towers, then of Tower Bridge and The Shard on the south bank. This part of the walk passes the South Bank Centre, a cultural quarter. The café and Skylon restaurant in the ❷ **Royal Festival Hall** are good places for refreshments with a fine view. Alternatively, beyond Waterloo Bridge stop at one of the cafés in Gabriel's Wharf, where galleries sell crafts. Go on to the ❸**Oxo Tower**, which contains designer shops, a bar, a restaurant and an observation terrace on the eighth floor.

Panoramic view of the City

> **!** MARCO ⊕ POLO TIP
>
> *Borough Market*   **Insider Tip**
>
> For a touch of class with oysters and white wine, or fish dishes, try Wright Bros. Oyster & Porter House (11 Stoney Street); for a more modest meal of sandwiches, baguette or cake, Konditor & Cook is next door (10 Stoney Street). Or buy a chorizo burger, paella and other exotic offerings from one of the market stalls.

Then walk under Blackfriars Bridge to **Southwark**, once a district of drinking dens, theatres and brothels. The great bulk of Bankside Power Station, now home to the art collection of the ❹****Tate Modern**, is on the right; on the left the intricate structure of the Millennium Bridge leads straight up to St Paul's. Just a little further, ❺****Shakespeare's Globe Theatre** provides an opportunity to experience Elizabethan-style theatre. Continue to the Gothic splendour of ❻*** Southwark Cathedral**.

It may well be time for a break by now. For this there is no better place than **Borough Market**, London's gourmet market. It lies next to Southwark Cathedral under the arches of the railway tracks leading to

London Bridge Station. Cooked-food stalls sell meals to take away, and around Borough Market in Stoney Street, Park Street and Bedale Street are many pubs and restaurants. The last stage of the route passes the spectacular new **7** **City Hall** on the way to **8** ****Tower Bridge** and, for the energetic, crosses the river to the ****Tower.**

Tour 3 **The West End**

Start and finish: Piccadilly Circus
Duration: min. 3 hours

Shopping, parks and royalty is the theme of this walk through some of the most exclusive districts of the city, including places with royal connections.

In the heart
of West End

Start at **1** ***Piccadilly Circus** and follow the impressive curve of Regent Street to the main shopping area of the West End. Not to be missed here are the department store, **2** **Liberty** and, if there are

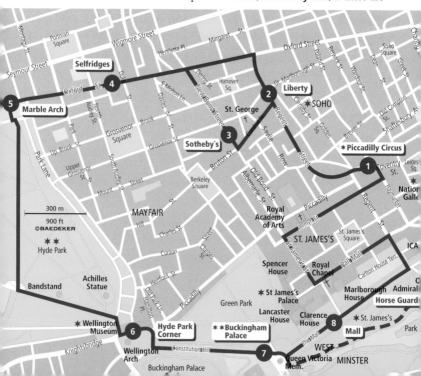

children in the group, Hamley's toy shop. Oxford Circus is the junction of Regent Street and the bustle of Oxford Street, which is also lined with shops and department stores selling everything from luxury goods to bargains. An alternative route to Oxford Street goes along Conduit Street and New Bond Street, site of the world-famous auction house ❸ **Sotheby's** and highly exclusive boutiques. A »must« for Oxford Street shoppers is the upmarket department store ❹ **Selfridges**.

Continue to the north-east corner of ****Hyde Park**, well-known for ❺ **Marble Arch** and Speakers' Corner. Any route through Hyde Park is a delight. The long way goes west round the Serpentine lake to the Princess Diana Memorial Fountain, with a stop for coffee at the Lido. Whichever route you take, leave the park at ❻ **Hyde Park Corner** where the Wellington Arch celebrates the victor of the Battle of Waterloo, who lived nearby at Apsley House, and various war memorials commemorate the dead of the world wars. From here cross Green Park to ❼ ****Buckingham Palace** and continue through ***St. James's Park** to Horse Guards Parade – or if you still have energy, proceed along ❽ **The Mall** to Carlton House Terrace and up the steps to Pall Mall. Turn left along Pall Mall and walk past London's clubs to ***St. James's Palace**, one of the city's few Tudor buildings. Finish with a stroll through the St James's district. This can take some time, as high-class gentlemen's outfitters, tobacco and pipe shops and the exclusive department store Fortnum & Mason provide plenty of distractions. Emerge from St James's at ***Piccadilly Circus** and continue to Chinatown for lunch or dinner.

Through Hyde Park

Soho – Creative People, Drinkers and Intellectuals

Tour 4

Start: Soho Square
Finish: Golden Square
Duration: 2 hours

Soho still has a dubious reputation. There is some justification for this, although it is a colourful and creative district that was originally built as a place for aristocrats to live.

❶ **Soho Square** (Tube: Tottenham Court Road) was laid out in the 1680s with the aspiration to make it a top address. The statue of Charles II in the gardens at the centre of the square and St Barnabas House at the south-east corner are reminders of this time. Soon Soho

Centre of Soho

went down in the world, becoming an immigrant quarter. St Patrick's Church on the east side, now splendid with marble and gilding, replaced a Roman Catholic church for a poor Irish congregation on the site where the Venetian courtesan Teresa Cornelys held masked balls in the 1760s and was hostess to Casanova. No. 1 Soho Square in the north-west corner is the headquarters of Paul McCartney's company. In the cellar is a reconstruction of studio no. 2 in Abbey Road, where the Beatles made recordings. A short walk away (via Carlisle Street, then left at the first crossroad) in charming ❷ **St. Anne's Court**, they recorded »Hey Jude« in 1968 in the Trident Studio, which still exists.

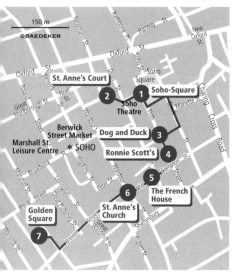

Greek Street leads south from Soho Square. Customers at the Gay Hussar restaurant on the left once included General Eisenhower, the Queen of Thailand, Soviet spies and Mick Jagger. From here turn right into Bateman Street to ❸ **The Dog and Duck**, a pub with a wonderful 1890s interior of mirrors, glass and wood. A memorial plaque on the west side of Frith Street, immediately south of its junction with Bateman Street, honours Dr John Snow, who investigated the deaths of people who had used a local pump in 1854 and was the first to show that contaminated drinking water was the cause of cholera. Five years previously over 50,000 Londoners had died in a cholera epidemic. Bateman Street leads to Dean Street, where Karl Marx lived in poverty at no. 28 on the right for six years from 1850. One of his six children fell victim to cholera.

Music and history

Return to Frith Street and head south. In 1764–65 the eight-year-old Mozart lived at no. 20. Opposite it is London's most famous jazz club, ❹ **Ronnie Scott's**, where Jimi Hendrix gave his last live performance. Continue to Old Compton Street, today a centre of the city's gay scene, where there are many places to stop for coffee or lunch. In the post-war decades the drinking dens of this area were run by some legendary landlords and frequented by a mixed clientele. All sorts of rumours surrounded the Thursday Club at no. 29–31 Old Compton Street in the 1950s, as Prince Philip used to escape the restrictions of palace etiquette here for alcoholic lunches with a carefully chose circle including actors such as Peter Ustinov. The Coach and Horses (in Greek Street south of Old Compton Street), dating from 1849, was a haunt of gangsters, corrupt policemen and artists in those days, but is respectable now. ❺ **»The French House«** (no. 49 Dean Street) was the unofficial headquarters of Charles de Gaulle and his entourage during the Second World War. This pub is also notable as the place where the inebriate poet Dylan Thomas mislaid the only manuscript of his radio play »Under Milk Wood« in 1953.

Walk west along Old Compton Street to Wardour Street, the northern end of which is a centre of the British film industry, then turn left and go a few paces southwards to the garden, formerly a cemetery, by the tower of ❻ **St. Anne's Church**. The strange top of this tower, all that remains of the church following war damage, was described as »crossed beer barrels« by an architectural historian. The churchyard is a quiet place for a break in noisy Soho, and also the last resting-place of the essayist William Hazlitt (1778–1830), whose home at no. 6 Frith Street is now the Hazlitt Hotel, and of a German adventurer named Theodor von Neuhoff (1694–1756), who fought unsuccessfully for Corsican independence, was declared king of the island and later is said to have pledged his kingdom in return for release from a debtors' prison in London.

Some calm

In Brewer Street a corner of seedy old Soho remains. Past sex shops and strip clubs continue west, then turn right into Lower James Street and follow it to ❼ **Golden Square**, which was laid out in the early 18th century for aristocratic residents. A few buildings remain from this time, including two on the west side that once housed the Portuguese embassy. From here it is not far to the shops on Regent Street and the Tube station at Piccadilly Circus.

Seedy old Soho

Spitalfields – an Immigrant Quarter for 300 Years

Tour 5

Start: U-Bahn-Station Aldgate East
Finish: Spitalfields Market
Duration: 1.5 – 2 hours

Spitalfields lies immediately to the east of the banking district of the City of London. Although the money earned in the City is noticeable in the shops and cafés, everyday life here is still marked by the Bangladeshis and students who live here and by the area's Huguenot and Jewish past.

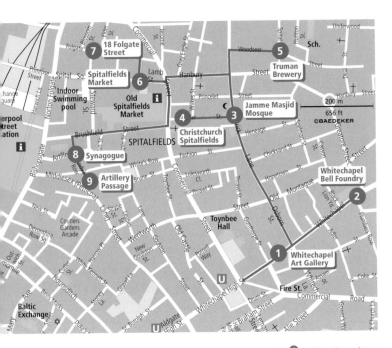

Arts and crafts Next to Aldgate East Tube station, exit 3, stands ❶ **Whitechapel Art Gallery**, built in 1901 in the Arts & Crafts style. With the neighbouring library, whose rooms are now part of the gallery, it was an important cultural institution for the poor population of the East End, a »university of the ghetto«, and is today one of the leading exhibition spaces for contemporary art in London. The main road, Whitechapel High Street, leads east to Osborne Street. If you have time, a detour of about 400m/450yd further east to ❷ **Whitechapel Bell Foundry** is recommended. Probably the oldest company in England, it has been based in Whitechapel since 1570. Its best-known product is Big Ben, the bell that gave its name to the clock and tower.

Whitechapel Bell Foundry: 32 Whitechapel Road, museum Mon–Fri 9am–5pm, tours of the foundry by appointment, www.whitechapelbellfoundry.co.uk

Banglatown Osborne Street leads directly to Brick Lane and »Banglatown«, a quarter dominated by immigrants from Bangladesh where a host of curry houses line the street. Monica Ali's novel »Brick Lane« describes the life of Bangladeshis in London around the year 2000, when the scene here was a little more diverse than it is today, for example through the presence of clothes shops selling saris.

On the left in Fashion Street is the Moorish Market, built in 1905 and now used as a business college. At the corner of Fournier Street and Brick Lane note the ❸ **Jamme Masjid Mosque**, the only building in Britain that has served three major religions: Built in 1743 by Huguenots, i.e. Protestants expelled from France, under the name Église Neuve, it later became a mission for converting Jews to Christianity – without success, as in 1897, in the wake of immigration by tens of thousands of Jews from eastern Europe, the church became a synagogue. After the Second World War, the Jewish community gradually dispersed, and the synagogue was then converted into a mosque in 1975. A few paces further up Brick Lane on the right the letters »CH. N. Katz« can be seen above a window. This was the last Jewish shop in the area. Until the late 1990s it sold paper bags and string.

Walk along Fournier Street past fine Georgian houses to see the striking church architecture of ❹ **Christchurch Spitalfields**, designed by Nicholas Hawksmoor (1714–29), or turn right from Fournier Street into Wilkes Street and right again into Princelet Street, where the houses give an impression of the prosperity of Huguenot silk weavers in the 18th century. Examples of the exquisite embroidered clothes that they made for high society can be seen in the ▶Victoria & Albert Museum. Some of the houses have long rows of windows in the attic. Their purpose was to provide light for the delicate work of sewing and embroidering, a facility appreciated by the Jewish tailors who worked here in the 19th and 20th centuries. Back on Brick Lane, head north to the site of the long-closed ❺ **Truman brewery**, which has been taken over by all kinds of creative activities, from cutting-edge fashion and media companies to artists' studios. Cheap places to eat, night clubs and well-attended Sunday markets round off the attractions.

Tailors' quarter

Follow Brick Lane back south and turn right into Hanbury Street (noting the weavers' windows in the attics of nos. 24–26), then cross busy Commercial Street to reach ❻ **Spitalfields Market**. The western part of the market halls, dating from the 1880s, was pulled down to make place for shiny new buildings after the fruit and vegetable market moved out in 1991, but it is still possible to enjoy market atmosphere, especially on Sundays, when the whole area is a bustling scene of buying and browsing.

Market life

To the north of Spitalfields Market, the neighbourhood around Folgate Street has many examples of restored 18th-century houses. One of them, ❼ **18 Folgate Street**, was the home of Dennis Severs, who made the house into an enchanting reconstruction of life 300 years ago, a walk-through work of art without electric lighting. Returning to and passing the market, follow Fort Street as far as Sandys Row to the only remaining ❽ **synagogue** in this area, which occupies a building dating from 1854. From here go left through the charming little ❾ **Artillery Passage**. Here and in Spitalfields Market the cafés and restaurant provide refreshment after the walk.

❶ www.dennissevershouse.co.uk

Excursions

In the vicinity   The best destinations for a short excursion from the centre of London are ****Greenwich**, the wonderful park and plant houses in ****Kew Gardens**, the majestic ****Hampton Court Palace** or, for a stroll on the banks of the Thames, **Richmond**. To see a residence of the royal family, take a trip to ****Windsor Castle**.

Farther away   Many places within 100km/60 miles of London that are well worth seeing can easily be reached by rail or bus (from Victoria Coach Station).

Arundel in the South Downs (80km/50 miles south of London) is one of the most attractive small towns in the south of England. The castle of the dukes of Norfolk dominates the town (train from Victoria Station).

The attractions of **Brighton**, a popular resort on the south coast (80km/50 miles south of London) are the funfair on the Victorian Palace Pier and other seaside pleasures (train from Victoria Station).

Richmond is worth the excursion

The city of **Canterbury** (75km/45 miles south of London) has one of the most beautiful cathedrals in England (train from Victoria Station or Charing Cross).

Ascot, just a few miles to the south-west of Windsor Castle, is the place where high society meets every June to watch the horse races and admire the ladies' hats during Ascot Week. On Thursday, the day of the Gold Cup race, the royal family comes in coaches from Windsor Castle (trains to Ascot from Waterloo Station).

In the university town of **Cambridge** the medieval colleges are open to visitors (train from Liverpool Street Station).

Oxford, one of the world's oldest university cities (90km/55 miles north-west of London) is in historical and architectural terms arguably Britain's second most important city after London. Its attractions are the colleges, cathedral, gardens and High Street – not to forget the student life (train from Paddington).

SIGHTS FROM
A TO Z

The British Museum with its wonderful Great Court, Buckingham
Palace, Trafalgar Square and the famous Tower Bridge – just a few
of the highlights for visitors to London

All Hallows-by-the-Tower

✳ **K 5**

Location: Byward Street, EC 3
Tube: Tower Hill
Tours by arrangement   or www.allhallowsby
tel. 020 7481 2928   thetower.org.uk, £5

All Hallows, the oldest church in London, is within sight of the Tower. Samuel Pepys watched the Great Fire of 1666 from its tower.

London's oldest church

The church was founded in 675 by monks from Barking Abbey, re-built in the 13th to 15th centuries, severely damaged in the Second World War and reconstructed in 1957. It has a 14th-century crypt and a tower dating from 1658, which is typical of the Commonwealth period. In 1666 Admiral **Sir William Penn**, father of the founder of Pennsylvania, saved All Hallows from the flames of the Great Fire by ordering the surrounding houses to be blown up. For some of those condemned to die in the Tower, for example Sir Thomas More in 1535 and Archbishop William Laud in 1645, All Hallows was their last place of rest before they mounted the scaffold.

Inside the church the remains of an arch, partly built from Roman masonry and bearing the date AD 675, are evidence of Anglo-Saxon origins. Two crosses have survived from this period. In the museum in the **crypt** a model of Roman Londinium, items from the Roman and Saxon periods and a font cover attributed to Grinling Gibbons are on display. The parish register records that William Penn the Younger was baptised in All Hallows on 23 October 1644 and that John Quincy Adams (1767–1848), sixth president of the USA, married here in 1797 while he was the American ambassador in London.

St Olave

Seething Lane, the street in which Samuel Pepys lived, branches off from Byward Street opposite All Hallows and leads to the church of St Olave on Hart Street, one of the few churches in the City left un-touched by the Great Fire. First recorded in the 13th century, and dating in its present form from about 1450 with a tower built in 1732, it is dedicated to the Norwegian patron saint King Olaf II, who is thought to have fought against the Danes on this site in alliance with the Anglo-Saxon king Ethelred in 1014.

It was the **parish church of Samuel Pepys**, who was laid to rest here (memorial on the south wall). In 1672 Pepys commissioned John Bushnell to produce a bust in memory of his wife Elizabeth, who is also buried here. The pulpit is by Grinling Gibbons.

Bank of England · Royal Exchange · Mansion House

──────── ✴ J / K 5

Tube: Bank

Three buildings close to Bank Tube station, the Bank von England, the former Royal Exchange and the official residence of the Lord Mayor, represent financial power and political authority in the heart of the City.

BANK OF ENGLAND

❶ Threadneedle Street, EC 3

The Bank von England, known since James Gillray's caricature at the time of the Napoleonic wars as »The Old Lady of Threadneedle Street«, extends along Threadneedle Street and Bartholomew Lane.

The Old Lady of Threadneedle Street

The old centre of high finance: the Bank of England (left), the Royal Exchange (right), with the Duke of Wellington in the middle

It was founded in 1694 as a private company on the proposal of the Scotsman William Paterson in order to finance the King William's War, the conflict against France in North America. This makes it the world's second-oldest central bank, only the Bank of Sweden being older. The bank issues banknotes and is responsible for monetary policy.

The fact that the nation's gold reserves are stored in its vaults has inspired crime novelists to fictional break-ins, but everything kept here is, needless to say, »as safe as the Bank of England«. Sir John Soane (1753–1837) was the architect of the original, single-storey bank building, which was completed in 1833 and given far-reaching alterations by Sir Herbert Baker from 1924 to 1939. Baker left Soane's façade and Corinthian columns on the south and west fronts untouched but built a new, seven-storey office building behind them.

Bank of England Museum

Admission to the Bank of England Museum (entrance in Bartholomew Lane) is free. Banknotes, coins and a reconstruction of the Stock Office, the banking hall designed by Soane, can be seen inside.
❶ Mon–Fri 10am–5pm; entrance on Bartholomew Lane

*Royal Exchange

With its imposing Corinthian columns the Royal Exchange dominates its surroundings. It was founded by **Sir Thomas Gresham** in 1565 and awarded the title »royal« by Elizabeth I in 1571. A statue at the back of the building and the weather vane in the shape of Gresham's crest, a grasshopper, commemorate the founder. The classical style of the present Royal Exchange, completed in 1844, is the work of Sir William Tite. The first building was destroyed in 1666 during the Great Fire, and in 1838 its successor also burned down. The relief by Sir Richard Westmacott in the tympanum represents »Commerce and the Charter of the Exchange«.

No trading takes place here any more. The broad steps are traditionally the place from which a new monarch is proclaimed. Share trading ceased here in 1939. In the 1980s part of the stock exchange returned, but since a thorough restoration in 2001, this historic exchange has served as an upmarket shopping centre. The London Stock Exchange is now based in Paternoster Square next to St Paul's Cathedral. The equestrian statue of the Duke of Wellington, without stirrups, that stands in front of the Royal Exchange was cast from captured French cannon. Every day at 9am, noon, 3pm and 6pm the **glockenspiel** still plays English, Welsh, Scottish, Canadian and Australian tunes.

Lombard Street

Since the Middle Ages the banking centre of London has been Lombard Street to the right of the Royal Exchange. The street takes its name from money-lenders from Lombardy. The bank signs are a reminder of times past: Illiterates could recognise their bank by its coat of arms, such as the horse of Lloyd's (1677), the three crowns of Coutts, the crown and anchor of the National Westminster Bank, the anchor of Williams and Glyn's, Alexander's artichoke and Barclay's eagle. In 1563 Martins took over the grasshopper emblem from Gresham, who lived here. In 1691 **Lloyd's Coffee-house**, the cradle of Lloyd's of London (▶Leadenhall Market), moved here from Tower Street. The window façade of the coffee house has been reconstructed in the National Maritime Museum in Greenwich. Today a great deal of banking business is not carried out in and around Lombard Street but in the towers of Canary Wharf in Docklands (MARCO POLO Insight p. 184). Although it is not very attractive from the outside, St Mary Woolnoth, (1716–27) at the start of Lombard Street is in fact a Baroque gem. With its blue plasterwork ceiling it is deservedly considered the masterpiece of Nicholas Hawksmoor, a pupil of Wren.

Mansion House, **the official residence of the Lord Mayor of London**, was built in Palladian style by George Dance the Elder between 1739 and 1753. It lies a short distance to the south of Bank station on Mansion Place. Below the Corinthian portico and pediment decorated with scenes of the rise of London, the Lord Mayor stands during official ceremonies. The hour-long tour of the building shows furnished reception rooms, an exquisite collection of Dutch 17th-century paintings (including works by Frans Hals, Jacob van Ruisdael and Jan Steen) and the banqueting hall. Although it is known as the Egyptian Hall, it is modelled not on Egyptian architecture but on the description of an »Egyptian room« in the *Ten Books of Architecture* of the Roman architect and military engineer Vitruvius. Eleven prison cells from the period when Mansion House had the additional function of a court of law can also be seen.

Mansion House

Tour: Tue 2pm; £6

St Stephen Walbrook directly adjoins the south side of Mansion House. It is the Lord Mayor's parish church. During construction of the church between 1672 and 1679, Sir Christopher Wren is thought to have studied the problems of dome-building before he undertook the incomparably larger dome of ▶St Paul's Cathedral. The dome of St Stephen Walbrook, borne by Corinthian columns, rises above an altar made from travertine stone by Henry Moore (1987) and derisively known as »the camembert«. Wren's original pulpit and altar are still in place.

*St Stephen Walbrook

Temple of Mithras   Construction work for the Bucklersbury office block on Queen Victoria Street, which leads south-west from Mansion House, uncovered remains of the Roman Temple of Mithras, which was in use for a period of over 250 years from AD 90. Items found on the site are on view in the ▶Museum of London.

London Stone   The purpose and origin of London Stone on the wall of the building at 111 Cannon Street are not totally clear. Does it represent the »navel of London«? One thing is known for certain: The rebel Jack Cade proclaimed himself »Lord of the City« here in 1450.

British Library

✴ G 3

Location: 96 Euston Road, NW 1
Tube: King's Cross / St Pancras
🕐 Mon–Sat from 9.30am,
Sun 11am–5pm

Admission: free
www.bl.uk

Bibliophiles should not miss the permanent exhibition in the British Library.

The British Library was established in 1972 as a merger of several institutions, first and foremost the library of the British Museum. Bequests by Sir Robert Cotton, Robert Harley, Sir Hans Sloane and Charles Townley, in addition to the Royal Library donated by George II in 1757, formed the basis of the collection; in 1823 George III's library was acquired. Owing to the lack of space in the old premises in the ▶British Museum, a new building designed by Colin St John Wilson was opened in 1997. Today the library's holdings amount to 14 million books. The glass book-tower at the centre accommodates George III's King's Library.

Some of the library's greatest treasures are on show in the ***John Riblat Gallery**: an original of the Magna Carta from 1215, the Lindisfarne Gospels from the early 8th century, a Gutenberg Bible, a Mercator atlas dated 1569, the original manuscripts of Handel's *Messiah* and the Beatles song *Yesterday* in Paul McCartney's hand, Lord Nelson's last letter to Lady Hamilton, notes by Alexander Fleming about the discovery of penicillin, Isaac Newton's first commentaries on gravity and mirror-image notes by Leonardo da Vinci. At the computer terminals visitors can leaf through documents – a treat not to be missed!

Insider Tip

St Pancras Station   While the architecture of the British Library may be politely ignored, this definitely does not apply to the neighbouring St Pancras Station

Luxury hotel connected to a railway station: St Pancras Station

and its luxury hotel, a **cathedral of the railway age** in Gothic Revival style. London's last great railway station, it opened in 1868 along with the hotel designed by George Gilbert Scott. The hotel closed in 1935, but following an expensive restoration its tradition was revived in 2011. To get an impression of its magnificence, pass from the waiting room of St Pancras International station into the hotel bar, which is the old ticket office. Note the capitals of the columns here: They depict neither demons nor acanthus leaves but railway motifs.

** British Museum

✦ G 4

Location: Great Russell Street
Tube: Russell Square,
Goodge Street
Entrances: Great Russell Street,
Montague Place
❶ Daily 10am–5.30pm,
Fri until 8.30pm

Tours:
Tours daily from
11am, »eye opener«
(introduction to a room, 30–40 min),
programme from information desk
and internet
Admission: free
www.britishmuseum.org

Seven million visitors every year make the British Museum one of London's most visited attractions. Its collections rank among the world's finest.

! *»A History of the World ...* Insider Tip

... in 100 Objects« is the title of a highly successful series of BBC radio broadcasts given by Neil MacGregor, director of the British Museum. His choice of exhibits from the museum illustrates the development of human civilisation. The objects are marked in the museum.

They encompass art, monuments and everyday items from Egypt, Assyria, Babylon, Greece, the Roman Empire, the rest of Europe and Asia. In 2004 the ethnographic exhibits from Africa, Oceania and Australia, which had been kept elsewhere for many years due to a shortage of space, returned. The origins of the museum are the medieval manuscripts collected by Sir Robert Cotton (1570–1631), a similar collection owned by Robert Harley, Earl of Oxford (1661–1724) and his son, and above all a bequest by the scientist Sir **Hans Sloane** (1660–1753) that was instrumental in the foundation of the museum by act of parliament in the year of Sloane's death. The money for premises was raised by lottery, and Montague House chosen as the site in 1759. Following the addition of enormous quantities of further items to the collections, it was decided to erect a new building in the classical style. Robert Smirke designed the new museum, which was begun in 1823 and completed in 1843 by his brother Sydney. When the ▶British Library moved out, space became available, particularly in the Great Court. This permitted the return of the ethnographical collections from the Museum of Mankind, which no longer exists.

**Great Court und Reading Room The entrance now leads directly to the Great Court (photo p. 152), which Sir Norman Foster has enclosed with a glass dome. The Great Court contains the famous circular Reading Room where, among others, Karl Marx, George Bernard Shaw and Mahatma Gandhi once worked. Here Foster has created the largest covered square in Europe, a breathtaking architectural space. New galleries, the café and museum shops have been placed around and below the Reading Room, which was completed in 1857 to a design by Sydney Smirke. The Reading Room, now open to visitors, has been restored to its original appearance and is used for special exhibitions, for which admission is usually charged.

OUTSTANDING EXHIBITS

Only a fraction of the collection, currently estimated to contain 8 million items, is on show, and it is quite impossible to visit even this small part in its entirety. The principal rooms are described below. Under the heading »Visiting« the museum website proposes routes with a duration of one hour and three hours.

This extensive gallery is devoted to large-scale Egyptian sculpture. The outstanding items are a colossal bust of Ramses II from West Thebes and the ****Rosetta Stone**. The latter was found in the Nile delta in 1799 by a French officer, Captain Bouchard, and fell into British hands in 1802. The inscription in three languages (Egyptian hieroglyphics in the hieratic and demotic styles and a Greek translation) on this tablet of black basalt dating from 195 BC made it possible to decipher hieroglyphics – a milestone of research into ancient history.

Room 4

Unique treasures of Assyrian civilisation are exhibited in these rooms. Room 10 contains **reliefs from the reign of Assurbanipal depicting a lion hunt**. In the other rooms are reliefs from the palaces of Nimrod and Nineveh, massive winged bulls with human heads from the palace of Sargon in Chorsabad and a black obelisk bearing a description of the deeds of Shalmaneser III.

Rooms 6–10

The Nereid monument (4th century BC) is an impressive example of a tomb from Hellenistic Asia Minor (Lycia).

Room 17

Room 18 contains the famous ****Elgin Marbles**, the sculptures and frieze from the Parthenon in Athens brought to London in the early 19th century by the Earl of Elgin. They include the Horse of Selene from the east pediment of the temple. Selene's triumphal chariot was

Room 18

Powerful: monumental Egyptian sculpture

British Museum

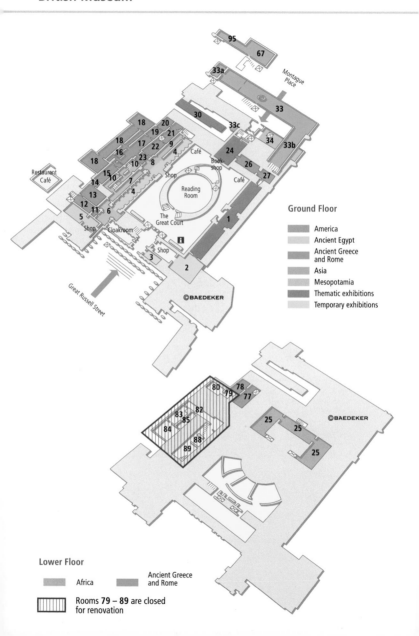

95
67
33a
Montague Place
33
30
33c
18
20
33b
19
21
34
17
9
18
22
16
4
Café
24
18
23
8
Book shop
26
15
10
27
Restaurant Café
14
7
Shop
Café
13
4
Reading Room
12
11
6
1
5
The Great Court
Shop
Cloakroom
ⓘ
3
Shop
2
Great Russell Street
©BAEDEKER

Ground Floor

America
Ancient Egypt
Ancient Greece and Rome
Asia
Mesopotamia
Thematic exhibitions
Temporary exhibitions

80
78
79
77
83
82
85
84
25
25
©BAEDEKER
88
89
25

Lower Floor

Africa
Ancient Greece and Rome

Rooms **79 – 89** are closed for renovation

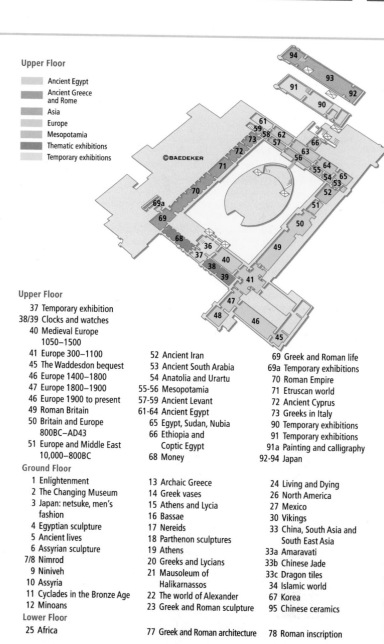

Upper Floor

- Ancient Egypt
- Ancient Greece and Rome
- Asia
- Europe
- Mesopotamia
- Thematic exhibitions
- Temporary exhibitions

©BAEDEKER

Upper Floor

- 37 Temporary exhibition
- 38/39 Clocks and watches
- 40 Medieval Europe 1050–1500
- 41 Europe 300–1100
- 45 The Waddesdon bequest
- 46 Europe 1400–1800
- 47 Europe 1800–1900
- 46 Europe 1900 to present
- 49 Roman Britain
- 50 Britain and Europe 800BC–AD43
- 51 Europe and Middle East 10,000–800BC

Ground Floor

- 1 Enlightenment
- 2 The Changing Museum
- 3 Japan: netsuke, men's fashion
- 4 Egyptian sculpture
- 5 Ancient lives
- 6 Assyrian sculpture
- 7/8 Nimrod
- 9 Niniveh
- 10 Assyria
- 11 Cyclades in the Bronze Age
- 12 Minoans

Lower Floor

- 25 Africa

- 52 Ancient Iran
- 53 Ancient South Arabia
- 54 Anatolia and Urartu
- 55-56 Mesopotamia
- 57-59 Ancient Levant
- 61-64 Ancient Egypt
- 65 Egypt, Sudan, Nubia
- 66 Ethiopia and Coptic Egypt
- 68 Money

- 13 Archaic Greece
- 14 Greek vases
- 15 Athens and Lycia
- 16 Bassae
- 17 Nereids
- 18 Parthenon sculptures
- 19 Athens
- 20 Greeks and Lycians
- 21 Mausoleum of Halikarnassos
- 22 The world of Alexander
- 23 Greek and Roman sculpture

- 77 Greek and Roman architecture

- 69 Greek and Roman life
- 69a Temporary exhibitions
- 70 Roman Empire
- 71 Etruscan world
- 72 Ancient Cyprus
- 73 Greeks in Italy
- 90 Temporary exhibitions
- 91 Temporary exhibitions
- 91a Painting and calligraphy
- 92-94 Japan

- 24 Living and Dying
- 26 North America
- 27 Mexico
- 30 Vikings
- 33 China, South Asia and South East Asia
- 33a Amaravati
- 33b Chinese Jade
- 33c Dragon tiles
- 34 Islamic world
- 67 Korea
- 95 Chinese ceramics

- 78 Roman inscription

originally drawn by four horses. Two of them are in Athens and one has been lost. Most of the surviving parts of the Parthenon frieze are also here.

Rooms 21, 22 These rooms focus on Hellenistic art from Asia Minor, with items from the mausoleum of Halikarnassos and the Temple of Artemis in Ephesos.

Room 40 In Room 40, which is dedicated to the Middle Ages, the **Sutton Hoo hoard** is on display. The ship burial of a 7th-century Anglo-Saxon king (Raedwald or Sigebert) was discovered in Sutton Hoo in Suffolk. It contained weapons, jewellery and coins. A further wonderful treasure in these rooms are the **Lewis Chessmen,** pieces of walrus ivory named after the Hebridean island on which they were found.

Room 49 One of the main attractions in the room devoted to Roman Britain is the Mildenhall Treasure, found during ploughing by a farmer in 1942. It comprises 34 pieces of silver plate from the 4th century AD, including **the Great Dish**, a silver bowl decorated with representations of Bacchus, Hercules and other figures from Greek and Roman mythology. The bearded mask at the centre is probably Oceanus, the god of the sea, surrounded by nymphs. The bronze bust of Emperor Hadrian was salvaged from the Thames.

> **!** MARCO⊕POLO TIP
>
> *Don't miss!* **Insider Tip**
>
> - Rosetta Stone: the deciphering of hieroglyphics
> - Elgin Marbles: sculptures from the Parthenon
> - Lion hunt reliefs from Assyria
> - Lewis Chessmen
> - Reading Room: where Mahatma Gandhi and Karl Marx studied

Room 50 The Lindow Man in room 50 is a 2000-year-old mummy of a man thought to have been ritually killed and buried in a bog in Cheshire after being strangled. His stomach contained seeds of mistletoe, the holy plant of the druids.

Room 56 The theme of this room, Mesopotamia, is illustrated by finds from the royal burial ground at Ur, including the »Royal Game of Ur«.

Rooms 61–63 The famous Egyptian collection places its emphasis on **mummies** and **sarcophaguses**. An exhibit unusual for its form and posture is the mummy of Katebet from the 18th or 19th dynasty.

Rooms 70/71 The life of the Etruscans and ancient Romans is the subject of these two rooms. The Portland Vase, a masterpiece from the 1st century BC named after the dukes of Portland, can be seen here. It is one of the finest known examples of Roman glasswork.

** Buckingham Palace

F 6/7

Location: The Mall, SW 1
Tube: St James's Park, Victoria,
Green Park
❶ late July to early October
daily 9.30am–6.30/7.30pm,
last admission 4.15/5.15pm

Ticket reservation
www.royalcollection.org.uk.or
tel. 020 7766 7300
Admission: £19.75

Buckingham Palace is the London home of the reigning monarch. When the royal standard is flying, the Queen is at home and at her place of work, attended by a staff of more than 300 persons.

However, the palace has been an official residence only since 1837, when Queen Victoria moved here from ▶St James's Palace. It was built on the site of a mulberry orchard laid out for James I and presented to the Duke of Buckingham by Queen Anne. In 1703 the Duke of Buckingham commissioned a plain brick-built house, which King George III bought for his bride Charlotte in 1762. In 1825 George IV gave **John Nash**, his court architect, the task of rebuilding the house, but the costs of the project escalated so much that Nash was dismissed and the work entrusted to Edward Blore, who completed it in 1837. In 1846 the east wing facing ▶The Mall was added, including the balcony from which the royal family wave to the public, and in 1853 the Ball Room, with a length of 36m/120ft then the largest room in London. In 1913 Sir Aston Webb gave the east wing its classical façade. The park of Buckingham Palace is the largest private garden in the city (see MARCO POLO Insight p. 266). The palace is used for receptions and banquets, and is also the place where the Queen and the Duke of Edinburgh have their offices.

Royal residence

In late summer visitors are admitted to 19 of the more than 600 rooms, most of which date from the time of George IV. They include the **Throne Room**, the **State Dining Room** and the remarkably fine private collection in the **art gallery**. The twelve private apartments of the royal family in the north wing remain closed, of course – though visitors would not meet any blue-blooded residents, as the royal family take their holiday at Balmoral Castle in Scotland at this time of year. A break for tea or coffee in the **Garden Café** on the West Terrace is consolation for their absence.

In front of the palace is the Queen Victoria Memorial planned by Sir Aston Webb and executed by Sir Thomas Brock. Queen Victoria, a mother of nine of small stature, is shown surrounded by allegorical figures of Victory, Endurance, Courage, Truth, Justice, Science, Art and Agriculture.

Victoria Monument

London visitors love it: Guards Parade

*Changing of the Guard

▶ MARCO POLO Insight p. 168

For those who arrive in good time, the base of the monument is the best place for watching the Changing of the Guard. At about the same time a squadron of the Household Cavalry coming from changing the guard at Horse Guards (▶Whitehall) rides past the palace on the way to its headquarters in Hyde Park Barracks. Five infantry regiments of the Royal Guard do duty at Buckingham Palace: the Scots Guards (founded in 1642), the Coldstream Guards (1650), the Grenadiers (1656), the Irish Guards (1900) and the Welsh Guards (1913). They all wear the famous bearskin caps and uniforms with scarlet jackets. To learn about their history go to the **Guards Museum** in Wellington Barracks.

Changing of the Guard: May–July daily 11.30am, rest of the year every other day at 11.30am

Guards Museum: Birdcage Walk, daily 10am–4pm, closed mid-Dec to Jan; admission £5; www.theguardsmuseum.com

Queen's Gallery

The Queen's Gallery in Buckingham Palace Road occupies the site of the Queen Victoria Chapel, which was destroyed by a bomb in 1940. Changing exhibitions of items from the extensive royal art collections are shown here.

❶ Daily 10am–5.30pm, last admission 4.30pm; admission £7.50

The Royal Mews, the stables built by John Nash in 1826 at the south corner of Buckingham Palace park, contain an exhibition of the coaches and automobiles of British monarchs, which are still used on special occasions. Pride of place goes to the eight-ton Golden State Coach built in 1762 for George III, which has been used for coronations since 1820. Its harnesses and trappings for eight horses are regarded as the finest in the world. Also on display are the Irish State Coach, bought in 1852 by Queen Victoria and now used for the journey to the opening of Parliament, and the glass coach acquired by George V in 1910, which is used by the bride and groom at royal weddings. Needless to say, Rolls Royces and Bentleys bearing the royal coat of arms, as well as some horses, can also be admired.

*Royal Mews

❶ Apr–Oct daily 11am–5pm, Nov–21 Dec and Feb Mon–Sat 10am–4pm; admission £8.25

* Camden Markets

✳ E / F 2

Location: north-east of Regent's Park
Tube: Camden Town
www.camdenlock.net

Until it was discovered by the hippie and alternative scene, Camden Town was just another London suburb. Today it is a magnet for Londoners and above all tourists, who come in search of exotic items.

The wares in the shops on the High Street, at Camden Market in Buck Street, the Lock Market (on the Regent's Canal), the Canal Market and the Stables Market under the railway arches are often outlandish, in-your-face and reasonably affordable: new and second-hand clothes, shoes and boots, CDs and vinyl records, jewellery and crafts, souvenirs and kitsch, Asian, African and esoteric goods, piercing and tattoos, all the essentials for Goths and punks or for a perfect monster party. In the middle of it all there are considerable numbers of good-quality Asian, African, Caribbean and Arabian food stalls to revive flagging shoppers. Camden markets are an unmissable seven-days-a-week experience, though preferably not at weekends, when the crush is almost unbearable. The Stables Market is well worth seeing and full of atmosphere, as the stands here occupy the old Victorian stables of the hospital for barge horses.

Those who are not in the mood for buying (which is hardly possible here) can watch from the bridge on the Regent's Canal or the patio of the adjacent pub as narrowboats pass through the manually operated

At Regent's Canal

Changing the Guard

Almost every morning at 11.30am, thousands of spectators watch the ceremony of Changing the Guard in front of Buckingham Palace. The five regiments of Royal Foot Guards take turns to provide security for the monarch. At the same time of day, a detachment of the Household Cavalry rides past the palace on its way to Horse Guards.

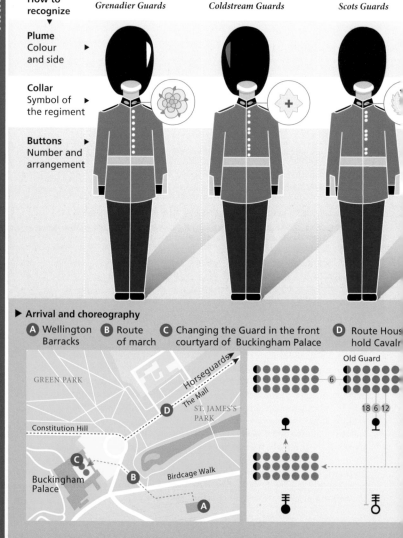

How to recognize ▼	*Grenadier Guards*	*Coldstream Guards*	*Scots Guards*
Plume Colour and side ▶			
Collar Symbol of the regiment ▶			
Buttons Number and arrangement ▶			

▶ **Arrival and choreography**

Ⓐ Wellington Barracks   Ⓑ Route of march   Ⓒ Changing the Guard in the front courtyard of Buckingham Palace   Ⓓ Route Household Cavalry

GREEN PARK

Horseguards

The Mall

ST. JAMES'S PARK

Constitution Hill

Ⓓ

Buckingham Palace

Ⓒ

Ⓑ

Birdcage Walk

Ⓐ

Old Guard

6

18 6 12

Schedule for
Changing the Guard

Irish Guards   *Welsh Guards*

► **The bearskin cap**
Officers' caps are made from
the skin of female North
American brown bears, dyed
black. Caps for rank-and-file
soldiers are made from the
thinner skin of black bears.

Officers

Rank and file

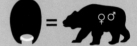

£250–550
680g

45.72 cm/
18 inches

► **Stocks**
In 2009–10 the Royal Foot
Guards used 1900 bearskin caps
according to official figures.
Each is worn for at least 50 years.
39 were restored and 139 new
ones purchased.

⬤ Offiicer of the day

⬤ Relief officer of the day

⬤ Commander of the guard

◑ Commander of the file

● Soldiers of the new guard

◑ Commander of the file

● Soldiers of the old guard

6 Paces / Distance

New Guard

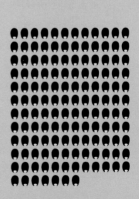

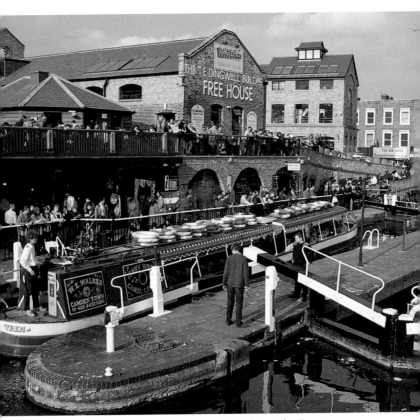

Camden Lock is the heart of the bustle in Camden Town

lock. To take in the activity on along the canal, walk along the tow-path to Regent's Park (about 20 min) and continue from there to Little Venice (a further 30 min).

∗ Chelsea

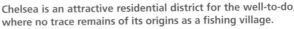 ✦ B – E 8/9

Location: south-west of the city centre
Tube: Sloane Square

Chelsea is an attractive residential district for the well-to-do, where no trace remains of its origins as a fishing village.

Chelsea emerged from centuries of obscurity when it caught the eye of Henry VIII, who chose the area as the site of a country palace, now long gone. Sir Thomas More, who lived here for many years, brought high politics to Chelsea. In later centuries scientists, artists and writers such as Joseph Banks, Algernon Charles Swinburne, Oscar Wilde and Thomas Carlyle followed his example. The quiet atmosphere came to an end in the Sixties and Seventies, when Chelsea was the centre of Swinging London – it was in King's Road that Mary Quant opened her boutique and invented the mini-skirt. Mick Jagger and Keith Richards moved in and, when they got older, Johnny Rotten and Sid Vicious took their place. One celebrity has never left: **James Bond**, whose London address is Royal Avenue, Chelsea.

From a fishing village to a top address

King's Road takes its name from the fact that from 1719 to 1830 it was reserved for the king on his way to Hampton Court or for those in possession of a royal permit. It starts at **Sloane Square,** which is named after Sir Hans Sloane. Here, in the Royal Court Theatre, the premiere of John Osborne's Look Back in Anger was staged in 1956. From Sloane Square the road passes right through Chelsea, bordered by pubs, cafés and shops of every kind, especially fashion and antiques. The most beautiful building on King's Road is **The Pheasantry** (no. 152), dating from 1765. **Chelsea Old Town Hall**, built in 1887, is well-known to antique collectors: The antique and art fairs held here in spring and autumn are among the leading events of this kind in the world. Somewhat further away and actually not in Chelsea, but well worth a detour, is the loveliest Art Nouveau architecture in London, **Michelin House.** This building dated 1911 (corner of Sloane Ave and Fulham Rd) is the home of a top restaurant, Bibendum, an oyster bar and a design store.

King's Road – Memories of Swinging London

A few minutes' walk from Sloane Square, the renowned Saatchi Gallery reopened in October 2008 on King's Road in premises worthy of the collection: the **Duke of York's Headquarters,** which date from 1801 and were once a school for army officers. The gallery is devoted to changing exhibitions of the works of young, less-known artists.

*Saatchi Gallery

❶ Daily 10am–6pm; free admission; www.saatchi-gallery.co.uk

Further along from the Saatchi Gallery, turn left into Cheltenham Terrace, follow it to Franklin's Row and continue to the Chelsea Royal Hospital. Founded in 1682 by Charles II as a home for army veterans, it is home to more than 400 **Chelsea Pensioners.** They are soldiers over the age of 65 who have served for at least 22 years. They still wear the traditional uniform of the Duke of Marlborough's time: scarlet in summer, dark blue in winter, always complemented by a three-cornered hat or a peaked cap and military decorations. The original Royal Hospital building, by Sir Christopher Wren, was ex-

*Chelsea Royal Hospital

These gentlemen are enjoying their retirement in the Chelsea Royal Hospital

tended by Robert Adam from 1765 to 1782; it was finally completed by John Soane in 1819. In the main building the **Great Hall**, the beautifully panelled dining room, is open to visitors. It is adorned with royal portraits, replicas of standards captured in the wars against America and France and a mural depicting Charles II on horseback. The **chapel**, which remains as Wren built it, has a Resurrection done in 1710 by the Italian painter Sebastiano Ricco. A colonnade leads to the Figure Court. The centre of the court is occupied by a bronze statue of Charles II, a masterpiece by Grinling Gibbons which is decorated with a wreath of oak leaves every year on 29 May, the foundation day of the hospital. This is a reference to Charles II's escape from Cromwell's army by hiding in a hollow oak tree. The pensioners receive double pay on this day.

The **museum** in the east wing is devoted to the history of the hospital and its residents.

The **Royal Hospital Gardens** extend to the river Thames. Each year in May they are the venue of the famous Chelsea Flower Show. Some of the cannon on show here were captured from the French at Waterloo.

Lighthouse Court, Great Hall, Museum: Mon–Fri 10am–12 noon, 2–4pm; free admission

National Army Museum

To see where the Chelsea Pensioners risked their lives, go to the National Army Museum in Royal Hospital Road. It is a slightly musty depiction of the history of the British army from 1415 to the present day. Among the curiosities is the **skeleton of Marengo, Napoleon's Arab horse** at the battle of Waterloo.

❶ Daily 10am–5.30pm; free admission; www.nam.ac.uk

Chelsea Physic Garden

Further along Royal Hospital Road on the left lies the Chelsea Physic Garden, founded in 1673 by the Society of Apothecaries for teaching purposes and cultivating medicinal herbs. The first cotton seeds sown in Georgia and the first tea bushes to be planted in India, which had been brought from China to England, came from here. There is a monument in honour of Sir Hans Sloane.

❶ Apr–Oct Mon 9.30am–5pm, Tue–Fri & Sun 11am–6pm, Nov–March daily 9.30am–5pm, admission £9.90; www.chelseaphysicgarden.co.uk

Cheyne Walk

Shortly before the junction of Royal Hospital Road and Chelsea Embankment, Cheyne Walk branches off to the right. The high-class nature of this address is shown by a selection of former and current residents: Keith Richards (no. 3), George Eliot (no. 4), Gabriel Dante Rossetti and Algernon Charles Swinburne (no. 10), James Bond author Ian Fleming (no. 21), Mick Jagger and Marianne Faithfull (no. 48), James McNeill Whistler (no. 101) and J.M.W. Turner (no. 119). Nos. 19–26 was the site of Henry VIII's Tudor palace, built in 1537 and demolished in 1753, where Anne of Cleves, Princess Elizabeth (the future Elizabeth I), Lady Jane Grey and later Sir Hans Sloane lived.

Do not fail to make a short detour to the Thames: From the elegant **Albert Bridge** (1873)), which leads across to **Battersea Park** with its Japanese Peace Pagoda, children's zoo and Pumphouse Gallery, there

A giant structure: Battersea Power Station beyond Battersea Bridge

is a fine view downriver to **Battersea Bridge** (1890) and, on the south bank, a U-shaped building which is the office of the architect Sir Norman Foster. Beyond this are the four towering chimneys of **Battersea Power Station**, which was decommissioned in 1983.

A second detour leads to Cheyne Row and the house (no. 25) of the Scottish writer **Thomas Carlyle** (1795 – 1881).

Carlyle's House: March–Oct Wed–Sun 11am–5pm; admission £5.10

Crosby Hall Cheyne Walk ends at Roper's Garden close to Crosby Hall, the remains of a fine townhouse built by the wool merchant Sir John Crosby on Bishopsgate in the 15th century. Most of it burned down in the 17th century, and the surviving Great Hall was moved here in 1910.

*Chelsea Old Church From here Old Church Street leads back to King's Road. On the right is Chelsea Old Church, a 12th-century foundation extended by **Sir Thomas More** in 1528 through the addition of the More Chapel, in which his first wife is buried. The two Renaissance capitals are said to be the work of his close friend Hans Holbein. In the inscription to be seen in the chapel, More asked to be laid to rest next to his wife – however, after his execution his body was buried in the Tower and his head impaled on London Bridge. There is a plaque to the author Henry James, whose grave is here. The Lawrence Chapel was the scene of the **secret marriage between Henry VIII and Jane Seymour**.

Other notable features are Bernini's monument to Lady Jane Cheyne (1699) on the north wall, the family memorial of the goldsmith Sir Thomas Lawrence in the Lawrence Chapel and the funeral monument of Sarah Colville (1632). The final resting-place of the scientist **Sir Hans Sloane** is the south-east corner of the churchyard by the seated figure of Sir Thomas More.

** Courtauld Institute Gallery

✧ G / H 5

Location: Somerset House, Strand, WC 2
Tube: Temple
❶ Daily 10am–6pm

Admission: £7
(Mon until 2pm free)
www.courtauld.ac.uk

The Courtauld Institute Gallery, one of the world's most exquisite art collections, exhibits paintings belonging to London University. The home of the gallery is Somerset House.

Somerset House previously accommodated the Royal Academy (▶p. 256), the Royal Society and the Society of Antiquaries, and was built for this purpose between 1777 and 1786 by Sir William Chambers on the site of the 16th-century palace of the Lord Protector Duke of Somerset. Chambers designed a building in the Palladian style with its main entrance on the Strand and an imposing, almost 200m/650ft-long façade facing the Thames. For this reason the best view of the building is from Waterloo Bridge. When Somerset House was built, the arcades on Victoria Embankment, intended to be used for market stalls, were from time to time subject to flooding by the Thames; the central arch served as a water gate. In the courtyard concerts are held in summer, and an ice-rink is set up in December and January for skaters. The east wing is occupied by the world-renowned **King's College** of London University.

Somerset House

The core of the gallery, a bequest by Samuel Courtauld (1865–1947), is one of the most important collections of French Impressionist and

Gallery

A highlight at the Courtauld: Manet's *Bar at the Folies Bergères*

post-Impressionist works outside France. Further acquisitions were Lord Lee of Fareham's collection of Italian Renaissance painting and British portraiture, Count Antoine Seilerne's Princes Gate Collection (Renaissance and Baroque), and lastly the Roger Fry Collection of works by British and French artists of the late 19th and early 20th centuries.

European art from 1300 to 1500 is on the ground floor. The rooms on the first floor cover the early Italian Renaissance through to Baroque painting and British portraitists of the 18th century – outstanding works here include *Adam and Eve* by Lucas Cranach the Elder (room 2-1), *The Flight to Egypt* by Jan Brueghel the Elder (room 4), Rubens's designs for the *Deposition* in Antwerp Cathedral (room 3-1), an *Ecce Homo* by Anthon van Eyck (room 3-2) and Goya's *Francisco de Saavedra* (room 4-1). The focal point of the rooms on the upper floor and at the same time the highlight of the gallery are the Impressionist works: Renoir's *La Loge* (room 6), Manet's *Dejeuner sur l'herbe* (room 6) and his famous *Bar at the Folies-Bergère* (room 6), as well as works by Gauguin, Monet, Seurat and van Gogh's *Self-portrait with Bandaged Ear* (room 7). Rooms 10 and 11 are devoted to British and French painting since 1900 respectively.

✶ Covent Garden

✶ G 5

Location: Covent Garden, WC 2
Tube: Covent Garden, Charing Cross, Leicester Square

Covent Garden is one of London's liveliest spots, especially at weekends, when it is a stage for street acrobats and buskers who parade their skills to passers-by.

From a vegetable market to a piazza

The name refers to a medieval »convent garden« granted to John Russell, first Earl of Bedford, by Edward VI. In 1631 the fourth earl commissioned **Inigo Jones** to design buildings for the site. Jones created an Italian piazza. With the exception of St Paul's Church, however, little of this remains today. From 1670 London's flower and vegetable market was situated here. In the 18th century Covent Garden, with its gambling dens, pubs and brothels, was London's main entertainment district. In 1832 the city authorities cleaned up the area and moved the market into the Central Hall; in 1974

! Insider Tip

Frenzy

MARCO ⊕ POLO TIP

To find out what went on in Covent Garden before 1974, watch Alfred Hitchcock's **Frenzy** – a great thriller as well as a source of information. Hitchcock knew the area well: His father was a Covent Garden merchant.

the market moved out again, and cafés and shops took up residence in Central Hall. The **Cabaret Mechanical Theatre** on the lower floor presents all kinds of strange contraptions. In the Jubilee Hall an antiques market is held on Mondays, on other weekdays a general market and at weekends a crafts market. The wholesale market is now held south of the Thames at Nine Elms.

The handsomest barn in the whole of England« was Inigo Jones's verdict on the church opposite Central Hall that he built in 1633: The Earl of Bedford had said »I would have it not much better than a barn«. St Paul's Church is popularly thought to be »back to front«: Jones originally planned to place the altar in the west, but the clergy opposed this solution and he was forced to close off the portico facing the piazza – the place where Professor Higgins first saw Eliza Doolittle – which he had originally planned as the entrance. Access to the church is therefore from the west, which is regarded as the back of the church.

St Paul's Church

The location of St Paul's Church in London's theatre district has made it the actors' church. No place of worship apart from ▶Westminster Abbey and ▶St Paul's Cathedral has so many graves of well-known Londoners of the 18th and 19th centuries, including many actors. In addition to the floral wreaths carved by Grinling Gibbons on the west entrance (1721), it is worth looking at funeral monuments such as those of Gibbons and the painter Sir Peter Lely.

> **MARCO POLO TIP**
>
> ❗ *Bar with a view*   Insider Tip
>
> The terrace on the second-highest storey of the Royal Opera House provides an excellent view over the roofs of London. To reach it, take the escalator from the bar in the Floral Hall (entrance on Bow Street or from the ticket office).

The Royal Opera towers above the north-western side of the square. It originated as the Theatre Royal Covent Garden, founded by John Rich in 1732. The present building was completed in 1856 to designs by E. M. Barry and is the third on the site, its predecessors of 1732 and 1809 having burned down. Today it is the home of the Royal Opera and the Royal Ballet. The restoration of 1999 integrated Barry's Floral Hall, which was conceived as a ballroom and concert hall but let to market traders in 1887 for financial reasons.

*Royal Opera House

The classical main façade of the opera house faces Bow Street, almost exactly opposite the former Bow Street Police Station, where Henry Fielding established London's first police force, the Bow Street Runners, in the 18th century. **Casanova and Oscar Wilde** were among the occupants of its cells (MARCO POLO Insight p. 340).

Bow Street Police Station and Magistrates' Court

London Film Museum	London Film Museum, which features interactive attractions, is privately run and is not restricted to British film but also presents Hollywood blockbusters. ❶ daily 10am–6pm, Sun until 7pm; admission £14.50; www.londonfilmmuseum.com
Theatre Royal Drury Lane	Russell Street leads to the Theatre Royal Drury Lane. From 1663 it was the site of the King's Servants Theatre, where the actress Nell Gwynne, mistress of King Charles II, trod the boards. The original theatre and two successors burned down. The present one was built in 1812 by Benjamin Wyatt. Occasionally a ghost is said to emerge from the wall on the left and hover over the auditorium.
*London Transport Museum	The London Transport Museum in the eastern corner of the piazza, now reorganised after a thorough renovation, tells the story of passenger transport in London. The collection is much more than just a row of old vehicles: Visitors are encouraged to enjoy a hands-on experience, and the exhibition beneath the Victorian arches of the market hall has been equipped with state-of-the-art museum technology. It covers the period from the 19th century to the present. Many different types of the famous red double-deckers are on show, ranging from a horse-drawn bus of 1870 to a 1930s trolleybus, a horse-drawn

Nostalgic buses in London Transport Museum

tram dating from 1882 and an electric tram of 1910. The Tube occupies a prominent place, with a steam locomotive of the Metropolitan Railway, the world's first underground railway, dating from 1866. There is an extensive collection of photos and a famous poster exhibition. Special mention goes to Harry Beck, the creator of the Tube network map, which has remained essentially unchanged to this day.

🕐 Sat–Thu 10am–6pm, Fri 11am–6pm; admission £15; www.ltmuseum.co.uk

✳ **Docklands**

 ✦ **L – N 5 – 7**

Location: East of Tower Bridge

To the east of the City lies London's largest redeveloped area of recent times, the »up-stream docks« of Wapping, Limehouse & Poplar, Surrey Docks, the Isle of Dogs and the Royal Docks, which finally closed in 1981.

They were once the economic heart of the British Empire, a place where goods from all over the world were unloaded. *Baedeker's London and its Environs* reported as follows in 1900:

London Docks, lying to the E. of St Katharine Docks, were constructed in 1805 at a cost of 4,000,000l., and cover an area of 100 acres. They have three entrances from the Thames, and contain water-room for about 400 vessels, exclusive of lighters. Their warehouses can store from 170,000 to 260,000 tons of goods (according to description), and their cellars 121,000 pipes of wine. At times upwards of 3,000 men are employed at these docks in one day. Every morning at 6 o'clock may be seen waiting at the principal entrance a large and motley crowd of labourers … Nothing will convey to the stranger a better idea of the vast activity and stupendous wealth of London than a visit to these warehouses, filled to overflowing with interminable stores of every kind of foreign and colonial products; to these enormous vaults, with their apparently inexhaustible quantities of wine; and to these extensive quays and landing-stages, cumbered with huge stacks of hides, heaps of bales and long rows of casks.

From:
Baedeker's
London and
its Environs,
1900

When the docks moved further downstream, London Docklands lost their purpose, fell into decay and became an area with social problems. From 1981 to 1998 the government authorised the construction of a £25 billion business district with planned employment for 200,000 and housing for 115,000 people. In accordance with the wishes of the then prime minister, Margaret Thatcher, no restrictions were placed on the investors' plans. This gave rise to criticism that the

The DLR is a convenient link to the Docklands

needs of the poor were not considered. After millions of square feet of new office space remained empty, investors turned to housing and retail developments, and life came to the Docklands.

Getting there The **Docklands Light Railway** (DLR) connects Tower Gateway and Bank stations in the City with the Docklands and goes on to ▶Greenwich. The driverless computer-controlled trains move on raised tracks that follow the route of 19th-century railway lines. The Tube (Jubilee Line) also has a Docklands link but the DLR is a pleasanter way to travel. The Docklands can also be reached by water on the Riverbus connection to Canary Wharf Pier run by London Transport.

SURREY DOCKS

Surrey Docks on the south bank of the Thames extend eastwards from ▶Tower Bridge to Greenland Docks in the bend of the river at Rotherhithe. Quays for trade in wood and grain were built on this stretch of the river bank as early as the 14th century. In 1620 the Mayflower left Rotherhithe for Southampton and Plymouth to carry the **pilgrim fathers** to North America.

Butler's Wharf The old warehouses of Butler's Wharf and the Anchor Brewery east of Tower Bridge were among the first properties to be converted to a fashionable residential and business complex. The street Shad Thames behind Butler's Wharf conveys a good impression of how the area used to look.

*Design Museum The Design Museum at the end of Butler's Wharf overlooks the Thames. Here everyday articles from vacuum cleaners to coffee cups and cars have been gathered under one roof. The museum remains open for temporary exhibitions while a move to the former building of the Commonwealth Institute in Kensington, planned for November 2015, is being prepared. From the café terrace there is a wonderful view of ▶Tower Bridge and St Katharine Docks opposite; the museum shop sells all kinds of design in miniature.

❶ Daily 10am–5.45pm; admission £12.40; http://designmuseum.org

Between 1825 and 1843 **Marc Isambard Brunel** built the Thames Tunnel, a technical marvel of its time, to connect Wapping with Surrey Docks. The pumphouse is now a museum. A good place to take a break near the museum is the pub **The Angel** (101 Bermondsey Wall East), which goes back to the 15th century.

Pumphouse Museum

Pumphouse Museum: Daily 10am–5pm; free admission; www.thepumphouse.org.uk

WAPPING, LIMEHOUSE AND POPLAR

Wapping, Limehouse and Poplar docks stretch along the north bank of the Thames from Tower Bridge to the Blackwall Tunnel. They were in use from the 16th century and reached their peak in the 18th and 19th centuries, when the main commodities unloaded here were rice, tobacco and wine. Poverty and a high crime rate were a stark contrast to the hive of commercial activity here: **Execution Dock** in Wapping was the site of the gallows on which many a pirate swung.

St Katharine Docks, on a site where ships had anchored since the 12th century, was opened in late autumn 1827. A number of handsome warehouses such as Ivory House (1852), which was originally used for storing ivory, the harbourmaster's house and the pub **Dickens' Inn** have survived into modern times.

St Katharine's Dock

The upper floors of Tobacco Dock Warehouse, which dates from 1811, were used to store tobacco and sheepskins, the cellars for wine and rum. Nearby the media magnate **Rupert Murdoch** has built the headquarters his company News International, generally known as Fortress Wapping – a glance suffices to understand the nickname. **The Prospect of Whitby** east of Tobacco Dock has been in business since 1502, which makes it probably the oldest pub on the Thames. The stone floor testifies to its early dates.

Tobacco Dock

Near Limehouse Basin, Nicholas Hawksmoor built St Anne's Limehouse church in 1730. The pyramid in the churchyard, sometimes reported to have been intended to top the church tower, is a mystery.

St Anne's Limehouse

One of the few new buildings not lambasted by the architectural critics was the printing works of the Financial Times in Poplar, designed by **Nicholas Grimshaw** and built of glass, steel and aluminium.

Financial Times Printing Press

Docklands

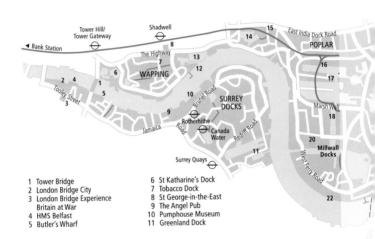

— Docklands Light Railway
⊖ London Underground

1 Tower Bridge
2 London Bridge City
3 London Bridge Experience Britain at War
4 HMS Belfast
5 Butler's Wharf

6 St Katharine's Dock
7 Tobacco Dock
8 St George-in-the-East
9 The Angel Pub
10 Pumphouse Museum
11 Greenland Dock

ISLE OF DOGS

The Isle of Dogs is the area that the docklands redevelopment transformed most fully. The names of the docks, East India and West India Docks, indicate the trade that was carried on here. However, the Isle of Dogs was not only a place for trade in colonial goods. Its quays and manufacturing works made it London's centre of heavy industry in the mid-19th century. The area has now acquired a completely different character as a place for offices and housing with attractive architecture such as The Cascades, a residential development by **Piers Gough**, the South Quay Plaza office complex and John Outram's Pumphouse on Stewart Street, but also controversial new buildings such as Canary Wharf.

*Museum of London Docklands

The buildings in the northernmost of the West India Docks, which date from 1802 and 1803, are the last remaining multi-storey warehouses from the Georgian period. The Museum of London Docklands at no. 1 is devoted to the history of the docks. The atmosphere

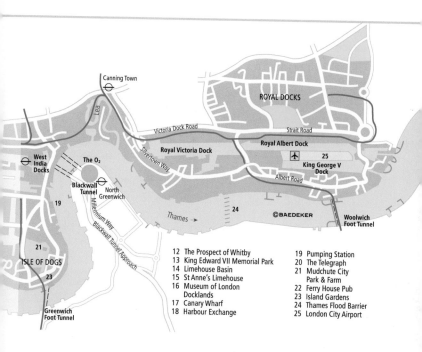

12 The Prospect of Whitby
13 King Edward VII Memorial Park
14 Limehouse Basin
15 St Anne's Limehouse
16 Museum of London
   Docklands
17 Canary Wharf
18 Harbour Exchange

19 Pumping Station
20 The Telegraph
21 Mudchute City
   Park & Farm
22 Ferry House Pub
23 Island Gardens
24 Thames Flood Barrier
25 London City Airport

of the old warehouse and the scenes recreated there give the museum its character. It is superbly equipped with loving attention to detail. Visitors can stroll through the dark alleys of the harbour quarter to the sounds of singing from a pub and the cries of the street hawkers. Children learn how to load a ship and can take an underwater trip wearing a diving helmet.

❶ Daily 10am–6pm; free admission; www.museumoflondon.org.uk/docklands

Tomatoes and bananas from the Canary Islands used to be handled at Canary Wharf. Its redevelopment was the most spectacular of the Docklands projects, with a 244m/800ft-high office block designed by **Cesar Pelli**, until 2012 the tallest building in Britain, towering above it. After its opening, a shortage of tenants gave the tower the nickname London Space Centre – »space« here meaning not the universe but empty office space. In the meantime, the Canary Wharf district has become the city's second thriving **financial centre** alongside the historic City of London.

Canary Wharf

A Centre of World Finance

In 1571 Queen Elizabeth I ceremoniously opened the Royal Exchange, which today under the name London Stock Exchange (SE) is among the world's leading places for trading. At the London Metal Exchange the world market price for gold has been fixed since 1919. The big investment banks, however, have mostly moved out of the City to Canary Wharf. More than 300,000 people work in finance in London, almost as many as in New York and almost five times as many as in Frankfurt.

Main exchanges
trade volume
(billion US dollars)

NYSE Euronext US (New York)
13 700

NASDAQ (New York)
OMX US
9585

equals a
trade volume
of **10 billion $**

▶ **Trading volume fluctuates greatly**
The graph shows volumes of trade, which are subject to enormous fluctuation: if a share is bought and sold several times, its purchase price enters the trading statistic every time.

Toronto, Canada
Boston, USA
New York, USA
London, UK
Geneva, Switzerland
Zurich, Switzerland

Trading volume of the most important international exchanges (billion US dollars)

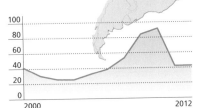

100
80
60
40
20
0
2000
2012

The GFCI-Ranking

The Global Financial Centres Index is an important method of evaluation for observers of stock exchanges. It compares the competitiveness of the world's leading places for trading. In addition to economic data on the country concerned, it takes account of the level of education and training, the availability of employment, and political criteria. This ranking produces different results from lists according to the volume of trade.

▶ **Important finance centres GFCI rank (points)**

1 New York	786
2 London	784
3 Hong Kong	761
4 Singapore	751
5 Zurich	730
6 Tokyo	722
7 Seoul	718
8 Boston	715
9 Geneva	713
11 Frankfurt am Main	709
14 Toronto	651

Japan Exchange Group (Tokyo)
6516

Shenzhen Stock Exchange
3911

Shanghai Stock Exchange
3785

London Stock Exchange Group
2315

NYSE Euronext Europe
1722

Deutsche Börse (Frankfurt)
1383

Korea Exchange (Seoul)
1334

TMX Group (Toronto)
1333

Frankfurt, Germany

Shanghai, China

Seoul, South Korea

ong Kong/Shenzhen, China

Singapore

Tokyo, Japan

▶ **Highly concentrated**
The world's leading trading places are in Europe, North America and Asia. The Middle East, Africa and South America have no globally significant financial centre.

Hardly anything remains of the old docks. Today Canary Wharf is a site for the dealings of international finance

Millwall Docks Two buildings stand out at Millwall Dock: the steel-and-glass construction of South Quay Plaza and Harbour Exchange. The London Arena is a multi-purpose hall seating 12,000 people.

Mudchute Park & Farm For those who are in this area with children, it is worth paying a visit to Mudchute Park & City Farm, where there are lots of animals and places to have a picnic in leafy surroundings.

❶ Farm Tue–Sun 9am–5pm, park daily; free admission; www.mudchute.org.

ROYAL DOCKS

The Royal Docks occupy an area to the east of the river Lea. In 1855 Victoria Dock was opened. Albert Dock followed in 1880. The chemical, cable manufacturing and food industries set up here, but progress had its price: In January 1917 an explosion in a TNT factory killed 73 people. In 1922 the last of the large docks, King George V Dock, went into service. Since 1987 London City Airport has been in operation on the site.

✳ THAMES BARRIER

On 8 May 1984 the world's largest moving flood barrier, 520m/570yds wide, went into operation in the Thames. Nine piers support a steel barrier consisting of ten enormous gates. It takes about half an hour for the hydraulic arms to lift the gates into position. This protects large areas of the counties of Essex and Kent from flooding. In the visitor centre there is an excellent audio-visual show about the construction and the working of the barrier. Boat trips run by Thames River Services leave from Greenwich Pier for the barrier gates.

❶ Woolwich, SE 18; DLR: Pontoon Dock; Thu–Sun 10.30am–5pm; admission £3.75; Thames River Services tel. 020 7930 4097

Some distance to the south-east of the barrier is the Royal Arsenal, where the Royal Artillery Museum is located.

Royal Artillery Museum

❶ North Greenwich, then bus 161, 422, 472 to Woolwich; Tue–Sat 10.00am–5pm; admission £5.30; www.firepower.org.uk

Dulwich

✳ **Outer suburb**

Location: Southwark, SE 21 / SE 22
Tube: Brixton
Train: West Dulwich from Victoria,

North Dulwich from London Bridge

No more than six miles south of the centre of London, the scene changes abruptly to the village atmosphere of Dulwich, the site of lovely Georgian houses, London's only surviving customs barrier and Dulwich College.

The college was officially founded in 1619 by **Edward Alleyn** (1566–1626), a wealthy Shakespearean actor and a bold bear-baiter, as the College of God's Gift for »six poor men and six poor women«. In fact he had already acquired Dulwich Manor and begun building work in 1605.

Dulwich College

The gallery possesses **one of the most important collections of Old Master paintings** in Europe. The basis of its holdings were the collection of the art dealers Noël Desenfans and Francis Bourgeois, who had not intended to amass these treasures: Between 1790 and 1795 they bought art all over Europe for King Stanislaus II of Poland, who wanted a picture gallery worthy of his court. However, after the Third Partition of Poland, his kingdom no longer existed. Following the death of Desenfans in 1807, Bourgeois donated the paintings to Dulwich College, on whose grounds London's first public art gallery

*Dulwich Picture Gallery

opened in 1814 in a building designed by Sir John Soane. Through its placement of skylights, it was to be a model for the architecture of many later galleries.

The works on display include paintings by Rembrandt, Jan van Ruisdael and Aelbert Cuyp, British 17th- and 18th-century portraits by, among others, Sir Peter Lely, Sir Godfrey Kneller, William Hogarth, Thomas Gainsborough and Sir Joshua Reynolds, paintings by Italian masters (including Raphael, Paolo Veronese, Guercino, Canaletto, Tiepolo), among them the oldest work in the collection, Piero de Cosimo's *Portrait of a Young Man* from 1500, works by Flemish artists (Rubens, van Dyck, David Teniers), Spanish masters (Bartolomé Murillo among others) and French painters (Watteau, Poussin and Le Brun). Desenfans and Bourgeois are buried in the so-called Mausoleum, surrounded by their treasures; the pictures are hung close together in the 19th-century fashion. Those who visit the chapel on a Tuesday afternoon (and only then) should take a look from the cloister to see whether **Christ's Chapel of God's Gift** is open. Edward Alleyn is buried there, and on the north wall hangs a copy of Raphael's *Transfiguration of Christ* by one of his pupils.

❶ Gallery Road; Tue–Fri 10am–5pm, Sat–Sun 11am–5pm; admission £6; www.dulwichpicturegallery.org.uk

Crystal Palace Park Crystal Palace Park (train from Victoria Station) was the site of the Crystal Palace, the focal point of the Great Exhibition of 1851, Sir Joseph Paxton's masterpiece of wrought iron and steel. In 1854 the palace was brought here from Hyde Park and remained a popular attraction until it was destroyed by fire in 1936. A model in the ▶Museum of London shows what it looked like, and some scanty remains are displayed in the **Crystal Palace Museum**. The site of the Crystal Palace is now the National Sports Centre and a park in which 33 life-size plaster casts of prehistoric animals were placed under the direction of Richard Owen, who coined the term »dinosaur«.

❶ Train: Crystal Palace from London Bridge or Victoria.
Crystal Palace Museum: Anerley Hill: Sat–Sun 11am–3.30pm; free admission; www.crystalpalacemuseum.org.uk

Fleet Street

✳ H 5

Location: Between Temple Bar and Ludgate Circus
Tube: Blackfriars, Temple

»Fleet Street«, once the »Street of Ink«, is no longer a synonym for the press, as most newspaper publishers have moved out, for example to the ▶Docklands.

Fleet Street, a main thoroughfare of the City of London, takes its name from the little river Fleet, down which the bloody effluent from Smithfield Market once flowed into the Thames. It was covered over in the mid-18th century after a drunken butcher fell in and froze to death. In the late 15th century **Wynkyn de Worde** moved his printing press here from Westminster. In 1702 the Daily Courant was the first daily newspaper to be published, and Fleet Street became the centre of British newspaper publishing. The buildings in which newspaper publishers, their editors and printers once worked are still standing, but they have been taken over by insurance companies and brokers. Reminders of its golden age as the heart of the newspaper business are the Daily Mail building between Bouverie and Whitefriars Street, the Daily Mirror building on Fetter Lane, the Daily Express building at the corner of Shoe Lane and no. 135 Fleet Street, the Daily Telegraph building. No. 85 is still the address of Reuters. Today Fleet Street is increasingly a symbol for English justice, as it is in the orbit of the Inns of Courts in ▶The Temple and the Royal Courts of Justice on ▶The Strand.

»Street of Ink«

? MARCO ● POLO INSIGHT **Did you know**

... that the first water-flushed toilet for gentlemen in Britain was opened on 2 February 1852 in Fleet Street? Ladies had to wait more than a week longer: Their water closet was inaugurated on 11 February in Bedford Street close to Covent Garden.

Temple Bar Memorial, erected in 1880 at the boundary between the City and Westminster and crowned by a griffin, marks the beginning of Fleet Street. Temple Bar, a gate built by Wren in 1680 upon which the heads of decapitated persons were placed on spikes, once stood here. The gate has now been re-erected in Paternoster Square north of ▶St Paul's. When the monarch pays a formal visit to the City, he or she is still obliged to request permission to enter from the Lord Mayor at Temple Bar. The entrance to the ▶Temple is here.

Temple Bar

Child's Bank, the oldest bank in London, was founded in 1671 »at the sign of the marigold« at no.1 Fleet Street, now the Bank of Scotland.

Child's Bank

The house at no. 17, opposite Chancery Lane, is one of the few buildings that survived the Great Fire of 1666. It was constructed in 1610 on the site of a house that went back to the 12th century. Inside is Prince Henry's Room with a wooden ceiling, the centre of which bears the coat of arms of Henry, Prince of Wales and son of James I (not open to the public at present).

Prince Henry's Room

St Dunstan-in-the-West on the opposite side of the road (no. 186a) is named after St Dunstan (909–988), bishop of London. The church

St Dunstan-in-the-West

All media institutions have left Fleet Street. Paul Julius Reuter, founder of the famous news agency, remains

existed in the 11th century and survived the Great Fire, but was re-built in 1831, when the clock dating from 1671, whose bell is tolled by two giants, was re-installed; it was the first church clock in London that struck the quarter hours. The oldest remaining statue of Elizabeth I (1586) can be seen on the south wall.

The pub Ye Olde Cheshire Cheese (no. 145) is easy to miss, as its entrance lies in the narrow passage Cheshire Court, but it is worth keeping an eye open for the tavern, which was rebuilt after the Great Fire and frequented by many notable writers, including Samuel Johnson, Charles Dickens and Arthur Conan Doyle. The atmosphere in the dimly lit pub and its historical associations make it a good place to take a break.

Ye Olde Cheshire Cheese

Samuel Johnson did not have far to go for a drink, as he lived on Gough Square, a little further north from (via Fetter Lane and W. Harding St) 1748 to 1759. One of the works he wrote here was his famous dictionary

Dr. Johnson's House

❶ May–Sept Mon–Sat 11am–5.30pm, Oct–April until 5pm; admission £4.50

St Bride's is the parish church of the newspaper business. It was first mentioned in the 12th century; the present church was rebuilt in 1957 to Wren's original designs after his building of 1701 burned out in the Second World War.
At 70m/230ft the tower of St Bride's is the tallest of any Wren church, supposedly prompting London confectioners to use it as the model for their wedding cakes. The church contains memorial plaques to a number of celebrities from the worlds of the press, art and literature. A Roman floor can still be viewed in the museum in the crypt, where there is an exhibition about the history of the church and its connections to the newspaper and printing trades: Wynkyn de Worde operated his printing press on this site.

St Bride's

The Old Bailey, or Central Criminal Courts as they are officially called, were built between 1902 and 1907 and take their popular name from the street on which they are sited. As is only right and proper for a court of law, the dome of the building is crowned by a bronze figure of Justice with a sword and scales – but closer inspection reveals that she is not blindfold, as she usually is. Members of the public can watch proceedings from the gallery. Bags, cameras and mobile phones are not allowed inside the building, but can be left for safe-keeping in the pub opposite. From the 13th century London's main jail, the infamous **Newgate Prison**, stood on this site. From 1783 to 1868 criminals were publicly executed in front of the prison, a spectacle that unfailingly brought good business to the landlord of the now-demolished Magpie and Stump opposite. On such days he added a special »execution breakfast« to the menu. Close by in **St Sepulchre Church** a handbell is on show: the »execution bell« that tolled the last hour of the condemned.

Detour to the Old Bailey

Public gallery: Mon–Fri 10am–1pm, 2pm–5pm

Gray's Inn

✦ H 4

Location: Gray's Inn Road, WC 2
Tube: Chancery Lane

Gray's Inn is one London's four legal schools (Inns of Court). The other three are Middle Temple and Inner Temple, situated in the ►Temple, and ►Lincoln's Inn.

Gray's Inn is thought to have existed since the 14th century. Its name derives from the former owners of the estate, the Lords de Gray. The main entrance is on High Holborn beneath a 17th-century arch next to the Cittie of Yorke pub. The interior of Gray's Inn, including the Great Hall, in which Shakespeare's Comedy of Errors was first performed in 1594, is open to the public only during the London Open House Weekend (►p. 92). Otherwise visits are limited to a walk around the garden, once a popular place for duelling, and a look at South Square with its statue of the philosopher and statesman Francis Bacon, the most famous member of Gray's Inn, who lived here from 1576 to 1626. The garden is open at midday.

*Staple Inn Opposite the junction of Gray's Inn Road with High Holborn is Staple Inn. It was once the home and business premises of wool merchants and later served as student accommodation for future barristers of Gray's Inn. As it stands today, the inn was built in 1586 and is the only surviving **Elizabethan timber-framed structure** in London.

✳✳ Greenwich

✦ Outer suburb

Location: East of the city centre
River Bus: Greenwich Pier
DLR: Cutty Sark, Greenwich

www.rmg.co.uk
www.visitgreenwich.org.uk

Greenwich, situated on the south bank of the Thames about 10km/6 miles from Tower Bridge, is one of the most charming parts of London, a place of pilgrimage for everyone who wants to study the history of seafaring at first hand and also an area of wonderful parks and architecture.

Greenwich is the birthplace of British sea power. Warships were built here in the reign of Henry VIII, and officers of the Royal Navy were trained here. Greenwich became world-famous for its observatory,

The figurehead of the *Cutty Sark* illustrates Robert Burns's poem Tam O'Shanter

traditionally the lodestar of navigation for sailors from the West, as the world's shipping is governed by Greenwich time and the **zero meridian** was fixed here. »Maritime Greenwich« in its entirety was declared a World Heritage site by UNESCO.

The new visitor centre, Discover Greenwich, in the Pepys Building next to the Cutty Sark provides a first orientation on these subjects. As well as being a ticket and souvenir shop and providing information, it has an exhibition on the history of maritime Greenwich, in which finds from the excavation of Henry VIII's palace and personal items belonging to this king are on display. The Greenwich Meridian is illuminated on a large model of the city.

Discover Greenwich Centre

★★ CUTTY SARK
🕐 Tue–Sun 10am–5pm; admission £13.50; bookings at www.rmg.co.uk/ cuttysark or tel. 0044 20 8312 6608; admission by timed ticket only

The Cutty Sark was the last and most famous of the tea clippers that plied the »tea road« between England and China in the 19th century (►MARCO POLO Insight p. 196). It was built in Dumbarton in Scotland in 1869 and was regarded not only as the most beautiful, but also, with its top speed of over 17 knots, as the fastest ship of its day – in 1871 it took only 107 days from Shanghai to London, and in 1889 on a voyage to Sydney it overtook the new steamship Britannia.

It was not taken out of service until 1954. The name, meaning »short shirt«, comes from Robert Burns's poem Tam O'Shanter, which describes how the witch Nannie pulls the tail from Tam's grey mare, as shown on the ship's figurehead. In 2007 a devastating fire destroyed much of the ship, but fortunately the masts, figurehead and other items had been removed for restoration. Following reconstruction work, the Queen herself reopened the Cutty Sark in 2012. The ship is now raised above the ground on supports so that the elegant form of its hull can be admired from below. The exhibition on board tells the story of the ship and the tea trade, with mementoes of voyages to China, Ceylon and India.

✹✹ ROYAL NAVAL COLLEGE

❶ Buildings daily 10am–5pm, grounds 8am–6pm; free admission

Former college for British naval officers

The Royal Naval College in the former Greenwich Hospital was the place of training for naval officers. Edward I (1272–1307) had a palace built here. In 1428 the Duke of Gloucester chose the site for his Bella Palace, which Henry VII in turn converted into Placentia Palace. This royal residence and Greenwich had strong connections to **Henry VIII:** He was born here, and for 20 years he ruled from here; here he married Catherine of Aragon and Anne of Cleves, here he signed Anne Boleyn's death warrant. His daughters, Mary I and Elizabeth I, were also born in the palace. Henry ordered the construction of shipyards in Greenwich and in 1512 watched the launch here of the first English four-master, Great Harry. Under Oliver Cromwell the palace was used as a prison and then demolished.

From 1696 it was replaced by the **King William Building** (the southwest side) and the **Queen Mary Building** (the south-east side), which housed a sailors' home founded by Queen Mary II in 1694.

> ! **MARCO ⊕ POLO TIP**
>
> *To and from Greenwich* **Insider Tip**
>
> To make an enjoyable event of the journey to Greenwich, take the DLR to Island Gardens and walk under the Thames through the Greenwich Foot Tunnel of 1902 (but first admire the view which Canaletto painted of the Royal Naval College from the river bank). Return by River Bus to the Tower or Westminster.

These buildings, designed by Sir Christopher Wren but not completed until 1751, were constructed around parts of a new palace for Charles II, begun by John Webb in 1664 but abandoned owing to shortage of money. The public have access to only two rooms. The **Painted Hall** in the King William Building, was completed in 1707 and decorated in the years to 1727 by Sir James Thornhill with the paintings to which it owes its name. The ceiling celebrates William of Orange and Mary as peace-makers, triumphing over tyranny in the person of Louis XIV. In the south-west corner there is a portrait of the Royal Astronomer **John Flamsteed**. The **chapel of the Queen Mary Building** was also built to designs by Wren, but not completed until 1752 by Thomas Ripley. »Athenian« Stuart restored it after a fire in 1779. Benjamin West's altarpiece depicts the shipwreck of St Paul.

✱✱ NATIONAL MARITIME MUSEUM

ⓘ Daily 10am–5pm; free admission; www.rmg.co.uk

The National Maritime Museum is probably the world's largest museum of ships and navigation. Its extremely impressive exhibits tell the story of British sea power since Henry VIII's time. The collections are housed in the west wing of the Queen's House, which was added between 1805 and 1816. Until 1933 the west and east wings were occupied by the Royal Hospital School for sailors' sons. The museum opened in 1937. The Queen's House and Royal Observatory are also part of the National Maritime Museum.

In the National Maritime Museum

Monarchs of the Ocean

Tea clippers, the fastest vessels of their day, transported goods between China and London. The merchants who could deliver the first fresh tea of the season made a handsome profit. This was the origin of the legendary tea races. In 1866 the Fiery Cross, Ariel, Taeping and Serica competed. Taeping won after 120 days with a lead of only 20 minutes. The Cutty Sark, shown here, never won a tea race but was regarded as the fastest ship of its class in 1885.

Foremast

▶ **»Cutty Sark«**

Date of launch	23 Nov 1869
Length	85.35m/280ft
Width	10.97m/36ft
Laden weight	2747 t
Crew	28 – 35
Sails	43
Mast height	46.3m/152ft

Top speed
17.15 knots (20mph)

Cargo capacity 1700 t
equals approx. 240 elephants

Surface of sails 3000m²
equals approx. half a football pitch

Fore Royal

Fore Topgallant

Fore Upper Topsail

Fore Lower Topsail

Fore Course

Jib

▶ **Bigger and bigger, faster and faster**
Classes of historic trading ships

Cog (approx. 24m/80ft)
Typical northern European
trading vessel, especially
between the 12th and
14th centuries

Fluyt (approx. 50m/165ft)
Dutch ship, used for the
colonial trade in the
18th century

Clipper (approx. 85m/280ft)
The biggest and fastest
wooden sailing ships ever built,
especially in the 19th century

Main mast

Mizzen mast

Main Royal

Mizzen Royal

Main Topgallant

Mizzen Topgallant

Main Upper Topsail

Mizzen Upper Topsail

Jigger

Main Lower Topsail

Mizzen Lower Topsail

Main Course

Mizzen Course

▶ Halfway round the world
The tea clippers' route

London

Fuzhou, China

Sydney, Australia

London–Fuzhou approx. 26,400 km/16,400mi
London–Sydney approx. 22,200 km/13,800mi
Sydney–London approx. 23,700 km/14,700mi

▶ All kinds of cargo
As well as tea, clippers transported mail, spices, ice – and even slaves.

Tea	Fruit
Spices	Ice
Wool	Mail
Opium	Slaves

▶**Full-rigged ships**
The tea clippers were full-rigged ships. This means that they had at least three square-rigged masts attached to lateral beams.

©BAEDEKER

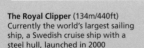

The Royal Clipper (134m/440ft)
Currently the world's largest sailing ship, a Swedish cruise ship with a steel hull, launched in 2000

Container ship (up to 397m/1300ft)
Can carry up to 11,000
6m/20ft-long containers

The Sammy Ofer Wing opened in 2012 with a new main entrance, café, museum shop, archive and Compass Lounge, which allows visitors to explore the museum interactively. This wing introduces the section of the museum entitled **»Voyagers: Britons and the Sea«** on the relationship of the British to the sea, including personal stories. Original exhibits are complemented by the Horizon Screen, a 20m/70ft-long, wave-shaped surface for projecting films and images.

Ground floor   The old part of the ground floor takes up the themes of London's role as a port since 1700 and the life of England's greatest naval hero, Admiral **Horatio Nelson**. The numerous mementoes of Nelson on display include the uniform he was wearing when he died at the Battle of Trafalgar. The magnificent state barge built in 1732 for Frederick, Prince of Wales is also on display. A further section is devoted to the discovery of America and the exploration of the North-West Passage.

On the **first floor** subjects are arranged geographically. Trade with Asia, which was mainly conducted by the East India Company, is explained with the help of superb model ships, sailors' diaries, portraits, navigational instruments and products from the Far East such as Japanese and Chinese swords. The section about the Atlantic trade and slavery is presented with many works of art, marine charts and traded goods from the New and the Old World.

On the **second floor** a particularly fine section is devoted to the construction of warships from 1650 to 1815: Every ship in the English fleet started as a model that had to be presented to the Admiralty; the collection contains a large number of these original models. The model-makers' attention to detail is astonishing. The two remaining

Greenwich

Foot Tunnel
Thames
Trafalgar Tavern
Trinity Hospital
GREENWICH MERIDIAN
Hoskins
Greenwich Pier
Royal Naval College
Queen Mary's Building
Greenwich Park Road St.
Cutty Sark
King William's Building
Discover Greenwich
Trafalgar
Dreadnought Library
Romney Rd.
Vista
Greenwich Market
National Maritime Museum
Queen's House
Park
St Alphege
Greenwich Theatre
Greenwich
PRIME MERIDIAN
Fan Museum
Park
©BAEDEKER
Burney St.
Crooms Hill
King William Walk

200 m
600 ft

1 3
2 4
Royal Observatory
5
7
6
8

1 Flamsteed House
2 Flamsteed's Observatory
3 Meridian Building
4 Great Equatorial Building
5 Altazimuth Pavilion
6 South Building
7 Tea House
8 Conduit House

sections allow visitors to make discoveries for themselves: Children can find out about life at sea, and the Ship Simulator shows what it is like to pilot a large vessel into harbour.

** QUEEN'S HOUSE
❶ daily 10am – 5pm; free admission

The Queen's House by **Inigo Jones**, a building that inspired the architecture of many other houses but was never surpassed, is a masterpiece of the Palladian style in its symmetry, proportions and the superb quality of its marble floors, wrought-iron balustrades, and carved and painted ceilings. In 1616 Jones was commissioned to build an annexe to Placentia Palace by James I, who wanted a house in Greenwich fit for his queen, Anne of Denmark. James abandoned the project after Anne's death in 1619, but in 1629 Charles I gave Jones the task of completing it for his wife, Henrietta Maria. The cube-shaped Great Hall represents authentic Palladian style. From here Inigo Jones' **Tulip Staircase** wonderful Tulip Staircase, the first winding staircase in England without a central support, leads to the upper floor with the King's Apartment, which was never occupied, and the Queen's Apartment, which was at least used for a few years. Another very beautiful staircase leads down to the Orangery.

> **MARCO POLO TIP**
>
> **?** Don't miss   Insider Tip
>
> - State barge for Frederick, Prince of Wales
> - Mementos of Lord Nelson
> - Model ships made for the Admiralty
> - Virtual ship's bridge
> - Children's department
> - Marine paintings in the Queen's House

The National Maritime Museum possesses the **world's largest collection of marine painting**, including maritime scenes by such artists as van de Velde, Turner and Muirhead Bone as well as portraits of famous seamen by equally famous artists: Kneller, Lely, Hogarth, Reynolds, Gainsborough and Romney. Changing selections from the collection are presented in the Queen's House.

Marine painting

** GREENWICH PARK

Next to the grounds of the National Maritime Museum is Greenwich Park, created as a royal garden for Charles II by Le Nôtre, Louis XIV's landscape gardener, around the hill that served as a camp for a Danish army in the 11th century and on which today the Royal Observatory stands.

A place for recreation

From the Old Royal Observatory, the view takes in the Queen's
House and the Royal Naval College with the skyscrapers of Canary
Wharf in the background

****Old Royal
Observatory**

Flamsteed House, designed by Sir Christopher Wren and named
after the first royal astronomer, John Flamsteed, occupies an impressive site at the top of the hill. There is a wonderful view of the Queen's
House and Royal Naval College with the bend of the Thames and the
▶Docklands in the background; further right is The O2 (formerly the
Millennium Dome). Flamsteed House Until 1957 Flamsteed House
was the home of the Royal Observatory, which Charles II founded in
1675. A mast on the turret bears the time ball, a red sphere that since
1833 has dropped every day at 1pm as a signal for ships on the
Thames to set their clocks. **Time and navigation** are the guiding

themes of the exhibition in Flamsteed House, where four rooms are still furnished as they were in Flamsteed's time. The collection of historic instruments includes three **original Harrison chronometers**, the first chronometers which worked so precisely that they could be used for navigation at sea. The problem of determining longitude, for the solution of which the Admiralty established a prize of £20,000 in 1714, is explained for visitors.

The solution was to **define a zero (prime) meridian**. The British Admiralty naturally fixed its prime meridian on home territory, and so the zero line runs through the **Meridian Building** and divides the world into a western and an eastern hemisphere. To pass from one hemisphere to another, just walk across the steel strip in the ground. The exhibition inside the building contains among other items the Transit Circle, a large instrument designed by the seventh royal astronomer, George Bidell Airy, who used it in 1851 to calculate the position of the prime meridian even more exactly than before. The meridian received international recognition at a conference in Washington DC in 1884. A dome built for a 28-inch telescope installed in 1893, the largest in Great Britain, is the dominant feature of the **Equatorial Building**. The **Azimuth Pavilion** behind it was built in 1899 and now holds a telescope for observing the sun.

London's only public planetarium, the new and highly modern **Peter Harrison Planetarium**, adjoins the pavilion.

Flamsteed House: daily 10am–5pm; admission £7

Peter Harrison Planetarium: shows Mon–Fri from 12.45pm, Sat and Sun from 11am; admission £6.50

> **MARCO POLO TIP**
>
> *Trafalgar Tavern* Insider Tip
>
> The Trafalgar Tavern (along the bank of the Thames from the Cutty Sark) is an excellent place for a rest. At high tide the river splashes round the picture window. The pub has changed little since it opened in 1837. Dickens, who like prime ministers Gladstone and Disraeli came here often, chose it as the scene for a wedding party in *Our Mutual Friend*. The British cabinet once regularly met in the Nelson Room on the upper floor to dine on whiting.

Ranger's House

A new attraction for visitors to the Ranger's House, built in 1688 in the south-east corner of the park, is the **Wernher Collection**, a famous collection of jewellery and gems from the Middle Ages to the Renaissance that belonged to the diamond dealer Sir Julius Wernher (1850–1912).

❶ April–Sept Mon–Wed guided tours only 11.30am and 2.30pm, Sun 10am–5pm; admission £6.70

VILLAGE OF GREENWICH

Greenwich Market
The first place to go in the village is Greenwich Market, a fine old market hall where arts and crafts are the main items on sale.

St Alfege
St Alfege's Church was built in 1718 by Nicholas Hawksmoor to replace an older church where Henry VIII was baptised and which stood on the site where Danes murdered St Alfege in 1012. The present church retains some of Grinling Gibbons's wall decoration.

Fan Museum
The Fan Museum (no. 12 Croom's Hill) presents over 3500 fans from the 11th century to the present day, most of them dating from the 18th and 19th centuries.
❶ 12 Croom's Hill; Tue–Sat 11am–5pm, Sun noon–5pm; admission £3

THE O2 (FORMERLY MILLENNIUM DOME)
River Bus: North Greenwich Pier
Tube: North Greenwich, www.theo2.co.uk

At the turn of the millennium the wish to express British national pride through architecture was given a new manifestation: the Millennium Dome, planned as a high-tech showcase for a confident nation. A top architect, **Richard Rogers**, sited the world's largest tent on industrial wasteland in northern Greenwich that had previously been contaminated by heavy metals. The 50m/165ft-high Teflon roof of the tent, which has a diameter of 365m/2000ft, is held in place by twelve masts, each 100m/330ft in height. The structure holds 35,000 people, and ▶Wembley Stadium can be fitted into it twice over. A

Once Millennium Dome, now O2

second British star architect, **Norman Foster**, designed North Greenwich Tube station, which is also the largest in the world. Most of the costs of the dome, which totalled £758 million, were raised by a lottery and by private sponsorship, and the rest was intended to come from admission fees. However, the expected stream of visitors failed to materialise. Ambitious plans for later use of the dome came to nothing and potential buyers pulled out.

Since 2007 it has successfully been put to new uses under the name »The O2«. Its 23,000-seater arena is a venue for concert and other events. The tent also accommodates restaurants, a music club, cinema and exhibition space. During the 2012 Olympic Games it was the venue for the gymnastics and basketball competitions.

* Guildhall

J 5

Location: Gresham Street, EC 2
Tube: St Paul's, Bank
❶ Enquiries tel. 7 606 3030
Tours: (£6) Once per month for the
meeting of the Court of Common

Council; booking
required at
info@cityoflondontouristguides.com

From the 12th century, Guildhall was the seat of the Corporation of London (▸MARCO POLO Insight p. 204), which pursued policies against the interests of the monarch in Westminster. This age is long past, but the old power base of the City still plays an important role in the traditions and ceremonies of London.

Guildhall is a late Gothic building that dates back to 1411, but only parts of the outer wall, the Great Hall and the crypt remain. The rest was devastated in the Great Fire of 1666. Later additions and rebuilding, such as the neo-Gothic south façade of 1789, were destroyed in an air raid in December 1940. After the war the Guildhall was restored.

This part of the City was the Jewish quarter. Its memory is preserved in the name of the church **St Lawrence Jewry**, the official church of the Corporation of London to the south of Guildhall.

The Great Hall is reached from a porch, where the coat of arms of London bears the motto »Domine dirige nos« (Lord guide us). The hall, once the place where the Corporation assembled and the site of political events such as the trial of Lady Jane Grey in 1553, is now used for ceremonies, receptions, banquets and the monthly meeting of the Court of Common Council, the governing body of the City.

*Great Hall

The Corporation of London

The constitution of the City of London, the so-called Corporation of London, is based on rights established in the Middle Ages and still operates according to age-old practices.

The Corporation has the same rights as other boroughs, but in addition exercises other powers such as that of policing the City. The Court of Common Council, which roughly corresponds to a city council, meets in Guildhall. It consists of the **Lord Mayor**, 24 aldermen and 131 **common councilmen**, the representatives of the 25 wards of the City who are elected each December; the aldermen, who are elected for life, and the Lord Mayor, himself an alderman, also represent the wards. The Common Council emerged in the 12th century from informal meetings of the Lord Mayor with the aldermen and was officially elected for the first time in 1384.

The Lord Mayor ...

The Lord Mayor is elected on Michaelmas Day for a one-year term. For this purpose a meeting of the **liverymen**, the representatives of the livery companies, is held. The list of candidates is read out and two are chosen by show of hands. The aldermen then elect one of these two to be Lord Mayor. On the Friday before the second Saturday in November the Lord Mayor elect is sworn in by his predecessor in the **Silent Ceremony**, during which hardly a word is spoken. As part of a splendid procession on the following day, the **Lord Mayor's Show**, he goes to the Lord Chief Justice in a golden coach and takes his vows

A griffin guards the city boundaries

The City Guard awaits the Lord Mayor

of office. On the following Monday the Lord Mayor's Banquet, which the prime minister and members of the royal family attend, is held in honour of the outgoing Lord Mayor.

... and His Assistants

The position of sheriff is one of the traditional offices of the City. It has existed since the 7th century. The liverymen elect an Aldermanic Sheriff, who must be an alderman, and a Lay Sheriff, who does not have to be an alderman. They are charged with carrying out the orders of the High Court of Justice, and they accompany and assist the Lord Mayor, who is required to have served a term as sheriff. Further important offices are those of the Town Clerk (responsible for administration), the Chamberlain of

London (responsible for finances), the Comptroller and Solicitor (responsible for law and order), the Remembrancer (master of ceremonies) and the Secondary Sheriff and High Bailiff of Southwark.

The Livery Companies

The livery companies developed from medieval guilds, and their name derives from the robes worn by members. Nowadays they act mainly as charitable organisations. Of the 109 livery companies that exist today, the following, known as the **Great Twelve**, are the oldest: the grocers, fishmongers, skinners, haberdashers, ironmongers, clothworkers, vintners, salters, tailors, goldsmiths, drapers and mercers. Only the goldsmiths, fishmongers and vintners still have responsibilities for regulating their trade.

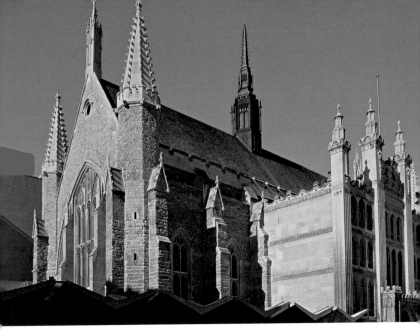

The Great Hall survived the Great Fire of 1666

The third-largest hall in England, it measures 50m/165ft in length and 29m/95ft in height and is decorated with the banners of the twelve great livery companies or guilds: Seen clockwise these are the grocers, fishmongers, skinners, haberdashers, ironmongers, cloth-workers, vintners, salters, tailors, goldsmiths, drapers and mercers. Their coats of arms appear again painted on the moulding, while the names of the lord mayors are shown on the windows. At the end of the hall is the minstrels' gallery, adorned with the figures of Gog (right) and Magog (left). On the south side are statues of William Pitt the Younger and Lord Mayor Beckford, an oak dresser with the sword and sceptre of the city, the Royal Fusiliers Memorial and the only remaining 15th-century window. On the north wall there are statues to Sir Winston Churchill, Admiral Nelson, the Duke of Wellington and the Earl of Chatham. Beneath the hall lies the **crypt**, which dates from the 13th to 15th centuries and has one of London's most beautiful groin vaults (open only for tours).

Guildhall Art Gallery & Roman Amphitheatre
Part of the art collection of the City of London, which goes back to 1670, is in the Guildhall Art Gallery. The remains of a Roman amphitheatre from the 1st century AD extending beneath the medieval structure were discovered in the front court in 1988 and can be viewed on the lower floor.

ℹ Mon–Sat 10am–5pm, Sun noon–5pm; free admission

The greatest treasures of the Guildhall Library, founded in 1420, are original designs for Shakespeare productions, a map of London from 1591 and a contract for the sale of a house with Shakespeare's signature. The collection of **600 clocks** belonging to the Worshipful Company of Clockmakers is also exhibited in the library.

Guildhall Library & Clockmakers' Museum

❶ Mon–Sat 9.30am–16.45pm; free admission

✳ Hampstead · Highgate

✳ **Outer suburb**

Location: North-west of the city centre
Tube: Hampstead

Hampstead has great charm. This district in the north of London with its healing springs has always attracted those in need of recuperation, but above all artists and writers.

John Keats, John Constable, Robert Louis Stevenson, D. H. Lawrence, George Orwell, Richard Burton and Peter Sellers have all felt at home here. Charles de Gaulle and Sigmund Freud also lived in Hampstead. The countryside around **London's highest ground** (145m/475ft above sea level) is shown in many landscape paintings – works by John Constable, for example.

Rural London

There is much to explore on a stroll around the up-and-down lanes of Hampstead Well. On the High Street and Flask Walk there are pretty shops, stylish houses and reminders of the time when Hampstead was a spa. Church Row is a beautiful row of Georgian houses leading to **St John's**, the burial place of John Constable. **Hampstead Cemetery** lies a little further away on Finchley Road and has welcoming pubs like the Holly Bush. A former pub, Jack Straw's Castle (12 North End Way), stands on a historic site: In 1381 Jack Straw, leader of the Peasants' Revolt, marched from here towards the City of London. Hampstead is notable for its museum houses: **Burgh House** on New End Square, built in 1703, is devoted to the history of Hampstead and has an excellent café.

Hampstead Well

MARCO POLO TIP

Kenwood Lakeside Concerts

Could there be a more romantic venue for open-air concerts? From June to September classical music is played every Saturday on the lawn of Kenwood House, which slopes like an amphitheatre down to a pond. The essential date is 4 July, when Handel's Fireworks Music is performed – with a robust pyrotechnical accompaniment, of course (www.picnicconcerts.com).

!

From Hampstead to Highgate Insider Tip

The trip to Hampstead can be combined with a beautiful walk to Highgate Cemetery. Starting in Hampstead, take the path through the woods at the end of Well Walk, go straight on across the heath, then between Highgate Ponds and up to Mernon Lane. Then go left up the steep Highgate West Hill, from which Swains Lane branches off to the right, and downhill to the cemetrey entrance. The walk from Hampstead takes about 45 minutes and shows that London can be quite hilly. On the way there is a view of the Millennium Dome in the distance in Greenwich and of The Shard. The best place for refreshments is the Flask pub on Highgate West Hill.

Fenton House dated 1693, is one of the oldest buildings in Hampstead. It contains a collection of historic keyboard instruments, all of which are still in working order.

The house at **no. 2 Willow Rd.**, which belonged to architect Ernö Goldfinger, is a classic example of 1930s residential architecture. If the name seems familiar, that is because **Ian Fleming**, the **creator of 007**, detested his neighbour Goldfinger and named an arch-villain after him.

The **Keats House** has many mementoes of the poet John Keats, who lived here from 1818 to 1829. He was inspired by the girl next door, Fanny Brawne, and wrote such famous verses as *Ode to a Nightingale* here.

Burgh House: Wed–Sun noon–5pm; free admission; www.burghhouse.org.uk www.burghhouse.org.uk

Fenton House: March–Oct Wed–Sun 11am–5pm; admission £6.50; www. nationaltrust.org.uk

No. 2 Willow Rd.: March–Oct Wed–Sun 11am–5pm (11am–3pm with guided tour only); admission £6; www.nationaltrust.org.uk

Keats House: March–Oct Tue–Sun 1–5pm, Nov–Feb Fri–Sun 10–5pm; admission £5; www.keatshouse.cityoflondon.gov.uk

Freud Museum

Lastly, a little to the south of Hampstead Well, there is very special museum: the house of **Sigmund Freud**, the founder of psychoanalysis, who fled to London from the Nazis in 1938. Freud's famous couch is of course the centrepiece.

❶ 20 Maresfield Gardens; Tube: Finchley Road; Wed–Sun noon–5pm; admission £6

Hampstead Heath

Hampstead's open space, the heath, is famous for its wonderful view over London. From **Parliament Hill** the city seems to lie at one's feet. The Celtic Queen Boudicca is said to be buried beneath a fenced-in hill further north-west.

Art-lovers should pay a visit to *****Kenwood House** built in 1616, to see the interior decoration done by **Robert Adam** from 1765 to 1769 for the Earl of Mansfield, as well as for the excellent collection of paintings belonging to the Earls of Iveagh, which includes works by Vermeer, Rembrandt, Reynolds, Romney and Gainsborough. For a freshly tapped pint, go to **The Spaniards Inn** (Spaniards Road), haunt of the highwayman Dick Turpin.

Kenwood House: April–Sept daily 10am–5.30pm, Oct until 5pm, Nov–March until 4pm; free admission; www.english-heritage.org.uk

London's best-known cemetery is located to the east of Hampstead in the well-to-do suburb of Highgate, on Swains Lane. To reach it, take the Tube to Archway, then a 15-minute walk via Macdonald Rd.

*Highgate Cemetery

(leaving the Tube left, then right), Salisbury Walk, Raydon St and Chester St to Swains Lane. The cemetery was established in 1839. The **western part** was closed in 1975 and has been cared for by the Friends of Highgate Cemetery since then. This section with its overgrown graves, truly a seques-tered spot – Bram Stoker found inspiration here for writing Drac-ula – is like a sample-book of Vic-torian funerary sculpture. For ex-ample, the owner of The Observer newspaper, Julius Beer, had a tomb for his eight-year-old daughter Ada modelled on the mausoleum of Halikarnassos in Asia Minor, and the 32 graves on the so-called Egyptian Avenue are based on royal graves from Egypt.

The **eastern part** of the cemetery, opened in 1856 and still in use, is the final resting-place of **Karl Marx** and his wife Jenny. To find it take the second left from the entrance. The grave is just beyond the second junction of paths.

The grave of Karl Marx

❶ Tube: Archway, then bus no. 210,143 or 271 to Waterlow Park and 5 min. walk through the park

Highgate Cemetery East: April–Sept Mon–Fri 10am–4.30pm, Oct–March until 3.30pm; Sat and Sun from 11am; admission £3

Highgate Cemetery West: (only as part of guided tour): March–Nov Mon–Fri 1.45pm (booking essential, tel. 020 83 40 18 34); Sat and Sun hourly 11am–4pm (tickets sold directly at the entrance, £7); www. highgate-cemetery.org

** **Hampton Court Palace**

✳ **Excursion**

Location: East Molesey, 25km/
16 miles south-west of the city centre
Train: Hampton Court from
Waterloo Station
Thames boat:
Hampton Court Bridge from
Westminster Pier (April– Oct)
❶ **Palace:** end of March to end of
Oct daily 10am–6pm, end of Oct to

end of March until 4.30pm
Formal gardens: summer
10am–7pm, winter until 5.30pm
Admission: £18.20(online: £17.05)
www.hrp.org.uk

**Hampton Court, on its bend in the river Thames, is one of the
most beautiful royal palaces in England and a fine example of
Tudor architecture.**

**Place of
history**
The Knights of St John built a manor on the site in 1236. It was leased
in 1494 by the courtier Giles Daubeney; in 1514 the Lord Chancellor,
Cardinal **Thomas Wolsey** (1475 – 1530) took over the lease. In the
years to 1520 he built the palace and led a luxurious life there that was

The entrance to the royal apartments is through Clock Court

in no way inferior to the splendour of the royal court, prompting John Skelton to write the satirical lines
The king's court / Should have the excellence,
But Hampton Court /Hath the preeminence.
In 1528 Wolsey fell out of favour with Henry VIII by failing to arrange Henry's divorce from Catherine of Aragon and lost his offices and possessions. The king took Hampton Court Palace for himself and had the Great Hall and extensions around Fountain Court built. Apart from Catherine of Aragon, all of his wives lived here; the **ghosts of Catherine Howard**, his fifth wife, and Dame Sybill Penn, the nurse of Elizabeth I, are said to haunt the rooms. Elizabeth, too, liked Hampton Court Palace; it was here that she heard the news of the victory over the Spanish Armada in 1588. Charles I lived here too – as king and as a prisoner of Oliver Cromwell. Major alterations were not made until the period of William and Mary: While the Tudor style of the west façade was preserved, the east wing and Fountain Court with the state apartments were rebuilt by Sir Christopher Wren. The palace has been open to visitors since 1838.

The way to the palace leads through Anne Boleyn's Gateway to Clock Court, which takes its name from the large astronomical clock made for ▶St James's Palace in 1540 and brought here in the 19th century. Here is an introductory exhibition about the palace.
State apartments

Access to **Henry VIII's apartments** is through Anne Boleyn's Gateway, which lead directly to the ****Great Hall**, built between 1531 and 1536, the most impressive room in the palace. Its outstanding features are a superb hammerbeam roof and wall tapestries, which were made in the 16th century on the basis of cartoons by the Flemish painter Bernaert van Orley and depict the story of Abraham. Shakespeare's theatre company performed before James I here in 1603. From the Great Hall, visitors reach the Great Watching Chamber (for the royal guard) and the Haunted Gallery, where Catherine Howard is the spook, before entering the **Royal Chapel**, which was built under Wolsey and furnished under Henry VIII. It was redecorated by Sir Christopher Wren, but he left the unique Tudor ceiling, resplendent in blue and gold, untouched. On either side of the entrance, the coats of arms of Henry and Jane Seymour are displayed.
A spiral staircase in the south wing of the Clock Court gives access to the Wolsey Rooms, the oldest in the palace, which were occupied by Henry VIII and Catherine of Aragon after Wolsey. They are now devoted to an ***exhibition on the life of the young Henry**: Paintings, including portraits by Hans Holbein, in combination with interactive terminals bring to life the period when the King was an active player on the European diplomatic stage and not yet derided as a womaniser and drinker.

After that visitors proceed up the ***King's Staircase** which has magnificent paintings by Antonio Verrio, into the **apartments designed by Wren for William III**, all of which were decorated by great artists of the Baroque period: woodcarvings by Grinling Gibbons, frescoes by Antonio Verrio, wrought iron by Jean Tijou, work in marble by John Nost. There are also paintings by Tintoretto and others in the King's Drawing Room. By contrast with the display of royal power in the Throne Room, the apartments of William III's wife Mary are modest, although there is a work by Sir Godfrey Kneller in the Queen's Guard Chamber.

The **Tudor Kitchens** are not to be missed. The beer cellar, wine cellar and the kitchens give an impression of the effort and expense involved in providing for the needs of a palace with 600 residents, who consumed 1240 oxen and 8200 sheep per year. **Cooking demonstrations** are usually held on the first weekend of the month.

Gardens A walk around the park and gardens takes in the Privy Garden, a private garden for William III; the Great Fountain Garden from the time of the same king; the Tudor and Elizabethan Knot Garden; and Wren's Broad Walk. The gardens are at their best in mid-May. The enormous *Great Vine, planted over 200 years ago in a greenhouse on the Thames by the landscape gardener Capability Brown, is an especially impressive sight with its diameter of 4m/13ft. Its annual yield of some 300kg/650lb of grapes is sold to visitors. Everyone visiting with children should venture into the *The Maze, which was planted in its present form in 1714. The covered Tudor tennis court on Broad Walk, where tennis is still played to the old rules, is a great rarity. The Lower Orangery facing the Thames houses a masterpiece of European art, one of the most important examples of Renaissance painting in existence: **Triumphs of Caesar, a cycle of nine enormous paintings by Andrea Mantegna (1431–1506) that Charles I acquired in 1629.

The Home Park with its ponds, long walks and deer extends over an area of 2.8 sq km/1.1 sq mi on the bend in the Thames.

? MARCO POLO TIP

Don't miss — Insider Tip

- Great Hall: glorious Tudor architecture
- *The Judgement of Paris*: painting by Lucas Cranach
- Young Henry VIII exhibition
- Tudor Kitchen: where 600 hungry people were fed
- The Maze: get lost for a while
- *Triumphs of Caesar*: cycle of paintings by Andrea
- Mantegna
- Tudor Tennis Court: where Henry VIII played

✳ Harrods

✦ **D 7**

Location: 87 – 135 Brompton Rd., SW 1
Tube: Knightsbridge
🕑 Mon–Sat 10am–8pm

After the Tower, British Museum, Buckingham Palace, Westminster Abbey and Big Ben, Harrods is the most-visited attraction in London. Nobody should miss a visit to Britain's largest department store.

In 1824 Henry Edward Harrod opened a shop for fabrics and haberdashery in Southwark. In 1834 he was a grocer in the East End, and in 1849 he moved close to Hyde Park in the expectation of doing good business during the Great Exhibition of 1851. His son Charles Digby Harrod extended the product range and built the department store that is now world-famous after a fire destroyed the old one in 1883.

From 1985 until it was sold for 1.5 billion pounds to Qatar Holdings in 2010, Harrods was owned by an Egyptian, Mohammed Al-Fayed, the father of Princess Diana's companion Dodi. By claiming that Prince Philip had Diana and Dodi murdered by the secret service, Al-Fayed achieved the feat of losing Harrods's privileged status as supplier to the royal family. The altar for Diana and Dodi in the staircase of the Egyptian Hall has remained under the new owners.

The richly decorated halls feel more like a cathedral for gourmets

All things for
all people,
everywhere

Mr Harrod's little shop has grown into an institution with **330 departments, a sales area of 90,000 sq m/970,000 sq ft** and a staff of 4000, who are proud to uphold the company motto: »All things for all people, everywhere«. Harrods is a theatrical experience. Fortnum & Mason (►p. 256) may have a touch more refinement – the staff at Harrods do not wear frock coats like their counterparts in Piccadilly – but the Brompton Road palace excels at capturing the limelight: Harrods is not just a department store, but has become a brand name. The chief difference between Harrods and its rivals is that Harrods has everything – and it goes without saying that, if something should be unavailable, Harrods will obtain it. There is no need to worry that shopping at Harrods is only for the well-off – it is also a store for normal purchases. Luxury is the attraction, however, which is why streams of tourists crowd through the portals and are granted admission so long as they are decently dressed, do not wear shorts or have rucksacks on their backs – and take no photographs! Once these conditions have been met, visitors are free to wander through the store and marvel at the nobly furnished **Egyptian Hall**, the enormous perfumery, the area selling exclusive gifts for gentlemen, the sports department with its top-quality cricket, golf and polo equipment, the departments for toys and school uniforms – the latter typically British in the eyes of foreign visitors – or any other of the almost 300 different departments. The absolute highlight, however, are the Victorian ****Food Halls** on the ground floor. It would be insulting to describe them as a supermarket.

> MARCO ⊕ POLO TIP
>
> *Picnic in Hyde Park*
>
> Surrounded by dozens of different kinds of Italian salami, French cheese and English biscuits, who could withstand temptation and walk out without buying anything? What pleasure could be greater than to take a well-filled bag from Harrods Food Halls and walk the short distance to Hyde Park for a picnic?

** Houses of Parliament

—————————————— ✦ G 6 / 7

Location: Parliament Square, SW 1
Tube: Westminster
Visitors' entrance: St Stephen's Entrance (west side)
www.parliament.uk

The seat of the upper and lower houses of Parliament is officially called The Palace of Westminster, because it stands on the site of an old royal palace.

The palace was built by Edward the Confessor and enlarged by William the Conqueror and William Rufus, for whom Westminster Hall was constructed between 1097 and 1099. A fire in 1512 spared only Westminster Hall, the 14th-century St Stephen's Chapel and the crypt. Westminster Palace was a royal residence until 1529, when Henry VIII moved to the nearby Whitehall Palace, and became the seat of Parliament in 1547: The House of Commons moved into St Stephen's Chapel, the House of Lords into a chamber at the south end of the courtyard. The architect of the present Houses of Parliament was **Sir Charles Barry** (1795–1860). His neo-Gothic design, built from 1839 after a fire destroyed most of the previous buildings in 1834, pays homage to ▶Westminster Abbey. The first official opening of Parliament in the new buildings took place in 1852, but construction was not completed until 1888. Following severe damage in the Second World War, Parliament buildings were restored between 1948 and 1950.

The heart of British democracy

There was uproar in 1605, when a group of conspirators led by **Guy Fawkes** tried to blow up Parliament. Fawkes, a staunch Catholic from Yorkshire, left Protestant England in 1593 to hire out his services as a soldier in the Spanish Netherlands. Increasingly repressive measures against English Catholics resulted in a plot against Parliament. For this purpose a man with military experience was needed: **Guy Fawkes**, who returned to England in 1604. He placed 20 barrels of gunpowder in a cellar below the House of Lords, but on 5 November 1605, before the fuse could be ignited, Fawkes was arrested, tortured, condemned to death and on 31 January 1606 hanged, drawn and quartered in Old Palace Yard. Every year since then a thorough search of the cellars has been made by officials in historic costume before the opening of Parliament (photo p. 217), and the Fifth of November, Guy Fawkes Day, is celebrated with fireworks and bonfires.

Gunpowder Plot

? MARCO ⊕ POLO INSIGHT

Visiting Parliament

There are two ways to visit Parliament: to watch debates free of charge or to join an guided tour.

Debates in House of Commons: Mon 2.30–10.30pm, Tue 11.30am–7.30pm, Wed 11.30am–7.30pm, Thu 9.30am–5.30pm, Fri 9.30am–3.00pm

Debates in House of Lords: Mon 2.30pm–10pm, Tue 2.30pm–10pm, Wed 3pm–10pm, Thu 11am–7.30pm, Fri from 10am

Tours: all year round on Saturdays between 9.15am and 4.30pm on timed tickets (£25); tickets available from www.ticketmaster.co.uk, tel. 0844 847 1672 or from the ticket office in front of the Jewel Tower (8.45am–4.45pm).

Next to Westminster Bridge stands the clock tower that is known around the world as **Big Ben**. Along with ▶Tower Bridge it is un-

Big Ben

** *Houses of Parliament*

The heart of British democrcay beats here – in the House of Commons , where important political decisions are taken, and in the House of Lords, which has lost much of its power in modern times. The annual occasion with the most lavish pageantry is the State Opening of the Parliament in November.

❶ Victoria Tower
With sides 23m/75ft long and a height of 102m/335ft, the Victoria Tower is the world's largest square tower when built in 1888.

❷ St Stephen' Entrance
The entrance for visitors

❸ St Stephen' Hall
The House of Commons met here from 1547 to 1837.

❹ Westminster Hall
The only surviving part of West-

minster Palace is a historic site. The trials of Richard II and Sir Thoams More, among others, were held here.

❺ Big Ben
London's best known landmark. The 97.5m/320ft-high tower was built in 1858–59. The clock-face is almost 8m/26ft in diameter, the hands of the clock are almost 4m/13ft long and the bell weighs 13 tons

❻ House of Commons
Read more:
▶MARCO POLO Insight p. 222

Houses of Parliament

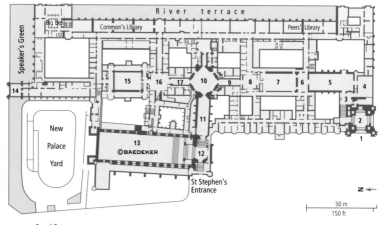

1 Royal Entrance	6 Prince's Chamber	10 Central Lobby	14 Clock Tower (Big Ben)
2 Victoria Tower	7 House of Lords	11 St Stephen's Hall	15 House of Commos
3 Norman Porch	8 Peers' Lobby	12 St Stephen's Porch	16 Common's Lobby
4 Robing Room	9 Peers' Corridor	13 Westminster Hall	17 Common's Corridor
5 Royal Gallery			

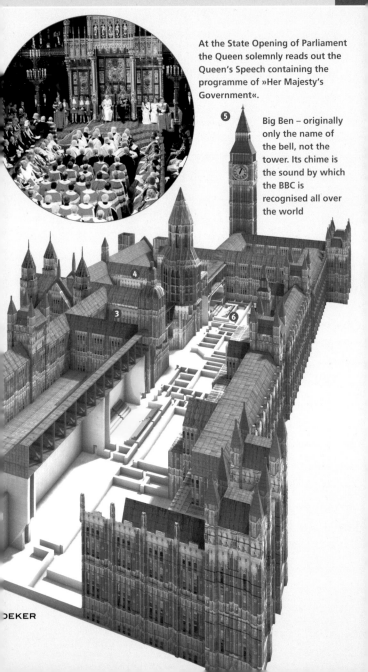

At the State Opening of Parliament the Queen solemnly reads out the Queen's Speech containing the programme of »Her Majesty's Government«.

5 Big Ben – originally only the name of the bell, not the tower. Its chime is the sound by which the BBC is recognised all over the world

4

3

6

Liveried yeomen make a search of Parliament before the opening – after all, Guy Fawkes tried to blow it up in 1605.

❶

❷

For the Ceremonial State Opening of Parliament Queen Elizabeth II and Prince Philip enter by the Royal Entrance in the Victoria Tower. Beyond is the Robing Room, where the monrach puts on the royal insignia.

©BAE

doubtedly London's best-known landmark. Big Ben is in fact the bell, but quickly became the appellation of the tower as a whole. Since New Year 1923 its chimes have been the signature of the BBC. The architectural counterpoint to Big Ben is the **Victoria Tower**, which was the world's largest and tallest square tower when it was built. The Union Jack flies from the Victoria Tower when Parliament is sitting.

Jewel Tower

The Jewel Tower opposite the Victoria Tower is one of the few surviving parts of Westminster Palace. Henry Yevele built it in 1366 as a store-house for the royal treasure. From the early 17th century it served as the House of Lords archive, and from 1869 to 1938 as the Weights and Measures Office. It now contains an exhibition about Parliament and the old Westminster Palace.
❶ April–Oct daily 10am–5pm, Nov–March Sat and Sun until 4pm; admission £3.50

Westminster Bridge

The best view of Parliament is from Westminster Bridge, which was built between 1856 and 1862. The stone structure that it replaced was the second bridge across the Thames after ▶London Bridge. The sculptural ensemble opposite Big Ben represents Celtic Queen **Boudicca**.

INSIDE PARLIAMENT

Royal chambers

The Queen passes through the 16m/52ft-high **Royal Entrance** in the Victoria Tower for the state opening of Parliament. The Royal Staircase leads up to the Norman Porch, beyond which is the **Robing Room**, where the Queen puts on the Imperial State Crown. The **Royal Gallery** is decorated with the coats of arms of the monarchs of England and Scotland. Two enormous frescoes by Daniel Maclise depict *The Death of Nelson and Wellington* and *Blücher after the Battle of Waterloo*. The next room, the **Prince's Chamber**, is the ante-room to the House of Lords. On the panelling are portraits of the Tudors. The reliefs below depict scenes from their reigns. Opposite the entrance is a white marble statue of Queen Victoria, flanked by Justice and Mercy.

House of Lords

The **Peers' Lobby**, immediately to the north of the House of Lords is paved with glazed tiles. Above the doors are the arms of the royal dynasties of England. From here the Peers' Corridor leads to the **Central Lobby**, an octagonal chamber between the House of Lords and the House of Commons with a 25m/82ft-high vaulted ceiling. The **House of Lords** is a magnificent room. The peers sit on red leather benches. In November 1999 they acquiesced in the loss of their own power by assenting to a bill that abolished automatic membership for hereditary peers. Until then no fewer than 646 hereditary peers sat in the House of Lords. The number has now been reduced to 92, who are joined by life peers and 26 Anglican bishops.

The ante-chamber to the House of Commons, the **Commons' Lobby**, is adorned by statues of 20th-century statesmen, including Winston Churchill and David Lloyd George. The seat of the Speaker, who chairs meetings of the House of Commons, is placed at the northern end of the chamber. The **start of a session** is marked by the call »Mr Speaker! – hats off – strangers!«. All those present stand up to allow a procession to pass. It is led by the sergeant-at-arms, who carries the golden mace over his shoulder and places it in front of the Speaker's seat. After this the session can begin. The Speaker follows him in gown and wig. A train-bearer, the Speaker's chaplain and a secretary bring up the rear. At the beginning of every session a prayer is held »for God's guidance«. The procession then leaves the chamber at the end of the session.

House of Commons

Westminster Hall, 79m/260ft long and 30m/98ft high, was built between 1097 and 1099, and suffered relatively little damage in the fire of 1299 that reduced the old Westminster Palace to rubble. Richard II (reigned 1377–1400) commissioned Henry Yevele to rebuild it; the carpenter Hugh Herland made the great **oak hammer-beam roof**. The 13 statues of English kings from Edward the Confessor to Richard II were placed here in 1385. From 1189 until 1821 coronation banquets were held in the hall. On these occasions the new monarch presented himself to the lords of the realm at the King's Table, fragments of which have survived. Oliver Cromwell was inaugurated as Lord Protector here in 1653. Westminster Hall has been the scene of some of the most moving events in English history: As the place in which the highest courts in the land met (1224–1882), it saw such famous trials as those of William Wallace (1305), Richard II (1399), Sir Thomas More (1535) and Charles I (1649). Westminster Hall is still used for ceremonial lying-in-state after the death of leading members of the royal family, most recently for Queen Elizabeth, the Queen Mother, in 2002.

Westminster Hall

> **?** *Late Revenge*
>
> **MARCO ⊕ POLO INSIGHT**
>
> After the restoration of the monarchy in 1660 under Charles II, nine men who were held responsible for the execution of Charles I were tried in Westminster Hall. The body of Oliver Cromwell, who had died in 1658, was exhumed, posthumously executed at Tyburn and his head placed on a spike on a tower of Westminster Hall, where it remained for 20 years.

MARCO⊕POLO INSIGHT

A Parliament with a Long Tradition

The British Parliament is one of the oldest in the world. With roots in the Anglo-Saxon period, it developed from a royal council to a democratic assembly. Many customs that resulted from this evolution are still upheld in the Houses of Parliament.

▶ **House of Commons**
Elected representatives of constituencies (MPs) sit in the lower house. The distance between the benches of the government parties and the opposition is the length of two swords.

▶ **House of Lords**
The upper house
nominated and 92
can propose and
prevent it from be
Parliament takes

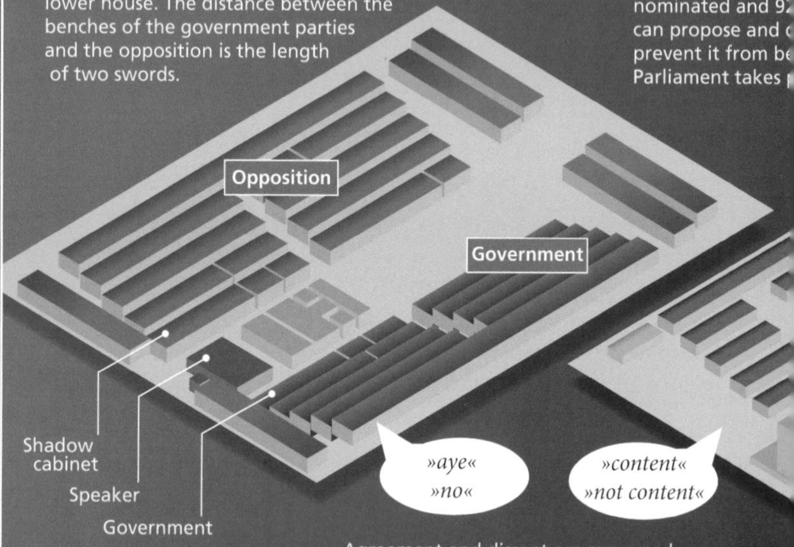

Opposition

Government

»aye«
»no«

»content«
»not content«

Agreement and dissent are expressed
in different ways in the two chambers.

Shadow cabinet

Speaker

Government

Serjeant at Arms
He is responsible for security and order in the House of Commons and is the only person in the chamber who is armed – with a sword. He carries the mace during the opening of Parliament

Black Rod
This officer of the House of Lords has a similar role to the serjeant at arms. He is always a member of the Order of the Garter and fetches members of the Commons at the state opening – when they first of all slam the door in his face.

Cat
An
attr

Spe
The
He
rep
vis-a
Hou

Coat of arms
of the Parliament

of life peers who have been
tary peers. The House of Lords
jislation, but not ultimately
sed. The ceremonial opening of
re.

▶ Robes and rituals
The two chambers of the British
Parliament are characterized by
centuries of history and customs.

Lord Speaker
Elected by the House of Lords, this
officer chairs debates like the Speaker
of the House of Commons. Until 2006
this role was performed by the
Lord Chancellor

Woolsack
During debates the Lord Speaker sits
on a large red seat stuffed with wool
from states of the Commonwealth.
The Woolsack dates from the 14th
century and symbolises the wealth
that England acquired
from the wool trade.

©BAEDEKER

Judges' Woolsack
This larger seat is occupied at the
State Opening of Parliament by the
senior judges. During debates any
member of the House of Lords
may sit on it

he Speaker's Eye
o wishes to speak stands up to
Speaker's attention.

r is elected by MPs.
hairs debates and
the House of Commons
e monarch and the
rds.

Dragging the Speaker
A newly elected Speaker is
gently dragged by his
parliamentary colleagues to
his chair, while he offers
token resistance: the job
of representing Parliament
to the monarch was not
a coveted one in past times

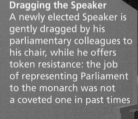

St Stephen's Hall   From 1547 until 1834 the House of Commons met in St Stephen's Hall. The mosaics depict the foundation of the chapel by King Stephen. The statues represent Norman and Plantagenet kings and queens and statesmen of the 17th to 19th centuries.

Hyde Park ·
Kensington Gardens
⚡ B–E 5/6

Location: West of city centre
Tube: Hyde Park Corner, Marble Arch, Lancaster Gate
www.royalparks.org.uk

Hyde Park, once the site of royal hunts, military exercises and duels, is now the place where London relaxes – for a picnic, a walk, sport or just to laze around.

** HYDE PARK

Where London relaxes   A walk through the park is a pleasure at any time of year, but especially in summer. In the morning, before the strollers, joggers and horse-riders arrive, Hyde Park is still quiet; at midday the office workers of the area eat their sandwiches on the park benches; and after work footballers and sunbathers take over the lawns.

In 1536 Henry VIII turned an area originally owned by Westminster Abbey into a park for hunting. In 1635 Charles I opened the park to the people of London, and the better-off residents adopted it as a place to be driven around in their coaches, to see and be seen. In 1851 Hyde Park was the venue of the Great Exhibition, for the 2012 Olympic Games of the triathlon and the 10-kilometre swimming (in The Serpentine).

Walk   The main entrance is the triple gateway at Hyde Park Corner built in 1828 by Decimus Burton. Its reliefs are scenes from the frieze of the Parthenon (►British Museum). Just behind it is the so-called statue of Achilles, cast from French cannonballs in 1822 by Richard Westmacott in honour of the Duke of Wellington. However, the statue is not the ancient god, but a copy of the horse tamer from the Quirinal in Rome. This did not prevent it from causing a scandal as Britain's first public representation of a naked man. From the grand entrance, three main paths cross the park from Hyde Park Corner: The Carriage Road on the left leads to the Albert Memorial (►p. 224), the East Carriage Road on the right past the **7th July Memorial** for the victims of the terrorist attacks in 2005 to Marble Arch and Speakers' Corner, and the path in the middle to **The Serpentine**, the lake created for George II's queen, Caroline of Ansbach, in 1730. A solar-powered boat now takes visitor on trips across The Serpentine. Near its east bank is the **Holocaust Memorial**, at its western margin the (Diana) **Princess of Wales Memorial Fountain**, to the north of the lake the Bird Sanctuary, in front of which is Epstein's naked spirit of nature, Rima. **Rotten Row**, which runs between The Serpentine and Carriage Road, is reserved for horse-riders. The name is a corruption of the French »Route du Roi«. It was laid out and illuminated for William III so that he could ride in safety to Kensington Palace.

Since 1872 Speakers' Corner has been the stage for all those who want to air their opinion about any subject on earth without fear of legal consequences. It is at its busiest on Saturdays and Sunday mornings. Karl Marx, Lenin and Jomo Kenyatta, the first president of Kenya, once spoke here. Idi Amin, the notorious former dictator of Uganda, often listened while he was a sergeant in the British army – but failed to learn his lesson in democracy.

Speakers' Corner

Breathing space: Hyde Park is a haven of peace in a busy city

Marble Arch Marble Arch, an island surrounded by traffic, can be seen from Speakers' Corner. The monumental arch was designed in 1828 by **John Nash** in the style of the Roman Arch of Constantine as the main gate to ▶Buckingham Palace. When the archway proved to be too narrow for the royal state coach, it was re-erected in 1851 in its present location at Tyburn, a place of execution from the 12th century until 1783. Criminals were brought here from the Tower or Newgate prison to die on the gallows, known as Tyburn Tree. Every execution drew crowds of onlookers.

** KENSINGTON GARDENS

Kensington Gardens lie to the west of the bridge across The Serpentine. Again it was Queen Caroline who was responsible for giving the park its – in comparison to Hyde Park– more formal layout from

1728 to 1731. It has been open to the public since 1841. At the end of the **Long Water**, the continuation of The Serpentine, is the **Italian Garden**, a gift from Prince Albert to Queen Victoria. Not far away at Lancaster Gate is the site of a small (closed) dog cemetery, established in 1880 on the wishes of the Duke of Cambridge. A walk along the west side of the Long Water leads to the most attractive monument in Kensington Gardens, the statue of **Peter Pan** made in 1912 by George Frampton. The little boy who never wanted to grow old is surrounded by all his animal and fairy-tale friends. Further along the path is the **Serpentine Gallery**, a showcase for changing exhibitions of contemporary art.

❶ Daily 10am–6pm, free admission, www.serpentinegallery.org

Albert Memorial In 1876, on the southern edge of Kensington Gardens, Queen Victoria unveiled Sir George Gilbert Scott's monument to her prince consort, **Albert of Saxe-Coburg and Gotha** (1819–61). The queen's original wish was to have a colossal monolithic granite obelisk, which was to have been financed by donations. However, the sum collected was insufficient, and a neo-Gothic monument was built instead.
The figure of Prince Albert, larger than life size, seated beneath a 58m/190ft-high canopy, holds in his hand the catalogue of the Great Exhibition of 1851, which took place largely on his initiative. On the marble reliefs that decorate the base are 178 figures of famous artists and scientists from all periods of history; the free-standing groups at

the corners represent Manufactures, Engineering, Commerce and Agriculture, and the ensembles at the corners of the steps symbolise Europe, Asia, Africa and America.

Albert Memorial Tours: March–Dec on the 1st Sunday in the month, 2pm and 3pm; meet at the monument; £6

Royal Albert Hall

Prince Albert looks across to the Royal Albert Hall, which he himself initiated. This oval hall with a circumference of over 210m/230yd was completed in 1871 to a design by the military engineers Captain Fowke and General Scott. Although the acoustics were widely known to be poor – they have since been improved – the interior with its enormous glass dome and the high quality of the music performed there made it one of London's most popular concert halls. Among other events, the famous Proms are held here each year (▶Enjoy London, p. 82).

* KENSINGTON PALACE

❶ March–Oct daily 10am–6pm; Nov– Feb until 5pm (last admission 1hr earlier); admission £16.50; tickets from www.hrp.org.uk or tel. 020 3166 6000

Kensington Palace, at the west side of Kensington Gardens, was the private residence of English monarchs from 1689 to 1760, but is now known all over the world as the **last home of Princess Diana**. Tens of thousands of mourners laid flowers at the palace gates after her death. Princess Margaret, the Queen's sister, lived here for 42 years, and in 2012 William and Kate, the Duke and Duchess of Cambridge, took up residence.

Kensington Palace was built as a country house in 1605 and bought by William III, who commissioned Sir Christopher Wren to convert it into his private residence. George I, who made it his official residence, had it altered by Colen Campbell and furnished by William Kent. The last king to reside here was George II. Queen Victoria was born in the palace and learned of her accession to the throne here. Queen Mary, grandmother of Elizabeth II, was also born here. William III, his wife Mary II, Queen Anne and George II all died in Kensington Palace. The statue of William III on the south side was a gift to Edward VII from Emperor Wilhelm II of Germany. To the east is a monument to Queen Victoria from her daughter Princess Louisa on the occasion of the Queen's golden jubilee.

Orangery

The Orangery on the north side used to be attributed to Sir Christopher Wren, but was probably the work of Nicholas Hawksmoor in 1704. The carvings by Grinling Gibbons that adorn it can today be examined over a cup of tea or coffee.

Triathlon in Hyde Park

Long-distance swimming in the Serpentine, cycle races in Regent's Park, equestrian events in Greenwich Park: The planners of the 2012 London Olympic Games resorted to historic sites for some competitions and planned new arenas for sustainable use after the games.

The good news was greeted with delight in London when the Olympic Committee announced its decision about the venue for the 30th Olympic Games at its meeting in Singapore on 6 July 2005. London's bid to hold the games in 2012 was successful in the fourth round of voting against competition from Madrid, New York and Moscow. The nomination of London was a historic decision, as the British capital is **the only city to have staged the Olympic Games three times**: in 1908, 1948 and 2012.

Planning and Investing

The third London Olympics were opened on 27 July 2012. The first records had already been broken, as the bids for European broadcasting rights brought the IOC €614 million. Thankfully it was impossible to break the record for construction and infrastructure costs: In 2008 Beijing raised the bar by spending the dizzying figure of 44 billion dollars. Admittedly, London's costs sprinted away from the original budget estimate of £2.9 billion to reach a sum of £11.4 billion, but this already looks modest following the 2014 Winter Olympics in Sochi, in which 51 billion dollars were invested.

Use of existing facilities helped to limit the spending: The ExCel Exhibition Centre for boxing, weight-lifting and wrestling, the O2 Dome for basketball and other sports, **Greenwich Park** for equestrian competitions and the Royal Artillery Barracks for shooting. Nobody was surprised that football was played at **Wembley** and tennis at **Wimbledon**, but who could have expected to see the triathlon in **Hyde Park**, with a ten-kilometre (approx. six miles) swim in the Serpentine? **Regent's Park** was the location for road cycling competitions, and there were breaches of hallowed tradition: **Lord's Cricket Ground** was being »hijacked« to stage the archery contests, and the Queen's mounted guards were treated to the sight of beach volleyball being played on **Horse Guards Parade**.

As for Sport ...

... the 2012 Olympics produced many highlights. The swimmer **Michael Phelps** became the most successful Olympic athlete of all time when he won his 22nd medal. The home team repaid huge investment in training facilities and personnel by coming third in the medals table behind the United States and China. The games were also the first at which every sport had female competitors, as women's boxing was included – and even Saudi Arabia and Qatar sent women athletes for the first time

The games are opened

After the Games

The Olympic Games always give rise to the same important question: What will happen when it is all over? This issue is one of the reasons why London's planners have opted to use a number of existing sports arenas. The new **Olympic Stadium** came with a price tag of £540 million. It will be the focal point of a redevelopment of the Lea valley, previously a decaying post-industrial wasteland, now christened the Queen Elizabeth Olympic Park. The stadium is being reduced in size and will be the home of West Ham United Football Club. The Aquatics Centre, unmistakably a work of Zaha Hadid, was also designed to be downsized after the games. The athletes' accommodation will be the new East Village, and a total of 10,000 homes are planned for the site over 15 years. London will benefit from an urban green area along the river Lea, with a northern section kept in a relatively natural state as a habitat for wildlife. Other institutions planned include a university specialising in sports science, digital media and green technology, a technology park and allotments. London visitors will find the ArcelorMittal Orbit, a steel tower with observation platforms at a height of 80m/260ft, a cable railway connecting the ExCel Exhibition Centre with the O2 Dome 50m/160ft above the Thames and the new Stratford tube station with its huge shopping mall.

The London Legacy project, as the Olympics post-development is called, seems to be on track to fulfil many of the promises about sustainable benefits that were made before the games

Refurbishment of state apartments

In 2012 the state apartments and gardens reopened after a thorough refurbishment. The aim was to produce a completely new and less formal presentation of the palace and its inhabitants over the last 300 years. Access to the **State Apartments** of William III and Queen Mary is given, as in the early 18th century, via the **King's Staircase**, with trompe-l'oeil paintings by William Kent from this period representing ambassadors and courtiers. The long **King's Gallery**, a room used for taking a walk in bad weather and adorned with portraits such as one of Charles I by van Dyck, looks as it did in 1727. The stories of Princess Diana and the 18-year-old Princess Victoria, who was wakened on 20 June 1837 in Kensington Palace with the news that she was now queen, illustrate the human side of palace life.

HYDE PARK CORNER

Wellington Arch •
Wellington Monument

Hyde Park Corner in the south-east corner of the park is the junction of three extremely busy roads: Park Lane, Knightsbridge and Piccadilly. Opposite the entrance to the park stands the Wellington Arch, a triumphal gate designed in 1828 by Decimus Burton to celebrate the victory of the Duke of Wellington (1769–1852) at Waterloo. Since 1912 a bronze sculpture representing Peace in a Quadriga has crowned the massive arch, replacing a 9m/30ft-high monument to Wellington. A new Wellington monument opposite Apsley House portrays the duke on his horse Copenhagen; an English grenadier, a Scottish Highlander, a Welsh fusilier and a northern Irish dragoon occupy the corners. Inside the arch are exhibitions on English monuments in the Quadriga Gallery; below the quadriga is an observation platform with views of Hyde Park and Buckingham Palace. Three further monuments are placed around Wellington Arch: the Royal Artillery War Memorial (1928), the Machine Gun Corps Memorial (1927) with a figure of the biblical King David, and a new memorial (2003) to the Australians and New Zealanders who fell in the two world wars.

> **?** MARCO POLO INSIGHT
>
> **Banned from London**
>
> The giant equestrian monument to the Duke of Wellington that stood on the Wellington Arch was much derided. Even Queen Victoria disliked it. Since 1885 it has stood in front of the Royal Garrison Church in Aldershot, 65km/40mi south-west of London.

● Wed–Sun 10am–5pm, admission £4

*Apsley House •
Wellington Museum

The victor of Waterloo and later prime minister looks across from his monument to Apsley House, his London residence. It was built by Robert Adam for Baron Apsley between 1771 and 1778, bought by Wellington's brother Richard Wellesley in 1807 and acquired by the duke in 1817. In 1819 he added the dining room, in 1828–29 the Corinthian portico the west wing with the Waterloo Gallery. The house, known as »No. 1 London«, was also re-faced in Bath stone and given expensive interiors in the Regency style. Many personal items preserve the memory of the **Iron Duke** – supposedly so called not because of his military victories but on account of the iron shutters that he installed on Apsley House after opponents of his policies smashed the window panes in 1832. The China and Plate Room on the ground floor is filled with silver and porcelain, including a dinner service from the royal Prussian porcelain manufactory presented to Wellington by the King of Prussia after the Battle of Waterloo, and the Egyptian Service that Napoleon intended as a divorce present for Josephine. The sabre that he wore at Waterloo can also be seen. The most impressive item in Wellington's home is in the stairwell: **Canova's statue of Napoleon**, twice life-size, depicting the French emperor naked except

Apsley House is a fitting setting for the Duke of Wellington's collection of paintings

for a fig-leaf. It was brought to London from the Louvre. The first-floor rooms contain paintings of the highest quality, many of which Wellington took from Joseph Bonaparte after the battle of Vitoria (1813). The outstanding works are Velázquez' *Water-seller of Seville*, Correggio's *Agony in the Garden* (Wellington's favourite painting) and an equestrian portrait of the Duke of Wellington by Goya, which hangs in the Waterloo Gallery, where Wellington entertained his comrades each year at the Waterloo Dinner. The centrepiece of the table, a gift from the King of Portugal, is now in the dining room.

❶ April–Oct. Wed–Sun 11am–5pm, Nov–March only Sat and Sun 11am–4pm; admission: £6.90

✳ # Imperial War Museum · Lambeth

✦ H 7

Location: Lambeth Road, SE 1
Tube: Lambeth North
❶ Daily 10am–6pm

Admission: free
www.iwm.org.uk

The Imperial War Museum in Lambeth is dedicated to British wars of the 20th century. In addition to all kinds of military hardware, impressive historical documents are on display here.

It was founded in 1920 and has occupied the former Bethlem Royal Hospital in Lambeth since 1936. The warship HMS Belfast (►South Bank) and the Cabinet War Rooms (►Whitehall), a large collection of aircraft at Duxford Airfield near Cambridge and the IWM North in Manchester are also part of the Imperial War Museum. At the centre of the London museum is a large hall in which planes, tanks and artillery-pieces are on display, including Field Marshal Montgomery's command tank, a British Spitfire fighter, a German Focke-Wulf FW 190, an American P-51 Mustang, a German one-man U-boat and the German »flying bombs« V 1 and V 2.

The rooms on the lower floor give a chronological account of the world wars, including some unique historical items such as Lawrence of Arabia's djellaba (Arab cloak), and a copy of Hitler's last testament. The Blitz Experience recreates the experience of being in a bunker during a German air-raid. A similar scene conveys the feeling of life in the trenches in the First World War. Other sections are devoted to post-1945 conflicts, secret service activities and the Holocaust.

Fighter aircraft of the Second World War in the Imperial War Museum

OTHER SIGHTS IN LAMBETH

Lambeth Palace is at the eastern end of Lambeth Bridge. It was built in the 12th century and has been the London residence of the archbishops of Canterbury for over 700 years. The **Lambeth Palace Library** shows its treasures in changing exhibitions.

Lambeth Palace

The Museum of Garden History is housed in the former church of **St Mary-at-Lambeth** close to the palace. It is particularly informative about the father and son named **Tradescant**, gardeners to Charles I. Both are buried in the churchyard, which is also the final resting place of **Admiral Bligh**, captain of the famous Bounty.

Insider Tip

Garden Museum: Sun–Fri 10.30am–5pm, Sat to 4pm; closed 1st Monday of the month; admission: £7.50; www.gardenmuseum.org.uk

Further north at the east end of Westminster Bridge, this museum tells the story of the life and work of the pioneer of modern nursing in a new presentation.

Florence Nightingale Museum

❶ Daily 10am–5pm; admission £5.80; www.florence-nightingale.co.uk

✶✶ Kew Gardens · Syon House

✦ **Outer suburb**

Location: Kew Road, Kew
Tube: Kew Gardens
River Tours: Kew from Westminster
Kew Gardens: daily from 9.30am;
admission £15

Kew Palace:
March–Sep daily
11am–5pm; admission £5.30
www.kew.org

A day in Kew Gardens, the Royal Botanic Gardens on the south bank of the Thames in the south-west of London, is almost a must. A trip to Kew means escaping from the bustle of the city into a leafy oasis. The idyll is spoilt only by the noise of aircraft flying in so low to land at nearby Heathrow Airport that visitors to the gardens can almost look in through the windows.

The gardens, Unesco World Heritage since 2003, are a place for serious scientific study as well as recreation: At Kew and Wakehurst in Sussex, the Royal Botanic Gardens cultivate 19,000 species, including some that have already died out in their natural habitat and many endangered ones; it is also a repository for the seeds of 30,000 species. Frederick, Prince of Wales laid out the first gardens here in the 1730s, but his widow Princess Augusta, who employed the architect William Chambers and the gardener William Aiton in 1751, is considered to be the true founder of the Royal Botanic Gardens. **Joseph Banks**, who had sailed around the world as a botanist with James Cook, became director in 1773. Banks's time saw the start of the expeditions to all parts of the globe that brought and still bring great numbers of exotic plants to Kew. Sir William Hooker, director from 1841, made Kew Gardens world-famous.

Kew Explorer The Kew Explorer is for everyone who finds the gardens too extensive. It is a gas-powered bus that runs around the gardens on a fixed route, stopping at eight places of interest, where ticket-holders can get on and off as often as they like. A day ticket costs £4 per person.

Botanical attractions Kew Gardens has a great many botanical attractions, from a small water-lily pond and a Japanese bamboo grove to the two gigantic Victorian glasshouses, the result of collaboration between the architect **Decimus Burton** and the engineer **Richard Turner**. The **Palm House**, constructed from 1844 to 1848, is considered the most important surviving iron-and-glass structure of its time; the species here include Seychelles palms, which have bigger seeds than any

Children enjoy the Treetop Walk, one of the more recent attractions in Kew Gardens

other plant. The **Temperate House**, begun in 1859, shelters plants from Africa, Australia and Oceania (closed until 2018 for restoration). The **Princess of Wales Conservatory**, opened in 1982, is home to plants that exemplify ten different climatic zones. The smaller Evolution House illuminates the theme of the development of plants over geological time. In the Arboretum visitors can look down on Kew's trees from the **Treetop Walk**, 18m/60ft above the ground. The **Marianne North Gallery** is devoted the life work of the eponymous painter of plants (1830–90), who painted 833 pictures on extensive journeys around the world. **Museum No. 1** displays unusual items from the botanical collection.

During his period of mental illness King George III lived in the modest-sized Kew Palace, which was built in 1631 for the Fortney family of merchants. Queen Charlotte, wife of George III, died here in 1818. Many items in the palace are associated with them.

Kew Palace

Queen Charlotte's Cottage	Queen Charlotte's Cottage is an early example of the longing for rural life. The royal family liked to come here to take tea. In a now-demolished compound, Queen Charlotte kept tigers and later kangaroos.
Pagoda and Japanese Gateway	Other charming buildings in the park are the 50m/165ft-high Chinese Pagoda, built by Sir William Chambers in 1761, and the Japanese Gate, a copy of a gate in the Nishi Honganji temple in Kyoto from the Anglo-Japanese Exhibition of 1912.
National Archives	The items on show in the museum of the **National Archives** in Kew (east of the Botanic Gardens) include Magna Carta, a letter by Jack the Ripper and the SOS telegram from the *Titanic*.

 Ruskin Ave; Tue–Sat 9am–5pm; free admission; www.nationalarchives.gov.uk

✴ SYON HOUSE · SYON PARK

? *Eventful family history*

Henry Percy, a close friend of Walter Raleigh, was a passionate alchemist and the first man to draw a map of the moon. He was thrown into the Tower for 15 years for alleged participation in the Gunpowder Plot: He had dined with one of the conspirators on the evening before the attempt to blow up Parliament. **Hugh Smithson's son James** founded the Smithsonian Institution in Washington DC. The **third Duchess of Northumberland** was the governess of Princess Victoria (later Queen Victoria).

Location: Brentford, Middlesex
Tube: Gunnersbury, then bus 237 or 267 to Brentlea Gate
Syon House: Mid-March–Oct Wed, Thu and Sun 11am–5pm
Syon Park: March–Oct Thu–Sun 10.30am–5pm
Admission: £12 (house and gardens; separate tickets for gardens at £7 also sold); **www.syonpark.co.uk**

Syon House is in Brentford on the north bank of the Thames. This house was founded in the 15th century as a monastery, which was dissolved in 1539 and converted to an aristocratic residence, bought in 1594 by **Henry Percy**, 9th Earl of Northumberland. Since then it has been a home to the Percy family, who have turned it into a jewel of interior decoration. This is above all the work of Hugh Smithson, first Duke of Northumberland. In the 18th century he hired the leading men in their fields, **Robert Adam** to design the interior and **Capability Brown** to landscape the park. In six of the rooms Adam created a classical interior unique in London with Roman columns, statues, antique furniture, paintings and elegant wall-coverings. The bedrooms including Princess Victoria's Bedroom were remodelled in the 1820s and 1830s.

Syon House is surrounded by a magnificent park in which Charles Fowler built a fine glasshouse, an inspiration for the Crystal Palace, in 1826–27 to house the ducal collection of exotic plants.   **Syon Park**

Two museums are worth a visit in Brentford. The **London Museum of Water and Steam** (look out for its tall tower) tells the story of London's water supply and contains a collection of 19th- and early 20th-century steam engines, including the »100 Inch«, the world's largest single piston steam pump. The **Musical Museum** at 368 High Street is a display of automatic musical instruments, from music-boxes to the Wurlitzer.   **Museums**

London Museum of Water and Steam: Green Dragon Lane/Kew Bridge Road; daily 10am–4pm; admission £11.50; www.waterandsteam.org.uk
Musical Museum: 399 High St; Fri–Sun 11am–5pm; admission £10; www.musicalmuseum.co.uk

Leadenhall Market

K 5

Location: Gracechurch Street, EC 3
Tube: Bank, Monument, Aldgate

At midday office-workers like to escape to the Victorian Leadenhall Market for a break in the Lamb Tavern or a restaurant, or to buy good-quality produce.

Here, on the site of the forum of Roman Londinium, there has been a market since the Middle Ages. From the 15th century poultry, eggs, cheese and other foods were sold here. Today it is hard to imagine that 34,000 geese per day were once slaughtered in Leadenhall Market. In 1881 Sir Horace Jones designed the Victorian halls that are now resplendent in green, beige and red; at the end of the 19th century the sale of poultry ended, and the market specialised in meat and fish. There is still a butcher here; gifts, jewellery and clothing are sold on the site too.

Leave the market by the entrance leading to Whittington Avenue and look up left to see the Lloyd's Building. Although it was completed in 1986, the Lloyd's Building remains one of London's most spectacular works of architecture. It was designed by a star architect, **Richard Rogers**. His ingenious idea was to put the inner parts of the building – lifts, stairs, pipes – on the outside. The only remaining part of the façade of the old building from 1928 is at the Leadenhall Street entrance. Lloyd's began in about 1688 as Edward Lloyd's coffee house in Tower Street, a meeting-place for captains, ship owners and mer-   **Lloyd's Building** chants, who made agreements to insure their ships and cargoes. The centre of the Underwriting Room, where business is transacted beneath the rostrum taken from the old Lloyd's Building, is occupied by the bell from the French frigate Lutine, which sank in 1799 and was insured at Lloyd's. The bell is rung still – once for bad news, twice for good news. To this day the name of every Lloyd's-insured ship that sinks is entered into a ledger on a desk next to the bell. The Adam Room, designed by Robert Adam in 1763 and taken out of the old Lloyd's Building, has been inserted on the 11th floor.

30 St Mary Axe   The tower known as »The Gherkin« (2004) is equally spectacular. Designed by **Sir Norman Foster** and **Ken Shuttleworth** for the Swiss Re insurance company, it rises to a height of 180m/590ft on the site formerly occupied by the Baltic Exchange building, which was destroyed by an IRA bomb in 1992. Foster's structure consists of intertwined spirals of steel. As an energy-saving measure, six storeys

Norman Foster's »Gherkin« shines above the City

are grouped into an atrium, through which air flows as through a chimney when the computer controls open the windows; this means that the air-conditioning rarely needs to operate. The Gherkin is now owned by a property company.

A little to the west lies St Helen's Bishopsgate, a 12th-century church, one of the loveliest and also most unusual in the City. St Helen's has two naves of equal size, because it was used simultaneously by nuns and the laity. The nuns assembled in the northern nave, while the southern one was reserved for the parish congregation. In the northern half the 15th-century steps, which gave access to the church from the nunnery, can still be seen. The most remarkable features are the funerary monuments: **Sir Thomas Gresham** († 1579), founder of the Royal Exchange, lies next to the nuns' choir. Alongside him is Julius Cesar Adelmare († 1636), an adviser to James I. William Pickering († 1574), ambassador to France and Spain, was laid to rest beneath a canopy tomb. Opposite this is the grave of Sir John Crosby († 1475); the tomb of Lord Mayor John Spencer († 1608) is by the south wall.

*St Helen's Bishopsgate

Liberty

 ✦ F 5

Location: Regent Street, W 1
Tube: Oxford Circus
❶ Mon–Sat 10am–8pm,

Sun noon–6pm
www.liberty.co.uk

While ▶Harrods boasts that it supplies almost everything, the department store Liberty takes pride in doing exactly the opposite: By no means is everything sold here, but what there is, is all the more refined.

Since its foundation in 1875 by **Arthur Lasenby Liberty** the store has been England's best address for fabrics, carpets, furniture and Oriental and Asian porcelain. Liberty made its name with printed silk fabrics of its own design. These products remain classics to this day, and every English country house worth its salt has furnishings in the proverbial Liberty Style. The present architecture of the store, dating from 1924, is a sight in its own right, starting with the Tudor façade on Great Marlborough Street and continuing in the wonderful sales areas, which rise as galleries around a spacious inner court. The warm and cosy atmosphere, quintessential Liberty Style, is provided by the wooden panelling.

MARCO ⬤ POLO TIP

! *A gift from London* Insider Tip

A throw, a scarf or a tie from Liberty in one of the company's own fabric designs is a souvenir that ought to please anybody.

This is not just any old wood: It came from the two last wooden ships of the Royal Navy, HMS Impregnable (launched in 1810) and HMS Hindustan (1841).

Lincoln's Inn

⊹ G / H 5

Location: Chancery Lane, WC 2
Tube: Holborn, Chancery Lane
Courtyards: Mon–Fri 7am–7pm
Chapel and gardens: Mon–Fri 12 noon–2.30pm

Other buildings:
only with a guided
tour, registration and information:
www.lincolnsinn.org.uk

Lincoln's Inn, established in the 14th century by the Earl of Lincoln, is one of London's four inns of court (associations for barristers) along with ▶Gray's Inn and the two inns of court in the ▶Temple. Its rolls of admission include such famous names as Sir Thomas More, Oliver Cromwell, John Donne, William Pitt, Horace Walpole, Benjamin Disraeli, William Gladstone and Margaret Thatcher. The complex of buildings is the best-preserved and handsomest of its type in London. For permission to enter, ask the porter in Chancery Lane; entry to the gardens and chapel is unrestricted.

Historic college for barristers

The gatehouse of 1517–21 bears the arms of Henry VIII, the Earl of Lincoln and James Lovell, Speaker of the House of Commons. Beyond it are the Tudor-style Old Buildings, which were altered in 1609. Straight ahead lies the Old Hall, on the right the Gothic chapel consecrated in 1623 and thoroughly restored in 1685 by Sir Christopher Wren. The Old Hall was built in 1485 and used until 1883 as the High Court of Chancery. Go past the chapel to reach the Great Hall and the library. Adjoining them are the Stone Buildings with New Square, built in 1680, to the left.

The quiet park behind Lincoln's Inn is a favourite spot for lawyers to take their midday break. Lincoln's Inn Fields was a place of execution in the Tudor and Stuart period. On the south side is the Royal College of Surgeons, home of the **Hunterian Museum**, the medical collections of the Scottish doctor John Hunter (1729–93).

Lincoln's Inn's Fields

❶ Tue–Sat 10am–5pm; free admission

Sir John Soane's Museum on the north side of Lincoln's Inn Fields is a treat for anyone who likes curiosities. The home of the architect (he designed the Bank of England and Dulwich Picture Gallery, for example) and teacher at the Royal Academy, Sir **John Soane**

*Sir John Soane's Museum

Shopping in style at Liberty

(1753 – 1837) is no ordinary museum, but a work of art. Soane showed his treasures – paintings, sculptures, architectural fragments and some oddities – to his students on the day before and the day after giving a lecture. Since his death nothing has been changed – right down to the positioning of even the smallest piece of bric-a-brac. The rooms seem somewhat untidy and over-full, but this constitutes their charm. The most notable works of art in the house are in the library and dining room: ceiling paintings by Howard in the library and dining room, a Reynolds and a portrait of Sir John Soane by Lawrence in the same rooms. Thanks to the ingenious folding walls, the Picture Gallery accommodates a large number of paintings, including twelve works by Hogarth (the series *The Rake's Progress* and *The Election*, several works by Canaletto and drawings by Soane. The Monk's Salon holds medieval art and more works by Canaletto in addition to paintings by Alcott and Ruisdael and, in the room next to it, by Watteau. Soane placed the sarcophagus of Sethi I, father of Ramses the Great, found in the Valley of Kings in 1817, in the Sepulchral Chamber in the basement.

❶ Tue–Sat 10am–5pm; free admission; tour Sat 11am (£10); www.soane.org

> **MARCO POLO TIP**
>
> **!**
>
> *Candlelight museum* **Insider Tip**
>
> The atmosphere of the museum is even more mysterious and enchanting on the first Tuesday of each month from 6pm until 9pm, when it is illuminated only by candlelight, but it is essential to arrive early. Tickets are sold from 5.30pm.

London Bridge

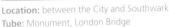 ✦ J / K 5 / 6

Location: between the City and Southwark
Tube: Monument, London Bridge

London Bridge is probably the biggest gap on a tour of the sights of London, as the historic bridge no longer stands here.

The words of the famous song, *London Bridge is falling down ...*, are untrue, as the bridge never fell down, though it was replaced twice. There was a bridge across the Thames on this site as early as the Roman period, in about AD 50. It is unclear whether the Anglo-Saxons repaired it, but the Normans built a new one, which was destroyed in a storm in 1091 and patched up again afterwards. A little further east **Peter de Colechurch** built Old London Bridge, the first stone bridge across the Thames, between 1176 and 1209.

Until the mid-18th century it was the only Thames bridge in central London.

Its 20 piers supported not just the roadway, but also houses with shops and even a chapel dedicated to St Thomas Becket. At the south end was a drawbridge, on the south tower of which the heads of the decapitated were placed on spikes. Among those who met this fate was Sir Thomas More. The houses were later pulled down to create passing-places, giving pedestrians refuge from the heavy traffic. Excellent models in the ▶Museum of London and in St Magnus-the-Martyr (▶p. 244) show how London Bridge looked in the Middle Ages. In 1831 John Rennie replaced it with a new bridge upriver. In its turn this five-arch structure made way for the present, aesthetically boring bridge in 1973. When word got out in 1968 of plans to demolish Rennie's bridge, the American millionaire Robert P. McCulloch bought it at auction and had it transported to the USA, where it now stands across Lake Havasu, Arizona. McCulloch vigorously denied the rumour that he had ▶Tower Bridge in mind and did not realise his mistake until the bridge was delivered.

✱ Madame Tussauds

✦ E 4

Location: Marylebone Road, NW 1
Tube: Baker Street
❶ Daily from 9am

Admission: £30,
cheaper online
www.madametussauds.com

The high admission price is not all that can be paid at Madame Tussauds, where many attractions are optional extras. Nevertheless, the waxworks is a magnet for visitors, who often queue for an hour in summer for admission.

Marie Tussaud (1761–1850) from Alsace learned the art of making wax figures from a German doctor named Phillippe Curtius in Paris in the 18th century. During the French Revolution this skill brought her some dubious commissions, when she made death masks of decapitated aristocrats. In 1802 she decided to move from Paris to England, taking with her a number of wax figures which she had inherited from Curtius. These formed the basis of the exhibition that opened in London in 1835.

Today the wax figures are constantly brought up to date. In addition to permanent exhibits such as the Queen and Muhammad Ali, it displays short-term celebrities who are removed again after one season.

The Mall

✦ F / G 6

Location: Between Admiralty Arch
and Buckingham Palace

Tube: Charing Cross

The generous width of The Mall makes it London's most impressive avenue and a parade route.

London's parade route
The royal family passes along The Mall from ▶Buckingham Palace on occasions such as Trooping the Colour, the Queen's official birthday. The Mall is used for military parades and decorated with flags to greet state guests. At other times four lanes of traffic thunder along it. The street was once much quieter. Until 1911, when **Sir Aston Webb** broadened the avenue to its present width, The Mall was a tranquil place to take a promenade, its original purpose when it was laid out in the reign of Charles II.

Admiralty Arch
Since 1910 the triple gateway of Admiralty Arch has marked the start of The Mall at Trafalgar Square. The Admiralty itself is nearby on Horse Guards Parade (▶Whitehall).

*Carlton House Terrace
This walk along The Mall starts from Admiralty Arch and heads towards Buckingham Palace. The row of brilliant white columns and pediments visible on the right is Carlton House Terrace, built in two sections by **John Nash** from 1827 to 1832 on the site of the old Carlton House, the residence of George IV before he became king. Carlton House was built in 1709 and demolished in 1829. Its size can be gauged from the portico of the ▶National Gallery, which formed part of Carlton House. The **Institute of Contemporary Art** (ICA) here
Insider Tip is one of London's leading avant-garde galleries. The ICA café is a popular meeting place for the art scene.
From the steps between the two halves of Carlton House Terrace, the **Duke of York Column** rises to a height of 38m/125ft. It is crowned by the figure of Frederick, Duke of York, who was appointed commander-in-chief of the British army in 1827 and was also notorious for his huge debts. This was said to be the reason for the height of the column – only at the top was the duke safe from his creditors. To meet the costs of erecting it, every soldier in the British army had to forgo one day's pay.

ICA: exhibitions daily 11am–6pm, Thu until 9pm; tickets tel. 020 79 30 36 47; www.ica.org.uk

? *Do you know*

... why the road surface of The Mall is red? It is meant to imitate a red carpet – heads of state, royalty and other celebrities pass along it often, and respect is paid to them in this way.

MARCO ⊕ POLO INSIGHT

A sight not seen every day: the Golden State Coach on The Mall, here for the Golden Jubilee of the Queen

---

* # Monument

◆ **K 5**

Location: Fish Street Hill, EC 3
Tube: Monument
🕑 Daily 9.30am–6pm

Admission: £4
www.themonument.info

As a memorial to the Great Fire of 1666 a Doric column 202 feet (61.5m) in height called simply The Monument was erected between 1671 and 1677.

It stands 202 feet from the spot in Pudding Lane where the fire broke out and was designed by Sir Christopher Wren and Robert Hooke. The Monument once stood in open ground at the northern end of the old ▶London Bridge. Although it is the world's tallest free-standing stone column, the surrounding buildings now hem it in and restrict the view from the observation platform, which was protected by railings in 1842 following six suicides. It is surmounted by a 4m/13ft-high urn with a golden ball of fire.

St Magnus-the-Martyr

From the Monument it is a short distance down Fish Street Hill to the Church of St Magnus-the-Martyr, which lies almost unnoticed between modern buildings. A church dedicated to the Norwegian Earl of Orkney, Magnus, who was martyred in about 1117 by his uncle Hakon and canonised in 1135, was recorded on this site at the northern end of London Bridge in the 11th century. The Great Fire destroyed the old church, and Wren replaced it from 1671 to 1676. The features of its fine interior are decorated Ionic columns, a pulpit designed by Wren and a lovely sword-rest made in 1708 (to the left of the altar).

The grave of **Henry Yevele**, one of the architects of ▶Westminster Abbey and bridge-master of London Bridge, is in St Magnus. To the left of the entrance is a model of the bridge. When the shops and houses on the bridge were demolished from 1756 in order to widen it, part of the church was also pulled down to make a passage through to Fish Street.

✳ Museum of London

✥ J 4

Location: London Wall, EC 2
Tube: St Paul's, Barbican, Moorgate
🕐 Daily 10am–6pm

Admission: free
www.museumoflondon.org.uk

The Museum of London in the Barbican complex, the largest city museum in the world, is a journey through 2000 years of history.

It presents Roman remains, including marble sculptures from the Temple of Mithras, weapons from the Anglo-Saxon period and furniture, clothing, documents and musical instruments from the Tudor and Stuart periods. The museum has reconstructions of a Roman kitchen and a cell from the old Newgate prison, as well as a shop and commercial premises from the time Victorian and Edwardian period. There is even an Art Deco lift from Selfridges department store. The Great Fire of London of 1666 is explained in detail, with the reasons, consequences and persons involved.

The sections from the 18th century to the present day have been remodelled. The displays on the 19th century, for example a Victorian shopping street, give a particularly lively and varied impression of the period when London, as the capital city of the British Empire, was at its zenith. The pride and glory of the collection is the golden Lord Mayor's Coach, made in 1757, which is taken out of museum once each year to convey the new Lord Mayor through the City.

** National Gallery

Location: Trafalgar Square, WC 2
Tube: Charing Cross
❶ Daily 10am–6pm, Fri until 9pm, guided tours daily 11.30am, 2.30pm,

Fri also 7pm; meet in Sainsbury Wing
Admission: free
www. nationalgallery.org.uk

The National Gallery, one of the world's most important collections of paintings, provides a more or less comprehensive cross-section of European art from the high Middle Ages until the late 19th century.

The façade of the National Gallery occupies the whole north side of ▶Trafalgar Square. The National Gallery was founded in 1824, when the government bought 38 paintings owned by the deceased banker and collector John Julius Angerstein and exhibited them in his house at 100 Pall Mall. From 1832 the gallery had its own building on Trafalgar Square to designs by William Wilkins, the work being completed in 1838. Wilkins integrated the colossal portico of Carlton House into the façade. The first extension, with a dome that gave the institution the nickname »national cruet-stand«, was made in 1876. The latest addition was the Sainsbury Wing in 1991. It was donated by the Sainsbury brothers, owners of the chain of supermarkets. Be-

MARCO⊕POLO TIP

? *Don't miss* Insider *Tip*

- Jan van Eyck: **The Arnolfini Portrait**
- Sandro Botticelli: **Venus and Mars**
- Hans Holbein the Younger: **The Ambassadors**
- Leonardo da Vinci: **The Virgin of the Rocks**
- Titian: **Bacchus and Ariadne**
- Rembrandt: **Self Portrait at the age of 34**
- Diego Velázquez: **The Rokeby Venus**
- John Constable: **The Hay Wain**

fore entering the gallery, stop on the terrace to enjoy the wonderful view of Trafalgar Square and ▶Whitehall. In front of the building is Grinling Gibbons's statue of James II as a Roman emperor (1686) and a copy in bronze of Houdon's statue of Washington in Richmond, Virginia.

SAINSBURY WING (PAINTING FROM 1260 TO 1510)

The so-called Wilton Diptych (room 53), a two-panel altar with a gilded background, which probably originated in France in about 1395, is a masterpiece of late Gothic painting. It shows the kneeling

The National Gallery, a Mecca for art lovers

King Richard II (1367–1400), presented to the Virgin by his patron saints John the Baptist, Saint Edward the Confessor and Saint Edmund.

Italian painting — Late Gothic painting from 14th-century Italy is represented by **Duccio di Buoninsegna** from Siena with an *Annunciation* and *Jesus Opens the Eyes of a Man Born Blind* with delicate colouring, fine linearity and a balanced, though not perspectival spatial composition (room 51). Early Renaissance painting in 15th-century Florence discovered perspective and a new view of man based on the study of anatomy and the ancient ideal of beauty. In this style **Piero della**

National Gallery (Main Floor)

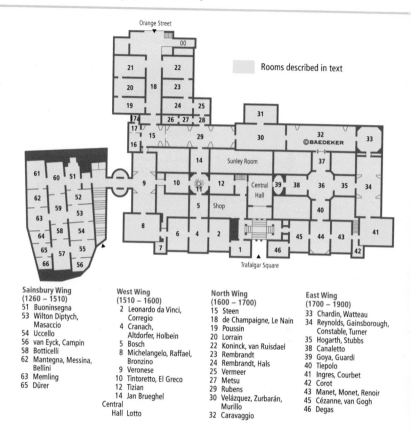

Orange Street

00

Rooms described in text

Sainsbury Wing
(1260 – 1510)
51 Buoninsegna
53 Wilton Diptych, Masaccio
54 Uccello
56 van Eyck, Campin
58 Botticelli
62 Mantegna, Messina, Bellini
63 Memling
65 Dürer

West Wing
(1510 – 1600)
2 Leonardo da Vinci, Correggio
4 Cranach, Altdorfer, Holbein
5 Bosch
8 Michelangelo, Raffael, Bronzino
9 Veronese
10 Tintoretto, El Greco
12 Tizian
14 Jan Brueghel

Central
Hall Lotto

North Wing
(1600 – 1700)
15 Steen
18 de Champaigne, Le Nain
19 Poussin
20 Lorrain
22 Koninck, van Ruisdael
23 Rembrandt
24 Rembrandt, Hals
25 Vermeer
27 Metsu
29 Rubens
30 Velázquez, Zurbarán, Murillo
32 Caravaggio

East Wing
(1700 – 1900)
33 Chardin, Watteau
34 Reynolds, Gainsborough, Constable, Turner
35 Hogarth, Stubbs
38 Canaletto
39 Goya, Guardi
40 Tiepolo
41 Ingres, Courbet
42 Corot
43 Manet, Monet, Renoir
45 Cézanne, van Gogh
46 Degas

Francesca painted the *The Baptism of Christ* (1442) against the background of an impressive landscape reflected in the water of the river Jordan (room 66). In the 1450s **Paolo Uccello** created the dramatic *Saint George and the Dragon* and in 1432, with extreme foreshortening, *The Battle of San Romano* between Florence and Siena as a tournament-like melée of many combatants (room 54). A comparison between **Massaccio**'s life-like, corporeal *Virgin and Child* (1426, room 53) and **Sandro Botticelli**'s mannered treatment of the lasciviously reclining figures of *Venus and Mars* (c.1485, room 58) illustrates the painting styles of the early and high Renaissance. **Andrea Mantegna** placed *The Agony in the Garden* (c.1460, room 62) in a barren, rocky landscape with a many-towered city, including the Colosseum and Trajan's Column in Rome as a backdrop. **Antonello da Messina**'s psychologically sensitive *Portrait of a Young Man* (c.1479) and his equally well-known *Saint Jerome in his Study* form a charming contrast to **Giovanni Bellini**'s official portrait of *Doge Leonardo Loredan* (c.1500; all room 62).

Early paint-
ing from the
Netherlands
and Germany

Robert Campin's *The Virgin and Child before a Firescreen* (c. 1430, room 56) is the starting point of the series of major old masters from the Netherlands. The background to the head of the Virgin, who is offering her breast to the infant Christ, is a wicker firescreen in place of a halo. The scene for **Jan van Eyck**'s life-like *Arnolfini Portrait* of 1434 (room 56) is an interior which the painter imbues with a remarkable intensity and spatial effect. **Hans Memling**'s altarpiece known as *The Donne Triptych* places the enthroned Virgin in the central panel, flanked by St Catherine and St Barbara, who are presenting the donor's family to the Madonna, while John the Baptist and John the Evangelist are shown on the side-panels (room 63). **Albrecht Dürer**'s portrait of his father is an expressive characterisation of old age (room 65).

WEST WING (PAINTING FROM 1510 TO 1600)

Painting from
Spain and
Italy

Leonardo da Vinci painted strongly modelled bodies with a subtle treatment of colour and light in intensely atmospheric landscapes, such as the *Virgin of the Rocks* (1483–1508, room 2), which depicts St John and the infant Christ in the presence of the Virgin and an angel praying and giving blessings in a rocky landscape. **Raphael** portrays the enthroned Virgin in *The Ansidei Madonna* with St John the Baptist and St Nicholas (1506) in a more contemplative mood as a sacra conversazione (room 8). His brilliant portrait of Pope Julius II (1512) is also on view. Italian Mannerist painting is represented by **Michelangelo**'s *The Entombment* (room 8).

The composition of its figures and the muscular bodies are a reference to the sculpture of Laocoön and his sons excavated in 1500–01. **Agnolo Bronzino** painted his *Allegory* in the 1540s in a coolly erotic manner with naked figures of Venus and Cupid, Jealousy tearing his hair, the mask-like portrayal of Fraud and an old man as the embodiment of Time (room 8). **Correggio** depicted his charming *Venus* *with Mercury and Cupid (The School of Love)* of 1520–25 in the style of the Holy Family and a delightful Madonna and child (*The Madonna of the Basket*) with Joseph's carpenter's shop in the background (both room 2). **Titian**'s meeting between *Bacchus and Ariadne* (room 12) is full of movement and drama, while **Andrea del Sarto** lends a pale and introspective face to his *Portrait of a Young Man* (room 8). **Lorenzo Lotto** presents a well-groomed Venetian lady as Lucretia (Central Hall). **Paolo Veronese** produced large-format scenes such as *The Family of Darius before Alexander* in a decorative and ceremonious style (room 10). **Tintoretto** painted a spectacular interpretation of *The Origin of the Milky Way* (room 10): Bodies are delineated in pulses of light as Juno casts away the infant Hercules who is drinking from her breast, at which a stream of divine milk is spilt over the heavens. **El Greco** bathes his religious works in flickering coloured light and paints his characteristically Mannerist, elongated figures, as in *The Agony in the Garden of Gethsemane* and *Christ driving the Traders from the Temple* (room 10).

There is also a sensitive portrait of a young woman by **Lucas Cranach the Elder** (room 4) and an expressive interpretation of *Christ Mocked (The Crowning with Thorns)* by **Hieronymus Bosch** (room 5). **Albrecht Altdorfer** and his *Landscape with a Footbridge* represent the so-called Danube school (room 4). In 1533 **Hans Holbein the Younger** from Augsburg painted *The Ambassadors* of France at the English court, Jean de Dinteville and Bishop Georges de Selve, in a tour de force of perspective technique with a variety of objects, such as a globe, sundial and musical instruments, that carry a deeper meaning (room 4). **Pieter Brueghel the Elder** produced an earthily rustic *Adoration of the Kings* (room 4).

Painting from Germany and the Netherlands

NORTH WING (PAINTING FROM 1600 TO 1700)

Peter Paul Rubens made a contribution to 17th-century Baroque painting with a charming portrait of his sister-in-law Susanne Fourment wearing a straw hat, *Le Chapeau de Paille*. Moving masses of human figures bathed in light and shade characterise his depiction of Peace and War: Peace naked and voluptuous, followed by Faith and Prosperity; on the right, by contrast, War in armour turns to flee with Discord, Pestilence and the goddess of war (both room 29). **Anthony van Dyck** was the leading court painter in England at the time of Charles I. His equestrian portrait of the king is one of his greatest works (room 31). **Frans Hals** (*Portrait of a Man Holding Gloves*, room 24), **Gabriel Metsu** (*A Man and a Woman Seated by a Virginal*, room 27), **Jan Vermeer** (*A Young Woman standing at a Virginal*, room 26) and **Jan Steen** (*Skittle Players outside an Inn*, room 15), on the other

Painting from the Netherlands

hand, depicted the world of the middle classes. Important landscape painters include **Jan van Goyen** with a river landscape (room 22), **Philips Koninck** with a landscape with houses in a wood, and **Jacob van Ruisdael** with a landscape with a ruined castle and a church (room 22). **Rembrandt** van Rijn enchants the viewer with his sensitive portraits in soft coloured light – his self-portrait, for example, or *Saskia as Flora* (both room 23). He created a novel combination of a historical painting with a religious theme in his famous early work *Belshazzar's Feast* (room 24).

Spanish, Italian and French painting

Diego Velázquez, the outstanding Spanish Baroque artist, is represented with a portrait of Philip IV of Spain and an erotic portrayal of the naked Venus looking at herself in a mirror, known as *The Rokeby Venus* (c.1650). **Francisco de Zurbarán** painted *St Margaret of Antioch* in the contemporary costume of a shepherdess and *St Francis in Meditation*. **Bartolomé Esteban Murillo** pleases with a cheerful portrait of *A Young Man Drinking* and the harmonious composition of *Christ Healing the Paralytic* (all in room 30). The first high point of Italian Baroque painting were the works of **Caravaggio**, which are characterised by strong contrasts of light and shade and powerful rendering of the body, as in *The Supper at Emmaus* (room 32). In France **Claude Lorrain** (room 20) painted landscapes and architecture with feeling, while **Nicolas Poussin** (room 19) preferred the severity of classicism. **Louis Le Nain** (room 18) portrayed the life of lower social classes, for example in *A Woman and Five Children* (1642). **Philippe de Champaigne** confirmed his reputation as a court portrait painter with his official portrait of *Cardinal Richelieu* (room 18).

EAST WING (PAINTING FROM 1700 TO 1920)

British Painting

William Hogarth's six-part *Mariage à la mode* (room 35) ventures a critical look at the hypocrisy of the nobility and bourgeoisie, using marriage customs as an example. **George Stubbs**, on the other hand, painted rustic scenes and thoroughbred horses (room 35) to please these social classes. **Robert Wilson** is the first major English landscape painter with his atmospheric renderings of the countryside of southern and central England. The portraits of **Joshua Reynolds**, for example *General Sir Banastre Tarleton* (room 36) or *Lord Heathfield* (room 34), combine individuality with a display of status. **Thomas Gainsborough** painted portraits such as *The Morning Walk for William and Elizabeth Hallet* (room 34), dissolving forms and colours in a manner that seems almost pre-Impressionist. With his naturalistic treatment of landscapes, **John Constable** stands at the threshold of the 19th century and had a lasting influence on later French outdoor

John Constable painted *The Haywain* in 1821

painting. *The unfinished Weymouth Bay, The Hay Wain* and *Salisbury Cathedral from the River* are among his great works (all room 34). The work of **J. M. W. Turner** developed from the romantic landscapes of the early years to late paintings that are almost non-representational. *The Fighting Temeraire* (1838) with its mood of diffuse light at the closing of the day depicts the last journey of a ship on its way to the breaker's yard; in *Snowstorm* dynamic whirls of colour emphasise the peril of a ship at sea. *Rain, steam and speed* is his title for a picture in which a train snakes through a landscape that dissolves and almost disappears in coloured light (all room 34).

Jean Baptiste Chardin painted delightful interior scenes and sensual still-lifes (*The Young Schoolmistress*), while **Antoine Watteau**'s *The Scale of Love* reveals him as an artist of the imaginary fêtes galantes of the Rococo in which dreams mingle with reality (all room 33). In the early 19th century **Eugène Delacroix** developed a style of painting that combined dynamic forms and colours, while **Jean Auguste Dominique Ingres** maintained a calm, classical manner, as the portrait of *Madame Moitessier* (room 41) illustrates. **Gustave Courbet**'s landscapes place him in the school of French Realism (room 41), whereas **Camille Corot** was an early exponent of outdoor painting (room 42). The Impressionists include **Edouard Manet** (*Music in the Tuileries Gardens*, 1862), **Claude Monet**, who visited London in 1870 in the company of **Camille Pissarro** (*The Thames*

French painting

below Westminster, room 43), **Pierre Auguste Renoir** (*The Umbrellas*, room 43), **Edgar Degas** (*Ballet Dancers*, room 46) and for a time **Paul Cézanne** (*Les Grandes Baigneuses*, room 45).

Spanish and Italian painting **Goya**'s sceptical view of human nature is particularly clearly expressed in his portraits of the *Duke of Wellington* and the legal scholar *Dr Peral* (both room 39). Artistic highlights of late 18th-century Venice included the airy Rococo painting of **Giovanni Battista Tiepolo** (room 40) and veduti by **Canaletto** (room 38) and **Guardi** (room 39), which captured the squares, canals, churches and views of the lagoon in ever-changing variations, often with photographic precision or in melting coloured light.

** National Portrait Gallery

— ✶ G 5

Location: St Martin's Place, WC 2
Tube: Charing Cross
🕐 Daily 10am–6pm, Thu and

Fri until 9pm
Admission: free
www.npg.org.uk

What counts in the National Portrait Gallery is not necessarily artistic quality, but the fame of the sitter.

The collection founded in 1856 today contains about 160,000 portraits – paintings, drawings, sculptures, photographs – of Britons who were famous in their time. The most interesting are on show in the permanent collection (▶photo p. 108).

Tour A chronological tour starts in the Tudor period on level 2. The outstanding paintings are of Henry VIII, life-size by Hans Holbein the Younger, several portraits of Elizabeth I, miniatures of Walter Raleigh and Francis Drake by Hilliard and a portrait of Shakespeare by John Taylor, the first acquisition made by the gallery. 17th-century portraits include those of Charles I and Charles II, Nell Gwynne, Oliver Cromwell, the Earl of Arundel (by Rubens) and Samuel Pepys. This is followed by the 18th century, with Sir Christopher Wren, Sir Isaac Newton, the Duke of Marlborough and Sir Robert Walpole (all by Sir Godfrey Kneller). There are self-portraits by William Hogarth and Sir Joshua Reynolds, and a portrait of Captain James Cook by John Webber. The section on the late 18th and early 19th century presents works such as Lord Byron in romantic Albanian dress, portraits of Lord Nelson and Lady Hamilton, Sir

Walter Scott (by Edwin Landseer) and the three Brontë sisters by their brother Branwell.

The Victorian period is well represented on level 1, with Queen Victoria herself and other notables such as Cecil Rhodes, Benjamin Disraeli, Henry James (by John Singer Sargent) and a caricature of Oscar Wilde. The other rooms and the Atrium Gallery are reserved for figures of the 20th century, ranging from Lawrence of Arabia, James Joyce, Sir Winston Churchill and John Maynard Keynes to John Major, Mick Jagger and Princess Diana and her sons.

** Natural History Museum

C 7

Location: Cromwell Road, SW 7   admission 5.30pm)
Tube: South Kensington   **Admission:** free
❶ Daily 10am–5.50pm (last   www.nhm.ac.uk

No one who takes children to London, and no one who is interested in nature, should fail to visit the Natural History Museum. For entertaining and easily comprehensible explanations of complex matters, with many opportunities to try things out for yourself, this is a marvellous museum.

On his death in 1753 the scientist Sir Hans Sloane left his extensive collections (50,000 books, 10,000 stuffed or preserved animals and 334 volumes of pressed plants) to the nation – the basis for the ▶British Museum. In 1860 it was decided to present the natural sciences separately. Alfred Waterhouse received the commission to design a new museum in Kensington. The result of his work, the Natural History Museum which opened in 1881, resembled a cathedral or a palace in the Romanesque style. The terracotta-clad façade, 230m/250yd long with two 64m/210ft-high towers, dominates this section of Cromwell Road. Expeditions to all parts of the world expanded the holdings. Sir Joseph Banks, who sailed around the world with Captain James Cook, was a particularly zealous collector. Charles Darwin also returned from his expeditions with new material. The museum is divided into a blue, a green, a red and an orange zone.

? *Don't miss* Insider Tip

MARCO ⊕ POLO TIP

- Dinosaur department
- Creepy Crawlies – your friends the insects
- The cocoon in the Darwin Centre – high-tech biology
- Model of the earth in the Red Zone

Central Hall   The main entrance leads into the imposing Central Hall. The 26m/85ft-long skeleton of a Diplodocus occupies the middle of the hall.

Blue zone   In the blue zone to the left of the Central Hall is the **dinosaur department**, where the world of Triceratops and Tyrannosaurus Rex comes to life. Videos, moving models and dioramas explain the evolution, body structure and way of life of these primeval creatures. The highlight is an extremely lifelike model of T Rex. The other departments in the blue zone are devoted to human biology – including a larger-than-life model of a human foetus – and the mammals. Fossil species and mammals that mankind has made extinct are on show; the 27m/89ft-long model of a blue whale hangs from the ceiling. The following sections are about fish, reptiles, amphibians and invertebrates.

Green zone   To the right of the Central Hall, the green zone holds a further high-light: the department for spiders and »creepy crawlies«. A huge mod-

The 26m/85ft-long skeleton of a Diplodocus in the Central Hall is a foretaste of the fantastic dinosaur department

el of a scorpion, no.1 Crawley House, containing drawers and cupboards that can be opened to see what kinds of bugs and insects crawl around in the home, and a walk-in termite mound are just two features of this highly entertaining and informative section. The ecology section opposite is less amusing but equally instructive. The exhibits in the next department, devoted to birds, include preserved specimens of extinct species like the dodo. On the first floor there are rooms on the evolution of species, primates, the varied world of plants and the position of humankind in evolution. The next part of the museum is given over to minerals and shells.

In an extension to the building the red zone, which has the history of the earth and geology as its theme, is no less spectacular. A lift takes visitors through a giant globe in which the diversity of Planet Earth is demonstrated. »Earth Today and Tomorrow«, about the earth's resources, has the 3.5-ton Cranbourne meteorite from Australia. There is a journey back to the Big Bang and easy-to-understand demonstrations of how earthquakes arise and volcanoes erupt. The section entitled »Restless Surface« shows how the wind and weather shape the surface of the earth.

Red zone

The **Darwin Centre**, the centre of the orange zone, opened in September 2002, and in 2009 the new extension was completed. Visitors are taken up through a 28m/92ft-high cocoon-like construction of concrete to a ramp, which leads down again via 40 interactive exhibits that provide a look at the work of scientists, with a view of laboratories behind glass and the opportunity to **put questions to the researchers**.

Orange zone

✳ Piccadilly Circus

✦ F 5

Location: City of Westminster, W 1
Tube: Piccadilly Circus

London's best-known public space, Piccadilly Circus, a synonym for Swinging London in the 1960s, is the »the hub of the world« for Londoners.

The first impression is one of confusion, however, because Piccadilly Circus is a noisy, frenetic place with nose-to-tail traffic: It is the junction of Regent Street, Piccadilly, Haymarket and Shaftesbury Avenue. After dark Piccadilly Circus takes on its role as the brightly lit heart of the West End. The **Shaftesbury monument** at the centre of the Circus, cast in aluminium by Sir Alfred Gilbert in memory of

The hub of the world

the Earl of Shaftesbury, is universally known as the Eros fountain, but in fact the figure represents the angel of Christian charity. The fountain on the corner of Piccadilly Circus and Haymarket is, by contrast, unambiguous: It represents the Four Horses of Helios. The stage and auditorium of the **Criterion Theatre** on the south side, opened in 1874, are subterranean. The London Pavilion on the north-east side, built in 1885 as a music hall, is now part of the London Trocadero entertainment complex and has been turned into a shopping arcade.

PICCADILLY

Gentlemen in high collars

Piccadilly, the street running from Piccadilly Circus towards ▶Hyde Park, may owe its name to the tailor Robert Baker, who made his fortune selling high collars known as pickadills in his shop on The Strand in the early 17th century and built a house on the vacant land that is Piccadilly today. Now as then, the street is the address of some of the longest-established and most exclusive shops in London.

*Fortnum and Mason, a department store founded in 1707, is one of the finest establishments on Piccadilly. It is famous for its truly aristocratic food hall with tail-coated staff behind the counters. The specialities here – apart from exorbitantly expensive hampers – are tea, biscuits and preserves.

Royal Academy of Arts

The Royal Academy was founded in 1768 and since 1869 has resided opposite Fortnum and Mason in Burlington House, which dates from 1664. In the courtyard is a monument to the first president, Sir **Joshua Reynolds** (1723–92). Such famous artists as Constable, Lawrence, Turner and Millais trained at the Royal Academy. The exhibition of works by contemporary British artists held annually from May until August attracts great attention, and the quality of the special exhibitions is extremely high. Selections from the permanent collection are shown in the John Madejski Fine Rooms, while the Sackler Gallery holds a treasure of the first order: the only sculpture by Michelangelo in England, a tondo of Mary, Jesus and the infant St John. Michelangelo made it for the Florentine patrician Taddeo Taddei immediately after completing his David. In 1823 Sir George Beaumont bought the work and bequeathed it to the academy.

Insider Tip

❶ Sat–Thu 10am–6pm, Fri until 10pm, free guided tour Tue 1pm, Wed–Sat 1pm and 3pm, www.royalacademy.org.uk

*Burlington Arcade

Close to the academy is Burlington Arcade, an exclusive shopping arcade built in the Regency style in 1819 for Lord Cavendish. More

The *Four Horses of Helios* on Piccadilly Circus

Teatime on Piccadilly   Insider Tip

Afternoon tea with cucumber sandwiches, scones and clotted cream is a stylish occasion but excessively expensive in big hotels like The Ritz and in the Fountain Restaurant at Fortnum and Mason. For more reasonable prices and a rooftop view, try the café on the top floor of the largest bookshop in England, Waterstones, (203 – 206 Piccadilly).

than 70 small shops supply essential articles for the gentleman and his lady: made-to-measure shirts, cashmere pullovers, hand-made shoes, articles for grooming and tobacco pipes. The house code of behaviour provides the best guide to the style of the arcade: *... a piazza for the sale of haberdashery, clothing and items, the appearance and smell of which do not cause offence. Whistling, singing, playing of musical instruments, the carrying of large parcels and opening of umbrellas are not allowed.* The arcade has its own guards, known as beadles. In their elegant attire of frock coats and top hats they ensure that visitors respect the rules.

Jermyn Street   The continuation of Burlington Arcade on the other side of Piccadilly (on either side of Fortnum and Mason) are the Piccadilly Arcades and Princes Arcades, which are no less exclusive. They lead to Jermyn Street, where a whole row of high-class outfitters caters for gentlemen of taste.

The Ritz Hotel   Since 1906 the Ritz Hotel at the corner of Piccadilly and Green Park has been one of the foremost addresses among London hotels. It is also a mecca for lovers of afternoon tea, which is taken in the wonderful Palm Court – not a cheap treat, but a stylish occasion for which a jacket and tie must be worn!

Regent's Park

✦ D / E 2–4

Location : Marylebone, W 1
Tube: Baker Street, Regent's Park, Great Portland Street

Once a royal hunting ground and later conceived as a green residential area for the wealthy, the park is now a popular place for leisure activities.

Recreation, not royalty   Henry VIII turned this area into a royal hunting ground in 1538 following the dissolution of the monasteries. Under the name Marylebone Fields, it kept this status until 1649. When **John Nash** (1752–1835) was commissioned by the royal family to landscape and develop Marylebone Fields in 1811, he envisaged a park with two circular avenues and residential terraces, as well as a palace for George, Prince of Wales, and fine villas; Nash also intended the ▶Regent's Canal to pass through the park. Work started in 1812, but the plans came to little – no palace was built and only eight villas, of which three remain, were completed. Regent's Park, open to the public since 1835, has become a place of recreation with children's playgrounds, areas for all kinds of sport and rowing on the boating lake. Plays and concerts are held in summer in the open-air theatre, while Queen Mary's Garden, a lovely rose garden and rockery, and the Victorian Avenue Garden are places to stroll. Since 1978 the principal place of worship for London's Muslim community, London Central Mosque, has stood at the western end of the park.

> ! MARCO ⊕ POLO TIP
>
> *Beatlemania* Insider Tip
>
> Close to Regent's Park is a sacred place for Beatles fans: the zebra crossing in front of the Abbey Road Studios, shown on the cover of the album of that name. From St John's Wood Tube station go west along Grove End Road, which leads into Abbey Road, then turn right. The studios are at number three. To find out more, join one of the Beatles tours organised by Original London Walks (tel. 7 624 3978, www.walks.com).

London Zoo occupies the northern end of the park. The world's oldest scientific zoo, it was founded in 1826 by Sir Stamford Raffles and Sir Humphrey Davy and is crossed by the ▶Regent's Canal. Its main attractions include the birds in the Snowdon Aviary, the gorilla compound opened in 2007 and the children's zoo. The entrances are on the Outer Circle, Prince Albert Road and Broad Walk.

London Zoo

❶ Daily from 10am, closing times vary according to the time of year; admission £22 in the high season; www.zsl.org

AROUND REGENT'S PARK

Several buildings by Nash show how Regent's Park might have looked. **Park Crescent**, built on the south-east side in 1821, is a fine example of a curving perspective of colonnaded façades. A tour around the park on the Outer Circle passes a number of Nash's terraces, such as **York Terrace** (1821) to the west of the crescent and, on the east side, **Chester Terrace** (1825), which has the longest uninterrupted colonnaded façade. Adjoining it is **Cumberland Terrace** (1828) with a figure of Britannia on the pediment relief.

*Buildings by John Nash

To the north of the zoo, on the far side of the canal, Primrose Hill rises to a height of 78m/260ft. It affords a good view of the city, and beyond it is the sought-after residential area of the same name with fine Victorian houses.

Primrose Hill

Lord's Cricket Ground

A short distance to the west of the park and beyond Regent's Canal is a place of pilgrimage for cricket fans: Lord's Cricket Ground, established in 1814 by the veteran cricketer Thomas Lord and now home of the **Marylebone Cricket Club**, which was founded in 1787. Alongside Wimbledon for tennis and Wembley for football, Lord's completes London's trio of sporting shrines. Lord's Museum tells the story of the ground and the game of cricket. Visitors can take a look at the urn containing the »Ashes«, the trophy for contests between England and Australia.

❶ Tours: £18; April–Sept daily 10am, 11am, noon, 1pm, 2pm, 3pm; for further dates see www.lords.org

Sherlock Holmes Museum

221B Baker Street: Everyone who has ever read a Sherlock Holmes story knows this address opposite the south-west entrance to Regent's Park. And indeed there really is a Sherlock Holmes Museum there today, though it does not take Holmes's powers of observation to notice that the museum is situated between number 237 and number 239. Visitors – who are greeted not by Mrs Hudson but by a doorman dressed as a Victorian policeman – can take a look at Holmes's flat on the first floor, where his violin and tobacco-pouch in the shape of a Turkish slipper on the mantelpiece are on display (►MARCO POLO Insight p. 262).

❶ Daily 9.30am–6pm; admission £10; www.sherlock-holmes.co.uk

REGENT'S CANAL

The Regent's Canal, opened in 1820 to connect the Grand Union Canal from Birmingham with London docks, was originally planned by **John Nash** to cut straight through ►Regent's Park, but it was feared that members of polite society taking a constitutional might be offended by foul-mouthed bargees, and the canal therefore makes a detour around the park. The canal starts in **Little Venice**, a genuinely romantic and peaceful canal basin where it is hard to believe that the hustle and bustle of London is all around. It is a good place to take a rest in one of the canalside cafés (take the Tube to Warwick Ave, or from Paddington Station the exit at the north end of platform 8 and follow the canal for five minutes). From Little Venice the canal passes through London Zoo to Regent's Park and Camden Lock. The following section to the Docklands and the Thames is, with the exception of the London Canal Museum, less

!

MARCO ● POLO TIP

On the tow-path — Insider Tip

An enjoyable alternative to a boat trip on the Regent's Canal (► p. 134) is a walk along the tow-path. The stretch from Camden Lock to Regent's Park, for example, takes about 30 minutes.

An idyllic scene on the Regent's Canal in Little Venice

interesting. The museum is housed in the ice-store of the ice-cream maker Carlo Gatti.

London Canal Museum: 12–13 New Wharf Road; Tube: King's Cross; Tue–Sun 10am–4.30pm; free admission; www.canalmuseum.org.uk

Regent Street

✦ F 5

Location: between Carlton House and Langham Place
Tube: Piccadilly Circus, Oxford Circus

Regent Street was London's most ambitious urban planning project when it was built. Today it is the city's finest shopping street.

John Nash planned the street to link Carlton House (▶p. 242) with ▶Regent's Park. In contrast to the park, which was to be a high-class residential quarter, the street was intended from the very beginning as a boulevard for promenading and shopping. Both take their name from the Prince Regent, later King George IV. Apart from All Souls

London's boulevard

MARCO●POLO INSIGHT

Mr Sherlock Holmes, Consultant Detective

The life of the greatest sleuth of all time, who described himself as a »consultant detective«, can be reconstructed only on the basis of his own statements and what was recorded by his companion and chronicler, Dr John H. Watson.

Sherlock Holmes was born in Yorkshire on 6 January 1854. In 1881, at St Bartholomew's Hospital in London, he first met **Dr John H. Watson**, who had come to him in search of accommodation. The two men moved into a flat in the house of the widow Mrs Hudson at the now-legendary address 221B Baker Street. Watson describes Holmes as a lean, muscular man with a remarkably acute intellect, who gathered information and possessed deep knowledge about all manner of strange crimes. He was also an outstanding chemist who had published a brilliant monograph on **140 Different Types of Cigarette Ash**, but took little interest in literature and philosophy, subjects on which he was positively ignorant. When he wanted to think, he played the violin – a genuine Stradivarius, though bought at a bargain price – and smoked cheap tobacco. His relationship to women was more or less non-existent, as he preferred his bachelor existence with Watson. However, there was one exception: **Irene Adler**, »The Woman«, who had proved to be a worthy opponent in the case of **A Scandal in Bohemia**.

Famous Cases

Holmes solved highly complex cases by applying his own method: close examination of the evidence; search for possible explanations; exclusion of what was impossible; consequent deduction. By this means he threw light on such famous criminal cases as **The Hound of the Baskervilles** and – the first jointly investigated case – **A Study in Scarlet**, a bestial murder in Lauriston Gardens near Brixton Road. This and many of his other investigations were carried out in London; one of the most spectacular was the secret of **The Sign of the Four**, a dangerous adventure involving a pact between convicts and a hoard of treasure. Holmes solved the case after a thrilling chase down the Thames from Westminster Pier on a steam-boat. In 1891 Holmes suc-

Here Sherlock Holmes is not looking at his friend Dr Watson, but at Arthur Conan Doyle, whom he also knew well

Holmes fighting with Professor Moriarty at the Reichenbach Falls

ceeded in closing the net around **Professor Moriarty**, the »Napoleon of Crime« and, incidentally, his former private tutor. On 4 May they had a dramatic encounter in Switzerland at the Reichenbach Falls near Meiringen in Switzerland. Moriarty gave Holmes time to write and leave behind a letter of farewell. However, after a short fight it was Moriarty who plunged into the abyss; Holmes realised that his own apparent demise represented an opportunity and allowed even Watson to believe that he, too, had met his death.

Holmes's Secret Life

Only Holmes's **brother Mycroft** knew the truth. By his own account Holmes spent the following three years travelling in the Himalayas and elsewhere and in carrying out research, on which he reported using the pseudonym »Sigerson«. Insiders claim that he went to the famous psychoanalyst Sigmund Freud in Vienna to seek a cure for his addiction to morphium; others believe that he took refuge in Cetinje, the capital of Montenegro, where he met Irene Adler again and lived with her for some years. This liaison is said to have produced a son, who went to the USA and had an illustrious career – as a detective. The name Rex Stout is often mentioned in this connection. However, in 1894, to the amazement of Watson, Holmes reappeared in Baker Street and once again successfully tracked down wrong-doers. In October 1903 he left Baker Street for Sussex to keep bees and conduct research into gelée royale. From here he solved his last case, bringing to book the German master-spy von Bork and thus saving the British Empire. Holmes died on 6 January 1957. His last words were reported to have been »Irene«, but devotees of the great man doubt the truth of this, pointing to his confession that »My brain has always governed my heart.«

Not rush hour but normality on Oxford Circus, where Regent Street crosses Oxford Street

Church, little remains from Nash's time as most of his buildings, dating from 1811 to 1825, were demolished when the street was remodelled between 1895 and 1927. The Quadrant, an elegant curved colonnade on the section beginning at Piccadilly Circus, was also pulled down at this time. A walk from here towards Oxford Circus leads past the opulent Café Royal, where Oscar Wilde was a regular guest, and on to **Hamley's**, the world's largest toyshop, and the high-class department store ▸Liberty.

*All Souls   The steeple of All Souls rises beyond Oxford Circus. This church, built between 1822 and 1824, is remarkable for two things: Firstly, it is the only church in London by John Nash (1752–1835), and secondly it is conspicuous for its unusual form, a colonnaded rotunda topped with a steeple surrounded by detached columns. All Souls is overshadowed by the BBC building on **Portland Place**, the street which leads to ▸Regent's Park between beautiful examples of the neoclassical architecture of the Adam brothers.

Richmond

✦ **Outer suburb**

Location: South-west of the centre
Tube: Richmond
River Tours: Richmond from Westminster

Richmond's quiet, rural character make this area on the south bank of the Thames in the south-west of London one of the best residential areas of the city and a pleasant destination for an excursion.

English monarchs appreciated its charm as long ago as the Middle Ages: In the 12th century Henry I owned a manor house here, which was extended to become Sheen Palace and replaced in 1501 in Henry VII's reign by Richmond Palace. Henry VIII quartered Anne of Cleves there after divorcing her, and Elizabeth I died in the palace. Only a few remains of these buildings survive around Old Palace Yard, including the gatehouse with the arms of Henry VII; Trumpeters' House was built in 1701 on the site of the middle gate of Richmond Palace.

Richmond Green once served for the recreation of palace residents and is now a pretty place with 17th- and 18th-century houses, narrow lanes, charming shops and pubs such as The Cricketers (1666) and The Princes' Head. The four eye-catching brick-built houses known as **Maids of Honour Row** were built in 1724 by the future George II for the court attendants of his wife.

*Richmond Green

To reach Richmond Hill take Hill Rise from Bridge Street, passing the elegant Terrace Gardens. From the hill there is a wonderful view over the green valley of the river Thames, on clear days as far as ▶Windsor.

Richmond Hill

South of Richmond village lies Richmond Park, an expanse of 1000 hectares/2470 acres (bus no. 65 from the Tube station). It was enclosed in 1637 in the reign of Charles I; herds of red and fallow deer still roam there. The special attractions are Isabella Plantation, an area of flowers and woodland created after the Second World War, and Prince Charles's Spinney, where some of England's oldest oak trees grow.

*Richmond Park

King Edward VIII was born in the **White Lodge**, which George II built; it was also the residence of the Duke of York, later King George VI, and today houses the school of the Royal Ballet. **Pembroke Lodge**, now a restaurant, was the home from 1847 of a prime minister, Lord John Russell, and later of his grandson, the philosopher Bertrand Russell. From King Henry's Mound there is a view of St Paul's Cathedral and the towers of the City 15km/10mi away.

Royal London

The British monarchy is the world's oldest, and London is the place where it is tangible. Its institutions cost tax-payers a good deal of money.

▶ **Residences and memorials**

A **Buckingham Palace**
The London residence of Queen Elizabeth II

B **Kensington Palace** Former home of Princess Diana, London residence of the Duke and Duchess of Cambridge, the Duke of Gloucester and the Prince of Kent

C **Clarence House**
Home of the Prince of Wales and the Duchess of Cornwall

D **St. James's Palace**
Still the official residence of the monarch, now home to the Princess Royal (Princess Anne)

E **Tower**
The Crown Jewels are kept here

F **Windsor Castle**
Private residence of Queen Elizabeth II

G **Princess Diana Memorial Fountain**

CAMDEN

London Zoo is attached to the park

WEST-MINSTER

KENSINGTON & CHELSEA

LAMBETH

WANDSWORTH

6 The largest enclosed city park in Europe

KINGSTON UPON THAMES

MERTON

©BAEDEKER

Ⓝ 3km/1.86mi

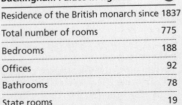

▶ **Buckingham Palace in figures** **A**

Residence of the British monarch since	1837
Total number of rooms	775
Bedrooms	188
Offices	92
Bathrooms	78
State rooms	19

▶ **When is the Queen at home?**

Queen is present: the royal standard is raised and four guards are on duty

Queen is absent: the Union Jack is raised and two guards are on duty

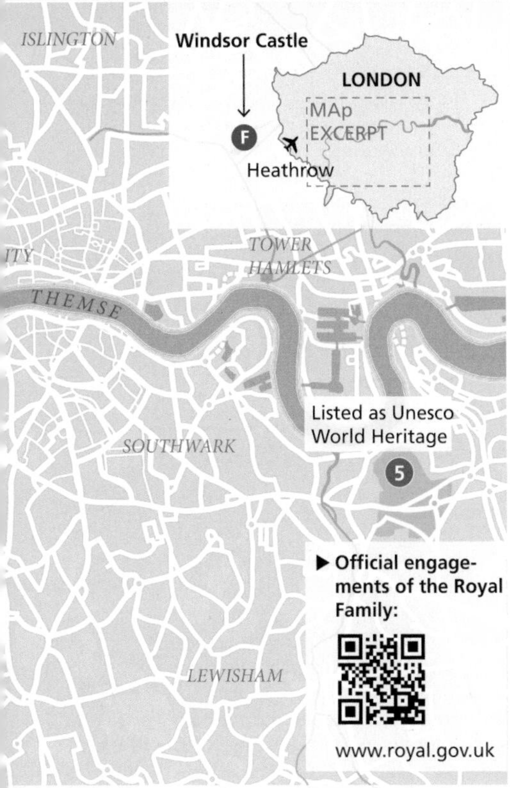

Windsor Castle

LONDON
MAp EXCERPT
Heathrow

F

ISLINGTON

TOWER HAMLETS

THEMSE

ITY

SOUTHWARK

Listed as Unesco World Heritage

5

LEWISHAM

▶ **Official engage-
ments of the Royal
Family:**

www.royal.gov.uk

▶ **Royal parks**

1 Hyde Park
2 Green Park
3 Kensington Garden
4 St. James's Park

5 Greenwich Park
6 Richmond Park
7 Regents Park
8 Bushy Park

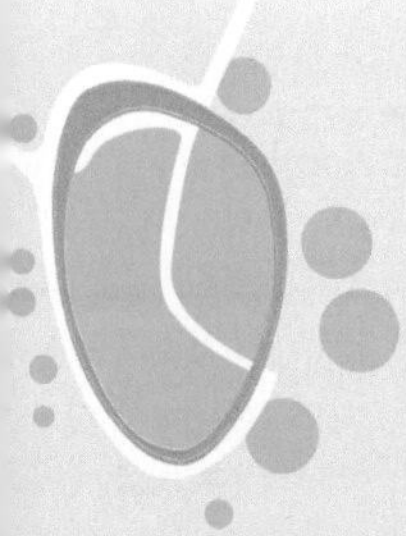

▶ **Size comparison**
(in hectares/acres)

Royal parks in London

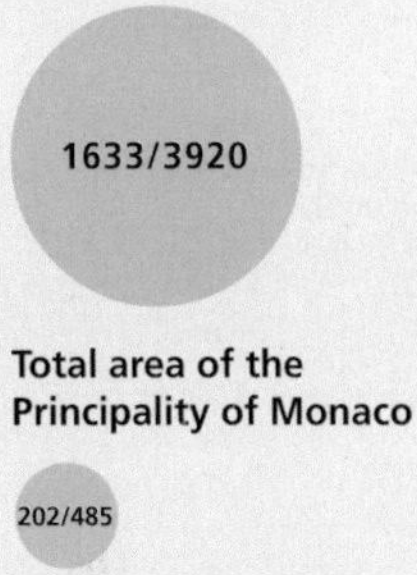

1633/3920

**Total area of the
Principality of Monaco**

202/485

▶ **The Sovereign Grant**
2013 (million pounds)

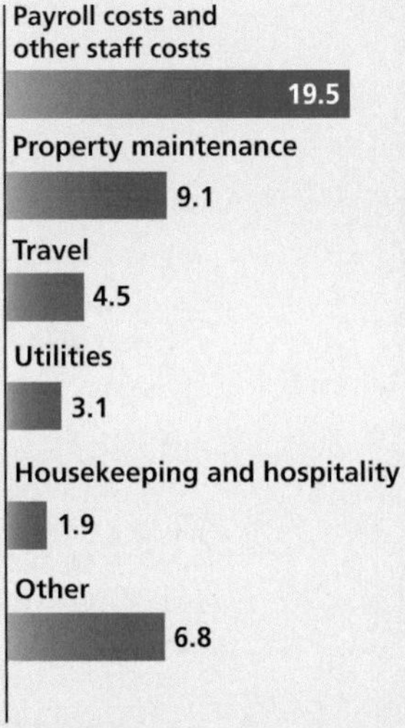

Payroll costs and other staff costs	19.5
Property maintenance	9.1
Travel	4.5
Utilities	3.1
Housekeeping and hospitality	1.9
Other	6.8

annual costs for each
British citizen

approx. £0.53

▶ **Diana Memorial Fountain** **G**

Cost	4.5 million pounds
Location	Hyde Park
Size approx.	50 x 80m/55 x 90yd

The water flows smoothly on one
side but foams on the other side
to symbolise Diana's life.

Ham House Ham House, built in 1610 for Sir Thomas Vavasour, lies on the Thames to the west of the park (bus no. 371 from the Tube station). Originally a modest country house, it was inherited in the mid-17th century by Elizabeth Murray, Countess of Dysart – her father was Charles I's »whipping boy«, i.e. he was beaten instead of the prince when Charles had misbehaved – who enlarged it after her marriage to the Duke of Lauderdale. Today house and park are owned by the National Trust (while the interior belings to ▶Victoria and Albert Museum) and remains largely as the Lauderdales left it. It is thus an opportunity to see a typical interior of wealthy aristocrats of the Stuart period. The collection of miniatures is itself a treasure.
❶ Bus no. 371 from Richmond Tube station; mid-March–May Mon–Thu, Sat, Sun 12 noon–4pm; June–Oct until 5pm; admission £9.90

✷ Royal Air Force Museum

——————————— ✳ **Outer suburb**

Location: Hendon, NW 9
Tube: Colindale
❶ Daily 10am–6pm

Admission: free
www.rafmuseum.org.uk

To see the Royal Air Force Museum, it is necessary to travel out to the northern edge of London, but one of the world's largest aviation collections makes the journey worthwhile.

The factory of an early aviator, Claude Grahame White (1879–1959), in the far north of London is the home of the Royal Air Force Museum. White learned to fly from Louis Blériot, in 1909 the first man to fly across the Channel, and ran a flying school, later an aircraft factory, in Hendon. In the museum, one of the largest of its kind in the world, more than 100 aircraft from the early days of military aviation to the present are on show, in addition to documents, medals and displays on technology.

Aircraft hangars Historic aircraft and other exhibits are spread over five large hangars. In White's factory hall veterans of the First World War can be seen. British and American bombers, including an Avro Lancaster and a B-17 Flying Fortress, are in the Bomber Hall; the Historic Hangars are devoted to planes of the Royal Air Force from the First World War to the present day. The Milestones of Flight Gallery exhibits such classic aircraft as the Blériot XI and Messerschmitt 262; 14 British, German and Italian planes that took part in the battle for England's skies in summer 1940 are in the Battle of Britain Hall. For hands-on experiments connected with flying, visitors are welcomed to the Aeronauts Interactive section.

★ St James's Palace

──────────── ✦ F 6

Location: Pall Mall, SW 1
Tube: Green Park
❶ No public access except for Sunday service in the chapels

St James's Palace, a little to the north of ▸The Mall, is an excellent example of Tudor-style brick architecture and one of the official residences of the monarch of the United Kingdom.

Its name preserves the memory of a leper hospital founded in the 12th century and dedicated to James the Lesser, Bishop of Jerusalem. In 1532 Henry VIII ordered its demolition and the construction to plans by **Hans Holbein the Younger** of the royal palace in which Charles II, James II, Mary II, Queen Anne and George IV were born. St James's Palace became the monarch's residence in 1698 after the fire in Whitehall Palace. This is the reason why ambassadors are still accredited to the Court of St James's, even though Buckingham Palace took its place as the home of the sovereign in the reign of Queen Victoria. St James's Palace is grouped around four courtyards. It accommodates many royal offices and is used for important ceremonies such as the proclamation of a new monarch. The palace is also the London home of Prince Charles and Princess Anne.

The home of Princess Anne

From St James's Street there is a view of the gatehouse, the sole surviving part of the original Tudor building, which bears the initials of Henry VIII. Behind lies the Colour Court with a 17th-century arcade.

Gate House

To the right of the gatehouse, visible from Stable Yard Road, lies Ambassadors' Court with the Chapel Royal of 1532. The painting of the coffered ceiling is said to be by Holbein. The weddings of William III and Mary II (1677), Queen Anne (1683), George IV (1795), Queen Victoria (1840) and George V (1893) took place in the chapel. Elizabeth I prayed here for the defeat of the Spanish Armada in 1588; in 1997 the body of Princess Diana was laid in front of the altar. George Frideric Handel was organist of the Chapel Royal. **York House** on the north side of the court was the home of Lord Kitchener from 1915 to 1916 and the Duke of Windsor from 1919 to 1930.

Chapel Royal

❶ Sunday services: from October to Good Friday, 8.30am and 11.15am

Queen's Chapel

Opposite the palace on Marlborough Road is the Queen's Chapel. It was built for Henrietta Maria, wife of Charles I; the commission was given to Inigo Jones, who made it the first Palladian church in England. Charles II married Catherine of Braganza here in 1661. 100 years later the chapel was again the scene of a royal wedding, when George III married Charlotte Sophie of Mecklenburg-Strelitz.
❶ Sunday services: from Easter to end of July, 8.30am and 11.15am

Clarence House

On Stable Yard Road, is Clarence House. It was the home of the Queen Mother until her death and now serves as Prince Charles's apartments. John Nash built the house in 1825 for the Duke of Clarence, the future King William IV.

Marlborough House

Beyond Carlton House Terrace and set back from the road is Marlborough House, headquarters of the Commonwealth Secretariat. It was built from 1709 to 1711 by Sir Christopher Wren for Sarah, Duchess of Marlborough. In 1850 it became the official residence of the Saxe-Coburg-Gotha family, including the later King Leopold I of Belgium, then of the future King George V (until 1910) and Queen Mary (from 1936 until her death in 1953).

Lancaster House

Lancaster House is almost at the end of The Mall. It is used by the Foreign & Commonwealth Office today but was planned in 1825 by Benjamin Wyatt for the Duke of York, who died before its completion. One of his creditors, the Marquis of Stafford, took over the house after its completion by Robert Smirke and Charles Barry in 1840 and named it Stafford House. The first Lord Leverhulme renamed it Lancaster House and donated it to the nation on the condition that it was used to house the Museum of London, which it did from 1914 to 1951. A comment made by Queen Victoria when she was welcomed to Lancaster House by the Duchess of Sutherland shows the magnificence of the interior: »I have left my house and come to a palace.«

Spencer House

Spencer House on St James's Place, an outstanding example of an 18th-century aristocratic residence, was the home of the earls of Spencer, the family of Princess Diana. Several of its magnificent rooms are open to visitors.
❶ Tours Sun 10.30am–5.45pm except Jul and Aug; admission £12

Pall Mall

St James's Street and Pall Mall, the main thoroughfares of London's clubland, meet in front of the gatehouse of St James's Palace. This district was and remains the home of the most famous London clubs (►MARCO POLO Insight p. 272). Pall Mall, in particular – the name derives from a game similar to croquet that was popular in the 17th century, paille maille – is the address of several exclusive institutions:

Nos. 36–39 are The Army and Navy Club, no. 104 is the Reform Club and no. 106 the Traveller's Club (both built by Sir Charles Barry, the architect of the ▶Houses of Parliament), while no. 116, the United Services Club, is the work of John Nash. About halfway along Pall Mall towards ▶Trafalgar Square and separated from it by a row of buildings, is one of the finest squares in the West End, ***St James's Square**. Henry Jermyn, Earl of St Albans, had it laid out in the 1660s. A wooden rotunda designed by John Nash and an equestrian statue of King William III occupy the centre of the square. Two of the surrounding buildings are particularly noteworthy: No. 15, Lichfield House, was built between 1764 and 1768 by »Athenian« Stuart for Thomas Anson and modelled on the Temple of Minerva in Athens; no. 20, Distillers House, is by Robert Adam, who built it from 1771 to 1774 for Sir Watkin Williams Wynn. George III was born in no. 31. Further along Pall Mall, on **Waterloo Place,** is the entrance to **Carlton House Terrace**, which has its main façade on The Mall. Several addresses of quality can be found here: no. 5 the Turf Club, no. 6 the Royal Society, no. 16 the Terrace Club. A short distance away on the right at no. 4 Carlton Gardens was the headquarters of Charles de Gaulle as leader of the Free French from 1940 to 1944. Nos. 7–9 housed the German embassy until 1939.

* St James's Park · Green Park

✳ E–G 6

Location: The Mall, SW 1
Tube: St James's Park, Green Park

St James's is London's oldest park and in spring and summer, when the flower-beds are in glorious bloom, its most beautiful.

The area was originally a marshy field which Henry VIII made into a hunting ground in 1532. James I established a menagerie with exotic animals, including several aviaries to the south, which is why the road on that side is called Birdcage Walk. Charles II, advised by the French landscape gardener **Le Nôtre**, converted the park into a formal Baroque garden. Finally **John Nash** was commissioned by George IV in 1829 to give the park its present appearance as a quintessential informal English garden and to turn Le Nôtre's canal into the lake seen today. *(Londons most beautiful park)*

Green Park was also used for Henry VIII's royal hunt. Charles II opened it to the public as Upper St James's Park without making any *(Green Park)*

Members Only

No sign marks the door. At most there is a uniformed doorman, who opens to allow gentlemen to enter. Passers-by on Pall Mall and St James's Street hardly notice that this is the heart of London's clubland.

The golden age of the club was the Victorian era. They were a refuge for gentlemen. Upon payment of fees for joining and for annual membership, the members had the club to themselves. They could dine in the restaurant, converse or gamble in the lounge and read in the library, obediently attended by servants – all in luxurious surroundings which by no means every member could have afforded himself. The social life of a true gentleman took place in the club. Only when he wanted to sleep was it necessary to go home. Under these circumstances a marriage was nothing but a burden. It was only logical that women were not admitted to membership, a rule that applies to this day in some clubs. There was a further inestimable benefit of club membership: Not everyone was permitted to join. To be exclusive and different from the others was (and is) the guiding principle of club life. The consequences of this were long waiting lists; the frequent foundation, on the part of those rejected by certain clubs, of new ones, which of course in turn took great care to ensure that only gentlemen worthy of the honour were admitted; and resulting animosities between some clubs.

Origins: the Coffee House

The story began in 1693 in White's Chocolate House, which under John Arthur had risen to become one of the most expensive coffee houses. Mr Arthur offered »gallantry, pleasure and entertainment« to his customers, which above all meant gambling for large sums and betting on the most far-fetched matters – as in the case of Lord Arlington, who in 1750 wagered £3000 on the question of which of two rain-drops would be the first to run down the window-pane. An »inner club«, to which not everyone was admitted, had emerged by this time and was to be the basis of London's oldest and most exclusive club, **White's Club**, which was officially founded several years later at 37-39 St James's Street. George IV, William IV, Edward VII, the Duke of Wellington, Sir Robert Walpole, William Pitt the Elder and of course Beau Brummell were all members. In 1760 opponents of Pitt's reforming policies led by the Prince of Wales formed **Brook's Club** at 60 St James's Street. These two clubs did not keep their political character for long. Almost 90 years later more important matters demanded members' attention, as a fierce dispute broke out over the issue of whether smoking should be permitted at White's, when up to that time only snuff had been allowed. With great reluctance a smoking lounge was installed, but the pro-smoking faction nevertheless founded the **Marlborough Club**.

Victorian Clubs

The Marlborough was founded in a period when clubs were springing up everywhere. For the armed forces there was the **United Services Club** and the **Army and Navy Club**, for fans of horse-racing the **Turf Club**. The **Garrick Club**, founded in 1831 at 15 Garrick Street by the Duke of Sussex, was a meeting place for writers, artists and actors, including Charles Dickens and W.M. Thackeray. Seven years earlier the author and politician John Wilson Croker had founded the **Athenaeum Club** at 107 Pall Mall, which aimed to bring together the intellectual elite of the nation. Croker had the honour of being the first to apply the term »Conservative« to the political party known as the Tories, who suffered a disastrous defeat in the 1832 parliamentary election; at this the remaining Tory members of parliament promptly founded a club for the preservation of Conservative values. It was named the **Carlton Club** after its second location, the Carlton Hotel, and is now at 69 St James's Street. To this day membership is restricted to those who espouse the principles of the Conservative Party; the club is a place of political dealings, where careers are made. All Tory prime ministers from Gladstone (in his Tory days) onwards have been members. In the same year the Whigs founded the **Reform Club** at 104-105 Pall Mall which has been celebrated in literature: It was the place where Jules Verne's **Phileas Fogg** wagered that he could go around the world in 80 days. A gentleman could, of

course, be a member of several clubs – but not of every one. The novelist W.M. Thackeray, for example, was a member of the Reform, the Garrick and the Athenaeum, but was never accepted for the Traveller's Club, which was a much more snobbish institution.

The Tradition Lives On

White's, Brook's, the Athenaeum, Carlton, Garrick and Reform are just a few of the most distinguished names from the golden age of the clubs. They all still exist, but the time when they were preeminent in society, and when the membership included an entertaining array of eccentrics and elderly military men asleep in the armchairs, is now as good as over. On the other hand, their influence should not be underestimated: To be a member of the right club can be extremely advantageous in career terms. The clubs still enjoy the penumbra of exclusivity, even though some have made truly revolutionary concessions to the modern age: The Reform Club, for example, decided to admit women (!) in 1981. It is, after all, proud of being progressive.

View across St James's Park to the rooftops of Whitehall

substantial alterations. Today Green Park is an expanse of grass and trees and shows no sign of once having been a popular place for duels. At the edge of the park facing Buckingham Palace is the memorial for Canadians who died in the two world wars. The memorial for the fallen from Asia, Africa and the Caribbean is at the west end of Constitution Hill, which forms the southern boundary of the park. At the north-western tip of the park opposite Wellington Arch (p. 232), the most recent large British memorial to the Second World War was unveiled in July 2012: the **Bomber Command Memorial** to 55,000 fallen crew members of British bombers.

✴ St Martin-in-the-Fields

                                    ✦ G 6

Location: Trafalgar Square, WC 2
Tube: Charing Cross

St Martin-in-the-Fields, the Admiralty church, rises above the bustle in the north-western corner of ▸Trafalgar Square.

The first written reference to a church on the site dates from 1222. It was rebuilt in 1542 for Henry VIII and again in 1726 to designs by James Gibbs, a pupil of Wren. Because St Martin's is the Admiralty church, the flag of the Royal Navy, the White Ensign, is hoisted on official occasions. It is also the church of the royal family, as ►Buckingham Palace belongs to the parish. Gibbs's new St Martin's was a masterpiece. With its Corinthian portico and slender, 56m/184ft-high tower, it became a model for many churches in the North American colonies. The royal coat of arms appears in the tympanum. The oval ceiling by the Italian stucco artists Bagutti and Arturi, the royal box to the left of the altar and the Admiralty box opposite

MARCO POLO TIP

! *Music in St Martin's* Insider Tip

The concerts in St Martin-in-the-Fields have an excellent reputation: evening programmes of classical and church music (featuring the chamber orchestra of the Academy of St Martin-in-the-Fields), lunchtime concerts with young musicians and jazz evenings in the Crypt Café. For information and tickets, see www.smitf.org.

are among the features to admire inside the church. William Hogarth, Sir Joshua Reynolds and Nell Gwynne, mistress of Charles II, are buried in St Martin's.

A »pearly« collecting money for a good cause

St Martin's has a special significance not only for kings and admirals, but also for a quite different group of people: the »**pearlies**«, a society composed of market traders from the East End who have a tradition of collecting for charity. Every October St Martin's is the venue for the **Costermongers' Harvest Festival**, when they wear suits and dresses covered in mother-of-pearl buttons and elect a pearly king and a pearly queen. Since the period when »Dick« Sheppard was vicar here (1914–27), St Martin's has also been one of London's main places of refuge for the poor and homeless.

St Mary-le-Bow
✦ J 5

Location: Cheapside, EC 2
Tube: St Paul's, Bank   www.stmarylebow.co.uk

St Mary-le-Bow has a special place in Londoners' hearts: Only those born within the sound of Bow Bells are considered true Cockneys.

Since the Middle Ages, the Great Bell of Bow has chimed every morning to wake the citizens of London, and every evening at nine to send them to bed. It marks the acoustic boundaries of the City. St Mary-le-Bow has Norman origins and was one of the first stone-built churches in London. Following the Great Fire Sir Christopher Wren rebuilt it from 1670 to 1683. The church suffered considerable

The Cockney church

damage in the Second World War and was not reconsecrated until 1964; the crucifix was donated by Germany. The name St Mary-le-Bow comes from the Norman arches of the crypt, a motif that Wren took up on the 73m/240ft-tall tower with its 3m/10ft-long weather-vane in the shape of a dragon. Several steps from the entrance to the medieval church can be seen next to these arches in the north-west corner of the Norman crypt.

** St Paul's Cathedral

✦ J 5

Location: Ludgate Hill, EC 4
Tube: St Paul's, Mansion House
❶ Mon–Sat 8.30am–4pm, galleries 9.30am–4.15pm

Admission: £16.50
www.stpauls.co.uk

St Paul's Cathedral, seat of the diocese of London and »parish church of the British Commonwealth«, is the largest and most famous place of worship in the City.

The second-largest dome in the world

The present cathedral with a massive dome that dominates its surroundings is the fifth church to stand on the site, which was probably once occupied by a Roman Temple of Diana. **Old St Paul's**, built in the 12th and 13th centuries, was one of the richest churches in the world. This large Gothic cathedral, burial place of the Anglo-Saxon King Ethelred among others, was severely damaged by fire in 1561, partially rebuilt by Inigo Jones (1627–42) and finally destroyed in the Great Fire of 1666. The architect of the present building, begun in 1675 and completed in 1711 as a successor to Old St Paul's, was **Christopher Wren**. The design was approved only after conflicts with the church commissioners, who found Wren's first plans too radical. The result was a compromise between Wren's original idea for the cathedral (shown by the model in the crypt) and the commissioners' wish to have a Latin cross as the ground plan. Despite this, St Paul's is undoubtedly Wren's masterpiece, the crowning glory of his life's work. The dome is the second-largest in the world after that of St Peter's in Rome. The wedding of Prince Charles and Princess Diana was held in St Paul's in 1981, the funeral service for the Queen Mother here in 2002.

? MARCO ⊕ POLO TIP

Don't miss Insider Tip

- Funeral monument of John Donne
- Tombs of Sir Christopher Wren, Admiral Nelson and the Duke of Wellington in the crypt
- Whispering Gallery
- View from the galleries of the dome

St Paul's Cathedral

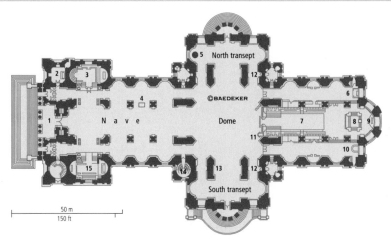

1 Main entrance
2 All Souls' Chapel
3 St Dunstan's Chapel
4 Wellington Monument
5 Font

6 Martyrs' Chapel
7 Choir
8 High altar
9 American Memorial
   Chapel

10 St Mary's Chapel
11 Pulpit
12 Entrance to crypt
13 Nelson Monument

14 To Whispering
    Gallery, library and
    dome
15 Chapel of St Michael
    and St George

Nave

This is one of the largest architectural spaces of any church in the world. All Souls' Chapel on the left has been used since 1925 as a memorial chapel for Field Marshal Lord Kitchener, who died in 1916. St Dunstan's Chapel, with a 17th-century oak screen and a mosaic by Salviati, is in the north aisle. Further along are memorials to the painter John Leighton, General Charles George Gordon and Prime Minister Lord Melbourne. The massive monument to the Duke of Wellington, who died in 1852, is by Alfred Stevens. In 1912 an equestrian statue by John Tweed was added to it. The two large allegorical groups on the monument represent Courage and Cowardice, Truth and Deceit.

Transepts

The baptismal font, statues of Joshua Reynolds and Dr Samuel Johnson, among others, and Holman Hunt's Pre-Raphaelite painting *The Light of the World* are in the north transept.
In the south transept the eye is drawn to John Flaxman's **Nelson Monument**, which has allegories of the North Sea, the Baltic Sea, the Mediterranean Sea and the Nile. The inscription on the base, Copenhagen – Nile – Trafalgar, refers to Nelson's greatest victories.

** *St Paul's Cathedral*

The second-largest church dome in the world after St Peter's in Rome is the result of a catastrophe: Old St Paul's burned down in the Great Fire of 1666 and had to be replaced. The new cathedral is Sir Christopher Wren's main architectural legacy.

❶ Mon – Sat 8.30am – 4pm; galleries 9.30am – 4.30pm; admission £16.50 . On Sundays open only for services.

❶ Towers
The two 47m/154ft-high towers house the peal of bells. There are twelve bells in the north tower, while »Great Paul«, cast in 1882 and at almost 17 tons the largest bell in England, hangs in the south tower.

❷ Nave, choir and transsept
St Paul's is 170m/558ft long and 75m/246ft wide at the transepts. Don't miss the view from the crossing at the centre of the church up into the dome – it is overwhelming!

❸ Dome
The dome is 111m/365ft in height from the ground to the cross. Two galleries, the Stone Gallery and the Golden Gallery, provide wonderful views over London.

❹ Crypt
Many famous Britons are buried in the crypt: Wellington, Nelson, Lawrence of Arabia and, of course, Christopher Wren.

❺ Pediment
The statue of St Paul at the top of the pediment, and those of the apostles James and Peter on each side, are by Francis Bird

Domes in comparison

Dome of the Rock (AD 690)
Jerusalem (Israel)
Diameter: 20m/65ft

Hagia Sophia (AD 737)
Istanbul (Turkey)
Diameter: 31m/6101ft

St Paul's (1708)
London (England)
Diameter: 34m/111ft

The Whispering Gallery, 33m/109ft above the floor of the cathedral, is notable not only for the best view of the paintings on the dome but also for a remarkable acoustic effect: Every whispered word can be heard on the opposite side of the dome.

Pantheon (AD 125)
Rome (Italy)
Diameter: 43m/141ft

Superdome (1975)
New Orleans (USA)
Diameter: 207m/679ft

St Paul's is Sir Christopher Wren's masterpiece. The entrance to the crypt, where he is buried, is at the northern pier of the crossing.

The choir stalls are the work of the famous wood-carver Grinling Gibbons.

©BAEDEKER

Santa Maria del Fiore (1436)
Florence (Italy)
Diameter: 42m/137ft

**Dome   The highlight of St Paul's is the view up to the dome. Eight mighty double piers with Corinthian capitals, each of them supported by four additional piers, bear the weight of the dome. The eight scenes from the life of the apostle Paul are the work of Sir James Thornhill. The mosaics were done by Salviati in the late 19th century.

Choir   The oak choir stalls, carved in masterly fashion in the atelier of **Grin-ling Gibbons** in the 17th century, are a veritable kaleidoscope of powerful images. The high altar with its cathedral-like vault was executed in 1958 by Dykes Bower and Godfrey Allan on the basis of drawings by Wren. The wrought-iron gates in the choir and choir aisles are all the work of the Huguenot Jean Tijou. In the American Memorial Chapel behind the high altar a roll of honour records the names of the 28,000 Americans stationed in Britain who lost their lives in the Second World War. The **effigy from the tomb of John Donne**, poet and dean of St Paul's, is situated in the south choir aisle. This is the only sculpture from Old St Paul's that survived the fire of 1666.

Krypta   Steps lead down to the crypt from both sides of the choir. It occupies the whole area beneath the church. The north part of the crypt houses the tombs of many famous persons, including the painters Constable, Turner, Landseer and Reynolds, as well as Sir Alexander Fleming, who discovered penicillin. T. E. Lawrence, better known as Lawrence of Arabia, is commemorated with a bust.

Finally, beneath the south aisle, is the plain tomb of the architect, Sir **Christopher Wren**. Wren's tomb is inscribed with the words »Lector, si monumentum requiris, circumspice« – »Reader, if you require a monument, look around you«. The **sarcophaguses of Wellington and Nelson** are also in the crypt. Nelson's marble tomb was originally intended as a sarcophagus for Cardinal Wolsey, Henry VIII's chancellor. The coffin containing Nelson's mortal remains was made from the mainmast of the French flagship L'Orient, sunk at the Battle of the Nile in 1798. Wellington's simple sarcophagus was made from Cornish granite; around it are the banners that were carried at his funeral procession – with the exception of the Prussian banner, which was removed during the First World War.

GALLERIES AND DOME

Triforium Gallery   143 steps lead to the triforium gallery above the south aisle, where plans and models of the earlier churches on the site are displayed. In the western part of the gallery various exhibits from the history of the cathedral are on display, including the Wren designs that were rejected by the church commissioners and other drawings.

The Whispering Gallery is reached from the library at the end of the Triforium Gallery. It takes its name from a peculiarity of the acoustics: Every word spoken in a whisper can be heard, even 48m/158ft away at the opposite side of the circle. This gallery is not only the best place to admire Thornhill's paintings on the dome, but also provides the most impressive view of the size and proportions of the nave.

Whispering Gallery

117 more steps remain to be climbed to the Stone Gallery, from where 166 further steps lead to the Golden Gallery at the foot of the lantern. On the way up an opening in the floor affords an awesome view down to the floor of the cathedral. The ball on top of the lantern is large enough to hold ten people.

Stone Gallery

Golden Gallery

PATERNOSTER SQUARE

Paternoster Square on the north side of St Paul's was completed in 2003. Since 2004 it has been the seat of the London Stock Exchange and big investment banks. The 23m/75ft-high Paternoster Square Column at its centre is also the ventilation shaft for the rooms below the surface of the square.

In front of the side entrance to St Paul's stands **Temple Bar**. Until 1878 this gate marked the west end of ▶Fleet Street, the boundary of the City of London. It was removed and sold in 1880 to the brewer Henry Meux, who re-erected it in the grounds of his country seat Theobald's Park. It was restored and placed on its present site when Paternoster Square was laid out.

* Science Museum

✦ C / D 7

Location: Exhibition Road, SW 7
Tube: South Kensington
🕐 Daily 10am–6pm

Admission: free
www.nmsi.ac.uk

The theme of the Science Museum is the history and role of the sciences, industry and technology.

For children, above all, it is a great experience. They can operate machinery and carry out many experiments: little ones on the lower floor in the Garden, up eight-year-olds on the ground floor in the Pattern Pod, and all ages in the Launchpad Gallery on the third floor.

The first section of the ground floor is a large hall presenting all kinds of ways to generate energy. The next area, reached by passing

Ground floor and first floor

a Foucault pendulum, is the Space Hall, where rockets and rocks from the moon are on display. The department that follows contains 150 of the most important exhibits in the museum, such as **Stephenson's locomotive Rocket**, built in 1829, and the **Apollo 10** space capsule.

The question »Who am I?« is answered in the extension on this level. The sections on the first floor are devoted to the making of materials such as iron and steel, glass and plastics, to telecommunications – with a telephone made by Graham Bell and a telegraph from the year 1846 – plastics, gas exploration, agriculture, meteorology, land surveying, the measurement of time and food, with **the world's oldest tinned food** (1823).

Second and third floor

The themes on the second floor are paper-making and printing (a typewriter from 1875 here has the original positioning of keys, valid to this day), mathematics and data processing – including the calculating machine **Engine 1**, constructed by Charles Babbage in 1832 – as well as navigation, ship-building and the earth's atmosphere.

The exhibitions on the third floor are concerned with science in the 18th century, health research and especially aviation. Visitors can carry out experiments on the physics of flying and admire the originals of aircraft such as the Vickers Vimy, in which Alcock and Brown were the first to cross the Atlantic in 1919, and a Gloster E 28/39, **the first British jet aeroplane**. The displays continue in the extension with interactive exhibits on science in the future. This section continues in the extension with interactive exhibits about the future.

Fourth and fifth floors

The fourth and fifth floors are all about medicine, for both humans and animals. The exhibits include the first working stethoscope (1818) and experimental apparatus used by Louis Pasteur.

Smithfield Market

✦ J 4

Location: Charterhouse Street/ West Smithfield, EC 1
Tube: Barbican, Farringdon
❶ Mon–Fri 3am–approx. 12 noon

Almost 500 tons of meat are bought and sold each day in the Victorian market hall at Smithfield. Since it opened in 1866 Smithfield Market has been London's main market for meat, and is now the only remaining wholesale market in the inner city.

Butchers, restaurants and food stores come here for poultry, cheese and other delicacies as well as meat. The market has a long history: A meat market recorded in the 10th century that was held on Fridays on the »smooth field« became larger as the centuries passed and by the mid-19th century was selling 220,000 cattle and 1.5 million sheep annually. This was accompanied by intolerable hygienic conditions, as most of the animals were slaughtered on site. The market was therefore closed in 1855, but in 1860 an act of parliament was passed to establish a market for meat and poultry. **Sir Horace Jones** designed the two main buildings, which still exist. Smithfield also has a history as a **site for festivities and executions**. In 1390 Richard II had Geoffrey Chaucer organise a tournament in which 60 knights from all over Europe took part. Executions drew large crowds: Here the Scottish folk hero William Wallace ascended the scaffold in 1305, the rebel Watt Tyler was beheaded in 1381 and 200 Protestants were sent to their deaths under Queen Mary in the mid-16th century.

London's
principal
meat market

> **? MARCO⊕POLO TIP** *For early birds …* Insider Tip
>
> If you want to catch the life of the market in full swing, get up early: the best time is around 7 o'clock in the morning. The pubs round about are all open then, so that market traders and party people who have left the mega-club Fabric opposite the market can quench their thirst.

AROUND SMITHFIELD MARKET

St Bartholomew-the-Great, **the oldest parish church in the City**, lies hidden behind a half-timbered 16th-century gatehouse to the south of the market halls. The church constitutes the remains of a hospital and monastery founded in 1123 by **Rahere**, who was also Henry I's court jester. By the time of the dissolution of the monasteries under Henry VIII it had been extended to a considerable size, but the nave was then torn down and the choir converted into a parish church; in the 18th century the buildings were used as a storehouse, shed, inn, smithy and printing-house, in which **Benjamin Franklin** worked in 1724.

*St
Bartholomew-
the-Great

The horseshoe arches in the choir and the billet mouldings are characteristic of Norman church architecture. Rahere, who died in about 1145, lies in a 16th-century tomb which shows him reclining and dressed in the black habit of the Augustinians. A crowned angel at his feet holds a shield with the coat of arms of the monastery. Other points of interest in the church are the alabaster tomb of Sir Walter Mildmay, chancellor of the exchequer to Elizabeth I, the early 15th-century font in which William Hogarth was baptised and the cloister built in 1405, which is entered through a Norman doorway with

St Bartholomew-the-Great is the oldest parish church in London

15th-century doors. The place where the nave once stood is now the small churchyard; the 13th-century gate that remains here was originally the entrance to the south aisle.

Charterhouse   The continuation of Charterhouse Street to the north of Smithfield Market leads to Charterhouse Square, where the courtyard of the Charterhouse, the London branch of the Carthusian order originating in the Chartreuse monastery, can be seen through the gatehouse. The London Charterhouse was founded in 1371 by Sir Walter de Manny and dissolved in 1535 by Henry VIII. Prior John Houghton, who attempted to resist, was hanged, drawn and quartered at Tyburn and one of his arms nailed to the gatehouse. The estate then came into the possession of, among others, John Dudley, Duke of Northumberland (executed in 1553) and Thomas Howard, Duke of Norfolk (executed in 1572 for conspiring with Mary Queen of Scots). In 1611 Thomas Sutton bought the Charterhouse and converted it into a home for the elderly and a school, which moved to Godalming in 1872 and is still one of the leading English public schools. Today the Charterhouse is home to 40 pensioners, who have to be members of the Church of England and either bachelors or widowers, and must have served as army officers or in the clergy.

To the north of the market (via St John Street and St John Lane) is St John's Gate, the former gatehouse of the priory of the Knights of St John. The Order of the Knights of St John was founded in the 11th century in Jerusalem, came to England in the 12th century and settled on this site in Clerkenwell in 1148. In 1381 Wat Tyler burned it down during his rebellion, and the prior was beheaded on Tower Hill. The priory was rebuilt in 1504, but shortly afterwards in 1537 the order was dissolved. The gatehouse, which dates from 1504, is the only remaining part of the priory. William Hogarth lived here for a few years when his father ran a coffeehouse in the gatehouse tower. From 1721 to 1723 St John's Church was built on the site of the priory church using the walls of its choir. The 15th-century altarpiece depicts the victory of the Knights of St John over the Turks at the siege of Rhodes. The Norman crypt (1140–80) has survived. Here the **Museum of the Order of St John** tells the story of the knights.

St John's Gate

❶ Mon–Sat 10am–5pm, Sat 10am–4pm, free admission; www.museumstjohn.org.uk

★ Soho

✦ F / G 5

Location: between Oxford Street, Charing Cross Road, Leicester Square, Piccadilly Circus and Regent Street

Tube: Oxford Circus, Tottenham Court Road

Soho, for a long time a byword for iniquity and vice, was once an aristocratic district. Today it is hardly more disreputable than similar inner-city districts and is a lively area of cafés and pubs where media people, office workers and normal citizens come to enjoy themselves.

It was one of Henry VIII's hunting grounds – hence the name »so-ho«, an old hunting call. In the 17th century, when the area was no longer used for the chase, nobles built their London residences here. In later decades they moved on to more fashionable districts, making way for immigrants from the continent of Europe and Asia, who gave Soho a more down-to-earth character. Not until the 19th century did Soho acquire its reputation as the red-light district par excellence; in 1958 street prostitution was banned, and since the local authorities' campaign in the 1980s to clean it up, Soho has become almost harmless. It does not take long to realise that the atmosphere is no more seedy in Soho than in other, similar parts of London. For many companies, an address in Soho is a mark of quality: The central location attracts film and record companies, publishers and advertis-

No longer a den of vice

ing agencies. The creative people from offices in Wardour Street and elsewhere have set their stamp on the local scene. The gay scene is at home in Old Compton Street. For food-lovers Soho is one of the best areas for delicatessens and restaurants. It is also a good place to buy ingredients for dishes from all parts of the world – on Berwick Street Market, for example, or in Chinatown. Lovers of exotic food flock to the restaurants in Soho. No part of London is more attractive to theatre-goers, as some of the best-known theatres in the West End are here (▶Practicalities, Theatre). The criminal underworld and shady establishments, bars and revues, pornography and prostitution still exist in places such as Great Windmill Street, but Soho is much more than this.

Soho – see it twice

▶ Tour 4, p. 147

The best way to get to know Soho is to go there twice – once during the day and again at night. Daylight hours reveal what has happened to **Carnaby Street**, famous for the flower-power scene in the 1960s. Until recently it was just another pedestrian zone with an unexciting range of retailers, but has become a busy shopping street with innovative little stores. In **Wardour Street** it is worth taking a look inside the church of **St Anne's Soho**, where one of the graves is that of Theodore, King of Corsica; after that go along **Dean Street**, where Karl Marx lived at no. 28 from 1851 to 1856, and stroll over to **Soho Square**, a haven of quiet with a statue of Charles II and the reconstruction of a Tudor garden shed in the middle of the square. Go back along **Greek Street** past the House of St Barnabas, built on the corner of Soho Square in 1746, which gives an idea of how Soho looked in its upper-class days, and on to the junction with **Old Compton Street**, the heart of Soho. Here the abundance of pubs, bars, cafés and restaurants is an opportunity to choose a place for a second visit in the evening. Frith Street branches off from Old Compton Street and is the home of **Ronnie Scott's Club**, London's best-known jazz club; straight ahead is the **Palace Theatre**, built in 1891 and today owned by Andrew Lloyd Webber. In 1910 Anna Pavlova made her London debut in the theatre. The Palace is on Cambridge Circus, from where **Shaftesbury Avenue** leads to Piccadilly Circus past some of London's most famous theatres, such as the Lyric (1888), the Apollo (1901), the Globe (1903) and the Shaftesbury Theatre (1911).

> ! **MARCO ◉ POLO TIP**
>
> *Dim sum* *Insider Tip*
>
> »Tiny bites to touch the heart«: This is the translation of dim sum, the best way to try authentic south Chinese food in Chinatown. The delicacies, in baskets and pots on a trolley, are wheeled through the restaurant, and guests take what they fancy for a standard price. Good places to eat dim sum are Yauatcha (15 Broadwick St., tel. 020 7494 8888) and Leong's Legends (4 Macclesfield St., tel. 020 7287 0288).

As everywhere in the world, Chinese New Year is celebrated in London's Chinatown with a procession

Leicester Square is the hub of the West End theatre world. This has not always been its role. After the second Earl of Leicester built a house here in 1631, other persons of rank such as Sir Isaac Newton, Sir Joshua Reynolds and William Hogarth followed. Statues of them are at the corners of the gardens, with a monument to Shakespeare in the middle. In the 19th century a number of music halls set up here. Today cinemas, especially the Empire and Odeon, dominate the square, which is why there is also a statue of Charlie Chaplin.

Leicester Square

An excellent way to round off an evening is a meal in Chinatown, which is concentrated around Gerrard Street, spilling over into Lisle Street and part of Wardour Street. This district, the centre of the 60,000-strong Chinese community in London, is a microcosm of China with exotic food stores, acupuncture practices, bookshops, hair-dressers, countless crowded restaurants, Peking ducks dangling in their windows, and even phone-boxes in the shape of pagodas. The language spoken on all sides is Cantonese. Chinatown developed from the late 1940s; before then most London Chinese lived around the docks in Limehouse.

*Chinatown – a slice of China

The Whole World in a City

London vies with New York for the title of the world's most cosmopolitan city. Its colourful mix of peoples is a result of colonial history and recent emigration from all over the world.

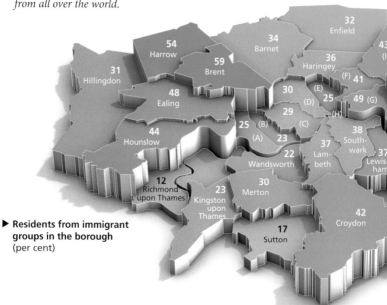

54 Harrow
31 Hillingdon
59 Brent
48 Ealing
44 Hounslow
34 Barnet
32 Enfield
36 Haringey
43 (I)
41 (F)
30 (D)
25 (E)
49 (G)
29 (C)
25 (B)
25 (A)
23
38 Southwark
37 Lambeth
37 Lewisham
22 Wandsworth
12 Richmond upon Thames
23 Kingston upon Thames
30 Merton
17 Sutton
42 Croydon

▶ **Residents from immigrant groups in the borough** (per cent)

▶ **Ethnic groups in London**
all of London

Caribbean 376,800	Black Africa 506,500	North Afrika 219,100	India 536,700

▶ **Religious diversity**
Although it is still not allowed for a Catholic to succeed to the throne, in London there are dozens of Hindu and Sikh temples, mosques and synagogues in addition to Anglican and other Christian churches.

Christians	56,2 %
Atheists	15,8 %
Muslims	8,5 %
Hindus	4,1 %
Jews	2,1 %
Sikh	1,5 %
Buddhists	0,8 %
Other	0,2 %
No information	8,7 %

▶ Rich Mix
Films, theatre, music, readings, comedy and club nights at the Rich Mix multicultural centre, 35–47 Bethnal Green Road, E 1

www.richmix.org.uk

A) Hammersmith and Fulham
B) Kensington and Chelsea, (C) City of Westminster (D) Camden, (E) Islington,
F) Hackney, (G) Tower Hamlets,
H) 24 City of London, (I) Waltham Forest

49 Redbridge
2 Newham
32 Barking and Dagenham
8 Havering
35 Greenwich
14 Bexley
13 Bromley

immigrant groups: 35%

▶ The colonial legacy
Former British colonies are still part of the Commonwealth. Big waves of immigration began early in London, and a multicultural society has a longer tradition here than anywhere else in Europe.

In 1920 the British Empire and English-speaking former colonies amounted to almost a quarter of the surface of the earth. In some former colonies, including Canada, New Zealand and Australia, the Queen is still head of state.

©BAEDEKER

Pakistan	Bangladesh	Asia (other)	China	other
194,600	202,500	260,500	112,500	317,400

How many peoples live in London?
60 out of 194 recognised nationalities are represented.

▶ Immigration will continue to increase
Change from 2001 to 2031 (forecast)

British residents

British residents from immigrant groups

100
%
0
2001   2031

South Bank

✦ G / H 6

Location: south bank of the Thames,
western part
Tube: Waterloo, Westminster

**The south bank of the Thames between Waterloo and West-
minster Bridge, originally a place of quays and small factories,
is now a cultural quarter and a place to stroll with a view of
Westminster and the City.**

**From an
industrial
area to a
cultural
centre**
The presence of industry made the area a prime target for German
bombing raids in the Second World War. After the completion of the
Royal Festival Hall in 1951, bombed wasteland gradually developed
into a cultural quarter, the South Bank Centre. At the start of the millennium it gained further momentum with the giant wheel, the London Eye, and the opening of the IMAX cinema in front of Waterloo
Station. A good place to begin a South Bank walk is the end of Westminster Bridge next to County Hall.

County Hall
The massive County Hall, built from 1912 to 1932, was the headquarter of the Greater London Council until 1986. Now it houses restaurants, hotels and the **London Sea Life Aquarium**, the largest in the
world according to its own advertising, where the highlights are
various tanks, an underwater tunnel through the shark basin and a
petting aquarium. The Aquarium's new neigbour is **London Dungeon** which claims to portray the cruel and bloody side of British
history: the murder of Thomas Becket, the plague, burning at the
stake, torture chambers and Jack the Ripper. In reality it is no more
than a collection of wax figures with gaping wounds, smeared in
artificial blood.
Sea Life Aquarium: daily 10am–7pm, admission £22.50;
www.visitsealife.com
London Dungeon: Mon–Wed, Fri 10am–5pm, Thu 11am–5pm, Sat
10am–6pm, Sun 11am–6pm; admission £25.20;
www.thedungeons.com

****London
Eye**
Beyond County Hall lie **Jubilee Gardens**, laid out in 1977 for the
Queen's 25th jubilee. Here stands the London Eye, designed by
David Marks and Julia Barfield (MARCO POLO Insight p. 292).
It turns full circle once every half hour, giving the passengers in its
32 glass capsules enough time to enjoy the amazing view, ranging
40km/25mi when the visibility is good.
❶ Daily from 10am; standard ticket £29.50;
www.londoneye.com

London illuminated

The South Bank Centre can hardly be regarded as an architectural triumph. Too much naked concrete gives it a cold atmosphere. The cultural attractions, however, are first class. The **Royal Festival Hall** was built in 1951 to designs by Robert Matthew and Leslie Martin. The **Queen Elizabeth Hall** has been a venue for symphony concerts, chamber music and solo concerts since 1967, the **Purcell Room** for chamber music. The **British Film Institute** (entrance under Waterloo Bridge) provides an opportunity not only to watch films in the institute's cinema but also to choose an item from the enormous BFI National Archive and watch it on a screen. The outside of the **Hayward Gallery**, which was built on top of the whole complex, as it were, shows what awaits on the inside: modern art. The building, a work of the New Style from 1968, is divided into two levels, equipped with excellent artificial lighting. The gallery stages temporary exhibitions of modern art of extremely high quality.

The **National Theatre**, which has three auditoria: the Lyttelton Theatre, the Olivier Theatre – named after its first director, Sir Laurence Olivier – and the Cottesloe Theatre.

South Bank Centre

The London Eye

In terms of urban planning it was a bold move to place the London Eye in one of the most prominent places in the city – opposite the Houses of Parliament and Big Ben on the banks of the Thames. London set a trend by doing so, as big wheels are such a source of fascination that other cities have built their own similar landmarks since then – some of them bigger, of course.

▶ **Children hit on the idea**
The idea of building a giant wheel comes from Bulgaria and derives from observing children who had attached small seats to a large wheel and turned it.

▶ **The Ferris Wheel**
George Washington Gale Ferris (1859–96), a bridge builder from Pittsburgh, constructed the world's first modern giant wheel for the World Exhibition in Chicago in 1893, and gave this type of wheel its name in the English-speaking world.

Locations

1893 Chicago, Illinois

1895 Chicago near Lincoln Park

1904 St. Louis, Missouri

1906 finally dismantled

©BAEDEKER

80m/262ft

▶ **Big wheels compared**

56m/184ft

Roue de Paris
2000

65m/213ft

Vienna big wheel
1897

135m/443ft

London Eye
2000

161.53m/
530ft

World's tallest church
Ulm minster
(for comparison)

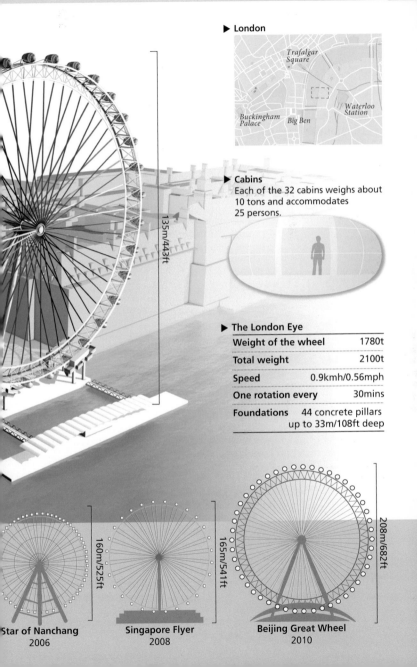

▶ London

Trafalgar Square

Buckingham Palace   *Big Ben*

Waterloo Station

135m/443ft

▶ Cabins

Each of the 32 cabins weighs about 10 tons and accommodates 25 persons.

▶ The London Eye

Weight of the wheel	1780t
Total weight	2100t
Speed	0.9kmh/0.56mph
One rotation every	30mins
Foundations	44 concrete pillars up to 33m/108ft deep

160m/525ft

165m/541ft

208m/682ft

Star of Nanchang
2006

Singapore Flyer
2008

Beijing Great Wheel
2010

National Theatre: tours Mon–Fri 10.15, 10.30am, 12.15, 12.30, 5.15, 5.30pm; Sat 10.30am, 12.15pm; price: £8.50; www.nationaltheatre.org.uk
Royal Festival Hall, Queen Elizabeth Hall, Purcell Room, Hayward Gallery: www.southbankcentre.co.uk, tickets tel. 020 79 60 42 00
British Film Institute: bfi.org.uk

Oxo Tower   The Oxo Tower on Barge House Street is not a youthful building, but it is now more up-to-date than ever: This 1930s block with a tower, formerly a factory for the production of the Oxo beef drink, was converted into a trendy apartment and commercial building. The expensive bar and restaurant on the 8th floor have made it part of a cool scene. The observation platform can be visited without the need to dine in the restaurant.

Further on ...   Energetic visitors can continue the walk along the riverbank beyond Blackfriars Bridge to the ▶Tate Modern, ▶Southwark and ▶Tower Bridge.

Southwark

⎯⎯⎯⎯⎯⎯⎯⎯⎯⎯⎯⎯⎯⎯⎯⎯ ✶ H – K 6

Location: south bank of the Thames, eastern part
Tube: London Bridge

As long ago as Roman times the men of Londinium frequented dubious taverns and visited prostitutes at the south end of London's first bridge.

London's first   In this respect little changed until the 19th century, except that bull
red-light   fights, bear-baiting and theatres added to the range of entertainments
district   in the red-light district. The brothels were pulled down to make way for quays and warehouses, most of which have now been converted into apartment buildings.

✶ SOUTHWARK CATHEDRAL

❶ Mon–Fri 8am–6pm, Sat and Sun 8.30am–6pm

Fine Gothic   Southwark Cathedral, the seat of the diocese of Southwark, is Lon-
architecture   don's most beautiful Gothic church after ▶Westminster Abbey. According to tradition a ferryman's daughter named Mary founded a convent here. It became known as St Mary of the Ferry. In 1106 Gifford, Bishop of Winchester, ordered the building of a large church, now called St Mary Overie, meaning »over the river«. This church burned down and was rebuilt from 1207 by Bishop Peter de Rupibus. The lower part of the 55m/180ft tower, the crossing, and the choir

and retro-choir date from this period. The nave, added in the 13th century and remodelled in 1469, was rebuilt between 1890 and 1896 by Sir Arthur Blomfield.

The 12th-century Norman doorway to the cloister has been pre-served in the **north aisle**. To its right the original wooden roof bosses are visible. Look for Judas Iscariot (in a kilt!) being swallowed by the devil. The poet **John Gower** (1330–1408) is buried under the sixth window. The effigy is a reclining figure resting its head on his books Speculum Meditantis, Vox Clamantis and Confessio Amantis. The north transept with its Norman arches is the site of a monument in memory of the quack Lionel Lockyer († 1672), who claimed to be able to make miraculous pills from the rays of the sun. A monument in the north choir aisle portrays John Trehearne, a favourite of James I, with his family. Trehearne and his wife are shown holding a tablet with the inscription: »Had kings a power to lend their subjects breath, Trehearne thou shouldst not be cast down by death«. The

Inside

Southwark Cathedral: one of the oldest Gothic buildings in London

! *The George Inn* Insider Tip

Diagonally opposite the entrance to Borough Market, an entry leads from Borough High Street to the George Inn – just the right place for a pint in historic surroundings. This pub dating from 1676 is London's only remaining galleried coaching inn. The creaking floorboards and scrubbed tables go back to the days when wagoners stopped here in Southwark before delivering their goods in the City on the other bank of the Thames. In summer there are tables outside in the courtyard.

wooden effigy of a knight from the late 13th century in the corner is one of the oldest of its kind in England.

The **choir**, which was divided to create a retro-choir, dates from about 1273, making it one of the oldest Gothic church buildings in London. The high altar with its 13th-century columns was made in 1520. The **south choir aisle** is the burial place of **Lancelot Andrewes**, Bishop of Winchester, who died in 1626. He translated the New Testament into English. The interesting features of the south transept, built around 1310, include the coat of arms and cardinal's hat of Cardinal Beaufort, half-brother of King Henry IV. Finally, in the south aisle, the Shakespeare window and the Shakespeare monument memorial to William Shakespeare of 1912 are also worthy of note. Southwark Cathedral is the burial place of Shakespeare's brother Edmund, who died in 1607, and Lawrence Fletcher, who leased the Blackfriars Theatre and the Globe Theatre in partnership with Shakespeare and Burbage. Part of the 13th-century arcade has survived next to the font.

AROUND SOUTHWARK CATHEDRAL

Borough Market A few yards away from the cathedral under the railway arches of the tracks to London Bridge Station is a market hall built in 1851. Borough Market was mentioned as early as 1276; it is now a high-class market for food-lovers with stalls selling much more than the traditional fruit and vegetables. A great range of snacks are on offer, and tempting cafés and restaurants have set up round about the market.
❶ Mon–Wed 10am–3pm »open for lunch«; Thu 11am–5pm, Fri 12 noon–6pm, Sat 8am–5pm; www.boroughmarket.org.uk

Old Operating Theatre and Herb Garret In today's St Thomas Street opposite the market, a hospital is recorded in the 12th century. It moved to the west of London in 1862. All that remains, now in the roof of St Thomas's Church, is the gynaecological **operating and lecture theatre**, which gives an impression of medical practices in the era before antiseptic hygiene. The collection of medical instruments here is equally sobering.
❶ Daily 10.30am–5pm; admission £6; www.thegarret.org.uk

LONDON BRIDGE STATION

London Bridge Station at the south end of London Bridge is the oldest in the city: On 14 December 1836 the first train steamed into this station. The area is now being upgraded to the **London Bridge Quarter**, which includes open spaces, the office and shopping complex The Place and above all a skyscraper that is already a London landmark: **The Shard**, designed by Renzo Piano, which lives up to its name with sharp-edged glass walls that reach 310m/1017ft high. The investor is the royal family of Qatar. 72 of the 87 storeys can be used. In addition to office floors, viewing galleries and a luxury hotel on

London Bridge Quarter

The Shard: an exclusive address in a down-at-heel district

floors 34 to 52, there are ten huge apartments for super-rich clients on floors 53 to 65. The Shard is thus a fitting symbol for the different faces of London: On the one hand it has been built in Southwark, one of the poorest inner-city districts, with high youth employment. On the other hand it demonstrates the continuing vitality and conspicuous wealth of this restless city. At a height of 244m/800ft three glassed-in terraces that are open to the public at an exorbitant price (»The View«) provide an unbeatable view of London and its surroundings.

The View: daily 9am–10pm; admission £29.95 (online: £24.95); www.theviewfromtheshard.com

The London Bridge Experience
The London Bridge Experience endeavours to cast as gruesome a light as possible on medieval London.
● 2–4 Tooley St.; Mon–Fri 10am–5pm, Sat and Sun until 6pm; admission £23; www.thelondonbridgeexperience.com

ON THE THAMES

Hays Galleria
Hays Galleria is on the Thames side of the London Bridge City shopping centre. The rattling, spouting and hissing steel sculpture in the middle is David Kemp's *The Navigator*.

»HMS Belfast«
HMS Belfast, the Royal Navy's last large cruiser, is anchored at Symons Wharf. The 11,500-ton ship, launched in 1938, was involved in operations including the sinking of the Scharnhorst in 1943 at the North Cape and the D-Day landings in Normandy in June 1944. After the war, HMS Belfast was on service in the Far East before being decommissioned in 1963. The cruiser is now a museum ship and part of the ►Imperial War Museum.
● March–Oct daily 10am–6pm; Nov–Feb until 5pm; admission £15.50; www.iwm.org.uk

City Hall
The egg-shaped leaning glass building on the bank of the Thames close to HMS Belfast is London's new city hall, designed by Sir Norman Foster and opened in 2002. In the basement you can explore London on foot: The floor is a huge aerial picture of Greater London measuring 16 x 16 m/52 x 52 ft and consisting of 200,000 individual images.
● Mon–Fri 8am–8pm

St Mary Overie Dock
A reconstruction of Sir Francis Drake's legendary **Golden Hind** lies in St Mary Overie Dock to the west of Southwark cathedral.
● Daily 10am–5.30pm; admission £6; http://goldenhinde.com

Winchester Palace Ruins
A few steps further on, the riverbank path passes the ruins of the 12th-century Winchester Palace, the London residence of the

powerful bishops of Winchester. The high wall of its great hall with a rose window gives an impression of the magnificence of palace.

Clink Street takes its name from the dungeon of Winchester Palace. The Clink Prison Museum is devoted to the history of this infamous prison and its inmates, many of whom were prostitutes, drunkards and debtors.   **Clink Prison Museum**
❶ July–Sept daily 10am–6pm, Oct–June Mon–Fri 10am–6pm, Sat and Sun 10am–7.30pm; admission £7; www.clink.co.uk

Vinopolis takes visitors on a »wine odyssey« with information about how wine is made, including tasting and sales of wine, whisky, beer and cocktails at high prices.   **Vinopolis**
To enjoy a drink in authentic surroundings without paying the high price, go to **The Anchor pub**, which has a pleasant terrace on the Thames. The inn has existed since the 17th century, the present building since the 18th century.
Vinopolis: wine tasting packages from £27, www.vinopolis.co.uk

The headquarters of William Shakespeare's theatre company lay in today's Park Street to the south of The Anchor. It was just one of several Elizabethan theatres in Southwark. The round, thatched theatre was built in 1598 but closed again in 1644, as the plaque in Park Street records. Thanks to years of efforts by the American actor **Sam Wanamaker**, the world of Shakespeare lives again, though a little further to the west. The plays are performed in the open air, as they were 400 years ago, regardless of the weather. An exhibition explains the history of the Elizabeth theatre. An insight into Shakespearian theatre times provide the Sam Wanamaker Playhouse Tours.   ****Shakespeare's Globe Theatre**
❶ Exhibition: daily 9am–5pm; theatre tours Mon 9am–5pm, Tue–Sat 9.30am–12.30pm, Sun 9.30–11am; admission £13.50 (exhibition and tour); Sam Wanamaker Playhouse: call tel. 7902 1500 for further information

The Queen honoured the opening of Globe Theatre with her visit

The excavations of the first theatre on Bankside, **The Rose** (1587), where Christopher Marlowe's plays were produced, Edward Alleyn trod the boards and Shakespeare learned his trade, can be seen on »open saturdays« from 10am to 5pm.

✳ **The Strand**

 ✳ **G / H 5 / 6**

Location: between Trafalgar Square and Temple Bar
Tube: Charing Cross, Aldwych, Temple

The Strand is the main thoroughfare from the west of London to the City. Its name derives from a long-gone path on the banks of the Thames.

Today the street is lined with old-established pubs and hotels, many of which were founded in the 19th century when the Strand was the focus of London's entertainment scene.

Craven Street

Starting from the Trafalgar Square end of the Strand, Craven Street branches off to the right. For almost 29 years house no. 36 (now a museum) was the home of Benjamin Franklin; the German poet Heinrich Heine stuck it out for just three months at no. 32 and recorded his impressions of London in his *English Fragments*: *Send a philosopher to London; but a poet on no account! Send a philosopher and place him on a corner of Cheapside, where he will learn more than from all the books at the last Leipzig fair, and as the flood of humanity surges around him, a sea of new thoughts will rise before him, the eternal spirit that hovers above will waft in his face, the best-hidden secrets of human society will suddenly be revealed to him, the pulse of the world will sound in his ears ... But do not send a poet to London! This naked earnestness in all things, this colossal uniformity, this machine-like activity, this irksomeness of pleasure itself, this excess of London crushes the imagination and tears the heart to pieces.*
Benjamin Franklin House: multimedia show Wed–Sun 12 noon, 1pm, 2pm, 3.15pm, 4.15pm, £7; Mon tours at the same times, £3.50
www.benjaminfranklinhouse.org

> **!** MARCO ⊕ POLO TIP
>
> *Stamp collectors* **Insider Tip**
>
> ... can spend happy hours on The Strand and in its side streets, as a number of dealers have their shops here. The largest and best-known is Stanley Gibbons (no. 339); it is also worth looking in Cecil Court Stamp Shop (6 Cecil Court), Malcom Sprei (2 Savoy Court) and Michael Chipperfield (1 Southampton St.).

Savoy Hotel

Beyond Bedford Street on the left is the Adelphi Theatre, built in 1881 and refurbished in 1930 in the Art Deco style. Further along on the other side of the street is the legendary Savoy Hotel, the first hotel to have electric light and an en-suite bathroom for every room. The founder of the hotel and the owner of the Savoy Theatre, Richard D'Oyly Carte, employed a certain César Ritz, who later became a competitor, as his first hotel manager. Next door is an old-established restaurant, Simpson's in the Strand, a bastion of traditional English roast beef, which may be cheaper elsewhere but is nowhere better.

The Savoy Chapel is also extremely close to the hotel. Its official name is the Queen's Chapel of the Savoy, as it is the queen's private property in her capacity as Duke of Lancaster. It was built in the late Perpendicular style in the reigns of Henry VII and Henry VIII on the site of the Savoy Palace, which was destroyed in the Peasants' Revolt of 1381 (turn right into Savoy Street, then right again into Savoy Row). **Savoy Chapel**

On the right, beyond the approach to Waterloo Bridge, is Somerset House, where the ▶Courtauld Institute Galleries and King's College are located. Further along is the church of St Mary-le-Strand, first mentioned in records in the 13th century, in its present form completed in 1724 by James Gibbs. Here Bonnie Prince Charlie secretly converted from Catholicism to the Anglican faith in 1750. Charles Dickens' parents were married here in 1809. **St Mary-le-Strand**

A little way on is St Clement Danes. Sir **Christopher Wren** built it in 1681 and James Gibbs added a tower in 1719. The name derives from a Danish church that stood on the site in the 9th century. This church is well known to London children from the song *Oranges and Lemons*, which the bells chime out each day at 9am, noon, 3pm and 6pm. The song refers to the custom that the traders of Clare Market on Drury Lane treated the children of St Clement Danes on every market day. A children's service still takes place in the church annually in March, when every child is given an orange and a lemon. St Clement Eastcheap near The Monument also claims to the church behind the song. **St Clement Danes**

St Clement Danes was almost completely destroyed on 10 May 1941 by German bombs and reopened in 1958 thanks to donations by the Royal Air Force. Since then it has been the main church of the RAF, as shown by the badges of 800 RAF units set into the floor of the church, the rolls of honour with the names of 125,000 members of the Allied air forces who lost their lives in the Second World War, the altar and font of the Dutch and Norwegian air forces in the crypt, the organ donated by the US Air Force and, in front of the church, memorials to Lord Dowding and **Air Marshal Arthur Harris**, known as Bomber Harris for his advocacy of air raids in the Second World War. The third memorial outside the church represents the 18th-century man of letters **Samuel Johnson**, who belonged to this parish.

From here it is not far to the fortress-like Royal Courts of Justice or Law Courts, a magnificent Victorian building completed in 1882. **Royal Courts of Justice**

Not a medieval castle but a court of law:
the Royal Courts of Justice

This is a court for civil cases – criminal trials are held at the Old Bailey (p. 191). The figures of two Chinese and a gilded lion mark the entrance to **Twinings**, an old-established supplier of tea that began in 1706 as Tom's Coffee House. The Strand ends a short distance further on at Temple Bar Memorial, the boundary between Westminster and the City; from here eastwards, the road is called Fleet Street.

Cleopatra's Needle   A detour down to the Thames at Waterloo Bridge leads to Cleopatra's NeedleCleopatra's Needle, an Egyptian obelisk of pink granite situated on Victoria Embankment below the bridge. It was presented to the British Crown by the viceroy of Egypt, Mohammed Ali. After a stormy voyage that cost the lives of six sailors it was placed here in 1878 and immediately nicknamed Cleopatra's Needle. The hieroglyphs on the obelisk, which was erected in Heliopolis in about 1500 BC, praise the deeds and victories of Thutmosis III and Ramses the Great. The counterpart to this obelisk stands in Central Park in New York.

** Tate Gallery

The Tate Gallery opened in 1897 in a neoclassical building by Sidney R. J. Smith on Millbank by the Thames in Pimlico. The basis for the gallery was a donation by the sugar manufacturer and art collector Sir Henry Tate. It is one of the world's greatest art collections.

The collections of the Tate Gallery are on display in two separate places: British art from the 16th to the 20th century in the old gallery on Millbank (Tate Britain) and international art of the 20th and 21st centuries in Bankside Power Station on the south bank of the Thames (Tate Modern). The two galleries are connected by the Tate Boat, which runs every 40 minutes. The Tate has branches in St Ives and Liverpool.

❶ www.tate.org.uk

** TATE BRITAIN ✦ G 7 / 8

❶ **Location:** Millbank, SW 1
Tube: Pimlico
Daily 10am–6pm; free admission
Late at Tate Britain: readings, films, discussions on the first Friday in the month

The rooms in Tate Britain either have a theme or are devoted to a particular artist. The earliest work is *A Man in a Black Cap*, painted in 1545 by John Bettes. The 17th century is represented by painters such as Anthony van Dyck (*Lady of the Spencer Family*) and William Dobson (*Endymion Porter*, 1643–45). There are many illustrations by the draughtsman and engraver **William Blake** (*Newton*, 1795–1805). One of the most famous works in the collection is **William Hogarth**'s *O the Roast Beef of Old England*, 1748. A large part of the gallery presents landscapes, including paintings by Thomas Gainsborough, Joshua Reynolds, George Stubbs, Edwin Landseer and Henry Fuessli, and particularly by **John Constable** (*Chain Pier, Brighton*, 1826–27). Among the notable 19th-century artists are John Everett Millais and James Abbot McNeill Whistler (*Nocturne in Blue and Gold: Old Battersea Bridge*, 1872–75). Representatives of modern British art include Lucian Freud, David Hockney and Gilbert & George.
In the **Clore Gallery**, designed by James Stirling, the ****best works from the oeuvre of J.M.W. Turner** (1775–1851), including his watercolours are on display.

Where power was once generated, modern art is now exhibited: the Turbine Hall of the Tate Modern

** TATE MODERN ✦ J 6

❶ **Location:** Bankside Power Station, SW 1
Tube: Blackfriars, Southwark;
Daily 10am–6pm, Fri and Sat until 10pm; free admission

To house the Tate's modern collection the Swiss architects Herzog de Meuron converted Bankside Power Station, which was built by Giles Gilbert Scott shortly after the Second World War – a good reason for even those who are not keen on modern art at least to take a quick look inside at the gigantic dimensions of the building. From the top floor there is a fantastic view of the City. The Swiss architects are working on an eleven-storey extension that is built to the south of the existing building. At 64m/210ft it will be as tall as the chimney of the power station. Exhibition spaces are also being created in the oil tanks beneath Bankside Power Station.

The original, somewhat free hanging, which took a good deal of criticism, was altered in 2006 for a classic grouping on the basis of themes and periods. Among the highlights are **Claude Monet**'s *Water Lilies*; Cubism is represented by, for example, Georges Braque (Mandola, 1909–10) and Fernand Léger. *Woman Crying* and other works by Pablo Picasso are on show, as is a key work of abstract art, **Vassily Kandinsky**'s *Cossacks* from 1911. Among the Dadaist and

Surrealist artists are Giorgio de Chirico, Max Ernst, Paul Klee, Salvador Dalí and Joan Miró; Expressionism (Karl Schmidt-Rotluff, Max Beckmann), Pop Art (**Andy Warhol**'s *Marilyn Diptych*; Roy Lichtenstein's *Whaam!*), Minimal Art and Conceptual Art are also well represented in the Tate Modern.

London's newest Thames bridge, the intricate Millennium Bridge by Norman Foster and Anthony Caro, connects the Tate Modern with the City, leading to ▶St Paul's. It is an especially fine sight when illuminated at night.

*Millennium Bridge

* The Temple

✳ H 5

Location: Fleet Street, EC 4
Tube: Temple

Opposite the Temple Bar Memorial on ▶Fleet Street, a small arch leads into the Temple, a charming, almost secret Georgian jumble of buildings, alleys and legal schools.

Charles Dickens described the Temple in *Barnaby Rudge*: *There are, still, worse places than the Temple, on a sultry day, for basking in the sun, or resting idly in the shade. There is yet a drowsiness in its courts, and a dreamy dulness in its trees and gardens; those who pace its lanes and squares may yet hear the echoes of their footsteps on the sounding stones, and read upon its gates, in passing from the tumult of the Strand or Fleet Street, »Who enters here leaves noise behind.« There is still the plash of falling water in fair Fountain Court ...*

The inns of court, corporations of and schools for barristers, developed in the reign of Edward I, when clerics were replaced by laymen as lawyers and judges (▶p. 192). In the 12th and 13th centuries the Temple was the English headquarter of the Order of Knights Templar, founded in 1119 in Jerusalem. After the dissolution of the order in 1312, its property came into the possession of the Crown. It was then granted to the Earl of Pembroke and passed after his death to the Order of the Knights of St John, who rented it to a corporation of lawyers. Since then the Temple has been the lawyers' district, as it lies only a stone's throw from the Royal Courts of Justice.

From Fleet Street the entrance to the Middle Temple is through Wren's gatehouse. The former members of this inn include Sir Walter Raleigh, Sir Thomas More, Thomas de Quincey, W. M. Thackeray and Mahatma Gandhi. Down the slope lies **Middle Temple Hall**, which

Middle Temple

was built in 1572 as a dining and assembly hall. Most of the original panelling, the carved screen, the double hammer-beam roof, the glass decorated with coats of arms and the table made from the wood of Sir Francis Drake's Golden Hind survived bombing in the Second World War. An equestrian portrait of Charles I by Sir Godfrey Kneller hangs on the end wall. Shakespeare's *Twelfth Night* was first performed in this hall on 2 February 1602.

Inner Temple

On the left beyond the Fountain Court is a passage to the Inner Temple. Inner Temple Hall contains statues of Templar knights and knights of the Order of St John. White and red roses grow in the **Inner Temple Gardens** in memory of the houses of York (white) and Lancaster (red), which feuded during the 15th-century Wars of the Roses. Shakespeare set a decisive scene from Henry VI relating to the Wars of the Roses in this garden.

Inner Temple Gardens: Mon–Fri 12 noon–3pm

Temple Church

The Temple Church consists of the original Norman round church of 1185, which was modelled on the Church of the Holy Sepulchre in Jerusalem, and a chancel added in 1240 in the Early English style. Sir Christopher Wren renovated the church in 1682. It holds a rare treasure, **nine effigies of Templar knights** in black marble from the 12th and 13th centuries; one of them, its slab below the head-rest decorated with a foliage relief, is said to portray William Marshal, Earl of Pembroke († 1219) and brother-in-law of King John, regent during the minority of Henry III. The author **Oliver Goldsmith** (1728–74) is buried in the churchyard.

❶ Usually Mon, Tue, Thu, Fri from 11am, Wed from 2pm; admission £4; www.templechurch.com

Funeral effigies of Templar Knights in the Temple Church

** **Tower of London**

⊹ K 5 / 6

Location: Tower Hill, EC 3
Tube: Tower Hill, Tower Gateway
❶ March–Oct Tue–Sat 9am–5.30pm,
Sun, Mon 10am–5.30pm; Nov–Feb
Tue–Sat 9am–4.30pm, Sun, Mon
10am–4.30pm (last admission
1 hour earlier)

Tours: every half
hour from Middle Tower; last tour
3.30pm (summer), 2.30pm (winter)
Admission: £22 (online: £20.90)
www.hrp.org.uk

The Tower is arguably the most important historic site in England. It is the place where the Crown Jewels, one of London's most popular visitor attractions, are kept.

The Tower lies outside the old city wall. Its irregular conglomeration of buildings is surrounded by a crenellated wall and a deep ditch. There was probably a fortress here on the Thames as early as the Roman period. The Tower originated in the reign of William the Conqueror, who began construction of the White Tower in 1078. From the 12th to the 14th century it was continually enlarged and strengthened. It was often besieged, but never captured. Until the time of James I it served as a royal palace, but it has also been a prison, mint and treasury – the Crown Jewels are still kept here. It was the site of an observatory, until a new one was built in ▶Greenwich, and a menagerie until 1834.

A historic site

The history of the Tower reflects the history of England. The large number of prisoners held here included David II of Scotland (1346–57), John the Good of France (1356–60), James I of Scotland (1406–07), Charles, Duke of Orléans (1415), Elizabeth I (1554, before she became queen), Walter Raleigh no less than three times (1592, 1603–16, 1618) and William Penn (1668–69). Some of those executed or murdered within its walls were Henry VI (1471), the »little princes in the Tower« Edward V and his brother, the Duke of York (1483), Thomas More (1535), Henry VIII's wives Anne Boleyn (1536) and Catherine Howard (1542), Thomas Cromwell (1540) and the nine-day queen Lady Jane Grey (1554). The last death sentence to be carried out in the Tower was the execution of a German spy in 1941.

> **❗ Jump the queue** *Insider Tip*
>
> **MARCO ⊕ POLOTIP**
>
> The Tower is one of London's most-visited tourist attractions. To save time, buy a ticket beforehand. They can be purchased up to seven days in advance at www.hrp.org.uk/TowerofLondon or tel. 0844 482 7799. Those in possession of an advance ticket can use a separate entrance.

The Tower of London is English history in concentrated form

*Ceremony of the Keys The Tower is officially guarded by 35 Yeoman Warders (»Beefeaters«, probably so called because they were given plenty of beef to eat in past centuries), who wear the traditional uniform from Tudor times. They are responsible for helping and supervising tourists, but also for closing the main gate every evening in the Ceremony of the Keys, a ritual which has been performed unchanged for 700 years by the commander of the Tower, the Chief Warder. To witness the ceremony it is necessary to apply for a pass in writing at least six months in advance by sending a franked, self-addressed envelope. The ceremony starts at 9.40pm; the pass must be shown at 9.30pm at the main entrance.

❶ Apply to: The Ceremony of the Keys, Waterloo Block, HM Tower of London, EC 3N 4AB

Location The ground plan of the Tower is an irregular pentagon with an area of over 5 hectares (12 acres). The outer courtyard (Outer Ward), probably built in the 14th century under Edward I, is bounded by a wall with six towers and two bastions. The Inner Ward is defended by a wall with 13 towers built in the 13th century in the reign of Henry III. The entrance is in the south-west corner, originally the site of the Lions' Gate, which took its name from the former royal lion enclosure.

OUTER WARD

A stone bridge flanked by the Middle Tower and Byward Tower (password tower), both built in 1307 by Edward I, spans the moat. Opposite the Byward Tower stands the Bell Tower, built in about 1190 during the reign of Richard I, in which **Mary Tudor** imprisoned her half-sister **Elizabeth** for two months.

Bell Tower

Traitor's Gate is situated between the walls. In the period when the Thames was the main way of travelling from the Palace of Westminster to the Tower, prisoners who had been condemned in Westminster were brought in through this gate.

Traitor's Gate

St Thomas's Tower was built above Traitor's Gate in 1242 during the reign of Henry III. Together with the Wakefield and the Lanthorn Tower it survives from the medieval palace, as a reconstruction of Henry's bedroom in St Thomas's Tower shows. The Wakefield Tower held the Crown Jewels until 1968. Henry VI, the last king from the house of Lancaster, was killed here while at prayer in 1471. The cage with the Tower ravens is at the exit. The hall in which the trial of **Anne Boleyn** was held stood next to this tower.

St Thomas's Tower · Wakefield Tower

The Bloody Tower, which was built under Richard II, stands opposite St Thomas's Tower. Here Richard III imprisoned the sons of his deceased brother Edward IV (»the little princes«), who were ten and twelve years old, and is said to have murdered them in 1483. 200 years later their skeletons were found in the White Tower. **Sir Walter Raleigh** was kept prisoner in the same tower, generally in comfortable conditions, for a total of 13 years and used the time to write parts of his *History of the World*. He was eventually beheaded in 1618 for disobedience to the king.

Bloody Tower

Between Cradle Tower and Well Tower is the passage to Tower Wharf, built in 1228, where artillery salutes are fired to mark the accession and coronation of monarchs and the birth of princes and princesses. This is the privilege of the Honourable Artillery Company (H.A.C.), the oldest British military unit. It was founded by Henry VIII in 1537 as the Brotherhood of St George.

Tower Wharf

Tower

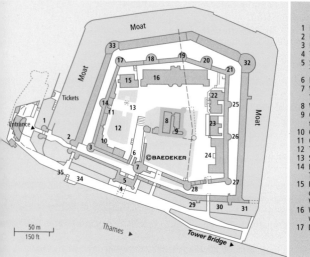

1	Middle Tower	18	Flint Tower
2	Byward Tower	19	Bowyer Tower
3	Bell Tower	20	Brick Tower
4	Traitor's Gate	21	Martin Tower
5	St Thomas's Tower	22	Fusiliers' Museum
6	Bloody Tower	23	Former Hospital
7	Wakefield Tower	24	Workshop
8	White Tower	25	Constable Tower
9	Chapel of St John the Evangelist	26	Broad Arrow Tower
10	Queen's House	27	Salt Tower
11	Gaoler's House	28	Lanthorn Tower
12	Tower Green	29	Cradle Tower
13	Scaffold site	30	Well Tower
14	Beauchamp Tower	31	Develin Tower
15	Royal Chapel of St Peter ad Vincula	32	Brass Mount
16	Waterloo Barracks with crown jewels	33	Legge's Mou
17	Devereux Tower	34	Tower Wharf
		35	Queen's Stair

INNER WARD

Queen's House

The Queen's House, a pretty timber-framed building from the time of Henry VIII, is on the left in the Inner Ward. Here **Anne Boleyn** and **Lady Jane Grey** spent their last days, **Guy Fawkes** was interrogated, and **Rudolf Hess** was imprisoned.
Yeoman Gaoler's House Next to it is the house of the Yeoman Gaoler, who still attends ceremonies wearing period uniform and carrying an executioner's axe.

Beauchamp Tower

The three-storey Beauchamp Tower (1199–1216) is named after Thomas Beauchamp, Earl of Warwick, who was imprisoned here (1397–99) by Richard II. Other nobles have left their mark here, including John Dudley, who carved a relief, and Lord Guildford Dudley, husband of Lady Jane Grey, who wrote »Jane« on the wall. The exhibition **Prisoners of the Tower** on the lower floor tells of the fate of others who were locked up here.

Scaffold Site

At the place of execution the condemned were beheaded with an axe. Henry VIII made an exception only for Anne Boleyn: She died by the sword. However, most executions took place outside on Tower Hill; to be executed within the Tower was a privilege allowed only to **Lord**

Hastings, **Anne Boleyn**, **Catherine Howard** and **Jane Grey**, the Countess of Salisbury and the Earl of Essex.

The Chapel Royal of St Peter ad Vincula (»St Peter in Chains«) was built in about 1100 and altered in the 13th century. It is the burial place of many of the executed, including Sir **Thomas More** (executed in 1535), Anne Boleyn (1536), Thomas Cromwell (1540), Catherine Howard (1542), Lord Seymour of Sudeley, Lord High Admiral (1549), the Duke of Somerset (1552), John Dudley, Earl of Warwick and Duke of Northumberland (1553), Jane Grey and Guildford Dudley (1554), Robert Devereux, Earl of Essex (1601), James Fitzroy, Duke of Monmouth (1685) and Simon, Lord Lovat (1747).

Chapel Royal of St Peter ad Vincula

The **Fusiliers' Museum** on the east side of the Inner Ward displays mementoes and trophies of the old-established regiment of Royal Fusiliers, which is based in the Tower. Next to it is the hospital, behind that the east inner wall with the Constable Tower, the Broad Arrow Tower and the **Salt Tower**. Hugh Draper, who was confined here in 1561 accused of sorcery, inscribed a horoscope on the wall. From 1605 to 1621 Henry Percy, Earl of Northumberland, accused on involvement in the Gunpowder Plot, was imprisoned in the tower on the north-east corner, the **Martin Tower**, with a cook, three scientific assistants, a library and his own skittle alley, as well as access to other prisoners such as Sir Walter Raleigh. An exhibition about the history of the Crown Jewels now occupies the tower.

East Wall

The Waterloo Barracks take up the whole north side of the Inner Ward. The Crown Jewels are displayed here (see below). A point of interest behind the barracks is the Bowyer Tower, in which George Plantagenet, first Duke of Clarence is said to have been drowned in a butt of Malmsey wine on 18 February 1478.

Waterloo Barracks

** CROWN JEWELS

The Crown Jewels are the biggest draw for tourists in the Tower. Visitors glide past the treasures on an moving walkway. Most of the jewels date from after 1660, as the ancient regalia and jewels were melted down after the execution of Charles I during Cromwell's government.

No photography

St Edward's Crown was newly made of pure gold for the coronation of Charles II and is the crown used at coronations. Nevertheless, the **Imperial State Crown** was commissioned for the coronation of Queen Victoria in 1837; Elizabeth II still wears it at the opening of parliament. It is set with over 2800 diamonds and other precious stones, including a large spinel ruby at the front which Pedro the

The finest of the Crown Jewels

Imperial
State Crown

St Edward's
Crown

Cruel of Castile donated to the Black Prince in 1369 and Henry V wore on his helmet at the battle of Agincourt. One of the two **Stars of Africa**, which were cut from the largest diamond ever found, the **Cullinan**, is also set into the crown. At the back is the Stuart sapphire, which is said to have been in the possession of Edward the Confessor. The **Imperial Indian Crown**, made in 1911, has an emerald weighing more than 34 carats and over 6000 diamonds. The most famous diamond in the world was used for **Queen Elizabeth's Crown**. This is the legendary, 108-carat **Koh-i-Noor** (»mountain of light«). It belonged to the Rajah of Lahore, Runjit Singh, but was taken from him by the British in 1849 and presented to Queen Victoria. The crown was made for the consort of George VI, the Queen Mother, who died in 2002. The second **Star of Africa**, at 530 carats the largest cut diamond in the world, is set into the **Royal Sceptre**; the ball of **St Edward's Sceptre**, which weighs 40kg/90lb, is said to contain a piece of the True Cross of Christ. Among the other exhibits are the silver font in which children of the royal family are christened, the golden vessel for anointing-oil in the shape of an eagle and the Anointing Spoon, the only item remaining from the 12th-century regalia.

? MARCO POLO INSIGHT

The ravens in the Tower

The six ravens which hop around in the Tower (plus a seventh that is kept in reserve in a cage by the Wakefield Tower) bear the responsibility of protecting the kingdom of England. It is said that the monarchy will fall if they should ever leave the Tower. There is little danger of this happening, however, as their wings have been clipped and no pains are spared to keep them safe. They are also the reason why the Royal Observatory moved to Greenwich: When the Royal Astronomer Flamsteed demanded the removal of the ravens, Charles II decided in favour of the birds and the astronomer was packed off.

WHITE TOWER

Oldest part of
the Tower

The White Tower, the most important Norman fortress in England, takes its name from the original building material, white stone from Caen in Normandy. In 1078 William the Conqueror ordered its construction on the site of two bastions built by King Alfred in 885. Gundulf, later Bishop of Rochester, was responsible for the design, and

Ranulph Flambard, Bishop of Durham, completed the work in about 1100, after which he took up residence as the very first prisoner. The bones of the little princes murdered in the Bloody Tower were found in 1674 below the stairway leading to the first floor. The four-storey tower is 28m/92ft high, and its walls are three to four metres thick. In the 17th century the cupolas were added to the corner towers and the façade was renewed by Sir Christopher Wren.

Royal Armouries

The White Tower houses the royal collections of weapons and armour, which goes back to the reign of Henry VIII. They include light weapons, hunting weapons, magnificent suits of armour for war and tournaments, European weapons and armour from the Middle Ages to the 19th century, as well as Henry VIII's personal arms and armour.

Chapel of St John the Evangelist

The Chapel of St John the Evangelist, built in about 1080, is on the first and second floors of the south-east tower. With its robust round columns, cushion capitals and the Norman arches of the apse it is one of the finest buildings in England in the Norman style.

** Tower Bridge

✦ K 6

Location: Whitechapel, EC 1
Tube: Tower Hill   www.towerbridge.org.uk

Tower Bridge, a wonderful example of Victorian engineering and architecture, ranks alongside Big Ben as London's best-known landmark.

Construction began in 1886 to plans by Horace Jones and John Wolfe Barry and was completed in 1894. The bridge has been painted red, white and blue only since 1977 – before that it was battleship grey. Two 82m/270ft-long suspension bridges connect the banks with the neo-Gothic towers, which stand on foundations sunk 7.5m/25ft into the bed of the Thames. The two moving bascules between the towers are 9m/30ft above the water level at high tide; when the bridge was raised, a high-level walkway was originally open to allow pedestrians to cross the river; today admission is charged for this. It takes only one minute to raise the bascules to let large ships through. This spectacle can nowadays be seen several times a week; it used to take place up to fifteen times each day. Tower Bridge is now a museum about itself: The **Tower Bridge Exhibition** in the towers tells the story of the bridge; the old steam engines and hydraulic equipment are also open to visitors.

✱✱ *Tower Bridge*

Tower Bridge competes with Big Ben as London's most famous land-mark. With a little luck visitors can watch how the bridge is raised. If you don't want to take a chance of missing out on this, check the sched-ule at http://www.towerbridge.org.uk to find out when the bridge will be raised and the name of the ship that will be passing through.

Tower Bridge Exhibition: April–Sep daily 10am–6.30pm, Oct–March 9.30am–5pm; admission £9

❶ North tower

Like the south tower, the north tower is 65m/215ft high and stands on a pier weighing 71,120 tons – the heaviest in the world at the time they were built. The entrance to the exhibition about the bridge is in the north tower.

❷ High-level walkway

The walkway between the two towers is 33.5m/110ft above the roadway and 42.4m/139ft above the average water level. In 1912 Frank McLean flew a bi-plane through the gap between it and the roadway.

❸ South tower

The exhibition continues in the south tower with insights into the everyday life of the people who built the bridge.

❹ Steel frame

The towers consist of a steel frame clad with masonry. A total of 11,481 tons of iron and steel, 37,477 tons of concrete, 20,320 tons of cement, 29,696 tons of bricks and 30,480 tons of stone were needed to build the bridge.

❺ Bascules

Each of the bascules weighs 1,220 tons and is based on a see-saw mecha-nism, rotating 86° in one minute.

❻ Passage through the bridge

When the bascules are raised, ships of up to 10,000 tons gross weight can pass through the 61m/202ft-wide opening. In 1952 a full double-decker bus had to make the jump across the gap when the bridge opened. The bus was still on the roadway because the bridge-keepers had misinformed the driver.

The bridge opens about twenty times a week

John Wolfe Barry
revised Jones' design.

...bascule is worked by four
...raulic engines. They were
...ginally powered by three
...epower pumping systems
...e engine room below the
...h approach of the bridge.

Horace Jones produced
the basic design: a bridge
with a roadway that
could be raised.

❶

❺

❻

©BAEDEKER

Each
hyc
or
300-hors
in t
sou

** Trafalgar Square

G 6

Location: Westminster, SW 1
Tube: Charing Cross

Trafalgar Square is every bit as busy as ▶Piccadilly Circus but much more attractive and harmonious in appearance. It is London's most majestic square.

The square takes its name from Admiral Nelson's victory over the Franco-Spanish fleet off the Spanish coast near Cape Trafalgar on 21 October 1805. It was designed by **John Nash**. Work began in 1829 but was not completed until 1851 by **Charles Barry**. Barry was responsible for the terrace on the north side in front of the ▶National Gallery, from which there is a superb view down ▶Whitehall to Big Ben and Parliament.

Nelson's Column

Nelson's Column rises to a height of 56m/184ft in the centre of the square. It was erected between 1840 and 1843 to a design by William Railton, who modelled it on a column of the Temple of Mars Ultor in Rome. The **statue of Horatio Nelson** at the top is over 5m/16ft high; before the admiral was put into position, 14 stonemasons had dinner on the platform. The bronze reliefs on the base cast from French cannon depict scenes from Nelson's four great victories: the Battle of the Nile (1798) is on the north side, the Battle of Copenhagen (1801) on the east, the Battle of St Vincent (1797) on the west, and on the south, the Battle of Trafalgar with the scene of the dying admiral who urged his fleet with his famous last words »England expects that every man will do his duty.« The four monumental lions by Edwin Landseer were added in 1868, the two fountains designed by Sir Edwin Lutyens in 1948.

A number of **other monuments** have been placed on Trafalgar Square: On the east side is Henry Havelock, who conquered Lucknow in India (the column to the right of it was placed there as a hiding place for a policeman, who could watch the goings-on around the square through a slit and phone for reinforcements), in the northeast corner George IV, between the fountains General Gordon, and on the west Charles James Napier, who conquered Sind in India. The pedestal in the north-west corner is a curiosity. After 150 years of

> **MARCO POLO INSIGHT**
>
> **?** *Do you know*
>
> ... that a yard is defined as the distance from the tip of Henry I's nose to the end of his thumb when his arms were outstretched? This, at any rate, is the traditional explanation. Try it out on the standard yard in Trafalgar Square.

Simply majestic: Trafalgar Square

discussion about what kind of monument should be placed on it, the decision was finally taken in 1999 to exhibit regularly changing modern sculptures and installations under the name **Fourth Plinth Project**. On the traffic island facing Whitehall stands an equestrian statue of Charles I by Le Sueur from 1633. It marks the position of **Charing Cross**, the site of the last of twelve crosses that Edward I placed along the route of the funeral procession of his wife Eleanor from Nottinghamshire to Westminster. The old British measures of length (**Imperial Standards of Length**) are set in brass into the balustrade on the north side of the square: one foot, two feet and one imperial yard.

The most noteworthy buildings on Trafalgar Square, apart from the ▶National Gallery and ▶St Martin-in-the-Fields, are Canada House on the west side and South Africa House on the east side. On the south-west corner Admiralty Arch leads to ▶The Mall. To the south is ▶Whitehall, to the south-east the ▶Strand and to the north Leicester Square and ▶Soho.

Canada House, South Africa House

** Victoria & Albert Museum

⭑ D 7

Location: Cromwell Road, SW 7
Tube: South Kensington
🕐 Daily 10am–5.45pm,
Fri until 10pm

Tours hourly 10.30am–3.30pm
Admission: free
www.vam.ac.uk

Queen Victoria's husband, the Prince Consort Albert of Saxe-Coburg and Gotha, conceived the idea of an institution that would collect arts and crafts of the highest quality and inspire would-be craftsmen. It became a world-class museum.

Many items from the Great Exhibition of 1851, which were put on show in Marlborough House from 1852, formed the basis for this »Museum of Manufacturers«. After five years the collection moved to South Kensington. In 1899 Queen Victoria laid the foundation stone for the present building, designed by **Sir Aston Webb**.

More than a museum café: the Morris Room at the V & A

PLANNING A VISIT

The V & A is one of the world's major art museums, and also one of the largest. The problem is that its multitude of departments and exhibits can be confusing. The broad division of the museum into four themes helps visitors to get their bearings: Asia, Europe, Modern, and Materials and Techniques. It is also easy to lose your bearings in the museum shop, which sells everything from knick-knacks for souvenir hunters to high-quality reproductions for art lovers.

This tour of the museum stays on levels 0 (lower ground floor) and 1. Some fine medieval art is at the very beginning on level 0: in room 8 the ivory Symmachi panel (c. AD 400), the Eltenburg reliquary shrine made in Cologne around 1180, the 12th-century **Gloucester candlestick** and a rare 13th-century Flemish silver hand reliquary. On the floor above, rooms 50a to 50d are devoted to sculpture and architectural decoration of the late Middle Ages and Renaissance, for example a marble-and-alabaster screen from s'Hertogenbosch (1600–13) and church furnishings and tombs from Italy. On the same level, rooms 26, 27 and 16a contain religious sculpture from 1300 to 1600 and stained glass, including magnificent 16th-century windows from German monasteries. The absolute highlight of this section is in room 48a: **the cartoons that Raphael produced** in 1515–16 as designs for the wall-hangings of the Sixtine Chapel.

Europe in the Middle Ages and Renaissance

MARCO ❁ POLO TIP

Don't miss — Insider Tip

- The Gloucester candlestick: 12th-century silver (room 8)
- Raphael cartoons: the designs for the Sixtine Chapel (room 48a)
- The Ardabil carpet: a superb 16th-century Persian carpet (room 42)
- Tippoo's Tiger: a macabre mechanical figure (room 41)
- Paintings by John Constable (rooms 603–620)
- Morris Room, Gamble Room und Poynter Room: the superb interiors of the first museum restaurant in England

The second tour on various levels of the museum leads to British arts and crafts and famous large-scale sculpture. Masterpieces such as Michelangelo's David, the Portico de la Gloria from Santiago de Compostela, the bronze doors of Hildesheim and – in two halves – Trajan's Column can be admired as plaster casts in the Cast Courts. Rooms 5–58 and 118–125 (level 4) present **British crafts from 1500 until 1900**. Here are the entire music room from Norfolk House am St James's Square (1756) with exquisite carpentry and wood carvings, silk fabrics woven by Huguenots, Roubiliac's statue of Handel, Henry VIII's writing box, the suit worn by James II for his wedding and the earliest English fork. The largest exhibit is the Great Bed of Ware from the White Hart Inn in Ware, which plays a part in Shakespeare's *Twelfth Night*. It measures 3.6m/12ft in length and breadth.

Materials and techniques

Victoria and Albert Museum

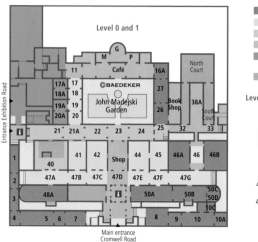

Europe

Asia

Material and techniques

Modern

Exhibition Road
building projects

Temporary exhibitions

Level 0 and 1
- 1–7 Europe 1600–1800
- 8–10 Medieval and Renaissance 300–1500
- 21–24 Sculpture
- 26–27 Sculpture 1300–1600
- 40 Fashion
- 41 South Asia
- 42 Islam
- 45 Japan
- 44,47E China
- 46A,B Cast Courts
- 47A–C South East Asia
- 47G Korea
- 48A Raphael Cartoons

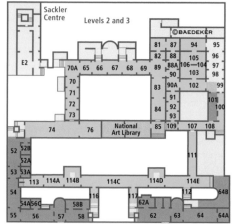

Levels 2 and 3
- 52–58 Britain 1500–1760
- 62A–64B Medieval and Renaissance 300–1600
- 65–70A, 89 Silver
- 81–82, 87–88A Paintings
- 83–84 Sacred Silver
- 90 Prints and Drawings
- 91–93 Jewellery
- 94 Tapestries
- 100 Photographs
- 102, 107 Leighton
- 103–106 Theatre and Performance
- 111, 117 Sculpture
- 113, 114E, 116 Ironwork

**13th-century Flemish hand
reliquary (room 10)**

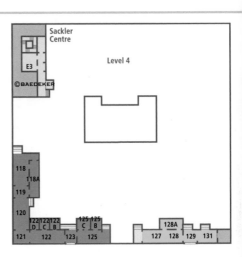

Level 4
118–125   Britain 1760–1900
127–128A Architecture
129   Contemporary Glass
131   Glass

Level 6
133–135   Furniture
136–146   Ceramics

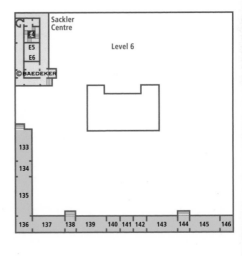

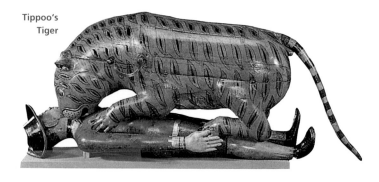

Tippoo's Tiger

Asia On level 1 is Asian art, starting with China in the T. T. Tsui Gallery (room 44), where the many techniques on display include ceramics from the Tang dynasty (700–900), furniture of the Ming dynasty (1368–1644) and an imperial throne taken from the South Palace in Beijing that was made under the Qing dynasty (1750–1820). In the following section there are objects from Japan, including a collection of netsukes and a 13th-century Buddha sculpture. The most precious piece in the Islamic department is the **Ardabil carpet**, which was produced in Ardabil carpet 1539–40 for Safi-al Din, the founder of the Safavid dynasty.

The Indian department is the largest collection of Indian art outside the subcontinent; it contains **Tippoo's Tiger** among other items, a late 18th-century wooden mechanical toy made for the Sultan of Mysore that shows a tiger devouring a British soldier. Its mechanism imitates the roars of the tiger and the cries of the victim.

More departments The departments on level 3 are highly recommended: the outstanding collections of silver, the Ironwork Gallery with its huge range of items and the jewellery collections (rooms 91–93), where a golden 7th-century Irish torque is just one of the exhibits. Not to be missed are the **paintings by John Constable** on level 3 in room 87: The V & A owns the world's largest collection of Constables. The adjacent rooms are home to the outstanding Ionides Collection, which ranges from painting of the Italian Renaissance to the Pre-Raphaelites and the French Impressionists.

Morris, Poynter & Gamble Rooms The museum café not only offers an enormous range of dishes and refreshments but is itself a work of art, as renowned artists of the time designed it: The Green Dining Room with windows by Edward Burne-Jones and Philip Webb was the creation of William Morris, while Edward Poynter designed the Grill Room with its Dutch tiles and James Bamble the main room with proverbs related to eating and drinking in the windows. Together these rooms form **the world's oldest museum restaurant**.

BROMPTON ORATORY

The V & A's immediate neighbour is the Roman Catholic Brompton Oratory, the church of the Oratorian Order. The order was founded in 1575 by St Filippo Neri in Rome and was introduced to England in 1847 by John Henry Newman, later Cardinal Newman, whose statue stands in the courtyard.

The church was built between 1854 and 1884 by Herbert Gribble in the Italian Renaissance style. The nave is the third-largest in England after those of Westminster Abbey and York Minster. The most notable features are figures of the apostles of Carrara marble from Siena Cathedral, the Renaissance altar in the Lady Chapel, which came from the Dominican church in Brescia, and the altar of the St Wilfred Chapel, which was originally in Maastricht Cathedral.

Brompton Cemetery in West Brompton is the largest place of burial in London.

✳ V & A Museum of Childhood

✦ M 3

Location: Cambridge Heath Road, E 2
Tube: Bethnal Green
🛈 Daily 10am–5.45pm
Admission: free

www.museumofchildhood.org.uk

The former Bethnal Green Museum of Childhood in East End of London, now part of the Victoria and Albert Museum, is the largest British collection of toys.

In 1872 Bethnal Green Museum opened in an unusual Victorian building that originally stood in South Kensington and housed items from the Great Exhibition of 1851 After completion of the ▶Victoria and Albert Museum, the glass and wrought-iron structure moved to Bethnal Green. Its charming exhibits range from games, oriental toy soldiers and European teddy bears to Matchbox and Corgi cars and a great variety of dolls and dolls' houses and clothes, including dolls' wedding dresses from the 19th and 20th centuries. Temporary exhibitions are held on the upper floor, and of course there is also an interactive area.

* Wallace Collection

E 5

Location: Manchester Square, W 1
Tube: Baker Street, Bond Street
◐ Daily 10am–5pm

Admission: free
www.wallace
collection.org

The Wallace Collection has a high-quality and unusually wide range of art and applied art of diverse origins, as well as a stylish café-restaurant in the courtyard.

The fourth Marquis of Hertford, who lived mainly in Paris, built on his forebears' passion for art by developing the family collection into one of the very finest quality; the widow of his son Richard Wallace (1818–90), who had expanded it further, bequeathed the collection to the nation. Since 1900 the Wallace Collection has been housed in 25 rooms of Hertford House, which was built between 1776 and 1788 for the Duke of Manchester and conveys a good impression of an aristocratic residence of the period. Many rooms contain pieces by the French furniture makers Boulle (1642–1732), Cressent (1685–1768) and Riesener (1734–1806) and are furnished with Sèvres porcelain, bronzes and majolica. Rooms 5 to 8 are devoted to weapons and armour.

The mecca of England's football: Wembley Stadium

The outstanding items, however, are miniatures, such as a portrait of Holbein by Horenbout in rooms 20 and 21, and above all paintings, including Lawrence's *George IV and Countess of Blessington* in room 1, works by Clouet and Foppa in rooms 3 and 4, religious subjects by Murillo in rooms 12 and 19 and views of Venice by Canaletto and Guardi in rooms 13 and 14. 17th-century Dutch and Flemish masters are on show in rooms 15 to 19, including paintings by Rubens (*The Holy Family, Isabella Brandt, The Rainbow Landscape*), Rembrandt (*The Good Samaritan*), ***Frans Hals** (*The Laughing Cavalier*) and several works by Nicolaes Berchem; as well as Velázquez (*Lady with a Fan*), Titian (*Perseus and Andromeda*), Reynolds (*The Strawberry Girl* and a number of fine society portraits), Gainsborough (*Mrs Robinson*) and Philippe de Champaigne. Apart from works by Sir Joshua Reynolds, the following rooms mainly display French paintings by, for example, Fragonard (*The Swing*).

Paintings and miniatures

Wembley Stadium
———————— ✳ **Outer suburb**

Location: Wembley, HA 9
Tube: Wembley Park   at tel. 0844 800 27 55; price: £16
Tours: bookings   www.wembleystadium.com

Wembley Stadium is the mecca of English football. At the inauguration and opening match on 28 April 1923, the cup final between Bolton Wanderers and West Ham United, 240,000 (!) people crowded into the stadium. The athletics contests of the Olympic Games in 1948 took place here.

Nothing remains of the old Wembley. It was demolished in 2003 and has been replaced by the world's most expensive stadium, designed by Sir Norman Foster and costing 800 million pounds. For this amount English football got the second-largest stadium in Europe after the Nou Camp in Barcelona and an architectural marvel. Its emblem is a steel-lattice arch 315m/345yd long set at an angle of 22°, which rises to a height of 133m/436ft and supports the whole north roof and more than half of the weight of the closing part

? MARCO⊕POLO INSIGHT

Football is not everything

The old Wembley Stadium was the venue for legendary open-air concerts. The artists with the most appearances were:
• Michael Jackson: 15 (1.1 million tickets sold)
• Rolling Stones: 12
• Fleetwood Mac: 10
• Madonna: 9
• U 2: 9
• Elton John: 7
• Tina Turner: 7
The new stadium too is used for concerts, of course. Take That hold the record so far, having played on eight consecutive evenings in 2011.

of the roof. The new stadium was inaugurated in 2007 with the final of the FA Cup. In front of the main entrance is a bronze statue of **Bobby Moore** (1941–93), captain of the England team that won the World Cup at Wembley in 1966. This story and many others can be heard during a stadium tour.

SHRI SWAMINARAYAN MANDIR

❶ 105–119 Brentfield Road, Neasden, NW 10; Tube: Wembley Park, then bus no. 206) or Stonebridge Park and 15 mins walk (signposted); exhibition daily 9am–6pm; admission £2; www.mandir.org

The largest Hindu temple outside India is situated on Brentfield Road to the south-east of Wembley. British Hindus raised the money for this astonishing, 21m/69ft-high building, for which 2800 tons of sandstone and 2000 tons of Carrara marble were used. The building materials were transported to be worked in India, and the construction was then completed in London in a matter of weeks. The result – wonderful sculptures of the Hindu pantheon of gods – is open for visits by non-Hindus, who can find explanations in the exhibition entitled Understanding Hinduism. There is an excellent vegetarian restaurant on the car park opposite the temple.

✹✹ Westminster Abbey

✦ **G 7**

Location: Broad Sanctuary, SW 1
Tube: Westminster
❶ Mon–Fri 9.30am–4.30pm, Wed until 7pm, Sat 9.30am–2.30pm

Admission: £18
www.westminster-abbey.org

Westminster Abbey, officially named The Collegiate Church of St Peter in Westminster, is not only one of London's greatest tourist attractions but also a »normal« place of worship for the faithful.

For this reason the stream of tourists is channelled along a route beginning at the north door and exiting through the west door. An Anglo-Saxon church is thought to have occupied this site as early as the 7th century. To distinguish it from the Abbey of St Mary-of-the-Graces further east, known as Eastminster, the church was given the name Westminster. Following destruction by the Danes, **Edward the Confessor** refounded the church in 1065. Starting in the reign of Henry III, Edward the Confessor's building was replaced in its turn by the present church in the Early English Gothic style. In 1388

The west entrance to Westminster Abbey

Henry Yevele built part of the abbey, which had been destroyed by fire in 1298. In 1506 **Abbot Islip** added the roof vaults. The Gothic-style façade with its two 68m/223ft-tall towers was built between 1735 and 1740 by **Nicholas Hawksmoor**, a pupil of Wren. Today Westminster Abbey is 156m/171yd long and 61m/67yd wide at the transepts. The height of the nave, 34m/112ft, makes it the tallest Gothic church interior in England. Since the beginning of the Church of England under Henry VIII, Westminster Abbey has been a »royal peculiar«, subject directly to the Crown. With the exception of Edward V and Edward VIII, all English kings since William the Conqueror in 1066 have been crowned here, and from the death of Henry III to the funeral of George II in 1760 most English kings were buried here. Royal weddings have been less numerous here – a total of 16 so far, the latest being that of William and Kate, Duke and Duchess of Cambridge, in 2011. Persons of national significance are still buried in the abbey or honoured with a memorial tablet.

NORTH TRANSEPT

The north door leads to the north transept, known as Statesmen's Aisle. The memorials to be seen on the right include those for **William Pitt the Elder** († 1778), the statesman and judge Lord Mansfield († 1793) and Warren Hastings († 1818), Governor General of

Statesmen's Aisle

India; on the left are memorials to Lord Norris († 1801) in St Andrew's Chapel, the dramatic tomb of Elizabeth Nightingale († 1734) by Roubiliac in St Michael's Chapel and that of Sir Francis Vere († 1608), a military commander under Elizabeth I, in St John's Chapel. The memorial to Admiral Peter Warren († 1752) is at the ambulatory railing. In front of it is the grave of prime minister **William Ewart Gladstone** († 1898) and next to it the memorial to **Sir Robert Peel** († 1850; MARCO POLO Insight p. 340).

ROYAL CHAPELS

North ambulatory
On the left is the way to the royal chapels through the north ambulatory, where the two-storey Islip Chapel is situated. The funerary monument to Abbott Islip († 1532), a builder of the church, is in the lower part, a chapel of remembrance for the Medical Corps in the upper part. Adjoining it is the Chapel of St John the Baptist. The graves here include that of Thomas Cecil, Earl of Exeter († 1622), counsellor to James I. The place to Cecil's left was intended for his second wife, who declined to be buried here as the place of honour on the right was occupied by Cecil's first wife. Further on, in the Chapel of St Paul, are the graves of Sir Rowland Hill († 1879; at the front), originator of the penny postal stamp, and **James Watt** († 1819; on the right).

**Chapel of Henry VII (Lady Chapel)
Twelve steps of black marble lead to the funeral chapel of Henry VII, built from 1503 to 1519 under the direction of Robert Ertue, Henry's court architect. The nave of the chapel, with its rich decoration and beautiful vault, is a magnificent example of the Perpendicular style. The tombs of Henry VII and his wife are by the Florentine sculptor **Torrigiani**. The marriage of Henry VII († 1509) and Elizabeth of York († 1502), who are portrayed as recumbent figures of gilded bronze, united the houses of Lancaster and York and ended the Wars of the Roses. James I lies in the same vault; George II and Edward VI, among others, have their final resting place in front of the tomb of Henry VII. Above the monument are the banners and wonderfully carved stalls of the Knights of the Order of the Bath.

Innocents' Corner is in the aisle on the left. Sophie and Mary, daughters of James I who died at the age of just three days and two years respectively, are buried here. Next to these graves is a small sarcophagus with the remains of the sons of Edward IV, who were murdered in the ▶Tower; at the front are the tombs of Queen Elizabeth I († 1603) and Queen Mary (»Bloody Mary«; † 1558), Elizabeth's Catholic half-sister.

The small funeral chapels contain the marble tomb of the Duc de Montpensier († 1807), brother of the »citizen king« of France, Louis

Westminster Abbey

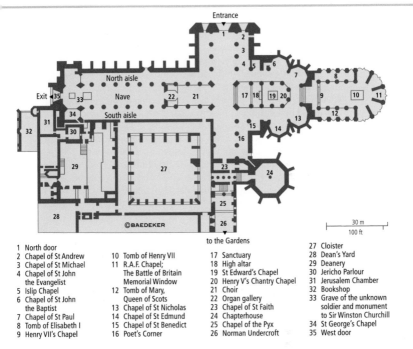

Entrance

1 North door
2 Chapel of St Andrew
3 Chapel of St Michael
4 Chapel of St John
   the Evangelist
5 Islip Chapel
6 Chapel of St John
   the Baptist
7 Chapel of St Paul
8 Tomb of Elisabeth I
9 Henry VII's Chapel

10 Tomb of Henry VII
11 R.A.F. Chapel;
    The Battle of
    Britain
    Memorial Window
12 Tomb of Mary,
    Queen of Scots
13 Chapel of St Nicholas
14 Chapel of St Edmund
15 Chapel of St Benedict
16 Poet's Corner

17 Sanctuary
18 High altar
19 St Edward's Chapel
20 Henry V's Chantry Chapel
21 Choir
22 Organ gallery
23 Chapel of St Faith
24 Chapterhouse
25 Chapel of the Pyx
26 Norman Undercroft

27 Cloister
28 Dean's Yard
29 Deanery
30 Jericho Parlour
31 Jerusalem Chamber
32 Bookshop
33 Grave of the unknown
   soldier and monument
   to Sir Winston Churchill
34 St George's Chapel
35 West door

Philippe; next to it is the Royal Air Force Chapel with the Battle of Britain Memorial Window; to the left of that is the tomb of John Sheffield, Duke of Buckinghamshire († 1723), and in front of it the tomb of **Anne of Denmark** († 1618), the wife of James I. Until 1661 Oliver Cromwell was also buried here. The noteworthy features of the aisle on the right are the tomb of Lady Margaret Douglas († 1577), daughter of Queen Margaret of Scotland, surrounded by her seven children, the **Tomb of Mary, Queen of Scots** recumbent effigy of Mary, Queen of Scots, who was beheaded in 1587, and the life-size figure of George Monk, Duke of Albemarle († 1670), who restored the house of Stuart to the throne. Charles II, William III and Queen Mary, and Queen Anne with her consort lie in the vault in front of the right-hand aisle.

Following on from Henry VII's Chapel is the **Henry V Chantry Chapel**. The recumbent figure of Henry V is without its head, which was stolen during the reign of Henry VIII.

**St Edward's Chapel

The wooden shrine of Edward the Confessor († 1066), which lacks its original decoration, stands in the centre of St Edward's Chapel above the apse of the old abbey church. The shrine, erected in 1269 in accordance with the wishes of Henry III, was for a long period a place of pilgrimage and the holiest place in the abbey. The old oak coronation chair of Edward I stands at the back wall of the sanctuary. For 700 years the **Stone of Scone**, the symbol of Scottish royal power made of sandstone from the west coast of Scotland, lay beneath the seat. The head of Jacob (Genesis chapter 28, verse 18) is said to have rested on the stone. Edward I brought the stone to London in 1296 as a sign of the subjugation of the Scots; it was not returned to Scotland until 1996. The sword of state and shield of Edward III are next to the chair. On the side walls it is worth noting (from the right of the chair) the plain tombstone of Edward I († 1308); the magnificent porphyry tomb of Henry III († 1272) with a mosaic; the tomb of Queen Eleanor († 1290), the first wife of Edward I, bearing an inscription in Old French; Philippa of Hainault († 1369), wife of Edward III; Edward III himself († 1377); Margaret Woodville († 1472), a daughter of Edward IV who died at the age of nine months; and finally Richard II, who was murdered in 1399.

Late flowering of the Perpendicular Style in the Chapel of Henry VII

In the first chapel of the south ambulatory, the Chapel of St Nicholas, is the marble tomb of Sir George Villiers, first Duke of Buckingham († 1606), and his wife; the wife of Henry V, Catherine of Valois, lay buried under it for 350 years and is now in the Henry V Chantry Chapel. The tomb of Elizabeth, Duchess of Northumberland († 1776) is a masterly work by Robert Adam and Nicholas Read (right). Among the finest monuments in the Chapel of St Edmund are those of William de Valence, Earl of Pembroke and half-brother of Henry III, who died in battle at Bayonne in 1296, with plaques of gilded copper and the recumbent effigy of the earl richly decorated with enamelwork (right); the tomb of Eleanor de Bohun, Duchess of Gloucester († 1399) shown as a nun (centre); the alabaster monuments to John of Eltham († 1334), the second son of Edward II (left), and Edward Talbot, Earl of Shrewsbury († 1617; right). The highlights of the Chapel of St Benedict are the alabaster tomb of Simon Langham († 1376), abbot of Westminster and archbishop of Canterbury, on the left; in the centre the grave of Lionel Cranfield, Earl of Middlesex († 1645), chancellor of the exchequer to James I, and that of **Anne of Cleves**, fourth wife of Henry VIII.

South ambulatory

SOUTH TRANSEPT · CHOIR · SANCTUARY

After the royal chapels, the route through the abbey goes left into the south transept. Statues and memorials to British poets have been placed on its south wall, east wall and in the floor, giving this part of the church the name »Poets' Corner«. The poets commemorated here include **Sir Walter Scott** († 1832), Oliver Goldsmith († 1774), John Gay († 1732), author of *The Beggars' Opera*, **William Shakespeare** († 1616), John Dryden († 1700), H. W. Longfellow († 1882), **Geoffrey Chaucer** († 1400), Percy Bysshe Shelley († 1822), Lord Byron († 1824), Robert Burns († 1796), Robert Browning († 1889), **Charles Dickens** († 1870), Lord Tennyson († 1892), Lewis Carroll († 1898), **Rudyard Kipling** († 1936), Dylan Thomas († 1953) and T. S. Eliot († 1965). On the right (the west side): a relief with a group of figures around the actor David Garrick († 1779); the novelist W. M. Thackeray († 1863), **Sir Laurence Olivier** († 1989) and above left a statue of George Frideric Handel by Roubiliac.

*Poets' Corner

The choir extends beyond the transepts into the middle of the nave. The sanctuary, the place where English sovereigns are crowned, faces the altar. Its marble mosaic floor, brought to London from Rome in 1268, is a masterpiece in the style of the Cosmati family. There are three very fine medieval tombs on the left: They belong to the founder of the house of Lancaster, Edmund Crouchback († 1296); Aymer de Valence, Earl of Pembroke († 1324); and Crouchback's wife, Ave-

Choir and sanctuary

line († 1273). The clergy sit on the right on the so-called sedilia, seats of oak that are probably situated above the grave of the 7th-century Saxon king Sebert. An eye-catching feature of the high altar, which Gilbert Scott designed in 1867, is Salviati's glass mosaic depicting The Last Supper.

CLOISTER

In its present form the cloister dates from the 13th and 14th centuries, but it was first built in the 11th century. Here too there are many graves, as well as a café. The Deanery, Jericho Parlour and **Jerusalem Chamber** (not open to the public), where Henry IV died, are on the west side of the cloister.

CHAPTER HOUSE · PYX CHAMBER · ABBEY MUSEUM

Chapter House The chapter house can be reached from the cloister or from outside the church through the entrance in Dean's Yard. A single column, a copy of the original made in 1866, supports the vault of the octagonal room (1245–55), which has a diameter of 20m/66ft. The architect was probably Henry of Reims. Remarkable features of the chapter house are the Roman sarcophagus in the vestibule and, in the octagon, the ribs around the six windows, the 13th-century tympanum above the doorway and the finest medieval tiled floor in Britain. The door in the vestibule, dating from 1050, may be the oldest in Britain. The chapter house was the meeting-place of the Great Council, the forerunner of Parliament, in 1257 and the House of Commons from 1282 to 1547; after that it was an official archive until 1865.

> **Insider Tip**
> *A precious wooden head*
>
> **MARCO POLO TIP**
> It is worth taking a close look at the effigy of King Edward III (1312–77) in the Abbey Museum: It is the oldest surviving wooden portrait of a monarch in Europe.

Pyx Chamber The Pyx Chamber (Chapel of the Pyx), part of Edward the Confessor's church, is the site of the oldest altar in the abbey. The name comes from the pyx, a wooden box that was kept here and held the samples of gold and silver coins used in the annual trial of the coinage of the realm.

Abbey Museum The Abbey Museum in the **Norman undercroft**, a survival from the time of Edward the Confessor, displays seals, documents, Mary II's coronation chair and the saddle, helm and shield of Henry V from the battle of Agincourt. The curiosity of the museum is a collection of life-size wax funeral effigies of prominent persons that were shown in the abbey at their funerals. The figures include those of Charles II, Elizabeth I, Mary II, William III, the Duke of Buckingham and Lord Nelson.

❶ Mon–Sat 10.30am–4pm

The College Garden, today used by Westminster School, is thought to be the oldest garden in England.

College Garden

❶ Tue–Thu; access from the Little Cloister

NAVE

From the cloister the tour enters the south aisle, where a memorial tablet to Lord **Baden Powell** († 1914), founder of the Scout movement, is set into the floor. On the right are the Abbot's Pew, a small oak gallery built in the 16th century by Abbot Islip, and memorials to the Methodist John Wesley († 1791) and **Sir Godfrey Kneller** († 1723), the last of these designed by the artist himself, the only painter commemorated in Westminster Abbey. The monuments on the left

South aisle

The choir and main altar of Westminster Abbey

include a bust of **Pasquale Paoli** († 1807), a Corsican national hero, and the memorial to William Thynne († 1584), a translator of the Bible.

Nave

Stone slabs in the nave cover the graves of, among others, the architects Sir Charles Barry († 1860) and Sir Gilbert Scott († 1878), the explorer of Africa **David Livingstone** († 1873), the inventor **Robert Stephenson** († 1859), and the prime ministers Andrew Bonar Law († 1923) and **Neville Chamberlain** († 1940). A short distance from the west doorway is the grave of the unknown soldier, who is buried in soil from Flanders, and the memorial stone to **Sir Winston Churchill** († 1965).

North aisle

Above the door to the north aisle is an allegorical monument to a prime minister, **William Pitt the Younger** († 1806). Pitt is portrayed as an orator, with History listening on the right while Anarchy on the left is in chains. Further notable monuments in this aisle commemorate William Wilberforce († 1833), one of the leading opponents of slavery; the statesman Charles James Fox († 1806); the poet **Ben Jonson** († 1637); the composers Orlando Gibbons († 1625) and **Henry Purcell** († 1695); William Croft († 1727), who like Purcell was abbey organist; and **Charles Darwin** († 1882). There is a window in honour of the engineer Isambard Kingdom Brunel († 1859) and on the left at the end of the choir the black sarcophagus of **Sir Isaac Newton** († 1726).

St George's Chapel

Before leaving the abbey it is worth taking a look inside St George's Chapel, which is dedicated to those who fell in the First World War. In addition to the memorial to Franklin D. Roosevelt, a 14th-century portrait of Richard II is particularly worthy of note.

AROUND WESTMINSTER ABBEY

Sanctuary

The Tudor gatehouse diagonally opposite the west door of the abbey to the left is approximately on the site where the abbey bell-tower and sanctuary once stood. This was a place of asylum for refugees, including the mother of Edward V, who gave birth to her son in the sanctuary.

Westminster School

Westminster School, one of the leading schools in London, lies to the south of the abbey buildings. It was first mentioned as a monastery school in 1339, but was refounded in 1560 by Elizabeth I. Former pupils include Dryden, Locke, Ben Jonson, Wren, Churchill, Peter Ustinov and Andrew Lloyd Webber. Shrove Tuesday is the occasion for **tossing the pancake**, when the school cook throws a pancake to the pupils. The one who grabs the largest piece receives a coin from the dean.

Middlesex Guildhall, built in 1913, faces Parliament Square. During the Second World War the Allied military courts sat here; today it is home of the Supreme Court. Memorial tablets in the entrance hall with the signatures of George of Greece, Wilhelmina of Holland and Haakon of Norway commemorate this.

Middlesex
Guildhall

St Margaret's Church to the north of Westminster Abbey, founded by Edward the Confessor in the 11th century and altered between 1488 and 1523 by Robert Stowell on the commission of the wool merchants of Westminster, has been the official church of the House of Commons since Palm Sunday 1614, when a service was held for the members of the house, mostly Puritans, for the first time. The church is also popular for the weddings of the English aristocracy. Winston Churchill, for example, married here. The main attraction of the church is the Flemish stained glass of the east window, a gift from the Spanish monarchs Ferdinand and Isabella for the marriage of Prince Arthur, the older brother of Henry VIII, to Catherine of Aragon. When the window arrived in London, Arthur had already died and Catherine was married to Henry. The glass was then sent to Waltham Abbey and bought back by Parliament in 1758. The most notable of the funerary monuments is that of **Sir Walter Raleigh**, founder of the state of Virginia, who is thought to have been buried here after his execution.

St Margaret's

Westminster Cathedral
✦ F 7

Location: 42 Francis St., SW 1
Tube: Victoria
❶ Mon–Fri 9.30am–5pm, Sat and
Sun 9.30am–6pm   **Admission:** £5
Tower viewing gallery Mon–Fri   **www.**
9.30am–5pm, Sat–Sun 9.30am–6pm   **westminstercathedral.org.uk**

Westminster Cathedral is the seat of the cardinal archbishop of Westminster and, along with Liverpool Metropolitan Cathedral, the most important Catholic church in England.

The 120m/395ft-long church was built between 1895 and 1903 in a Romanesque-Byzantine style to designs by John Francis Bentley. Its ground plan is that of a four-domed basilica. Next to the north-west door is the lift to the top of the 94m/308ft-tall St Edward's Tower with a view over much of London. Two columns of red Norwegian granite in the vestibule symbolise the precious blood of Christ, to which the cathedral is dedicated. Next to the left-hand column is a bronze image of St Peter, a copy of the famous seated St Peter from St Peter's Cathedral in Rome. The nave, the widest in England at 52m/170ft, has two aisles. The decoration work is still in progress; the mosaics of the chapels have been completed. The most interesting chapels are St George's Chapel, with the tomb of John Southwark, who died in 1654; the Chapel of St Thomas of Canterbury in the north transept, in which Cardinal Herbert Vaughan, who initiated the construction of the cathedral, is buried; and the Chapel of St Patrick and the Saints of Ireland, where the colours of Irish regiments from the First World War are kept. The crypt chapel, dedicated to St Peter, houses a collection of holy relics, including Thomas Becket's bishop's mitre and fragments of the Holy Cross.

✷✷ Whitehall

✧ G 6

Location: Westminster, SW 1
Tube: Westminster, Embankment, Charing Cross

The street Whitehall has become a synonym for the district from which Britain is governed.

Government quarter
The name comes from Whitehall Palace, which stretched for over half a mile from ▶Trafalgar Square to Westminster Bridge on one side, and from the Thames to ▶St James's Park on the other side. It originated in the 13th century as York Palace, the residence of the archbishops of York. Cardinal Wolsey extended this palace, and after his fall from favour, Henry VIII moved in and made it into a royal palace. He commissioned a great hall for festivities, a jousting ground and the Holbein Gate, a large Renaissance building close to the present site of the Cenotaph. James I had even more ambitious plans, which he entrusted to Inigo Jones and John Webb, but only the Banqueting House was actually built and is the sole part of the palace to have survived the fire of 1698.

FROM PARLIAMENT SQUARE TO TRAFALGAR SQUARE

Parliament Square
A walk along Whitehall begins at the ▶Houses of Parliament on Parliament Square. Around the lawn here are the flags of the Commonwealth states and monuments to British and American statesmen, of which the statue of Sir Winston Churchill is undoubtedly the most impressive. From here walk along Parliament Street towards Trafalgar Square.

The first street on the left, King Charles Street, divides the Public Offices, a large complex of buildings erected between 1868 and 1873. The northern part houses the Foreign Office, Commonwealth Office, the Home Office and the India Office Library, while the southern part is occupied by the Treasury.

Public Offices

Steps at the end of King Charles Street lead down to the Churchill War Rooms. The war cabinet directed British operations in the Second World War from these 19 bunker rooms. They have been kept as they were in 1945 with all sorts of interesting items, such as the telephone that Churchill used for his frequent conversations with US President Roosevelt. Even Churchill's simple bedroom has been preserved just as it was – although he preferred to watch the bombing raids from the roof or sleep in the Savoy Hotel. Some of the rooms have been converted into a Churchill museum, and there is an exhibition about life in the bunker.

*Churchill War Rooms

❶ Daily 9.30am–6pm; admission £17.50, www.iwm.org.uk

Opposite the Foreign Office in the middle of the road is the national monument for the fallen of the two world wars, the Cenotaph (from the Greek, meaning »empty grave«). It was designed by Sir Edward Lutyens and unveiled in 1920 on the second anniversary of the armistice of 11 November 1918 as a memorial to those who died in the »Great War«, as the First World War was known. After the Second World War the dedication was changed and now reads »The Glorious Dead«. There are no religious symbols on the Cenotaph, just the emblems of the army, air force, royal navy and merchant navy. On Remembrance Day, the second Sunday in November, representatives of the Commonwealth states gather at the Cenotaph at 11am to honour the fallen. The **Women at War Memorial** (2005) honours the work of British women in the Second World War. Its creator John Mills depicted uniforms and working clothes hanging as if in a changing room.

Cenotaph

On the left is a massive iron gate, guarded by police and besieged by tourists eager to see what lies behind. This is Downing Street, a modest but **famous cul-de-sac**. Since 1735, when George II put the house at the disposal of Sir Robert Walpole, **number ten** has been the prime minister's official residence. Number nine is home to the »chief whip«, number eleven is the residence of the chancellor of the exchequer, and number twelve accommodates the prime minister's press office. Numbers 13, 17 and 19 were never built, while numbers 14 to 16 were demolished. The street was constructed in the 1680s for the diplomat Sir George Downing. From outside the houses are plain-looking, but behind the façades surprisingly spacious. However, the tourists do not get a good look, as Downing Street has been

Downing Street

closed to the public since the gates were installed in Margaret Thatcher's time.

Dover House
The next building along is Dover House, headquarters of the Scottish Office. For most tourists Horse Guards is the highlight of Whitehall. Designed by William Kent and completed in 1753, symmetrically arranged around a small courtyard with an arched gateway and two sentry-boxes, it occupies the site of the former Whitehall guardhouse.

**Horse Guards
The great attraction, however, is not the building, but the soldiers on guard in front of it: a foot guard and two mounted soldiers of the Household Cavalry who keep to their posts regardless of the tourists scurrying around them. The Household Cavalry consists of the Queen's Life Guards with their scarlet coats and helmets with white plumes, and the Blues and Royals, who have a blue coat and a red plume. The Life Guards began as the personal bodyguard of Charles I, while the Blues and Royals originated as a regiment under Cromwell. The ** **Changing of the Guard**, which takes place every day in almost every weather, is an extremely popular tourist attraction. To

Duty done: A squadron of the Life Guards leaves Horse Guards and rides back to barracks

get a good view, it is advisable to arrive early. The Horse Guards are based in Hyde Park Barracks in Knightsbridge, and the long ride back to the barracks is timed so that they ride past ►Buckingham Palace at about the moment when the Foot Guards parade there. Behind the Horse Guards building and facing ►St James's Park is Horse Guards Parade. In June the official birthday of Queen Elizabeth II is celebrated here with the colourful pageantry of **Trooping the Colour**. However, normal tourists and Londoners can only glimpse this spectacle from a distance. The new **Household Cavalry Museum** presents the regimental history and offers a glimpse into the stables (entrance on Horse Guards Parade).

Changing of the Guard: Mon–Sat 11am, Sun 10am
Household Cavalry Museum: March–Sept daily 10am–6pm, Oct–Feb until 5pm; admission £7; www.householdcavalrymuseum.co.uk

On the opposite side of the road is the Banqueting House, the only part of Whitehall Palace to have been preserved in its entirety. It is the third building on this site but the first in London to be designed in the Palladian style. Charles I entrusted the work to **Inigo Jones**. Built between 1619 and 1622, it is a clear expression of Palladian principles: The horizontal lines marked by rows of windows on two storeys and alternating segmental and triangular pediments, the verticals by Ionic columns and pilasters on the ground floor and Corinthian columns and pilasters on the first floor.

*Banqueting House

The Banqueting House served as a hall for royal banquets and receptions and is still used by the royal family and government. History was made here: In 1533 the marriage of Anne Boleyn and Henry VIII took place in the previous building, in which Henry also died; Princess (later Queen) Elizabeth was conducted from here to the Tower. On 30 January 1649 Charles I had to pass through a window to the scaffold erected on Whitehall – a bust of him by Le Sueur above the entrance marks the spot. It was so bitterly cold on that day that Charles was given a second shirt for the execution. His successor Oliver Cromwell lived and died (1658) within the walls of the palace, and at the restoration of the Stuarts this was the place where Parliament swore fealty to the new monarch Charles II. William of Orange received the offer of royal sovereignty after the Glorious Revolution in the Banqueting House. The interior of the Banqueting House is a single room in the shape of a double cube, 38m/125ft in length, 18m/60ft in width and 18m/60ft in height. The glory of the room are the **nine allegorical ceiling paintings, with which Charles I commissioned Peter Paul Rubens** in 1635. The Apotheosis of James I is at the centre, and a further motif is the union of the crowns of England and Scotland. Rubens received £3,000 and a knighthood for the work.

❶ Mon–Sat 10am–5pm; admission: £6.60, www.hrp.org.uk

The London Police and Their Forebears

Until 1829 there was no police force for the whole of London, but only some unreliable bands of watchmen. Sir Robert Peel founded the institution that was to become world-famous: Scotland Yard

The first attempt to form a true police force was made in 1742 by the author Henry Fielding in his capacity as alderman of the City, and later by his brother John. The first of »Mr Fielding's people« were seven fearless men who pursued thieves and burglars, and went down in the history of London as the »**Bow Street runners**«, as their headquarter was in Bow Street near Covent Garden. In 1782 the City of London created a police force that kept watch during daylight hours as well as after dark. These men were dressed in capacious blue coats, as blue was regarded as the most suitable colour for lending dignity to an execution. In 1798 the Thames Police was founded to counteract river pirates, and in 1805 the Bow Street Runners were reinforced by a mounted unit known as »Robin Redbreasts« due to their red waistcoats.

Scotland Yard

London still lacked a police force that was responsible for the whole city and, above all, competent. **Sir Robert Peel** (1788–1850), home secretary, then created the **London Metropolitan Police** in the face of opposition from the City. This new force set up its headquarters in a building at the back of No. 4, Whitehall Place. Access to the building was through a yard with a now-

famous name: Scotland Yard, the best-known police force in the world, was born. It originally consisted of 3000 men clothed in blue uniforms and top hats. In 1839 the Bow Street Runners and the Thames Police were merged with it, but the same year saw the foundation of the separate **City of London Police**, which still exists today. It was not until 1842, following two spectacular murders, that the first criminal investigation department was founded in Scotland Yard. By the time the force acquired a new uniform – a cloak and the famous helmet – in 1864, it already had a considerable reputation, expressed in the nickname »Bobby«, which perpetuated the memory of Sir Robert Peel. The criminal investigation department was greatly expanded in the early 1870s. Its successes lie behind the fame of Scotland Yard, though detectives constitute only a part of the Metropolitan Police. Although they are not universally loved by local citizens, internationally the London police have a reputation for helpfulness. This, too, is rooted in tradition: From the very beginning they were unarmed.

To the right of the Banqueting House is the massive headquarters of the Ministry of Defence. The standards of the British armed forces fly from the roof of the building, which stands on part of the remains of Whitehall Palace: Henry VIII's wine cellar. In front are monuments to military men, including Sir Walter Raleigh and Field Marshal Montgomery.

Ministry of Defence

Beyond Horse Guards Avenue and next to the Banqueting House is the Old War Office. At the end of Horse Guards Avenue, overlooking the Thames, is a further survival of Whitehall Palace: Queen Mary's Terrace. Sir Christopher Wren designed the steps and quay in 1691.

Old War Office

Back on Whitehall there is a street on the right with the name Great Scotland Yard. Until the 16th century the Scottish kings had a palace here. However, Scotland Yard became a legendary address as the first headquarters of the London Metropolitan Police, founded in 1829 by Sir Robert Peel (MARCO POLO Insight p. 340). In 1890 the police moved out and since 1967 have been based in New Scotland Yard in Victoria Street close to ▶Westminster Abbey.

Scotland Yard

On the opposite side of the road is the Old Admiralty building. The older part is a work of Thomas Ripley dating from 1723–26, while the domed extension at the back was added between 1895 and 1907. From here ▶Trafalgar Square is only a few steps away. .

Old Admiralty

Wimbledon

✳ **Outer suburb**

Location: south London
Tube: Southfields
Bahn: Wimbledon ab Waterloo Station

Every summer Wimbledon, a desirable residential area with well-tended gardens about 10km/6 miles south of the city centre, is the venue for the world-famous tennis tournament.

The tournament has a strange history. The organiser, the All England Lawn Tennis and Croquet Club, originally existed only for the game of croquet. In 1877, when the club needed money to buy a roller for the lawn, the members hit upon the idea of staging a tennis tournament. Tennis was then coming into fashion, and the contestants' starting fees were used to buy the roller, which is displayed in a prominent position.

Mecca for tennis fans

Visitors to Wimbledon Lawn Tennis Museum in Church Road (gate 4) can find out everything they wanted to know about the »white

Wimbledon Lawn Tennis Museum

sport«, admire tennis equipment, see the famous trophies and even take a look at the hallowed turf of Centre Court. A holograph of John McEnroe in his changing room explains how things are for the players.

❶ Daily 10am–5pm; admission £12, with a tour £22; www.wimbledon.com

Wimbledon Common
There is more to Wimbledon than tennis: Wimbledon Common is a large expanse of woods and grassland, and a good place to take a walk to the **windmill** that was built in 1817 and is now a museum. **Southside House**, part of Wimbledon King's College School built in 1687, is undeservedly often overlooked. It is not just the home of the Pennington family, who live here as in the old days with candlelight and open fires, but a store of hidden treasures: paintings by Anthony van Dyck and Hogarth, Romney's portrait of Lady Hamilton, the necklace that Marie-Antoinette wore on the scaffold …

Wimbledon Windmill: end of March to end of Oct Sat–Sun 2–5pm; admission £2
Southside House: tours Easter Sun to last Sun in Sept, Wed, Sat, Sun 2pm, 3pm, 4pm; admission £9; www.southsidehouse.com

> **?**
> MARCO POLO INSIGHT
>
> *Did you know*
>
> … that the most successful Wimbledon contestant of all time was neither Pete Sampras nor Björn Borg, neither Steffi Graf nor Martina Navratilova, but Hugh Lawrence »Laurie« Doherty? Doherty won no less than 14 titles between 1897 and 1906: the singles from 1902 to 1906 and the men's doubles with his brother Frank »Reggie« Doherty from 1897 to 1905. To keep things in the family, Reggie held the singles title from 1897 to 1900.

** Windsor Castle

✳ Excursion

Location: Windsor, Berkshire, 35km/22mi west of London	Nov–Feb daily 9.45am–4.15pm, last admission 1 1/4 hours earlier
Bus: Green Line 700, 701, 702 from Victoria Station and Hyde Park Corner	**Changing of the guard:** April–July Mon–Sat 11am; Aug–March every other day
Train: From Waterloo or Paddington	**Admission:** £18.50
❶ March–Oct daily 9.45am–5.15pm,	**www.royalcollection.org.uk**

Everyone who stays in London for longer than just a few days should go to Windsor. The world's largest inhabited castle, and the one that has been a residence for longest, is well worth the trip.

History
Windsor Castle rises above the Thames on a chalk rock. Edward the Confessor was responsible for the construction of the first, wooden

castle. In about 1110 Henry I had the first stone structures built. In the reign of Henry II the wooden palisade was replaced by a stone wall with square towers, and Henry III extended the defences. In 1189 the English barons laid siege to the castle and defeated the Welsh troops of Prince John, later to be King John Lackland, who was forced to sign **Magna Carta** a short distance away in Runnymede. Edward III, born in 1312 in Windsor, tore down the old wooden castle and had William of Wykeham, bishop of Winchester, build further fortifications, including the Round Tower. The north terrace was added under Elizabeth I. In the reign of Charles II the castle was converted into a comfortable palace, but was little used and extended only when George III took up residence in 1800. George IV ordered thorough restoration work, which continued into the reign of Queen Victoria.

Windsor has been a **residence of the royal family for 900 years**. When the queen is at home, her standard flies from the Round Tower; but her rest is surely disturbed by the aircraft that take off from Heathrow and roar over the castle at low altitude. The buildings are grouped around two courtyards, the Lower Ward and Upper Ward, between which the Round Tower stands. The Lower Ward is bordered on the north by St George's Chapel; the apartments of state are situated on the north side of the Upper Ward.

Windsor Castle, the monarch's summer residence

LOWER WARD · MIDDLE WARD

The entrance to the Lower Ward is the monumental Henry VIII Gateway, built in the reign of that king. The south side of the court, between the Salisbury Tower and the Henry III Tower, was once accommodation for members of the Order of Military Knights of Windsor, founded by Edward III.

Horseshoe Cloisters

Horseshoe Cloisters, opposite the entrance gate, was built in the time of Henry IV and takes its name from the ground plan.
In the north-west corner lies the entrance to the **Curfew Tower**, which was built in 1227 under Henry II and is the oldest surviving part of the castle; it includes part of the dungeon and an escape tunnel.

Canons' Residence

A small courtyard situated towards the Thames houses the canons of St George's Chapel and the chapter library, both of which are part of Canons' Cloister, dating from 1333. In 1390 **Geoffrey Chaucer** spent time in the Winchester Tower in the north-east corner.

Deanery

A walk along the north side of St George's Chapel leads to the pretty Dean's Cloisters, built in 1356, and the Deanery.

**St George's Chapel

St George's Chapel is the **chapel of the Order of Knights of the Garter**. This remarkable example of late Perpendicular architecture was begun in 1474 by Edward IV on the site of a chapel of Henry I and completed in the reign of Henry VIII. The enormous window above the main entrance contains 75 stained-glass windows from the 16th century. They portray popes, kings, princes, military commanders, bishops and saints. Since 1882 the north and south façades have been adorned with the coats of arms and heraldic beasts of the houses of York and Lancaster: falcon, stag, bull, black dragon, hind and greyhound for York, lion, unicorn, swan, antelope, panther and red dragon for Lancaster.
In the bright interior, the eye is drawn to the wonderful fan vault of the nave. The 15th-century choir with its choir stalls carved from Windsor oak is truly magnificent. The rich detail of the carvings depicts scenes from the lives of St George, Edward III and the knights of the Garter. The coats of arms, swords and standards of 700 knights of the Garter are behind and above the choir stalls. The graves of **Henry VIII**, Jane Seymour and **Charles I** are in the centre of the choir. Below it is the Royal Tomb House, built in 1240, in which **George III**, **George IV** and **William IV** are buried. Further notable features are the Bray Chapel, now the bookshop, with the funerary monument of Sir Reginald Bray († 1503) in the south aisle; in the south-west corner the Beaufort Chapel with the tombs of the Earl of Worcester († 1526)

Windsor Castle

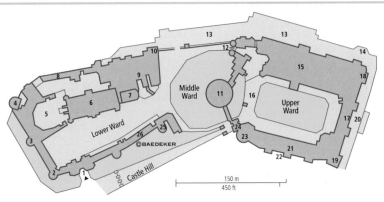

1 Henry VIII Gate
2 Salisbury Tower
3 Garter Tower
4 Curfew Tower
5 Horseshoe Cloister
6 St George's Chapel
7 Albert Memorial Chapel

8 Canons' Residence
9 Deanery
10 Winchester Tower
11 Round Tower
12 Norman Gate
13 North Terrace

14 Brunswick Tower
15 State Apartments
16 Charles II Statue
17 Private Apartments
18 Prince of Wales Tower
19 Queen's (Victoria) Tower

20 East Terrace
21 Visitors' Apartments
22 George IV Gate
23 Edward III Tower
24 St George's Gateway
25 Henry III Tower
26 Garter House

and the Duke of Kent, father of Queen Victoria; in the north-west corner the Urswick Chapel with a marble monument to Charlotte, a daughter of George IV, and diagonally opposite the tomb of **George V** and Queen Mary; among those buried in the north ambulatory are **George VI** (left) and Edward IV (right); in the south ambulatory **Edward VII** and **Henry VI**; in the south-east corner is the Lincoln Chapel with the tomb of the Earl of Lincoln († 1585) and his countess, and on the wall of the choir the Oxenbridge Chantry, with the sword of Edward III attached to its south wall.

The Albert Memorial Chapel is next to St George's Chapel. It was built by Henry VII as his funeral vault, but remained empty, as he was buried in ▸Westminster Abbey. James II used it as a Catholic chapel, and Queen Victoria ordered alterations to make it into a place of memorial for her consort, **Prince Albert**, after his death in 1861. It is lavishly decorated with marble, mosaics, sculpture and stained glass showing scenes from the Bible, members of the royal dynasty and relatives of Prince Albert, whose remains lie in a sarcophagus. To the right of it is the porphyry sarcophagus of the Duke of Clarence († 1892), the eldest son of Edward VII. The marble figure in Scottish dress by the west door represents the Duke of Albany († 1884).

*Albert
Memorial
Chapel

Round Tower The Round Tower rises majestically between the Lower Ward and the Upper Ward. It was built in the reign of Edward III on an artificial mound on which William the Conqueror had erected a keep. A wonderful panorama of the castle and Thames valley is the reward for climbing to the viewing terrace 24m/80ft above the ground.

UPPER WARD

The Upper Ward or Quadrangle is bounded by the state apartments in the north, the visitors' apartments in the south and the private apartments of the royal family in the east. A statue of Charles II made in 1679 stands on the west side of the courtyard.

State Apartments The state apartments are open to visitors when the court is not in residence. In their present form they are largely the result of alterations by Geoffrey Wyattville in the first half of the 19th century. A tour of the apartments leads from the terrace to the room in which **Queen Mary's Dolls' House, produced by Edward Lutyens in 1923, is displayed.

This is followed by the collection of porcelain in the China Museum and the **Grand Staircase**, which is dominated by Chantrey's statue of George IV and decorated with weapons and armour, including a suit of armour that belonged to Henry VIII. The **Grand Vestibule** is equipped with armour, standards and military mementoes such as a cloak that Napoleon wore. An exhibit which almost has the status of a holy relic is the bullet that killed Nelson at the battle of Trafalgar. The walls of the 30m/98ft-long **Waterloo Chamber**, decorated with carvings by Grinling Gibbons and an enormous Indian carpet, are hung with portraits of men connected with the events of the years 1813 to 1815, including Wellington, Blücher, Castlereagh, Metternich, Pope Pius VII, Tsar Alexander I, Friedrich Wilhelm III of Prussia and the English kings George III and George IV. From here turn left into the **Garter Throne Room**, where the Order of the Garter has been awarded since the reign of George IV. The large **reception room** adjoining is decorated in opulent Rococo style. Tapestries depicting the story of Jason and Medea and a large malachite vase, a present from Tsar Nicolas I, can be seen here. The queen's banqueting hall, the 14th-century **St George's Hall**, was destroyed by fire in 1992 but has now been restored. The paintings include works by van Dyck, Kneller and Lely. The next rooms were the **state chambers of the queen**. In the Queen's Guard Chamber armour, Indian cannon and a golden shield presented to Henry VIII by François I of France are displayed. The ceiling in the Queen's Presence Chamber with a portrait of Catherine of Braganza was painted by Antonio Verrio. The tapestries, which tell the story of Esther and Mordechai, continue in

St George's Chapel, the church of the Order of Knights of the Garter

the Queen's Audience Chamber, which also has a ceiling painted by Verrio. The Queen's Ballroom, built under Charles II for Catherine of Braganza, was hung in George IV's reign with paintings by Anthony van Dyck, including Charles I and his Family, The Children of Charles I, Charles I on Horseback and a self-portrait of the artist. The last room in the suite was the queen's private chamber and is now known as the Queen's Drawing Room. The works of art here include van Dyck's painting of Charles I's five children.

The highlights of the **King's Closet** and the **King's Wardrobe** are paintings by Holbein, Rubens, Rembrandt and van Dyck's famous ****Triple Portrait of Charles I**. Works by Canaletto and Gainsborough are hung in the next room, the King's State Bed Chamber; the King's Drawing Room has Rubens's Holy Family, and van Dyck's Saint Martin. The final room is the King's Dining Room with wood carvings by Grinling Gibbons, a fine ceiling painted by Verrio (1678–80) and a portrait of Catherine of Braganza by Jacob Huysmans.

Frogmore House and Mausoleum, the burial place of Queen Victoria, are in Home Park. It is open to visitors only for a few days in May and August (www.royalcollection.org.uk).

Home Park
Great Park

Honi soit qui mal y pense

In 1348 at Windsor Castle King Edward III founded the Most Noble Order of the Garter, the highest decoration that the kingdom of England can bestow.

The Queen in the dress of a Knight of the Garter

The occasion for the foundation of the order is said to have been a feast at which a lady lost her garter. The king picked up the garter and put it round his own leg, which aroused much laughter among the courtiers. Edward retorted that his knights would soon be honoured to receive such a garter. The Order of the Garter, modelled on Arthur's Round Table, was an attempt to establish a select band of men who would maintain knightly virtues in an era, the late Middle Ages, when it was apparent that chivalry was on the wane. Membership was confined to 26 knights or – in modern times – ladies, though this number can be exceeded through nomination of supernumerary knights by the monarch, who is the sovereign of the order. The order is awarded in a splendid ceremony in the Garter Throne Room at Windsor Castle. On ceremonial occasions the insignia of the order, which are on view **in room 46 of the British Museum**, consist of a heavy gold collar bearing a figure known as »The George«, on less important occasions a riband over the left shoulder with a badge called »The Lesser George«, in addition to the famous garter of dark blue velvet with the motto »Honi soit qui mal y pense«, meaning »dishonour to those who think it dishonourable«, which the knights wear below their left knee and the ladies on their upper left arm. The knights wear their regalia on the Monday of Royal Ascot week in June for a service in St George's Chapel.

WINDSOR · ETON

The town of Windsor with its half-timbered houses and inns dating from the 17th and 18th centuries, its narrow, crooked alleys and cobblestones presents an essentially medieval appearance. The Guildhall was designed by Sir Christopher Wren.

Windsor

Eton is just across the Thames bridge. The world-famous Eton College, founded in 1440 by Henry VI, is one of England's elite schools. Former pupils include Henry Fielding, William Pitt, Percy Bysshe Shelley, William Ewart Gladstone and the Duke of Wellington. The Lower School, for the younger boys, was built between 1624 and 1639, the Upper School from 1689 to 1692. The most remarkable feature of the buildings is the school chapel, built in 1441 in the Perpendicular style. Its late 15th-century wall paintings depict scenes from the life of the Virgin. The Museum of Eton Life tells the story of the college.

Eton

❶ Tours: end of April to early Oct daily during school holidays, in term time only Wed and Fri–Sun, 2pm and 3.15pm; £7

Legoland is a short distance out of Windsor on the B 3022 towards Ascot. The attractions of the 60ha/150-acre site are rides, a medieval castle, pirate ships, a miniature town and all manner of technical wonders made with the famous coloured bricks. A shuttle bus starts from Windsor parish church and opposite the Theatre Royal.

*Legoland Windsor

❶ www.legoland.co.uk

PRACTICAL
INFORMATION

How do you get from the airport to the city centre? How expensive is London? How do you get around once you have arrived? Read on to find out – ideally before you go!

Arrivals · Before the Journey

HOW TO GET TO LONDON

By air For visitors from overseas, except those who live near a Channel port or have a good connection to the Eurostar fast rail link, the quickest and cheapest way to get to London is by air. For those travelling from the more distant parts of Britain, too, a domestic flight may be preferable to a long trip on the congested roads or much-criticised rail network. London's five airports are served by a huge number of airlines offering direct flights from major intercontinental destinations, every country in Europe and almost all British airports. Luton and Stansted airports are the main destinations of low-cost flights.

By train Trains from the London region and other parts of Britain arrive at one of more than ten railway stations distributed around the perimeter of central London. Eurostar High-speed Eurostar trains from the European continent via the Channel tunnel between Calais and Folkestone arrive at the newly built St Pancras International station. Journey times from Paris are 2hr 15min, from Brussels around 2hr. Passengers from Europe who prefer a sea crossing take the route Hoek van Holland–Harwich arriving at Liverpool Street Station, or Calais–Dover, arriving at Victoria Station.

By car Congestion charge Traffic in inner London is so heavy that it is not advisable to take a car. If you do so, leave the car in the hotel car park. For private vehicles entering the city centre on working days between 7am and 6.30pm a congestion charge of £10 per day must be paid (e.g. at petrol stations). Eurotunnel Drivers from the European continent can choose between the ferry and the Channel Tunnel. The shortest ferry routes are Calais–Dover and Dunkirk–Dover. Eurotunnel operates a train service to transport cars through the tunnel every 15 minutes. Passengers stay in the car or can walk about in the carriage. The terminals have motorway connections: in France junction 13 on the A 16, in England junction 11a on the M 20.

By bus Journeys from other parts of Britain to London are generally cheaper and sometimes not much slower by coach than by rail. National Express runs services from all parts of the country to Victoria Coach Station; the cheapest long-distance connections from major British cities are offered by Megabus. National Express/Eurolines also runs services from many European destinations to Victoria Coach Station.

AIRPORTS
Heathrow
Location: 24km/15mi west of the city centre
Information: Tel. 0844 335 1801
 www.heathrowairport.com
Tube: Piccadilly Line every 5–10 min (5.04am–11.33pm daily); journey time approx. 45 min. The cheapest way into London. Note that there are three Tube stations (one for terminals 1, 2, 3 and one each in terminals 4 and 5)!
Rail: Heathrow Express to Paddington every 15 min; journey time 15 min from terminals 1, 2 and 3, 20 min from terminals 4 and 5; single ticket £21
Heathrow Connect via Ealing Broadway to Paddington every 30 min; journey time 25 min from terminals 1, 2 and 3, 35 min from terminals 4 and 5; single ticket £9.90.
Bus: National Express to Victoria Station in about one hour from Heathrow Central Bus Station (terminals 1, 2, 3), terminal 4 (stops 13, 14) and terminal 5 (stops 13–16). Taxi: expensive (approx. £45–50) and not necessarily fast due to congestion – the same applies to the other airports.

Gatwick
Location: about 40km/25mi south of London
Information: Tel. 0844 892 0322
www.gatwickairport.com
Rail: Gatwick Express, every 15 min, 30 min journey time to Victoria Station from 6am to 12.30am. First Capital Connect to London Bridge Station and St Pancras Station. (journey time 50 min). Southern via Clapham Junction to Victoria Station (journey time 35 min).
Bus: National Express to Victoria Station (approx. 65 min), easyBus to Earls Court.

Luton
Location: 50km/32mi north of London
Information: Tel. 01582 4051 00, www.london-luton.co.uk
Rail: Frequent services to various stations in central London (shuttle bus from terminal to station); journey time 20-25 min.
Bus: National Express to Victoria Station; journey time about 75 min; easyBus to Baker St.

Stansted
Location: 55km/35mi north-east of London
Information: Tel. 0844 335 1803, www.stanstedairport.com
Rail: Stansted Express every 15/30 min, journey time 45 min to Liverpool Street Station
Bus: various companies operate, e.g. to Victoria Station and Liverpool Street Station (journey times 45–80 min)

City Airport
Location: 10km/6mi east of city centre in Docklands
Information: Tel. 020 7 646 0088, www.londoncityairport.com
DLR: DLR station at City Airport, journey time to Bank Station about 22 min, to Canning Town Tube station 10 min.

AIRLINES
British Airways
Reservations: tel. 0844 493 0787
London phone numbers for some other major airlines in the English-speaking world:

Aer Lingus
Tel. 0871 718 5000

Air Canada
Tel. 0871 220 1111

Air New Zealand
Tel. 0800 028 41 49

American Airlines
Tel. 0844 499 7300

Delta Airlines
Tel. 0871 221 1222

easyjet
Tel. 0843 104 5000

Fly Be
Tel. 0871 0700 2000

Qantas Airways
Tel. 0845 774 7767

Ryanair
Tel. 0871 246 0000

United Continental Airlines
www.united.com

Virgin Atlantic
Tel. 0844 811 0000

RAIL TRAVEL
TO THE NORTH
Euston
Euston Road, NW 1

King's Cross
Euston Road, NW 1

St Pancras
Euston Road, NW 1
terminus of Eurostar trains through the
Channel Tunnel

TO THE EAST
Liverpool Street
Liverpool Street, EC 2

TO THE SOUTH
Charing Cross
Strand, WC 2

Victoria
Victoria Street, SW 1

Waterloo
York Road, SE 1

TO THE WEST
Paddington
Praed Street, WC 2

RAIL INFORMATION
In Britain
Tel. 08 45) 748 4950
www.nationalrail.co.uk

From Europe
Tel. 0044 20 7278 5240
Eurostar Tel. 08432 18 6186,
from outside UK 0044 1233 617 575
www.eurostar.com

BREAKDOWN SERVICES
Automobile Association (AA)
www.theaa.com Breakdown service:
Tel. 0800 887 766

RAC
www.rac.co.uk
Tel. breakdown service:
0333 2000 999

BUS INFORMATION
National Express bus
Tel. 08705 808 080
www.nationalexpress.com

Victoria Coach Station
Elizabeth Street/Buckingham Palace
Road

Megabus
Tel. 0900 1600 900
www.megabus.co.uk

CHANNEL TUNNEL
Eurotunnel: Tel. 08443 353 535
www.eurotunnel.com

IMMIGRATION AND CUSTOMS REGULATIONS

To enter the United Kingdom as tourists, citizens of many English-speaking countries (e.g. Australia, Canada, New Zealand, South Africa, USA) need a valid passport but no visa. Citizens of member countries of the EU or European Economic Zone need either a passport or identity card. Further information: www.ukba.homeoffice.gov.uk. Drivers must have a valid driving licence and the relevant car registration documents from their country of origin. Cars should be marked with the oval sign showing nationality.

Travel documents

Animals may be brought into the United Kingdom only if a microchip has been implanted for the purposes of identification and a test and vaccination for rabies has been carried out in an authorised laboratory at least six months in advance. Vaccination against ticks and worms is also required one or two days before arrival. Information from Visit Britain (▶Information).

Animals

Travellers from non-EU countries can import the following without paying customs duties: 250g of coffee, 100g of tea; 200 cigarettes or 50 cigars or 250g of tobacco; 4 litres of still wine and 2 litres of fortified or sparkling wine with up to 22% alcohol content or 1 litre of spirits with an alcohol content of over 22%, £390-worth of all other goods including perfume, gifts and souvenirs. Travellers within the EU are not subject to restrictions as tourists, though quantities higher than those needed for personal consumption should not be imported (e.g. more than 800 cigarettes, 10 litres of spirits and 90 litres of wine).

Customs regulations

Health

Citizens of Australia, New Zealand and some other countries are entitled to free emergency medical treatment through the National Health Service (helpline for non-urgent medical advice: tel. 111; www.nhsdirect.nhs.uk). Citizens of the European Union receive free medical treatment by the National Health Service and should carry their European health insurance card. Citizens from other states are advised to take out health insurance.

Doctors

PHARMACIES
HD Bliss
5 Marble Arch, W 1
Tel. 020 7723 6116, 9am–midnight

Zafash
233–235 Old Brompton Road, SW 5
Tel. 020 7373 3506; 24 hr

Boots the Chemist
A large number of branches all over
London, most with a pharmacy

EMERGENCY
Ambulance
Tel. 999

Private emergency services
Doctorcall tel. 020 75351888
Medcall tel. 0800 136 106
SOS Doctors tel. 0845 108 0446

HOSPITALS
See also www.visitlondon.com/
traveller-information

Information

IN LONDON
Tourist information centres
www.visitlondon.com
Victoria Station, SW 1
Tube: Victoria
Mon–Sat 7.15am–9.15pm, Sun 8.15am–
7pm
Liverpool Street Underground Station,
EC 2
Tube: Liverpool Street
Sat–Thu 8.15am–7.15pm, Fri 8.15am–
8.15pm
Euston Station, NW 1
Tube: Euston, daily 8.15am–6pm
Heathrow Terminals 1, 2, 3 Under-
ground station
Daily 7.30am–7.30pm
Piccadilly Circus
Piccadilly Circus, SW 1
Tube: Piccadilly Circus
Daily 9.15am–7pm
Greenwich, Pepys House
2 Cutty Sark Gardens
DLR: Cutty Sark
Daily 10am–5pm

City of London Information Centre
St Paul's Churchyard, EC 4
Tube: St Paul's
Mon–Sat 9.30am–5.30pm, Sun 10am–
4pm

London Information Centre
Leicester Square, Tel. 020 7292 2333
Tube: Leicester Square
Daily 8am–midnight

INTERNET
www.visitlondon.com
The official website of the London tourist office with a huge amount of information: sightseeing, hotel bookings, restaurants, maps, entertainment

www.timeout.com/london
Sightseeing, pubs, bars, restaurants,
shopping, kids etc. on the website of
the London listings magazine

www.londontown.com
Claims to be the number one internet

site for London, and certainly has a wealth of information

www.officiallondontheatre. co.uk
A comprehensive programme of London theatre, including shows and comedy; search function and ticket information

www.tfl.gov.uk
Everything you need to know about public transport, including timetables

www.londoneats.com
A comprehensive online guide to restaurants in London

www.capitalFM.com
Website of London's most popular radio station with a lot of information on the music scene

www.royal.gov.uk
The royals online

www.thebritishmuseum.ac.uk
www.nationalgallery.org.uk
London's two top museums have excellent websites. The online presentation of the National Gallery, in particular, is brilliant.

EMBASSIES IN LONDON
Australia
Australia House, Strand WC 2
Tel. 020 7379 4334
www.uk.embassy.gov.au

Canada
1 Grosvenor Square, W 1
Tel. 020 7258 6600
http://unitedkingdom.gc.ca

Ireland
17 Grosvenor Place, SW 1
Tel. 020 7235 2171
www.embassyofireland.co.uk

New Zealand
80 The Haymarket, SW 1
Tel. 020 7930 8422
www.nzembassy.com/united-kingdom

South Africa
South Africa House, Trafalgar Square, WC 2
Tel. 020 7451 7299
http://southafrica.embassyhomepage.com

USA
24 Grosvenor Square, W 1
Tel. 020 7499 9000
http://london.usembassy.gov/

Literature

Ben Weinreb/Christopher Hibbert: The London Encyclopaedia. MacMillan/St. Martin's Press/Papermac 1983 More about London than any other source. *Work of reference*

James Boswell: London Journal, 1762–1763. Edinburgh University Press 2004. Vivid portrait of 18th-century London. *Diaries and travel*

Samuel Pepys: Diaries – A Selection. Penguin, 2003 The vibrant life of 17th-century London in Pepys's famous diaries – not only valuable historical documents, but an extremely good read.

Monica Ali: Brick Lane. Black Swan, 2004. A story about the Bangladeshi community in the Tower Hamlets area set around one of London's most colourful streets.

Novels and stories

Sir Arthur Conan Doyle: The Complete Sherlock Holmes, Penguin 1981 Many of Holmes's cases were set in Victorian London.

MARCO ⊕ POLO TIP

! *London in the movies* **Insider Tip**

Frenzy: a murderer stalks women in Covent Garden market
The Man Who Knew Too Much: another Hitchcock. James Stewart stars in a thrilling showdown in the Royal Albert Hall.
A Fish Called Wanda: a zany comedy with John Cleese set in a criminal milieu. Not suitable for animal-lovers.
Notting Hill: Julia Roberts and Hugh Grant get romantic. The travel bookshop really exists: no. 13-15 Blenheim Crescent.
Vera Drake: a tragic masterpiece of social realism set in working-class London of the post-war years

Joseph Conrad: The Secret Agent. Everyman, 1992. Spy story in anarchist circles.

Daniel Defoe: Journal of the Plague Year. Penguin, 2003. An old man looks back on the Great Plague of 1665, 60 years after it devastated the city.

Charles Dickens: Oliver Twist. A Tale of Two Cities. Charles Dickens more than anyone else captured Victorian London in literary form.

Nick Hornby: High Fidelity. Penguin, 2000. The life of a thirty-something Londoner who works in a record shop.

Hanif Kureishi: The Buddha of Suburbia. Faber and Faber, 2000. Classic novel about growing up in the Asian community.

Colin MacInnes: Absolute Beginners. Allison and Busby, 2001. Cult novel about Fifties youth culture in Notting Hill.

Timothy Mo: Sour Sweet. Paddleless Press, 1999. Chinese immigrants open a restaurant and struggle to cope with life in England.

Zadie Smith: White Teeth. Penguin, 2001. An impressive literary debut about immigrant families in north London.

Barbara Vine: King Solomon's Carpet. Penguin, 1992. The London underground system is the main character in this dark thriller, written under Ruth Rendell's pseudonym.

Non-fiction

Peter Ackroyd: London, the Biography. Vintage, 2002. This mammoth but entertaining work on the life and history of London, organised by themes instead of chronology, has acquired the status of a definitive work.

George Orwell: Down and Out in Paris and London. Penguin, 2003. Orwell's report about living rough in the 1930s

Donald Rumbelow: The Complete Jack the Ripper. Penguin Books. The best book that has been written about London's most notorious criminal case

Iain Sinclair: London Orbital. Granta Books, 2002. The author walked right around the perimeter of the city and captured encounters and observations. The »psychogeographer« Sinclair has expressed his own highly personal view of London in a great deal of fictional and non-fictional writing.

Lost Property

Lost property can be reported to police stations. London Transport has its own lost property office for items lost on buses and the Tube.

TUBE, BUS, TAXI
London Transport Lost Property Office
200 Baker Street, NW 1
Mon–Fri 8.30am–4pm
Inquiries in person or online; forms are available at Tube stations and bus depots and from www.tfl.gov.uk/contact.

National Express Buses
In Victoria Coach Station opposite platform 21 or tel. 7730 3466

In railway stations
Ask in the station.

Money

The United Kingdom is a member of the European Union but not the EU currency union. Currency
The currency remains the British pound (pound sterling; £), equal to 100 pence (p, colloquially pronounced »pee«). There are banknotes for £5, £10, £20 and £50, and coins for 1 penny; 2, 5, 10, 20 and 50 pence; and £1 and £2.

There are no restrictions on the import or export of British or foreign currency from the EU. Travellers entering from non-EU countries must declare amounts in cash higher than £10,000.

? Exchange rates

£1 = US $1.58
US $1 = £0.63
€1 = US $1.13
US $1 = €0.88

Banks   The normal opening times of banks are Mon–Fri 9.30am–3.30pm, on main shopping streets until 5.30pm; some banks also open on Saturday mornings. Branches at Heathrow and Gatwick airports are open 24 hours per day.

Credit cards   Credit cards (Mastercard, Visa, Diners) are accepted in almost all
Travellers'   hotels, restaurants and shops, travellers' cheques at banks and in
cheques   many hotels.

Cash   Cash machines (ATMs) accept bank cards and credit cards. The loss
machines   of bank cards and credit cards should be reported immediately to the card company.

Changing   There are bureaux de change in larger hotels, in the department
money   stores Harrods, Dickins & Jones, Selfridges, John Barker and Marks & Spencer (Marble Arch and Oxford Street) and at many Tube and railway stations.
As their rates are normally less favourable than the official rate and they often charge high fees, it is advisable to use them only in emergencies.

Newspapers and Magazines

Newspapers   The first news-sheet appeared in Fleet Street in 1501. The conservative national newspapers are The Times, The Daily Mail, The Daily Telegraph, The Daily Express and The Sun. The left-wing or liberal papers are The Guardian, The Independent and The Daily Mirror. The Financial Times is not just for stockbrokers, but also has an excellent culture section. The Evening Standard is London's local paper. Sports enthusiasts read Sporting Life or The Racing Post.

City   Time Out, published every Tuesday evening, is an unbeatable source
magazine   for listings of events, night life, entertainment and restaurants. For the online version go to www.timeout.co.uk.

Sunday   There are Sunday versions of most of the daily papers, as well as
papers   scandal and sensation in The Sunday People and The Sunday Mirror.

International   International newspapers are available at many newsagents, espe-
press   cially in the City. A well-stocked newsagent for international papers is Moroni & Son, 68 Old Compton Street, W 1 (Tube: Leicester Square).

Post and Communications

POST

Post offices in London are open Mon–Fri 9am–5.30pm, Sat to 12.30pm. The post office on William IV Street next to Trafalgar Square has longer opening hours: Mon–Fri 8.30am–6.30pm, Sat to 5.30pm.

Postcards and letters weighing up to 20g to European countries cost 88p, to all other destinations worldwide £1.28. Stamps are on sale at post offices, newsagents and many souvenir shops.   Stamps

TELEPHONE

Most public telephones run by British Telecom (BT) can be operated with either coins (10, 20, 50 pence, £1) or credit cards The payphones operated by other companies take credit cards.   Public telephones

Calls abroad from a BT payphone cost at least £1. Charges are lower on weekdays between 6pm and 8am and at weekends.   International calls

The mobile phone network in the UK is compatible with mobile phones from Europe, Australia and New Zealand, but not with the North American system.   Mobile phones
If your phone is not compatible, consider buying a SIM card usable in Britain at a high-street store.

CALLING CODES AND SERVICE NUMBERS

In Britain
Tel. 020 for London

From abroad
Tel. +44 20

From London
to Australia: tel. 00 61
to Canada: tel. 00 1
to Ireland: tel. 00 353
to New Zealand: tel. 00 64

to South Africa: tel. 00 27
to USA: tel. 00 1

Operator
Tel. 100

Time of day
Tel. 123

Directory inquiries
for London tel. 142
outside London tel. 192
international tel. 153

Prices · Discounts

The most
expensive
city in Europe

London is one of the world's most expensive cities. Visitors notice this most of all when shopping and if they want to eat something other than fast food. It is a relief to find that many museums, including most of the major ones, do not charge for entry or only ask for a voluntary contribution. On the other hand some of the most popular sights, such as Tower and Madame Tussaud's, have steep admission charges. For a stay of a few days it may therefore be worth buying the rather expensive **London Pass**, which includes free entry to more than 60 attractions (e.g. the Tower) and other discounts. It is sold at all tourist information offices ▶Information) and many other outlets. A London Pass including travel by Tube, rail and the DLR cannot be purchased in London, but only before arrival. For information about prices and validity: www.londonpass.com. On public transport a Travelcard or an Oyster Card can save a good deal of money (▶p. 363).

MARCO ◉ POLO INSIGHT

? *Tipping and low-cost*

Restaurants: 10–15% if a service charge (often 12.5%) has not already been added
Pubs: no tips at the bar; 10–15% for waiter service if a restaurant is attached to the pub
Taxi: 10–15% or round up

Low-cost London
www.londonforfree.net/lists free or low-priced activities.

Time

Greenwich
Mean Time

The British time zone is Greenwich Mean Time: GMT. From the end of March to the end of October **British Summer Time** (BST: GMT plus one hour) applies. From the end of October to the third Sunday in March the clocks are put back again to winter time (= GMT).

Transport

Transport for
London

Transport for London runs the underground railway (Tube), buses and Docklands Light Railway. The Overground rail network complemenets these services. Tube and bus plans are available in all Tube stations. For information round the clock phone **tel. 020 7222 1234** or visit **www.tfl.gov.uk**.

Underground

London's most efficient transport system, for all its age and the problems of modernising it, remains the underground railway, generally known as »the Tube«. Trains run on 12 lines at very short intervals from about 5am to 1am. It is best to avoid the rush hours: 7.30am–9.30am and 4.30pm–6.30pm.

The **Docklands Light Railway** (DLR) connects the Docklands and Greenwich to the City (Mon–Sat 5.30am–12.30am, Sun 7am–11.30pm).

> **Insider Tip**
>
> MARCO POLO TIP
>
> *Underground animals*
>
> The map is world-famous. To find out about the animals that live on the London Tube, see www.animalsontheunderground.com

London's famous red double-decker buses – now only the modern types, with the exception of two tourist routes – operate from early morning until midnight. Buses always stop at the stops marked with a red or white sign, but at those marked »request« only when a sign is given to the driver. Night buses operate once or twice per hour after midnight. Most of the routes pass through Trafalgar Square. They are marked N before the bus number and only stop at bus stops marked N.

Bus

The transport network is divided into six zones. Single tickets are available at a minimum cash price of between £4.70 and £5.70, depending on the zone, which is expensive if you are travelling only in the two inner zones where most tourist attractions are to be found. A Travel Card for one or more days, or an Oyster Card (£2.20 for a short journey instead of £4.70) is a much better deal. Children under five travel free, under-fifteens pay half fare. Be sure to keep your tickets to show them or insert into the automatic gate at the end of the journey.

Tickets

It is almost always worth buying a Travelcard or an Oyster Card. The latter can be ordered online, and is needed for purchase of a seven-day, monthly or longer Travelcard. It is a plastic smartcard with stored credit which can be topped up. There is a refundable deposit of £5. Cards are also on sale at railway stations and most Tube stations. The one-day **Travelcard** is available without buying an Oyster Card. The **7 Day Travelcard** entitles the holder to unlimited travel at any time with all forms of transport including local trains for one week. The **Travelcard or Visitor Oyster Card** is purchased not in London but online before arrival in the city from http://visitorshop.tfl.gov.uk/. This service is available in over 50 countries worldwide in addition to the UK and saves delays on arrival. The price of a Travelcard depends on the number of zones selected (zones 1 and 2 usually suffice for visitors whose accommodation is within this area).

Save money: Travelcard and Oyster Card

At Tube stations – at least in the central zones – tickets have to be placed in a slot at the barrier to be registered. Always keep single tickets, as they are collected by staff or retained by the machine at the end of the journey.

Taxis   A feature of London almost as famous as the double-decker buses are the taxis, once **black cabs** without exception, but now in fact seen in a variety of colours. They can be hailed from the kerbside – if the FOR HIRE sign is lit up, the taxi is free. **Important: licensed taxis have a licence number!** Fares and supplementary costs are displayed in the taxi. The price is doubled for journeys longer than six miles (9.7km); journeys after 8pm also cost more.

Travellers with Disabilities

Internet sources   The websites of Visit London and Transport for London have useful information: www.visitlondon.com/accommodation/accessible/ is a source of information about accessible hotels. www.visitlondon.com/attractions/culture/london-attraction-accessibility gives further advice. www.tfl.gov.uk has a range of accessibility guides (click on Getting Around, then Transport Accessibility), including an audio map and a large-print map of the Tube and information about assistance services, and the brochure Getting Around London, which can also be downloaded.

Open Britain
www.openbritain.net
This website has a wealth of information for persons with disabilities on travel, accommodation, restaurants and sightseeing.

Artsline
www.artsline.org.uk
Information about arts and performance venues suitable for persons with disabilities.

Magic
c/o: Tate Modern Bankside, London SE1 9TG
http://magicdeaf.org.uk/
MAGIC is a group of museums and galleries in London that provide events and facilities for the deaf and hard of hearing: the British Museum, Courtauld Institute, Dulwich Picture Gallery, Geffrye Museum, Hunterian Museum, Institute for Contemporary Arts, London Transport Museum, Museum of London and Museum of London Docklands, National Portrait Gallery, National Maritime Museum, Photographers' Gallery, Royal Academy of Arts, Serpentine Gallery, Sir John Soane's Museum, Somerset House, Tate Britain, Tate Modern, Wallace Collection, Victoria & Albert Museum and the Whitechapel Art Gallery.

Tourism for All
7A Pixel Mill
44 Appleby Road
Kendal
Cumbria LA9 6ES
www.tourismforall.org.uk
Information about programmes, accessibility, transport facilities and much more, including special offers.

Weights and Measures

In 1995 the United Kingdom joined the rest of Europe by adopting the metric system, but with two important exceptions: the pint for beer and milk and the mile for distances on road signs.

Metric system with exceptions

BRITISH MEASURES	CLOTHING SIZES				
1 mile (mi) = 1.61 km	Europe:	36	38	40	42	44
1 pint (pt) = 0.568 litres	GB:	8	10	12	14	16

When to Go

London has a temperate climate. However, as it can be rainy or in summer too hot, the best time for a visit is spring (from May) and early autumn. The fogs for which London was once notorious are now unusual, as the air is much cleaner than it was 50 or 100 years ago.

Index

List of Maps and Illustrations

Photo Credits

Publisher's Information

1st Edition 2015
Worldwide Distribution: Marco Polo
Travel Publishing Ltd
Pinewood, Chineham Business Park
Crockford Lane, Chineham
Basingstoke, Hampshire RG24 8AL,
United Kingdom.

Photos, illlustrations, maps::
163 photos, 27 maps and and illustra-
tions, one large city map
Text:
Rainer Eisenschmid, Kathleen Becker,
John Sykes and Dr. Eva-Maria Blattner,
Maike Hachfeld, Martina Johnson,
Reinhard Strüber, Werner Voran
Editing:
John Sykes, Rainer Eisenschmid
Translation: John Sykes
Cartography:
Christoph Gallus, Hohberg; Franz Huber,
Munich; MAIRDUMONT Ostfildern (city
map)
3D illustrations:
jangled nerves, Stuttgart
Infographics:
Golden Section Graphics GmbH, Berlin
Design:
independent Medien-Design, Munich

Editor-in-chief:
Rainer Eisenschmid, Mairdumont
Ostfildern

Printed in China

Despite all of our authors' thorough
research, errors can creep in. The publishers do not accept any liability for thi
Whether you want to praise, alert us to
errors or give us a personal tip Please
contact us by email or post:

MARCO POLO Travel Publishing Ltd
Pinewood, Chineham Business Park
Crockford Lane, Chineham
Basingstoke, Hampshire RG24 8AL
United Kingdom
Email: sales@marcopolouk.com

FSC
www.fsc.org
MIX
Paper from
responsible sources
FSC® C011918

MARCO ⊕ POLO

HANDBOOKS

MARCO ⊕ POLO
TRAVEL HANDBOOK
ANDALUCÍA
INFOGRAPHICS · 3D ILLUSTRATIONS · PULL-OUT MAP
Insider Tips
NEW

MARCO ⊕ POLO
TRAVEL HANDBOOK
BARCELONA
INFOGRAPHICS · 3D ILLUSTRATIONS · PULL-OUT MAP
Insider Tips
NEW

MARCO ⊕ POLO
TRAVEL HANDBOOK
BERLIN
INFOGRAPHICS · 3D ILLUSTRATIONS · PULL-OUT MAP
Insider Tips
NEW

MARCO ⊕ POLO
TRAVEL HANDBOOK
DRESDEN
INFOGRAPHICS · 3D ILLUSTRATIONS · PULL-OUT MAP
Insider Tips
NEW

MARCO ⊕ POLO
TRAVEL HANDBOOK
FLORIDA
INFOGRAPHICS · 3D ILLUSTRATIONS · PULL-OUT MAP
Insider Tips
NEW

MARCO ⊕ POLO
TRAVEL HANDBOOK
GRAN CANARIA
INFOGRAPHICS · 3D ILLUSTRATIONS · PULL-OUT MAP
Insider Tips
NEW

MARCO ⊕ POLO
TRAVEL HANDBOOK
ICELAND
INFOGRAPHICS · 3D ILLUSTRATIONS · PULL-OUT MAP
Insider Tips
NEW

MARCO ⊕ POLO
TRAVEL HANDBOOK
LONDON
INFOGRAPHICS · 3D ILLUSTRATIONS · PULL-OUT MAP
Insider Tips
NEW

MARCO ⊕ POLO
TRAVEL HANDBOOK
NEW YORK
INFOGRAPHICS · 3D ILLUSTRATIONS · PULL-OUT MAP
Insider Tips
NEW

MARCO ⊕ POLO
TRAVEL HANDBOOK
PARIS
INFOGRAPHICS · 3D ILLUSTRATIONS · PULL-OUT MAP
Insider Tips
NEW

MARCO ⊕ POLO
TRAVEL HANDBOOK
ROME
INFOGRAPHICS · 3D ILLUSTRATIONS · PULL-OUT MAP
Insider Tips
NEW

MARCO ⊕ POLO
TRAVEL HANDBOOK
VENICE
INFOGRAPHICS · 3D ILLUSTRATIONS · PULL-OUT MAP
Insider Tips
NEW

www.marco-polo.com

London Curiosities

The only street in Britain where you drive on the right, a statutory right to peep through the bushes and public toilets that disappear into the ground – London is full of strange and unusual places and sights.

►A mummified philosopher

In his will the philosopher Jeremy Bentham (1748–1832) stipulated that his preserved and clothed corpse should be placed on his favourite chair and left there. It is still on view in University College – the head is made of wax, however.

►Lost rivers

Many tributaries flow into the Thames in London, almost all of them subterranean for most of their course. The sources of the river Fleet are the bathing ponds on Hampstead Heath, its mouth is below Blackfriars Bridge. The Walbrook flows beneath the Bank of England.

►Heritage-listed huts

13 wooden huts that were built in the 19th century as places for drivers of hansom cabs to have a rest and a meal are still standing. The ones in Grosvenor Gardens, Temple Place and in front of the Victoria & Albert Museum are in operation. Others stand empty on Russell Square and next to Embankment Station.

►London's beaches

The difference between low and high tide on the Thames in the city centre is several metre At low water many little beaches of pebbles, sand or mud appear. Amateur archaeologists known as mudlarks have made many remarkable finds.

►A parliamentary view

Some popular panoramic views are protected by law – in Greenwich Park, for example, on Parliament Hill in Hampstead and on Westminster Pier. The most famous statutory view presents St Paul's Cathedral through a gap in the bushes, ten miles away in Richmond Park.

►Patented protection against body-snatchers

200 years ago only the bodies of executed criminals could be dissected. The needs of medical research led to a thriving trade in bodies that had been dug up from cemeterie A patented coffin in the crypt of St Bride's Church shows how to prevent this.

►Urilifts

This is the name for an invention that appears out of the pavement in the evening when it is needed, a useful device to stop pub-goers from urinating on the street. They can be viewed or used on Bishopsgate/Middlesex Street, behind the Royal Exchange on Cornhill and in Watling Street.

►Please drive on the right!

Savoy Street, a very short stretch of road in front of the eponymous hotel on The Strand, is the only one in Britain where traffic drives on the right.